LUTHER S. HARRIS

Around Washington Square

AN ILLUSTRATED HISTORY OF GREENWICH VILLAGE

THE JOHNS HOPKINS UNIVERSITY PRESS

BALTIMORE AND LONDON

© 2003 Luther S. Harris
All rights reserved. Published 2003
Printed in the United States of America on acid-free paper
9 8 7 6 5 4 3 2 1

The Johns Hopkins University Press
2715 North Charles Street
Baltimore, Maryland 21218-4363
www.press.jhu.edu

Library of Congress Cataloging-in-Publication Data

Harris, Luther S.
   Around Washington Square : an illustrated history of
Greenwich Village / Luther S. Harris.
         p.   cm.
   Includes bibliographical references and index.
     ISBN 0-8018-7341-X (acid-free paper)
     1. Greenwich Village (New York, N.Y.)—History—
Pictorial works.   2. Greenwich Village (New York,
N.Y.)—History.   3. Washington Square (New York,
N.Y.)—History—Pictorial works.   4. Washington
Square (New York, N.Y.)—History.   5. New York
(N.Y.)—History—Pictorial works.   6. New York
(N.Y.)—History.   I. Title.
     F128.68.G8 H37 2003
     974.7′1—dc21   2002152159

A catalog record for this book is available from the British
Library.

CONTENTS

ACKNOWLEDGMENTS

I take pleasure in thanking the many people who helped make this book possible. First among them are Christopher Gray, author of the "Streetscapes" column in the *New York Times,* and Barbara Cohen and Judith Stonehill, who long ran the New York Bound Bookshop. Chris's columns and counsel and Barbara and Judith's delightful shop were a constant source of discoveries and inspiration, which were particularly welcome at a time in the late 1980s when I was stymied by the scale and complexity of the goal I had set.

A number of others played key roles in the book's long research phase. Wendy Shadwell and Helena Zinkham at the New-York Historical Society led me to finds among the society's vast collections, and Steven Miller, then curator of prints and drawings at the Museum of the City of New York, steered me through the museum's trove of material. Municipal Archives director Kenneth Cobb's knowledge of the city's collections proved invaluable, as did Gunther Pohl's grasp of the New York Public Library's local-history stacks. Archivist Thomas Frusciano and the late historian Bayrd Still assisted me with New York University's important archives. Seymour Durst, the recently deceased real estate magnate and New York City enthusiast, let me browse through his splendid cache of New Yorkiana. The late architect and preservationist Alan Burnham's library and his *New York City, the Development of the Metropolis: An Annotated Bibliography* (Garland, 1988) were a valuable resource and an early stimulus. So was historian Thomas Bender's *New York Intellect: A History of Intellectual Life in New York City from 1750 to the Beginnings of Our Own Time* (Knopf, 1987). Among the many collectors of photography, Larry Gottheim gave me the greatest assistance in finding rare nineteenth-century images.

In writing the book, more deserve special mention. Architectural historian Regina Kellerman and preservationist Christabel Gough graciously read early drafts of my manuscript, as did Madeline Rogers, editor of *Seaport Magazine,* who published an extract of my first chapter. Art historian and writer Avis Berman aided me mightily with the whole manuscript, and her *Rebels on Eighth Street* (Atheneum, 1990) was also an inspiration. Architectural historian Andrew Dolkart read and advised me on most of the manuscript, and historian and journalist Fred Siegel critiqued my last two chapters. I am indebted to Sylvia Warren and Michela Porta for their excellent editorial assistance, and especially to Sylvia, whose enthusiasm and encouragement were a joy. Finally, I thank Robert J. Brugger, my wise and knowledgeable editor and sponsor at the Johns Hopkins University Press, who helped me improve the text, edited the manuscript's images, and supported the inclusion of over 200 illustrations in the published work.

West Village   Greenwich Village   East Village

Placing Greenwich Village from Colonial Times to the Present. The Fifteenth Ward's nineteenth-century grid and today's "Village" designations are superimposed on part of a British colonial map, ca. 1767. "Greenwich," spelled out vertically to the left on the British map, spanned what are now West Village and Chelsea. "The Bowery Lane," running prominently from the lower right and bordering the grid, is presently the Bowery and Fourth Avenue, with today's East Village, to the right, on former Stuyvesant land between Houston and Fourteenth Street. Minetta Creek flows diagonally through the square from Fifth Avenue to MacDougal Street; it and other natural features of the land were leveled for the city's grid plan. The Hudson River (lower left) and East River (upper right) have original shorelines, since extended by landfill. This amazingly accurate map, which covered colonial Manhattan from its southern tip to about today's 50th Street, was produced by a British officer named Bernard Ratzer. It was based on expert and detailed surveys of the island. Colonial map courtesy of the New York Public Library.

INTRODUCTION

I moved to Washington Square in 1976, a bleak year in what had thus far been a bleak decade for New York City. For New Yorkers, the term "big MAC" was more likely to suggest the Municipal Assistance Corporation—a group formed the previous year to save the city from financial ruin by wresting fiscal controls from the hapless mayor—than fast food. Although Greenwich Village was not exempt from what some perceived as a mini–crime wave, and Washington Square Park seemed at times to be more drug market than tourist mecca, I soon developed a deep and abiding affection for that human-scaled patch of Manhattan Island that lies between the skyscraper canyons of midtown and Wall Street: Greenwich Village. As both a physical presence and a place in the American psyche, just what *is* "Greenwich Village" needs some explanation.

During the British colonial era (1664–1783), *Greenwich* denoted a group of country seats on the Hudson River, two miles north of Wall Street. Its namesake was the fashionable town of Greenwich on the Thames, located some five miles from the City of London. Settlements along the Hudson were called *villages,* hence the Americanized *Greenwich Village.* In 1832 boundaries were drawn for New York City's new Ninth Ward (an administrative district), enclosing much of that Greenwich Village (today's West Village), and the name stuck. Immediately east of the Ninth lay the patrician Fifteenth Ward, known as *Washington Square* after its centerpiece public space, and that name, too, stuck. Around 1910 a creative and rebellious bohemian enclave—born in the 1850s—formed around the square. Its members, mightily abetted by a fascinated press, repackaged the Fifteenth Ward as the quainter "Greenwich Village" and embraced the Washington Square Arch as their symbol of defiance. In decades to come, quaintness faded into a supercharged modernism and a fierce preservationist movement. This storied Greenwich Village, centered on Washington Square and located between today's West and East Villages, is the companion subject of my book. It is the neighborhood made famous by a cavalcade of world-famous writers, artists, and musicians who once lived or worked in this historic place.

Here, too, is a marvelous architectural mix, where nineteenth-century gems may be found on the same blocks as Modernist and Postmodern works. Within a half-mile radius of my own apartment on Lower Fifth Avenue can be found townhouses in the Federal, Greek Revival, Gothic Revival, Italianate, French Second Empire, Neo-Grec, and Queen Anne styles, as well as an extraordinary collection of nineteenth- and twentieth-century commercial buildings clad in Romanesque, Beaux Arts, French Second Empire, and contemporary facades designed by such giants as Richard Upjohn, James Renwick, Richard Morris Hunt, McKim, Mead & White, Louis Sullivan, and Philip Johnson. Many humble vernacular structures of quality, including tenements south of the square, add to the charm of this remarkably skyscraper- and superstore-free ensemble. Two outstanding examples of the many lovely early churches that dot the area are both magnificent Gothic Revivals: the Church of the Ascension, designed by Richard Upjohn and remodeled by Stanford White, with an altar mural and stained glass by John La Farge and an altar relief by Louis Saint-Gaudens; and Grace Church, designed by James Renwick Jr., whose specialty in the principles of Gothic architecture won him this grand commission at the age of 24.

As I strolled through some of the streets of the quarter, the New York evoked by Henry James and Edith Wharton seemed not so distant. What set of circumstances, I wondered, had made possible what I had begun to think of as Manhattan's renewable Eden—a place that glows in retrospect over successive periods of its history? What had made Greenwich Village such an important seedbed for the growth and flowering of culture in New York City, the United States, and indeed the world? And, most perplexing, how had so much of it survived?

The answers were not easy to come by. A few guidebooks and treatises painted an intriguing portrait, and I found some excellent sources recounting parts of the story, but most books seemed glib and superficial—not to mention inaccurate—and the pictorial record relied on a tired group of oft-published images. Cultural historians trying to analyze the worldwide fame of the district have focused on one or another aspect of its history, such as its elite residents, super-rich figures like the Astors and Vanderbilts, or on the literary and artistic bohemia that flourished in the years before World War I and during the 1950s, or on one of the neighborhood's high-profile talents from Poe to Pollock. Those who *have* tried to deal with the wider social and architectural history of the place have lumped together the West and Greenwich Villages. That approach, however, obscures the unique and important story of Greenwich Village, where the modern city first bloomed with new wide streets and new forms of housing—terrace rows—and is still much in evidence. Finally, most existing histories and monographs rely heavily and uncritically on secondary sources, thereby perpetuating errors and inventions. For example, contrary to some of the myths and legends abounding in the literature, no one was ever hung from Washington Square's "Hangman's Elm," and Lafayette certainly never witnessed 24 highwaymen being strung up from its branches.

My search for answers began with original sources: city council minutes and files, real estate tax and conveyance ledgers, directories, family histories and records, institutional and business inventories, newspapers, and the invaluable collections of the New-York Historical Society, the New York Public Library, the Museum of the City of New York, and the city's Municipal Reference Library and Archives. These institutions also have a wealth of engravings, paintings, and photographs. Long immersion in both municipal records and period newspapers gave me an understanding of the texture of the past that was obtainable in no other way. Tracking down images to document visually the long history of Greenwich Village led me through many private collections and family holdings. Several early discoveries filled important gaps in the city's history and heightened my detective's zeal. I found, for example, that the indefatigable efforts of one man, Mayor Philip Hone (1826–27), to create and promote the space were such that he truly deserved to be called the father of Washington Square.

In the end, it took 20 years of research to track down all of the answers I needed. This book is the culmination of those efforts.

Sifting through and organizing the material presented the challenge of a lifetime, but I finally determined that I could best sustain a cohesive narrative by dividing the epic's 200-plus years into eight roughly chronological chapters, each tied to a major theme. From 1797 to 1852 the square evolved from its rural setting, its first residences were built from the 1820s through the early 1850s, and Fifth Avenue grew from its Washington Square base to become the city's most fashionable thoroughfare. New York University's Gothic Revival edifice, built between 1834 and 1836, was one of the first arrivals on the square. The massive (for the time) space was far larger than needed to accommodate the small number of students (less than 150), so NYU rented out rooms. The building became a haven for artists around the square, and early residents included the artist and inventor Samuel F. B. Morse and the Hudson River School painter Daniel Huntington.

The neighborhood's first settlement in what is today's NoHo and the streets surrounding Washington Square were formally established in 1832 as a separate political jurisdiction—the Fifteenth Ward—and reached maturity as the home of New York's most powerful group of citizens by the 1870s. By the 1860s, the ward contained the best churches, residences, clubs, libraries, art galleries, hotels, stores, and theaters in the city. Known as the Empire Ward, it was Manhattan's shining "center city." In 1878 the district's first preservation battle was fought, when community activists successfully thwarted the city's attempt to install an armory in Washington Square. During the mid-nineteenth century, the square became the center of the city's cultural life. Hudson River School artists, the country's first important group of painters, were concentrated in the Studio Building at 51 West Tenth Street. Early arrivals there included John W. Casilear, John La Farge, Frederic E. Church, William M. Hart, Sanford Gifford, Jervis McEntee, Martin Johnson Heade, Emanuel Leutze, and William S. Haseltine. They would be joined later by Winslow Homer, Ralph Blakelock, Albert Bierstadt, and William Merritt Chase. John F. Kensett, another important painter of the group, had a studio nearby. A literary salon on Waverly Place showcased Edgar Allan Poe, and another, on East Eighth Street, provided a refuge for Herman Melville. A few blocks away, Walt Whitman and his irreverent circle—the beginnings of the country's bohemian tradition—could be found in Pfaff's cellar restaurant at 647 Broadway, a little above Bleecker Street.

Around the turn of the century, from 1879 to 1908, it seemed that the residential fabric of Greenwich Village, which was smack in the path of the city's burgeoning commercial growth and transportation routes, would be permanently damaged. However, the neighborhood organized to fight the inroads of business, and the great marble arch designed by Stanford White and dedicated in 1895 is at once a monument to residents' victory in that clash and a commemoration of George Washington's inauguration. Construction of the arch highlighted the work of two talented sculptors, Philip Martiny and Frederick MacMonnies; meanwhile, two of the country's greatest sculptors, Augustus Saint-Gaudens and Daniel Chester French, lived and had studios near the square.

From 1908 to 1920, the term *Greenwich Village,* centered on Washington Square, became synonymous with rebellion in the arts and in mores, and the area was universally recognized as America's supreme bohemia. The impact of gatherings at Mabel Dodge's salon at 23 Fifth Avenue and the Liberal Club at 137 MacDougal Street was felt nationwide, as was the influence of groundbreaking plays by Eugene O'Neill and the gritty urban paintings of the Ashcan School artists. The country also noted the equal roles taken by the Village's independent women as writers, artists, and rebels. Artists John Sloan, William Glackens, Everett Shinn, Ernest Lawson, and Maurice Prendergast had studios on or just off the square.

The real estate boom of the twenties produced residential rather than commercial buildings in Greenwich Village. During the thirties and forties, the creative energy unleashed in the city, most specifically in Greenwich Village, made New York the world's capital of art. Abstract Expressionists Jackson Pollock and Willem de Kooning lived and worked in the Village during this heady period of artistic development, as did the Realists Edward Hopper and Thomas Hart Benton.

In the fifties, hoards of tourists invaded Greenwich Village for a firsthand look at the haunts frequented by Beat Generation poets and writers influenced by Allen Ginsberg, Jack Kerouac, and William S. Burroughs. By the late sixties and early seventies, the Village was attracting from all over America folk singers inspired by Pete Seeger, Joan Baez, Bob Dylan, and other musicians who used their songs not just to entertain, but as a medium of protest. It was during this period that destruction of the district's buildings reached a peak, but some major preservationist battles were won as well. Robert Moses aroused the ire of thousands of residents—including Jane Jacobs, whose views of what a city should be were diametrically opposed—with his plans for a boulevard through Washington Square and a proposed Lower Manhattan Expressway. Once again, the residents prevailed, and the defeat of the expressway led to the salvation of what was to become SoHo. A New York state landmarks preservation law passed in 1965 and was upheld by the U.S. Supreme Court in 1978.

From 1979 to 2001, Greenwich Village and its environs experienced ongoing improvements. What was destined to become a hugely successful anticrime drive began in 1994 in Greenwich Village, and Eighth Street, which had fallen on hard times, became a business improvement district that is now, both East and West, becoming home to a colorful mix of thriving mom-and-pop shops and national chain stores. At the turn of the twentieth century, Astor Place was being transformed by Cooper Union's development from a sea of asphalt, complete with erratic physical remnants of its varied history, into extensive green space with a fashionable new hotel. But tragedy ensued. On September 11, 2001, the twin towers of the World Trade Center were erased from the Village's southern skyline in a monumentally horrendous terrorist act, with a devastating loss of life and a revisiting of the 1970s economic troubles. However, resilient New York City and the whole country continue to recover.

Because Greenwich Village has influenced the rest of Manhattan in numerous ways and has itself been affected by the larger currents in the city and the nation, it cannot be examined in isolation. Whenever I perceived it appropriate to move beyond strict geographic boundaries to discuss the district in a wider context, I have done so.

Inevitably, some readers will be disappointed by the omission of a favorite building, person, group, or bit of history. It was necessary to be selective, sometimes ruthlessly so, or the book would have ballooned into several volumes. Throughout, I have tried to include significant material that has not been reported before or has been reported inaccurately. My goal has been to choose well enough so that most of the book will be a revelation.

: : : : : :

AROUND WASHINGTON SQUARE

Washington Square North in the 1860s. Fifth Avenue enters in the middle of the view, just to the left of the carriage. Henry James set *Washington Square* here and allows his own nostalgia for the lost city of his childhood to assist him in evoking the area for his readers: "It was here, as you might have been informed on good authority, that you had come into a world which appeared to offer a variety of sources of interest; it was here that your grandmother lived, in venerable solitude, and dispensed a hospitality which commended itself alike to the infant imagination and the infant palate; it was here that you took your first walks abroad, following the nursery maid with unequal step, and sniffing up the strange odor of the ailanthus trees which at that time formed the principal umbrage of the Square, and diffused an aroma that you were not yet critical enough to dislike as it deserved; it was here, finally, that your first school, kept by a broad-bosomed, broad-based old lady with a ferule, who was always having tea in a blue cup, with a saucer that didn't match, enlarged the circle both of your observations and your sensations. It was here, at any rate, that my heroine spent many years of her life; which is my excuse for this topographical parenthesis" (Harper & Brothers, 1881, p. 24). Photograph by Anthony Brothers. Author's Collection.

: : : : : **1**

RISE OF THE SQUARE AND FIFTH AVENUE

1797–1852

ASHINGTON SQUARE, THE GREAT BUSTLING HUB OF MANHATTAN'S
downtown Villages, is both the mirror of its surrounding cultural and ethnic
diversity and a potent reminder of "old" New York. Henry James, who fixed
the square's early tone and value preeminently in our imagination with *Washington Square* and *The American Scene*, wrote that going there "was as if the
wine of life had been poured for you, in advance, into some pleasant old
punch-bowl." He also noted that as early as 1835 the "ideal of quiet and genteel retirement" was to be found in the handsome houses on the north side of
Washington Square. That living on the square was already desirable in the
1830s, when Dr. Sloper of *Washington Square* built his "modern, wide-fronted
house," is a telling index of how quickly perceptions can take hold. For Washington Square, with its air of dignity and preordination, was not even created
until the mid-1820s, and the decision to do so constituted a momentous event
in the annals of New York City, with consequences that shaped the growth of
the rest of Manhattan. Along with its instantaneous success as the domain of
the rich and eminent, the square helped lure the main development of Manhattan away from the avenues of the East Side. Similarly, its prestige would
preclude the construction of an enormous park on the East River. A more centrally situated park would be planned instead, its site pegged to the development of a Fifth Avenue stylishly anchored by Washington Square.[1]

But the square's impact on the social and cultural ramifications of the city
was more immediate. In the eighteenth and early nineteenth centuries, New
York had a few open spaces inherited from the colonial era—the Battery
(much smaller than it is now), Bowling Green, DeLancey's Square, and the
[City Hall] Park. DeLancey's Square, which under British rule had been ear-
marked for use as a residential square, was confiscated, divided into lots, and
sold by the city shortly after the Revolutionary War. So the city began its post-
colonial life with no new residential squares. Unlike London, which boasted
more than 20 of these enclaves by the 1820s, Manhattan possessed exactly
one—Trinity Church's 5½-acre Hudson Square, a private green laid out in
1803 and surrounded by Hudson, Varick, Beach, and Laight Streets. Though
the city had a hard-fought blueprint in the 1811 Commissioners' Plan that provided for squares as well as streets, large spaces in the sparsely populated upper
reaches of the island that had been marked for squares, a parade ground, and
a marketplace were being drastically reduced in size (fig. 1.1). Manhattan, its
commissioners chauvinistically and myopically explained in 1811, did not need
much "vacant space": "Certainly, if the City of New York were destined to
stand on the side of a small stream, such as the Seine or the Thames, a great
number of ample spaces might be needful; but those large arms of the sea
which embrace Manhattan Island, render its situation, in regard to health and
pleasure, as well as to convenience of commerce, peculiarly felicitous."[2]

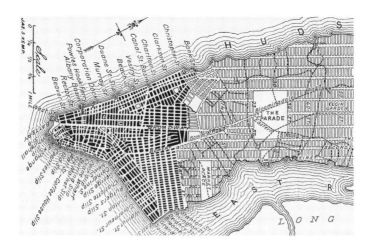

This benighted attitude did not change until the 1820s, when London's renowned West End emerged as the model that New Yorkers would adopt for their squares. Residents of fashionable precincts like St. James and Mayfair could look out on a square and view it as a kind of private park, their own bit of bucolic ground amid the sophisticated pleasures of town. A square, in contrast to a park, is given identity and form by its surrounding buildings. The typical London square required nine acres or less, with owners giving up a portion of their land to green space, the presence of which consequently raised the value of the adjoining land. New York landowners were ready to accept the idea.

Once covering much of what is now Washington Square was a 6½-acre parcel of the Herring Farm, sold at auction in 1797. The city, which happened to be searching for a new potter's field that year, bought the land for about $4,500. Later, the city sheriff had a public gallows erected approximately where the square's fountain is now. At the time, this area (near the present Waverly Place) was the natural choice for such bleak facilities because it was a rural northern suburb of the city and already the site of cemeteries owned by downtown churches. The property was far enough away, yet convenient to the population center located two miles to the south. Just three-quarters of a mile to the west lay the new state prison on the Hudson River, another source of supply for the field and noose. Episcopal minister William F. Morgan left this graphic description of the locale (fig. 1.2): "Large open fields stretched off yonder to the southwest. Old country seats still held their place. Old milestones were still in requisition along what was then a turnpike [the Bowery], unpaved, and lined with modest footpaths. Brooks and running streams diversified the landscape. Groves of patriarchal trees were in sight. Gardens under tillage, and pastures enclosed with rails, and flocks and herds—yes and hill and valley and bog were discernible in almost every direction."[3]

The isolation of the potter's field eroded over the next 25 years as urban growth spread northward. Houses were springing up above Canal Street, and several epidemics of yellow fever gripped the city, leaving thousands of fatalities in their wake. These and many other dead totaling 20,000 filled the trenches of the public burial ground to capacity. (In 1857 one physician de-

FIG. 1.2 (*above*) Bird's-eye view south from Union Place, named for the junction of the Bowery (left) and Broadway, 1828, as seen in an oil painting by Alburtus D. O. Browere. The leftmost church spire is that of St. Mark's, at what would soon be East Tenth Street. Within a few years, this bucolic scene would be replaced by Union Square and the regulated streets of the expanding city. © Museum of the City of New York.

FIG. 1.3 (*right*) Mayor Philip Hone, the "father of Washington Square," used his considerable influence to ensure not only that the square would be a reliable source of income for Sailors' Snug Harbor, but also that it would be developed to benefit the city as a whole. Portrait by John Vanderlyn, 1827. Courtesy of the Art Commission of the City of New York.

scribed Washington Square's former role as "our Golgotha during the dreadful visitations of the Yellow Fever of 1797, 1798, 1801, and 1803, and many a victim of the pestilence, of prominent celebrity, was consigned to that final resting place on earth, regardless of his massive gains or public service.")[4] In 1825, the city had to level the overflowing gravesite and went on to designate a new and larger potter's field on the block that now contains Bryant Park and the New York Public Library.

Six months after the old potter's field was cleared, New York elected as

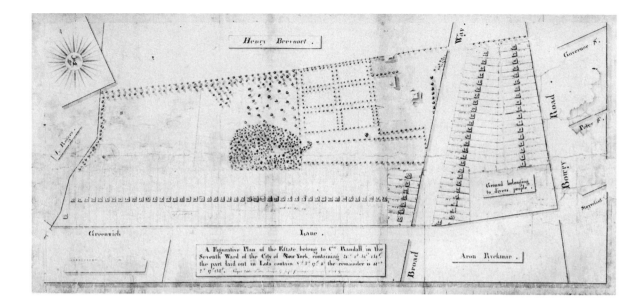

Within the map, visible labels: "Henry Brevoort .", "Way .", "Governor S.", "Road", "Poter St.", "Bowery", "Ground belonging to divers people .", "Stuyvesant .", "Greenwich", "Lane .", "Broad", "Aron Ryckman .", "A Figurative Plan of the Estate belong to Cpt Randall in the Seventh Ward of the City of New York, containing ..."

mayor a man who was destined to be one of its most illustrious and useful citizens. Soldier, patriot, philanthropist, politician, and diarist Philip Hone left his mark on the city in innumerable ways, from a host of charitable and cultural works that he supported to the invaluable record of New York events and society preserved in his journals (fig. 1.3). Hone served as investment advisor to Trinity Church, a patron of the Mercantile Library, a trustee of Columbia College, and a governor of New York Hospital, among other positions. As mayor, he emerged as the moving spirit and indefatigable force behind the creation of Washington Square.

When Hone took office in early 1826, the streets were closing in on the recently vacated potter's field, and the city's Common Council, of which Hone was a voting member, was pressed for a decision on its future. Hone was also an active trustee of Sailors' Snug Harbor, a prominent charitable trust founded to aid indigent seamen. The trust sorely needed rents from its property that spread eastward from the foot of Fifth Avenue, one of the city's newly created 100-foot-wide thoroughfares. What better way to raise that income than by creating a residential square of luxurious dimensions on adjoining land? To Hone's public-spirited yet pragmatic way of thinking, the old potter's field was a key to the destiny of the trust he was bound to help.

From 1831 to 1976, Sailors' Snug Harbor maintained on Staten Island a home for retired sailors and was largely associated with that borough, but the Harbor began as a powerful Manhattan-based charity well before Philip Hone served on its board. Its assets consisted of 21 acres of farmland in the heart of today's Greenwich Village, much of which touched directly on the northern boundary of the potter's field. The property was bounded by Fifth Avenue on the west and by Fourth Avenue and the Bowery on the east. Its northern edge was approximately East Tenth Street, and its southern border was a line near what is now Washington Square North and the eastern portion of Waverly Place (fig. 1.4). The farm was once owned by Thomas Randall, a New Yorker who made his fortune in privateering and trade (including the slave trade) in the years before American independence. As a rich merchant, he was involved in the early commercial and political life of the city, and in 1770 he was a founding member of the Marine Society of the City of New York. (Shipping fueled the city's growth, but government aid for needy sailors did not yet exist. The Marine Society, a precursor of Sailors' Snug Harbor, assisted distressed families of ship captains and other seamen through its membership donations.)

When Thomas Randall died in 1790, his farm went to his son, Captain Robert Richard Randall, who was also a privateer and merchant seaman. Thomas Randall's home had been at 7 Whitehall Street, but Robert Randall lived on the farm in a mansion inspired by a French countryside chateau. It had been built by the farm's last British owner, Andrew Elliot, Collector of the Port, who left with the British forces in 1783. Robert Randall had no immediate heirs, and on his death in 1801 he left the 21-acre Randall Farm in trust to charity. According to trust tradition, Alexander Hamilton was the Randall family lawyer who drafted Captain Randall's will and suggested that the land be left "for the purpose of maintaining and supporting aged, decrepit and worn-out sailors."[5] This proposal would—and did—appeal to Robert Randall, for he, as well as Hamilton and George Washington, along with many other illustrious Americans, was a member of the Marine Society. A provision of the will that especially ensured the clout of the new trust, to be called Sailors' Snug Harbor, named the most powerful group of people in the city as ex-officio trustees. Accordingly, the city's mayor and recorder, the chancellor of New York State, the president of the chamber of commerce, the president and vice-president of the Marine Society, and the rectors of Trinity and the First Presbyterian churches sat on the charity's board.

This nexus of influence notwithstanding, the trust did not lack for problems. As soon as Robert Randall's will was made public, distant relatives of the Randall family contested it, laid claim to the estate, and filed lawsuits that took nearly 30 years to settle. Moreover, the trust received no public tax support. By the terms of the Randall will, the proceeds from the real estate holdings were supposed to pay Sailors' Snug Harbor bills, and as early as 1817, the trustees realized that the Randall Farm would be best served by being developed and deployed as a long-term real estate investment, rather than as a rest home for sailors. That is, the mariners should be moved to a more distant—and less prime—spot, and housing and other facilities built for them there. But with an income of $4,242 in 1806, the year the trust was incorporated, and only $6,660 in 1817, the trustees wondered how they could adequately take care of their new charges, given the land, buildings, and staff that would be required. (As an indication of dollar value in the period, a fine row house on a good street cost $10,000.) The Randall will further stipulated that the trust could not sell its property. The trustees concluded that they would have to induce developers to build houses with long-term leases on their land. However, leaseholds, as opposed to freeholds, would be a very tough sell, as Trinity Church had discovered with its Hudson Square lots. Many years had passed before anyone could be persuaded to occupy those, yet the expected revenues had made it worth the wait.

In the early 1820s, the trustees of Sailors' Snug Harbor eyed the steady developments west and south of their land. A final yellow fever epidemic in 1822 again forced many downtown residents and businesses to flee northward. Most of them chose the growing settlement around Christopher Street near the Hudson River. This area (today's West Village) had grown due to flights of citizens from downtown since the first major outbreak of epidemic disease in 1791. Many wooden buildings were hastily constructed, one of them reportedly holding *300 boarders*. Meanwhile, to the south, large, elegant houses, some with marble fronts, were lining Bond and Bleecker Streets. This was the sort of construction that the trustees and other owners of land around the square wanted. Enter Philip Hone.

Along with his desire to improve New York City, Hone had to consider the financial well-being of Sailors' Snug Harbor, and he had an idea that would benefit both—a gracious square that would encompass the potter's field located next to a substantial portion of the old Randall Farm. A square would enhance the property value of the lots facing it and those in the vicinity, making developers more amenable to the prospect of leaseholds. Few were willing to invest in property improvements on land they did not own without other inducements. Trinity Church, despite its initial difficulties in attracting developers, might well have been a source for Hone's notion of using a square to endow a charity. By the 1820s, Hudson Square was a successful real estate venture, and the church, with Hone as its principal business advisor, surely knew how it benefited from higher rents on that square.

For all his knowledge and energy, Hone faced two stubborn obstacles. First, the area covering today's Washington Square wasn't on the Commissioners' Plan. Furthermore, the plan was not going to be easy to alter, particularly because the Fifth Avenue–Thompson Street connection (a line that bisects the square) was one of the very few through routes between the new streets and the old. Changes would also be impeded because in 1807 jurisdiction over the Commissioners' Plan had been transferred from local authorities to the state legislature precisely to avoid special interests. The plan was to be kept free of the manipulations of municipal politics and the pleadings of influential property owners. Second, land in Manhattan had become more and more expensive as the built-up city advanced northward. In 1826, an acre of the old potter's field was worth *23 times* what the city had paid for it in 1797. The city could profit handsomely from taxing lots there rather than maintaining it as a public space.

Hone's solution to these dilemmas was masterly. The Commissioners' Plan had marked a huge, 270-acre square in the center of the island above 23rd Street for military exercises and as a place to "assemble in case of need the force necessary to defend the City." Conceived during events leading up to the War of 1812, the "Parade" as it had been labeled on the 1811 Plan, was much reduced in size shortly after the war ended in 1814. When the Common Council, which included Hone, met in February 1826, the Parade's size and reason for being were questioned.[6]

The members considered eliminating it altogether or moving the Parade's function elsewhere in the city. In that same meeting, and not coincidentally, for Hone evidently had been able to muster strong support for his position, the council resolved that the recently vacated potter's field would be "appropriated for use by the Military and called the Military Parade Ground."[7]

Hone himself was no mere exploiter of the military's popularity. He had been a corporal in an artillery regiment during the War of 1812, and imbued with a zestful, patriotic spirit, he was proud of his country's men in uniform. Yet Hone also understood the value of splashy public displays of brass and flourishes, especially during an era when the military was made up of voluntary bands of local citizens. These citizen militia groups had been active in the War of 1812, but now their services were largely ceremonial. They marched in the parades that were a standard feature of public events, reminding spectators of the republic's brief but inspiring history and inciting feelings of unity and glory.

Hone ensconced the militia in the former potter's field, then decreed that the site be used to host the national jubilee for the fiftieth anniversary of the signing of the Declaration of Independence. Thus, in one masterstroke, Hone both enhanced the square's status and made it impregnable to routine or thoughtless development schemes, and the occasion itself, fortuitously enough, would be celebrated during his term of office. A related maneuver was to confer on the square a distinguished name with which no one could quarrel. In June 1826, in preparation for Independence Day, the Common Council officially changed the name of the new square to "Washington Military Parade Ground." Besides fitting in nicely with the celebration, the sacred name of "Washington" was well nigh irresistible. All of the surrounding north-south streets extending from downtown had been named for heroic generals of the Revolution, and how better to honor the commander-in-chief than with an entire reviewing ground devoted to his memory? Also, the name Washington significantly enhanced lot values. (Finding the parade ground's full-dress name cumbersome, the press at the time quickly shortened it to "Washington Square," or simply, "the square," as it also appears in these pages, though it would not achieve its landscaped "square" shape until 1828.)

New York in 1826, then a city of 170,000, barely seemed large enough to hold the multitudes attending the July 4 jubilee. Militia units from Philadelphia and Connecticut joined New York troops in marching through the downtown streets before proceeding to the recently covered gravesite. There, they were received by Governor De Witt Clinton, Mayor Hone, the Common Council, judges, generals, other officials, and thousands of everyday folk. Alderman Doughty of the Committee of Ceremonies and Mayor Hone addressed the crowd. The Declaration of Independence was read to shouts and applause, and the square was dedicated with its new name, Washington. The next day's *Evening Post* marveled that 10,000 guests had consumed "two oxen roasted whole" and "ponderous loads of beef, hams, etc., etc., and moistened by a plentiful supply of ale." All of this was laid out on "tables spread 400 feet in length" decorated with flowers and greens. The paper estimated that 50,000 people visited the square that day.[8]

With the square safely anointed and preserved as open ground, Hone led the Common Council toward enlarging it. The land area, after boundary adjustments, was about 6¼ acres, a respectable public space, but not a grand one. Much narrower than today's square, the potter's field was limited on the east by a strip of church cemeteries, and on the west by Minetta Creek, which ran southwest from the foot of Fifth Avenue to the corner of MacDougal and West Fourth Streets. At a mere 6¼ acres, the square would face tough competition for residential sovereignty over Bleecker, Bond, and Great Jones Streets, Hudson Square and the St. Luke's Church block, the Astor family's enclave on Lafayette Place, the Stuyvesant family's developments around Second Avenue, and Clement Clarke Moore's Chelsea. There was also Broadway, by far the most sought-after living address since the earliest days of the Nieuw Amsterdam colony, when it was named "Heere Straat" in the 1600s. "Heere Straat" meant "Gentlemen's Street," and the gentlemen of New York were loyal to Broadway as the premier place to be into the 1840s. Nevertheless, a more spacious square would draw moneyed residents, and nearby Broadway might well guarantee its appeal. Furthermore, recent news from London was instructive. In the 1820s Lord Grosvenor created Belgravia, the most prestigious residential scheme yet attempted in London. The crown jewel of the new neighborhood was Belgrave Square, laid out in 1826; it occupied 11 acres, including the land and perimeter streets, and was a brilliant success.

Increasing the size of Washington Square would be expensive and controversial. A single landowner, Alfred S. Pell, owned the western side up to Minetta Creek, which was primed for the sale of lots. Expanding to Wooster Street on the east and only as far as Sullivan Street on the west, the square would have encompassed the potter's field and the old church cemeteries (about one acre) and cost $17,000. This plan would have yielded a modest 7¼-acre square, although the Fifth Avenue entrance would have been far off-center. However, Pell offered a reasonable price for his land (the same price, proportionally, as for the church property), and the council opted for both the eastern and western extensions. Pell's 2½ acres, bounded on the west by Mac-Dougal Street, were bought for $43,550, forcing a burdensome assessment on landowners in the vicinity. Assessments paid for Washington Square, as they bankrolled such other public land improvements as streets and wells. This method of revenue complied with an 1813 assessment law that the state enacted as a companion piece to the 1811 Commissioners' Plan for streets. Buttressed by the strength of the law, in December 1826 the Common Council applied to the

New York State Supreme Court for the full-sized, 9¾-acre ground—or a magnificent 13¾-acre square including the adjoining streets. Assessments skyrocketed to $537.50 for a lot with a 25-foot frontage on the square—more than one-half the total taxable value of the lot. On top of that, the city raised the total taxable values by 80 percent. Ignoring the resentment of the assessed owners, the city could boast a 13¾-acre square whose lavish size beat London's best.

It had taken him almost the whole year, but by the end of his term, Philip Hone, the father of Washington Square, whose labors were indispensable to its genesis, had shepherded the square toward ultimate acceptance. The court would approve its expansion ten months later.

Soon after the Independence Day festivities, Hone's ambitions for the square met with a positive response. With the full-sized square practically assured, eight owners controlling 12 contiguous lots on Fourth Street facing the future Washington Square South built a uniform set of houses on their properties. This was the first important development on the square and also the city's first terrace row. Even though London had been building magnificent terrace housing for a century, and in the 1820s was lining Regent's Park with the most opulent yet seen, Manhattan had none. These designs might have offended New York's— and America's—more egalitarian instincts, as the reigning motivation of the typical London terrace was to give from a distance the appearance of a palatial residence to each individual row house. Nevertheless, the architectural consistency inherent in the terrace row could enclose a square magnificently. Here, on Washington Square South, the first step toward terrace construction was gingerly taken.

But success in the city's tight-knit and staid society of the early 1800s hinged on precisely who lived in the new square and how severe was any break with tradition. Most prominent among the owners was the wealthy merchant, soldier, and remarkably effective politician, Colonel James Boyles Murray (fig. 1.5). He had been an adventurous international trader for his father's firm during the Napoleonic wars (shipping guns to aid Haiti's slave revolt was one of the firm's myriad activities) and a soldier in the War of 1812. Colonel Murray was descended from an ancient Scottish peerage, and in 1814 he increased his wealth and influence through marriage to Maria Bronson. She was the daughter of Isaac Bronson, one of the country's richest financiers and bankers, and could trace her lineage to the first colonial settlers of New England. In addition to these stellar credentials, Isaac Bronson and the colonel's father,

FIG. 1.6 The Fourth Street
Row, drawn by Albert Lorenz in
1996, as the row appeared
ca. 1830. Its Federal style was
soon eclipsed by the Greek Revival, but its small front yards
had a momentous impact on the
city's development. Author's
Collection.

John Boyles Murray, had been Revolutionary War veterans—Bronson under
Washington's command and Murray under Lafayette. Murray received his
rank of colonel in 1817 and, after retiring from his artillery regiment in 1824,
accepted control of his father's business and invested largely in real estate. He
later represented the Washington Square district on the Common Council.
There, through the task of garnering public and political support, and through
other forms of initiative, he played the most critical role in bringing pure Croton water to the city and pushed for sewers, railways, and other major urban
improvements. (At that time in 1832, the cholera- and fire-plagued city mainly
depended on wells for water.) Murray's family built five of the twelve houses
in the row, and various members, including Colonel Murray and his younger
brother, the philanthropist and social lion Hamilton ("Ham") Murray, resided
there. Adding prestige were Alfred S. Pell, a descendant of the Westchester
Pells, and his wife, Adelia. He had secured the square's western 2½ acres at
market value for the city. She was the daughter of James Duane, the city's first
mayor after the Revolution, and granddaughter of Robert Livingston, the
proprietor of Livingston Manor on the Hudson. Also catching society's eye
was James Farquhar, leader of New York's assembly dances (forerunner of today's debutante balls). Farquhar, a prominent wine merchant, had leased the
Randall mansion north of the square, moving when the hill on which it stood
was leveled to build streets. With these and other row luminaries, the city's
elite approved and soon embraced the terrace-row concept.

Occupying most of the original long block between Thompson and Mac-
Dougal Streets, the row's unified design and imposing scale added a new twist
to the ubiquitous Federal style (fig. 1.6). The Fourth Street houses, typical of

the dwellings favored by the wealthy merchant class, were 25 feet wide, with three full stories and a fourth with a pitched roof and dormer windows. Their facades were entirely marble (as opposed to the brick surfaces of the city's contemporary Federal houses), their long parlor windows reached to the floor, and all the parlors gave out onto ornamental wrought-iron balconies that ran the width of each house. The elaborate stoops and doorways typical of the Federal style were sacrificed to the overall row design. Instead of the city's traditional high stoops, just a few steps gave access from the street, and a lintel, rather than an arched stone molding and fanlight, topped each doorway. All of the houses were graced with front yards enclosed with decorative iron fencing that extended across the entire length of the row. Although just ten feet deep, these grass plots were the city's first real front yards. Earlier row houses had been set back a few feet from the building line to accommodate stoops and permit access to cellars and basements. Otherwise, row houses in New York City and throughout the United States abutted the sidewalk or street. The land gave the row added elegance, with a hint of a forecourt such as only the grandest of London's houses possessed. Most of the west side of the square and all of the north side copied the idea, as did a number of other rows elsewhere in town. Generally, though, as row houses began to blanket Manhattan, front yards did not catch on, which further contributed to the singularity and refinement of Washington Square.

While they were being erected, the Fourth Street houses were first offered for sale under the frank heading "To Capitalists" in the *New York Gazette* of January 6, 1827. When they saw that affluent buyers were snapping up the new

FIG. 1.7 (facing page) Washington Square, view to the southeast from the square's west side in 1849, as engraved by James Smillie. Washington Square is depicted as it was originally laid out, although the fountain was not completed until 1852. In the distance, the crenellated towered New York University building and the Reformed Dutch Church have been shifted south by the artist to better serve the view. Generally, though, it is a fine image of the early square and its visitors. The engraving was made as an advertisement in the city directory for the Mt. Washington Collegiate Institution, which occupied the southeast corner of Fourth and MacDougal Streets (right). One of the town pumps is in use on the curb opposite the college. The chimneys and dormer windows of the Fourth Street Row trail off from the three corner buildings. Author's Collection.

residences, developers two blocks south on Bleecker Street, fearful of being left behind, built their own terrace rows. Although seven years ahead of the pack—an eon in the city's development rush—the trailblazing Fourth Street row put Washington Square on the residential map and raised property values.

Over the next two years the square prevailed against political change and stiff neighborhood opposition. Philip Hone, a Federalist and later a Whig, lost the next election (of 1827) to William Paulding, a Democrat. Despite Hone's loss, Paulding and the Common Councils of 1827 and 1828 firmly defended the square against fierce assessment protests. In October 1827, the court approved the council's request for the fully enlarged square, precisely denoting it as a "Public Place." (London's squares were private, as was New York's Hudson Square.) The council needed all the ammunition it could get because its opposition was formidable.

One of the strongest protests came from the Scotch Presbyterian Church, owner of the largest cemetery. The congregants had vigorously objected to the eastern extension to Wooster Street, not wanting their dead to be disturbed. (In 1819, just a block south of their property, 131 skeletons had been unearthed in building Fourth Street.) Why, other opponents asked, should they pay assessments for a nearby parade ground, when owners elsewhere, benefiting from proximity to a public market, didn't pay at all? The city duly took note but pressed on with the assessments. In July 1828, the Common Council listed nearly 15 percent of the assessed lots as delinquent and ordered them to be advertised and sold. By December, however, when the auction took place, owners were not eager to give up their property; fewer than 5 percent of the assessed lots still had taxes due on them. Perhaps a continuing real estate boom all over the city had taken some of the sting out of the assessments, although owners continued to object to them.

In spite of the assessment battle, work on the square was proceeding apace. On May 10, 1828, the *Evening Post* announced that the landscaping of Washington Square was nearly finished:

> Workmen are busily employed in putting a handsome fence around this spacious public square, by far the largest of any in this city. And laborers are busy in leveling and preparing the ground to be laid down to green turf, with neat gravel foot walks around the margin and across it from each extremity. When this work is completed and proper shade trees and shrubbery are beautifully set out over the whole square, it will afford a most delightful morning promenade. The improvements already made for the streets bordering upon it, and those in contemplation, will add to its beauty.[9]

Unlike later naturalistic landscapes promulgated by Olmsted and his generation of landscape architects, the design of Washington Square was formal. Its flat topography and geometrical walkways were similar to those of the squares of Paris and London. By the autumn of 1828, Minetta Creek had been carried away to the Hudson in a wooden sewer, grass was planted, and ailanthus trees lined the walks; the square was ready for parades and promenades in a beautifully finished setting. Despite all the leveling, preparing, and planting that the *Evening Post* described, not everything had been razed. The landscapers in charge were careful to preserve older buttonwood trees and elms as a part of its leafy green canopy. One survivor, the magnificent English elm at the northwest corner, is today the oldest tree in New York. (It is popularly known as the "Hangman's Elm," although no one was ever executed there.) An iron fence (the original was wood), a fountain, and lighting came later (fig. 1.7). The square even had its own caretaker; for all of 75 cents a day, one Isaac C. Osborn was hired as keeper in early 1829.

At a citizens' meeting in Tammany Hall in mid-November 1830, with ex-president James Monroe as chairman, plans were made to celebrate the revolution in France against the Bourbon restoration. (General Lafayette had made triumphal visits to New York in 1824 and 1825, and sympathy for the French was running high.) The upcoming Evacuation Day, November 25, 1830, the anniversary of the final withdrawal of British military forces from the city in 1783, was selected for the occasion. The indefatigable Hone accepted leadership of the arrangements committee, and he again made Washington Square the center stage for a production. The event outdid the Fourth of July jubilee of 1826, with tradesmen, social and business societies, the militia, and other groups forming a procession that stretched 2½ miles from downtown to the square. At the square itself, the latest manifestations of technological progress, including a steamboat, were displayed. Monroe's son-in-law, Postmaster Samuel Governeur, gave the oration in the presence of Monroe and Albert Gallatin, Secretary of the Treasury under Jefferson and Madison, and printers distributed copies of Governeur's speech to the horde in attendance. Memories of the Revolutionary War were fanned by the presence of veterans and patriots, two of whom had hauled down the Union Jack and raised the American flag when the British departed in 1783. Militia units assembled just north of the square fired a salute at the end of the ceremonies. For New Yorkers, now more than 202,000 in number, Washington Square had fulfilled its promise as a splendid new public space and a shrine of democracy. For Sailors' Snug Harbor, Philip Hone's extra promotional efforts had provided free advertising for their still vacant yet prime real estate holdings.

Prior to the celebration, the U.S. Supreme Court had ruled against the last relative's challenge to the Randall will, allowing the Harbor to proceed as it wished without further legal challenges. In the spring of 1831, the trust's long-held dream came true: a group of downtown merchants decided to lease the Harbor's 13 lots on the north side of the square for their new residences. Between 1831 and 1833 they erected a monumental redbrick and marble terrace, immediately dubbed the "Row," in a bold Greek Revival style. Prime movers in this endeavor were two of the city's most distinguished and influential merchants, business partners James Boorman and John Johnston (fig. 1.8). Boor-

FIG. 1.8 John Johnston, by Rembrandt Peale, ca. 1830s. Johnston was a founder of the Row, and his descendants helped sustain lower Fifth Avenue as a social center for over a century. Courtesy of The Metropolitan Museum of Art, Bequest of Noel Johnston King, 1980 (1980.77).

man leased the Row's prestigious Fifth Avenue corner, and Johnston leased two lots in the center.

Boorman's and Johnston's charitable natures alone could well have led them to favor Sailors' Snug Harbor lots; Boorman, in particular, gave his money and valuable time generously to public service, on a par with Philip Hone. But their connections with the Murrays of the earlier Fourth Street row may have cemented their decision. Boorman and Johnston also had Scottish roots, and Boorman had strong personal associations with the Murrays. He had been a downtown neighbor and friend of the public-spirited Colonel Murray, and was closely allied with Hamilton Murray in charitable work.

In *Washington Square,* Henry James, with his thumb unerringly on the social pulse of the times, placed his novel's protagonist in a mid-1830s Greek Revival residence similar to those on the Row, and he noted the rapid consecration of the square as the quintessence of upper-crust New York once these noble buildings were added.

With its stunning victories in court and in real estate, Sailors' Snug Harbor bought 130 acres on the north shore of Staten Island in May 1831, and five months later the cornerstone of its new asylum for sailors was laid there. The trust could begin caring for seamen on Staten Island with ample funds from the Randall Farm lots. Hone noted this landmark event in his diary, reflecting that the trust's property "has increased greatly in value within the last year and must be ample now for the object of [Randall's] munificent bequest."[10]

Another break for the trust and the square occurred when the Common Council created the city's Fifteenth Ward in March 1832, the year of the centennial of Washington's birth. Until then the square had been in the Ninth Ward, a large territory ranging from the Bowery to the Hudson River, between Houston and Fourteenth Streets. By 1831, there was sufficient population in the eastern part of the Ninth—that is, east of Sixth Avenue—to create a separate ward, which would have the square nearly in the center of it (fig. 1.9). As a distinct ward, the square and its immediate vicinity would have their own alderman on the Common Council (there was one for each ward) and the means to obtain their full share of benefits. Landowners around the square now had superb representation on the council. The Fifteenth Ward's first alderman was the notable Colonel James B. Murray, primary founder of the Fourth Street row. Judge Judah Hammond, Murray's successor and row neighbor, was elected in 1833; he was a politician and judge of the Marine Court, and had been a partner with Murray in creating the row. The ward's tax assessor was the rich and socially prominent John L. Ireland, who had married

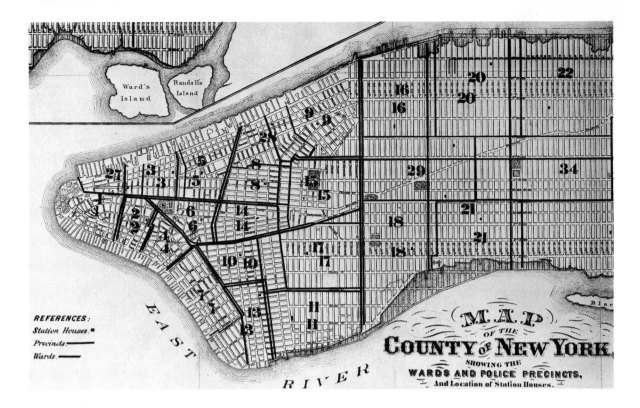

FIG. 1.9 Section of an 1870 ward map showing the city's police precincts. The Fifteenth Ward surrounding Washington Square and its Fifteenth Precinct have mostly coterminous boundaries. Cartographer unknown. Courtesy of NYC Municipal Archives.

into the wealthy Floyd family of Long Island. Ireland's father had purchased from the Herrings land that, in the grid, covered most of the square's original two southern blocks. Son and heir John L. Ireland kept a six-lot-wide swath through the center of the eastern block (about a third of the block's total area) for his double-lot house surrounded by an orchard and garden. His father had built the house on Amity Street (now West Third Street), with its back to the doleful setting of the potter's field; the carriage-house and stable wound up facing the square on Fourth Street. The aldermen assured that the square received plenty of improvements and the owners fair tax treatment.

While the Row was going up on the north side of the square, the University of the City of New York, later New York University (NYU), was planning its new building destined for the east side of it. James M. Mathews, D.D., the institution's first chancellor from 1831 to 1839, was the driving force behind both the building and the university itself as a nonsectarian training ground for the mercantile elite. Mathews wanted the best and got it, although at a crippling cost. NYU paid $40,000 in 1832 for the entire blockfront between Waverly and Washington Places, containing about 7¼ standard (25 × 100 foot) lots. The city's top architectural firm, Town, Davis & Dakin, was hired to execute the project, and they proposed an English Collegiate Gothic design, the style purposely evocative of Oxford and Cambridge (fig. 1.10). The builder engaged was Seth Geer, one of the two best in the city, and the building itself would be clad extravagantly in marble.

Construction took over three years to complete, amid continuing strife on

FIG. 1.10 New York University looking northeast across the snowy square in the early 1860s. The rear towered section of the building masked a pair of houses, one facing Washington Place (in the view) and the other facing Waverly Place. Photograph by Anthony Brothers. Author's Collection.

NYU's governing council. Buying the land had wiped out all but $66.46 of the university's funds. Nonetheless, Mathews forged ahead while the council's secretary and treasurer resigned, and the university sank heavily into debt. Additional construction costs soared to more than $150,000 by 1837, and to cover them professors were not paid. Some $25,000 was spent to incorporate a grand Gothic chapel in the building, another pet project of the chancellor, and even the university's books were mortgaged to cover this new expense. Whether or not it was any consolation to the many dissident council members or angry faculty, the chapel, which had an immense traceried window facing the square, was singled out as the most marvelous feature of the new building, itself picturesquely castellated and gabled. One observer proudly described Mathews's chapel in the *New-York American* of May 27, 1837:

> In the centre of the edifice, fifty feet wide, rising from the ceiling of the second story to the top, and running through from front to rear, is the chapel. As a work of art, this room is far in advance of any other in our country, a specimen of the pointed architecture of the age of Henry VII, the golden age of that style. It is florid, but not gaudy; rich, but not overwrought. All the parts are bold, prominent, and dignified. It carries the spectator back about three centuries, and nothing reminds him of the present but the arms of the nation, and the state and city, displayed on the flat of the ceiling.[11]

Contributing to the cost overruns was a problem concerning the building's dimensions. As the structure began to rise, builders and contractors complained that parts of the towers and buttresses were protruding a few feet over the building line. The university requested a variance. According to Mathews's appeal, refusal would mean that all the marble for the first three floors had to be redressed or shortened. Fearing a deluge of similar variance requests, the Common Council did refuse. Following this expensive delay, local stonecutters rioted in October 1834 over the use of convict labor on the project. To save money, the university had authorized Seth Geer to contract for Sing-Sing prisoners to work the marble. Geer was just finishing the marble Colonnade Row on Lafayette Place—another magnificent terrace row—using convict labor, and this common practice by him and other builders enraged the stonecutters. They had objected to the state legislature but with no success. This time the stonecutters converged on offending construction sites with rocks and brickbats. Units of New York's National Guard were called out, and they encamped in Washington Square for four days and nights to protect the NYU building until tempers cooled.

Despite numerous critics, Chancellor Mathews inspired strong and sustained backing, much of it from leaseholders on the Row. Seven of those thirteen affluent residents devoted substantial time and money to NYU during its tough early years. Two stood out as the university's strongest champions. One was John Johnston, a founder of the Row, who was an original shareholder in 1830 and was council vice president from 1835 to 1845. Johnston could be counted on to provide generous funds in times of need. The other pillar of strength from the Row, General James Tallmadge, was Mathews's most staunch supporter and defender. Tallmadge, one of the leadership Whigs, had assisted Mathews in organizing the university and was its council president from 1834 to 1846.

Five tumultuous years after acquiring the site, the chancellor finally got a striking new edifice for his scholastic experiment. With much pomp and ceremony, the building was dedicated on May 20, 1837. Its reviews in the highbrow press were excellent, and James Gordon Bennett's fledgling *Herald* liked it, too, adding a racier slant in July 1837: "Washington Square, in the 'west end' [an allusion to London's most fashionable neighborhoods] is rivaling the Battery, in the elegance and beauty of its fair promenaders. Last night the display was beautiful. The trees, broad expanse of sky, the solemn Gothic towers of the University, all heightened the scene. I observed one beautiful being in a blue silk hat, colored slippers, and pure white cambric dress, that is fit to set the world on fire. There will be a great rush, during these fine evenings, to elegant Washington Square."[12]

One byproduct of the university's early financial problems and small enrollments was its need to rent out a large part of its space. In 1835, with construction not yet complete, artists and other creative personalities had begun moving into the upper floors of the building. Samuel F. B. Morse, painter, inventor, and first president of the National Academy of Design, and the portraitist Daniel Huntington—both outstanding members of New York's early art world—became tenants in 1835. Before long they were joined by other illustrious residents. Alexander Jackson Davis, the influential architect who designed Federal Hall, liked his firm's building enough to establish his home and studio there. Samuel Colt, inventor of the revolver and later one of the nation's leading arms manufacturers, was another tenant. While in residence, he worked with Morse on the use of telegraphy for the remote detonation of mines as a harbor defense. Over the years these floors became an exotic combination of apartment house, scientific laboratory, clubhouse of the Hudson River School, and haven for one of the city's earliest bohemian communities.

While Mathews was engaged with his university, his South Reformed Dutch Church, near Wall Street, was destroyed in the Great Fire of 1835. The congregation split over where to move, with one group following Mathews uptown to Washington Square. He served as their pastor, using the university chapel until a new church could be built. Land on the eastern side of the square, covering approximately three standard lots just south of the NYU building across Washington Place, was purchased for $44,000 in 1837. Mathews and the other university officers must have been cognizant of the 240 percent increase in the cost of the church's lots over what NYU had paid in 1832, especially as 1837 was the year of a bad financial panic. The escalation in price since 1832 indicates the dramatic increase in the desirability of the square. Some of the demand came from downtown residents after the 1835 fire, which had left much of the area south of Wall Street and east of Broadway in ruins. The victims of the burnt district added to an already lively market for lots on the square and other streets nearby.

The architect of the new church, Minard Lafever, was already intimately connected with the square's history. In 1831, at the beginning of his architectural career, he won the competition for the design of Sailors' Snug Harbor's first buildings on Staten Island. By 1839, when he undertook the Reformed Dutch Church commission, he was widely known for his builder's guides and texts on architecture. For Mathews and his flock, Lafever designed a twin-towered Gothic Revival structure derived from English models. The building, which also featured a central traceried window, complemented Town, Davis & Dakin's work, but it had a contrasting exterior of rough-cut dark granite trimmed in red stone. Services were first held in the lovely new church in 1840, but unfortunately three small wooden stables blemished the lots south of it. Converted to shops, they commercialized the block for most of the nineteenth century. A lone residence on the Fourth Street corner was soon converted into a boarding house.

For more than half a century, the university building and the Lafever church graced the square with classical beauty, and they became beloved neighborhood landmarks. The NYU building in particular was one of the largest and most impressive in the city—a must-see for tourists and visiting

FIG. 1.11 (*left*) John Rogers Jr., real estate developer and fighter for Fifth Avenue's growth. His generation was the first to give up powdered hair and stockings for the forerunner of modern menswear. Artist and date unknown. Courtesy of Henry A. Chisolm.

FIG. 1.12 (*right*) Mary Rogers, daughter of John Rogers Sr., and wife of W. C. Rhinelander. As the model for Dr. Sloper's much mourned wife in *Washington Square,* James wrote that she had "the most charming eyes in the island of Manhattan." This portrait hung prominently in the Rhinelander home at 14 Washington North. Artist and date unknown. Courtesy of Mr. and Mrs. Charles D. Miller.

dignitaries. However hallowed and permanent they may have seemed, change was unstoppable, and they were swept away in the tide of commercial building that engulfed the area of the square in the 1890s. Henry James, on his American trip of 1904, visited Washington Square and decried what he saw. The new construction was "high," "impersonal," and "crude," and the effect of the new buildings on him was akin to "having been amputated of half my history." James was born in 1843 on Washington Place, two doors east of the old NYU building; when it was torn down, his birthplace had vanished or, in his words, been "ruthlessly suppressed."[13]

Meanwhile, Fifth Avenue, the square's major appendage, had competition from the other 100-foot-wide avenues. It had been laid out from the square to Thirteenth Street in 1824, and extending it further to the north would better its chances of becoming the premier avenue in New York. This improvement, of course, would benefit those with property along it. Along with the Sailors' Snug Harbor trust, George, John (fig. 1.11), and Mary Rogers (fig. 1.12) were among the owners with the most to gain. They were the children and heirs of the eminent John Rogers (fig. 1.13), Captain Randall's neighbor, who owned acreage immediately north of the square, west of Fifth Avenue (then Minetta Creek). In 1826 the Rogers heirs and other private owners petitioned the Common Council for an extension to 23rd Street, where the avenue would meet the Bloomingdale Road (part of present-day Broadway). However, owners of estates further north protested, and the extension was delayed until 1829. At the time, the Stuyvesants were planning lots and squares on their 300-acre farm crossed by eastside avenues, and Clement Moore was developing

FIG. 1.13 John Rogers Sr., Captain Randall's neighbor across Minetta Creek and a member with Randall in the Marine Society. Artist and date unknown. Courtesy of Henry A. Chisolm.

Chelsea around westside avenues. Fifth Avenue needed something more than its expanded Washington Square base to ensure its future.

Although the front yards of Washington Square had not caught on citywide, they proved to be the answer for Fifth Avenue when it was determined that part of the public street could be used. Several owners on Lafayette Place had proposed in 1831 that on their relatively secluded 100-foot-wide street (which originally ran between Astor Place and Great Jones Street), 15 feet of space on each side could be spared for front yards, and the city agreed. In 1832, Fifth Avenue owners followed suit, petitioning the Common Council for the same privilege up to 21st Street. In their proposal, they argued that traffic would be light, "located as this avenue is between two of our greatest streets [Sixth Avenue and Broadway] and terminating abruptly in Washington Square." Again, the city agreed, and in 1840, Fifth Avenue found an angel in Thomas E. Davis, a wealthy real estate developer with a stellar track record of buying and building on Bleecker Street and St. Mark's Place (Stuyvesant territory). In an 1840 auction following the Panic of 1837, Davis picked up over 400 lots on Fifth Avenue blocks north of Twentieth Street, for a few hundred dollars each, with plans to erect elegant residences there. (He built up the entire block between East 31st and East 32nd Streets.) In 1844 the privilege of having a yard was extended to 42nd Street, and with these spectacular inducements, New York's elite quickly placed their social and real estate bets. The *Evening Post*, which was closely tracking city progress, reported swift results. In April 1845, the paper informed its readers that "Contracts have been made for the erection of fine buildings on the 5th Avenue, as far as Murray Hill [34th to 40th Streets]." Nine months later, it announced that Fifth Avenue had essentially won its race with Second Avenue, its closest competitor, whose lot values and extent of development lagged far behind.[14]

Fifth Avenue soon possessed the finest houses in Manhattan. Their yards, filled with handsome plantings and lined with ornamental ironwork, imbued the avenue with a grandeur and gentility (fig. 1.14). By 1853, with Fifth Avenue's lead clinched by the official creation of Central Park (rather than Jones Wood), the guidebook *New York in a Nutshell* was touting Fifth Avenue as "the most magnificent street on this continent and likely to become the finest perhaps in the world."[15] *New York in a Nutshell* was one among a plethora of publications readied on the eve of New York's first World's Fair exhibition in 1853.

The intellectual *Putnam's Monthly* was also launched in early 1853. In Feb-

FIG. 1.14 This engraving from *New York in a Nutshell* (1853) emphasizes Fifth Avenue's width and its plantings. The view is south from Fifteenth Street, with the Church of the Ascension (Tenth Street) and First Presbyterian Church (Twelfth Street) towers (right). Artist and engraver unknown. Author's Collection.

FIG. 1.15 Fourteenth Street, south side looking east from Fifth Avenue, from "New York Daguerrotyped," *Putnam's Monthly*, 1853. The two grand Italianate houses on the corner were co-owned by the shipping magnates Paul Spofford and Thomas Tileston. They drew straws for the houses, with Tileston winning the more valuable corner property. Photographer and engraver unknown. Author's Collection.

FIFTH AVENUE.

East Fourteenth-street, from Fifth Avenue.

ruary its second issue commenced an important series titled "New York Daguerrotyped," which projected the city's image to the nation. A spread on private residences showed engravings of views on and from Fifth Avenue, beginning with the Row on Washington Square and going all the way up to 38th Street (fig. 1.15). Some buildings on other streets were included, but the message was clear—Fifth Avenue was the "noblest" among the "streets of greater beauty than any city of the old world can boast of." William C. Macready, the famous British Shakespearean actor, may have been the first foreign visitor to name Fifth Avenue as the nation's ultimate street, albeit in a backhanded way. During his American tour in March 1849 he had shown his scorn for the vulgarity of American audiences. "Let me die in a *ditch* in England, rather than in the Fifth Avenue of New York here," he cried.[16]

By the early 1850s, resplendent houses lined the north, west, and south sides of the square, built in the changing styles of the period. Federal and Greek Revival designs coexisted in the 1830s, but by the late 1840s, the Italianate style became the rage. Earlier styles were soon considered old-fashioned, if not *retardataire.* Also, within the established architectural style, society expected strict conformity. No laws or codes then ensured such uniform compliance, but social rigidity did, and it had the unintended benefit of fending off a hodgepodge of designs. Architects had begun promulgating Gothic-, Egyptian-, Oriental-, Elizabethan-, and Swiss-inspired styles among others. That sort of eclecticism would not be tolerated on Washington Square.

East of Fifth Avenue on Washington Square North stands the Row, the terrace that sparked the success of Captain Randall's charity. Its Greek Revival design was an English import that found new expression in the city. This all-encompassing design for residences—freestanding or in a row—was a unique solution within the larger Greek Revival movement. A Greek Revival doorway had been introduced in the city as early as 1829 on Bleecker Street. In the Row, however, white marble porches and stoops with balustrades displayed the style to dazzling effect. On the facades, smooth bricks set with narrow joints presented the rather austere look required. Dormers no longer projected from a steeply pitched roof. Instead, roofs were relatively flat with small rectangular attic windows in the fascia, and the rooflines were crowned with a continuous balustrade. Decorative iron fences, with a Greek key-and-leaf design, enclosed the front yards, further underscoring the visual consistency of the block. Today, even with the roof balustrade gone (owners removed it because it was a source of leaks), the unity, monumentality, and, above all, the timeless elegance of the houses at 1–13 Washington Square North are impressive.

West of Fifth Avenue, most of the houses north of the square were built of red brick in the Greek Revival style, like the Row, but with more brownstone than marble incorporated into their facades. Similar lease and deed restrictions created a uniform setback for yards across the entire north side. In 1828–29 George Rogers built the first of these houses—No. 20, in the middle of the block—just as the square was being finished. It was a seed venture for his family's vast holdings north of the square, but it failed to jump-start development. Having been the first owner or leaser to commence building on the north side of the square, his 12-foot-deep front yard set the standard for the yard depth of both northside rows. Rogers's house was big—37 feet wide—and in the Federal style, with a gabled roof and a carriageway; on its own, it stood like a manor house in a private estate. The Rogers themselves, however, chose to stay on fashionable Broadway, leasing No. 20 on the square first to the merchant James Buchanan, who was the British consul in New York. When development around the house picked up six years later, the Greek Revival style ruled. Number 20 kept its arched doorway and other Federal-era details

when it was enlarged to create an exclusive four-family apartment house in 1880, and it remains a commanding presence on the block.

At the Fifth Avenue corner, two Greek Revival houses were the finest on the western row and, indeed, the finest on the square (fig. 1.16). These splendid redbrick and marble residences, built in 1839–40, were 42 feet wide. The entrances, even grander than those on the Row, were flanked by wrought-iron balconies. Wealthy merchant William C. Rhinelander (fig. 1.17), who married the heiress Mary Rogers, lived on the corner at No. 14. It was designed by Richard Upjohn, the architect of Trinity Church. It was in the house next door, No. 15, built for the shipping magnate Gardiner Greene Howland, that Henry James chose to have reside the martinet Dr. Sloper and his heiress daughter in *Washington Square* (fig. 1.18). James describes the house as having "a big balcony before the drawing room windows, and a flight of white marble steps ascending to a portal which was also faced with white marble. In front of them was the square, . . . [with] inexpensive vegetation, enclosed by a wooden paling, which increased its rural and accessible appearance."[17] In 1852 George Rogers filled the long-vacant lots at Nos. 16 and 17 with then-fashionable Italianate brownstone houses, moving into No. 16 himself from Broadway. Rhinelander's mansion, as well as Nos. 15–18 are gone, but much of the block still survives.

On MacDougal Street between West Fourth Street and Waverly Place (now Washington Square West), Italianate designs predominated beginning in the late 1840s. A beautiful example was the house owned by the financier

FIG. 1.17 W. C. Rhinelander, 1850s daguerrotype. Henry James was given the basic plot for his novel *Washington Square* by the actress Fanny Kemble in London. In placing the story in the heart of the square, there is strong evidence that he based aspects of his characters on the Rhinelander family, whom he knew. They had a prominent, millionaire member, W. C., who fit the story's requirements nicely. Like Dr. Sloper, W. C. lived in a big house on the square and was a widower with an unmarried daughter, Serena, who became an heiress. Disinheritance, the novel's ominous threat, was not uncommon among W. C.'s set, but W. C. made news in 1876 when he disinherited his grandson and namesake because the young man had married a family servant. Photographer unknown. Courtesy of Mr. and Mrs. Charles D. Miller.

FIG. 1.18 Serena Rhinelander, 1850s daguerrotype. She was W. C.'s daughter and a likely model for Catherine Sloper. Serena was born in her father's home (then at 477 Broadway) and lived at 14 Washington Square for the remarkable period of more than 74 years. As a wealthy heiress on W. C.'s death in 1878, she gave generously to the churches and charities in which she was interested. Serena's gifts include the works of art in her family's Church of the Ascension on lower Fifth Avenue and the wonderful French Gothic–inspired Church of the Holy Trinity on East 88th Street. The latter was built on a huge property the Rhinelanders once owned, which extended from 85th to 93rd Streets and from Third Avenue to the East River. Photographer unknown. Courtesy of Mr. and Mrs. Charles D. Miller.

Joseph W. Alsop at the northwest corner of Washington Place (fig. 1.19). It had both a front and a side yard, and a distinctive canted bay window running the full height of the house. The west side of the square was developed well after the north, south, and east sides, with the Alsop residence not constructed until 1850–51. Today, 15- and 16-story apartment buildings dating from the 1920s line Washington Square West.

On Washington Square South, the pioneering
Fourth Street terrace row of 1827 stood alone for
years. It did not have company until the 1840s,
when three Greek Revival houses were built on the
vacant lots at the corner of MacDougal Street; the
corner building housed the Mt. Washington Collegiate Institute. To the dismay of the row's inhabitants, however, three undeveloped lots on the
Thompson Street end of the block, where the Judson Memorial Church now stands, became a coal
yard in the late 1830s. East of the terrace row, between Thompson and Wooster Streets, Federal-
style houses with Greek Revival touches went up.
This block was also forced to suffer several unsightly lots, some in the form of carriageways for
John L. Ireland and another wealthy Amity Street
resident, as well as a string of humble two-story
wooden shops on the corner opposite the coal yard.
The shops remained for a century.

With its Thompson Street entrance marred
(fig. 1.20), Washington Square South never had
the distinction of the posh north side. Laurens Street (now La Guardia Place)
was cut through the center of the eastern block in 1869. In that same fateful
year, a stately residence three doors east of Thompson Street became the
Home for Friendless Women, a rescue mission. Nine years later, noisy and
cinder-spewing elevated trains (els) ran over Amity Street, and by the 1890s
the entire neighborhood south of the square was filled with industrial lofts and
tenements. Still, southside residents could take pride in their location until the
el invasion. One such was John B. Ireland, son of John L., who built a house
on the square at the southwest corner of Fourth and Laurens Streets after the
cut. He lived there until 1879 on land that his family had owned since 1797.

In 1900 Sullivan Street was extended, and its cut into Washington Square
left a raw hole in the middle of the Fourth Street row. Later, an obnoxious six-
story garage and gas station were built facing the square near Wooster Street.
The garage was a long-lived eyesore, but it was a small irritant compared with
the continued destruction of buildings on the block between Thompson and
Laurens streets after 1927, which created a glaring scar in the middle of the
south side that lasted for 30 years. Except for the Judson Memorial Church
block, the rest of Washington Square South was razed in the 1950s and 1960s
to make way for new construction for ever-expanding New York University.

In addition to members of the city's higher society, many others, including tradespeople, artisans, family servants, hotel workers, seamstresses,
carters, and the like populated the Fifteenth Ward. The ward's most affluent

FIG. 1.20 Wooden shops on the east side of Thompson Street from Fourth to Third Street (right), 1905, in stark contrast to the grand dwellings (left) that once lined Washington Square South. The corner shop, here the "Arch Cafe," was the oldest structure on the square and would soon be occupied by a series of "garret" proprietors during the pre–World War I bohemian era. Photographer unknown. Courtesy of Brown Brothers.

homes had as many as eight servants in the 1850s. Mechanics Bank president Shepard Knapp, for example, lived at No. 2 on the Row with his wife, two sons, a daughter-in-law, and a grandson. The Knapps employed a German-born hostler and a black coachman, a German-born waiter, and five female servants—three Irish, one French, and one Welsh. Historian Bayrd Still estimated that three to five servants, mainly Irish-born females, constituted the neighborhood average during the mid-nineteenth century.

Today, only the north side of Washington Square retains something of the appearance that the entire square once had. In his 1846 book, *Annals and Occurrences of New York State, in the Olden Time,* Philadelphian John F. Watson praised the charming old square of pre-brownstone Manhattan, yet took care to appropriate that charm to the greater réclame of his own native city:

Philadelphians should feel themselves complimented by the general style of the whole square where [NYU] is situate[d]: the University itself being wholly of *white* marble, and the houses of the whole square being constructed after the manner of Philadelphia's best houses, of fine red brick, and all the window sills, and tops, and doorsteps of fine *white* marble. The *coup d'oeil* gives a sudden impression of summer sunshine, and presents the idea of cheerful and cleanly residences. The contrast of this place with other squares of the city, is certainly very agreeable, even to those who, like ourself have been sufficiently pleased with the frequent use of the grave and sober looking brown stone so often used in lieu of marble.[18]

FIG. 1.21 *Washington Square Park Fountain with Pedestrians,* looking east from the new fountain and a crowd of onlookers, ca. 1855. The columns in the far distance adorn the pair of houses at 714–716 Broadway at Washington Place. The NYU building (left) and the Reformed Dutch Church (right) face the square in the medium distance. Photograph by Silas A. Holmes, salted paper print, 11⅝″ × 16⅛″. Courtesy of The J. Paul Getty Museum, Los Angeles. © The J. Paul Getty Museum.

Major additions to Washington Square Park were made by 1850. In 1848 the city lavished $25,000 on an iron fence with gates at the street and corner entrances. Fences then had a functional as well as decorative purpose, protecting squares as all-important "lungs" of the city.[19] Gas streetlights were installed in 1849, and in January 1852 a fountain in the center of the square (not the present one) was completed (fig. 1.21).

In the span of a generation, Washington Square was conceived, developed, and lauded as the premier address in all of Manhattan. In the words of Henry James: "I know not whether it is owing to the tenderness of early associations, but this portion of New York appears to many persons the most delectable. It has a kind of established repose which is not of frequent occurrence in other quarters of the long, shrill city; it has a riper, richer, more honorable look than any of the upper ramifications of the great longitudinal thoroughfare—the look of having had something a social history."[20] No dukes or earls had guided its development as in London, where royals transformed West End estates into elegant residential districts radiating from the central nucleus of a square. Nevertheless, the area around Washington Square evolved very much like one of those London neighborhoods, with traditions and devoted citizens that maintained the square's dignity and helped its precious heritage to survive. In fact, so intertwined was the prestige of the square with its environs that "Washington Square" became a metaphor for New York's Fifteenth Ward, just as the name "Belgrave Square" stood for London's Belgravia district.

In 2003 the Village blocks around Washington Square remain a microcosm of New York City. The square's human vitality is matched by one of the city's most stirring vistas: the view through the majestic arch up Fifth Avenue. In immediate proximity to this view are still some of the most desirable residential blocks in Manhattan.

Bird's-eye view looking south from above Union Square, 1849. The whole of the Empire Ward is shown except for its northwest corner. The three wide roads entering the square at Fourteenth Street, are, from the left: the Bowery, Broadway, and University Place. The leafy green of Washington Square appears in the right center of the view, with Fifth Avenue extending from it to the lower-right corner of the print. The avenue is lush with trees and plantings in the front yards of the residences. At the bend in Broadway, Grace Church can be seen, disproportionately large, with the thick foliage of Lafayette Place just beyond. Despite some oversized buildings, the extrawide Broadway and University Place, and several immense-appearing ships in the distant harbor—all exaggerated because of their relative importance—the view is a fair representation of New York City's development by the middle of the nineteenth century. *Putnam's* introduced its 1853 series on the growth and architecture of the city with an engraving of this view, commenting, "New-Yorkers know that this point is rapidly becoming the centre of the city, and will in a few years be 'down town'" (February, p. 123). Lithograph by John Bachman. Courtesy of the Library of Congress.

: : : : : **2**

EMPIRE WARD

1832–1878

FOR WASHINGTON SQUARE TO FLOURISH, IT COULD NOT REMAIN an isolated strand of wealth. If the square was Manhattan's equivalent of Belgrave Square, the streets surrounding it would create the city's center of wealth, fashion, and influence only by themselves becoming cynosures of architectural elegance, material power, and civic responsibility. As well as the square proper, the old Ninth Ward east of Sixth Avenue was included in the newly created Fifteenth Ward in 1832—an area today known as Greenwich Village. This heavyweight product of redistricting would shortly be nicknamed the "Empire Ward" in deference to the political preferences and social clout of the movers and shakers who resided in it. The sobriquet was an allusion to New York State, which had earlier become known as the Empire State after it sponsored enormous economic growth by building the Erie Canal. The canal, which opened in 1824, was the crucial link that opened the country's interior to trade through the port of New York. Beyond the ward's early role in establishing commercial primacy for the city and nation, the ward became the setting for many of the country's major cultural and philanthropic achievements, urban development schemes, and protest movements throughout the nineteenth and twentieth centuries.

By the 1850s, a mercantile class with the capacity to patronize the arts and ameliorate moral and social ills was strongly established in Manhattan; it was time for the surging commercial metropolis of New York to contemplate challenging European capitals for cultural supremacy. It had become clear that more than just the money pits of Wall Street and the counting houses of South Street, where America's foremost entrepôt had sprung up, held the key to the city's future superiority. What, posited *Harper's Monthly* in 1854, made London, Paris, Rome, and Vienna each a metropolis beyond simple statistics of population density and square footage? "It is," the magazine declared, "the devotion of money to humane and permanent purposes—to the endowing of libraries, galleries, and institutions of every kind for the intellectual benefit of the population."[1] Would some of those who had applied themselves to the piling up of money use their wealth and leisure to transform New York and, by extension, America—that crude, boorish, uncivilized New World so often mocked and condemned by Europeans—into a locus of beauty, grace, and enlightenment?

Among the grandees who felt a need to enhance the reputation of their city and make a mark in ways other than the financial, many, including Philip Hone, chose to become residents of the blocks surrounding Washington Square. In 1836 he accepted a splendid offer of $60,000 (about three times what a fine new house on a choice residential street would have then cost) for his comfortable house on Broadway across from City Hall Park, making a sizable profit on the $25,000 he had paid 15 years before. With a number of recent developments from which to choose, Hone elected to move uptown to the Fifteenth Ward into a house on the southeast corner of Broadway and Great Jones Street. Hone paid $15,000 in 1836 for the prime oversized lot.

Over the next decade, this ward drew the wealthiest, most influential, and most talented people from New York City and elsewhere. By 1845, 85 percent of the richest citizens living in the city's northern wards resided in the Fifteenth. They overwhelmingly voted Whig, an upper-class party, which favored the consolidation of wealth in central banks as agencies of economic growth under a single sovereign power and which constituted the principal political opposition to Andrew Jackson's populism and policies of decentralization.

What made the area such an attractive place in which to live? First, it had as its anchor Washington Square, a green haven in a city with few such oases. Second, it contained within its boundaries sections of Fifth Avenue and Broadway, and Lafayette Place, long wide roads that stood in stark contrast to narrow byways in the lower city. Almost every street in the Fifteenth set a new standard of luxury, as they were significantly wider than most streets in New York and indeed in any other city in the United States.

Just as squares consume building lots yet at the same time increase the value of surrounding lots, so too can streets. Wider streets leave less acreage to sell or tax, but the adjoining land thus becomes more valuable. William Penn's 1683 plan for Philadelphia, which established the nation's earliest grid for a large city and became an important model for other burgeoning American cities, featured major and minor streets measuring 100 and 50 feet wide, respectively, a generous allotment very much ahead of its time. In the 1780s, New York City followed suit, decreeing a standard 50-foot width for all of the streets in its patchwork of grids except the aptly named Broadway, which was 80 feet wide.

New York's 1811 Commissioners' Plan topped the Philadelphia standard by mandating 100-foot avenues and 60-foot cross streets for Manhattan. (By contrast, the *widest* streets in London's new West End were 60 feet, twice the width of the typical streets in pre-Haussmann Paris.) In addition to advocating spacious residential streets, New York City's Common Council valued trees, planting them and paying property owners to do so. Old trees were even spared if their trunks were close enough to the curb line. Wider streets, in fact, needed trees. Where the narrow byways of ancient cities lacked any aspect of grandeur, their tightly packed buildings did, at least, provide shade from the broiling rays of the summer sun. Shopkeepers lined early New York's broad avenues with extensive sun-shielding awnings in commercial sections, but trees provided respite from the heat elsewhere, and all of the elegant enclaves had them.

Although the commissioners' grid would govern the Fifteenth Ward only north of Washington Square (too much development had already occurred below it), the southern part of the ward already possessed some extrawide

FIG. 2.1 Lafayette Place looking northwest from its terminus at Great Jones Street, 1860s. The view emphasizes the street's spacious 100-foot width, with broad sidewalks and front-yard incursions like St. Bartholomew's Church (right), surrounded by the Greek Revival iron fence. Most prominent is the lush leaf canopy formed by the profuse plantings. All of these attributes helped draw the wealthy to Lafayette Place and other enclaves that had generous landscaping. Photograph by Anthony Brothers. Author's Collection.

streets. The long multiblock stretch of Bleecker Street (60 feet wide) and Bond and Great Jones Streets (70 and 75 feet wide, respectively) were soon considered "the" locations for choice residential lots, which would be a safe but commutable distance from the city's bustling downtown business center. In 1834, the guidebook *New York as It Is* singled out those streets, as well as the 100-foot-wide Lafayette Place, boasting that several rows of houses there "may vie, for beauty and taste, with those of the finest Cities of Europe" (fig. 2.1).[2]

Two other grand thoroughfares radiated from Washington Square in the 1830s: 70-foot-wide Washington Place, which connected the square and Broadway, and 75-foot-wide University Place, which linked Washington Square and Union Square. Competing for the limited cohort of moneyed New Yorkers (in 1828, 8,000 people, or 4 percent of the city's population, possessed half the city's wealth), landowners sponsored development on these capacious streets and built speculative housing.

Of the ward's four east-west streets south of the square—Third, Fourth, Bleecker, and Houston—only Fourth and Bleecker Streets had the roomy 60-foot width. In the years before underground sewers were introduced, the channels in these two roadways operated as drains for the local watershed, and the city had at that time imposed the 60-foot standard for street width. Later, this extra width paid off in more valuable lots. Although Houston and Amity (as West Third was then known) Streets were also developed early with rows of first-class houses, they were less desirable because they were only 50 feet wide, holdovers from the 1780s plan.

Grafting the 1811 grid onto the city's old streets left a gap by two large blocks immediately north of the square that were not deep enough to be divided into one of the new 60-foot-wide streets. It did, however, permit the creation of a stately, 35-foot-wide London-like mews running midblock between the houses of Washington Square North and Clinton Place (now East and West Eighth Street). MacDougal Alley, west of Fifth Avenue, and Washington Mews, to the east, enhanced the prestige of Washington Square North and Eighth Street because residents were able to erect stables and carriage houses directly behind their townhouses. Residents enjoyed the convenience of having their horses and liveries available at a moment's notice, yet out of the sight and smell of a graciously conducted life. Two other long but narrower mews—Jones Alley and Shinbone Alley—served the large blocks between Bleecker and Bond Streets, and between Lafayette Place and the Bowery. What remains of them today are grimy crevices between tall loft buildings. All these mews were a practical exception in a city where stables coexisted with houses on many streets, ruining parts of neighborhoods in which their concentration was high.

An awkward block was created at the original foot of Sixth Avenue, where the streets had once converged at the ward's southwest corner. Here, two old paths were converted to Minetta Street and Minetta Lane, named for the ancient creek that still flows through the sewers beneath them. These substandard 30-foot-wide streets soon were lined with second-rate buildings—small houses and shanties—that stood in sharp contrast to the grander dwellings on the new broad streets of the ward.

By the 1850s the Fifteenth was filled with houses, many of them mansions. Two city food markets had opened nearby on Sixth Avenue and the Bowery in the early 1830s. Many small grocery, bakery, hardware, and other family-run stores providing household necessities could also be found on those ward boundaries and on the older streets south of Washington Square. Elegant shops were locating further north on Broadway, and by 1860 fashionable department stores had arrived in the ward. Churches punctuated the Fifteenth's skyline with lofty spires, and the residents attended local opera, concerts, theater, and ballrooms for entertainment, and to see and be seen. Gentlemen had their clubs, and neighborhood libraries, art galleries, and lecture halls offered attractions whose indubitable aura of refinement allowed them to be patronized by both sexes. There were even gymnasiums, which had arisen in the 1830s and 1840s to counteract the ill effects of sedentary urban life.

Yet, no matter how exclusive the neighborhood, no New Yorker felt free from the threats of fire and mob violence, scourges since colonial times. Wood construction, primitive fire-fighting equipment, poor communications, and

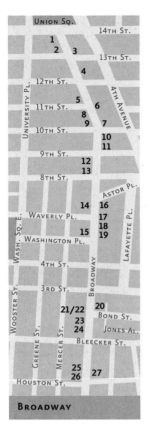

the lack of a paid professional fire department (until 1865) led to disastrous conflagrations. Nevertheless, fire and police protection were better in the Fifteenth Ward. A new reservoir, with hydrant distribution in the area, had been in use by firefighters since 1831, long before Croton water arrived in 1842 to service the rest of Manhattan. The police were backed up by the crack Seventh Regiment of the State National Guard, which was over 1,000 strong. The ward was also the healthiest of the built-up precincts. Doctors then knew little about how infections were transmitted, but the Fifteenth had the lowest population density of the developed wards, as well as superior drainage and better sanitation. The last was a definite advantage in an era when travelers, most famously Charles Dickens, complained that pigs were allowed to roam freely through the city's filthy streets, jostling women in their silks and parasols as they crossed Broadway.

In addition to Washington Square, Broadway, and the extrawide Lafayette Place, Bond and Great Jones Streets were the lures that first drew New Yorkers from downtown to the urban edge. The following guide progresses first from rich and varied *Broadway* through *Astor Place* and *Lafayette Place* and pioneering *Bond* and *Great Jones Streets* to the ancient *Bowery*. (Numbers in boldface type refer to bold numerals on the corresponding sectional maps.)

BROADWAY Even Charles Dickens liked Broadway, despite its dirt and occasional pigs. When he visited New York in 1842, sallying forth to "mingle with the stream" of humanity there, he was excited by "[t]he great promenade," "the many-coloured crowd and glittering shops," and "the lively whirl of carriages."[3] Then Manhattan's premier street, Broadway had long enjoyed the praise of visitors, though none so distinguished—or so discerningly critical—as Dickens. A few eager boosters went so far as to compare Broadway to Regent Street, London's royal thoroughfare. Broadway, of course, lacked the splendid unifying architecture designed by John Nash for the dashing Prince Regent, the future George IV. Nevertheless, running wide and straight for more than two miles from Bowling Green, and lined with poplars and the city's best buildings, Broadway must have been an inspiring sight.

Broadway's presence in the Fifteenth Ward practically guaranteed the ward's success. Wealthy and powerful citizens began building on Broadway above Houston Street in the 1820s, and in 1826, the same year that Washington Square was dedicated, the cornerstone was laid for St. Thomas' Church at No. 615 (**26**; see Broadway map), on the northwest corner of Broadway and Houston Street (figs. 2.2 and 2.3). In 1828, the well-to-do importer Allan Melville and his family moved to 675 Broadway (**22**); at that time, his son Herman was nine years old.

Peter Gerard Stuyvesant, a great-great-grandson of the legendary Dutch colonial governor, and overseer of the Stuyvesant family's vast lands, lived at 621 Broadway (**25**), just north of St. Thomas' Church. One of the city's top millionaires, Stuyvesant's wealth was minimally displayed in his 50-foot-wide,

FIG. 2.2 View northwest at Broadway and Houston Street, 1831. The Federal-style row adjacent to St. Thomas' Church has been democratized, with Peter Gerard Stuyvesant's house next to the church actually being substantially wider, by one and two windows, than the rest. Engraved by James Smillie. © Collection of the New-York Historical Society.

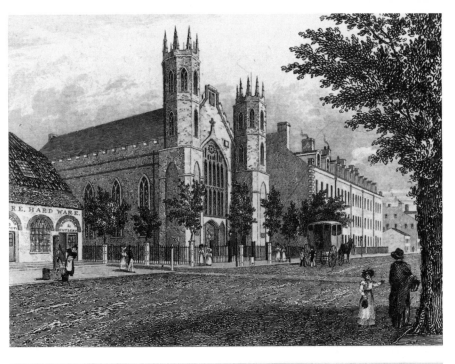

FIG. 2.2 View northwest at Broadway and Houston Street, 1831. The Federal-style row adjacent to St. Thomas' Church has been democratized, with Peter Gerard Stuyvesant's house next to the church actually being substantially wider, by one and two windows, than the rest. Engraved by James Smillie. © Collection of the New-York Historical Society.

FIG. 2.3 A fashion shoot on Broadway at Washington Place, 1835, with hat manufacturer Elisha Bloomer's unusual, marble Ionic-columned houses at 714–716 Broadway in the background. The country residence (left) from an earlier period would remain until 1847, when a Baptist church would replace it. Philip Hone rented No. 716 in the following spring, for $1,600 per year, while his house at Great Jones Street was being built. Lithograph by C. R. & J. B. Graham. © Collection of the New-York Historical Society.

double-lot house, which was otherwise nearly identical to its Federal-style neighbors. (The 1811 grid plan anticipated a standard 25-foot house width. In the 1820s and 1830s, homes of rich families could generally reach a 50-foot width without being considered too ostentatious, although this limit was continually pushed higher, particularly in corner residences.) The house two doors up, 32 feet wide, belonged to John Rogers, the biggest private owner of land north of Washington Square. Heeding the financial success of Hudson and

Washington Squares, Peter Gerard Stuyvesant donated Stuyvesant Square to the city in 1836 to promote his family's real estate holdings. Ten years later, he provided the land for St. George's Church. He remained at 621 until his death in 1847.

In 1834 Stuyvesant had been a beneficiary of and had lent his name to the ward's second cultural institution, Stuyvesant Institute. (The first was New York University.) The institute was organized in that year by leading citizens "for the diffusion of knowledge, by means of popular lectures, and to establish a reading room, library, cabinet of natural history, &c." By 1837 it was located in a handsome granite Greek Revival edifice covering 75 feet at 659 Broadway (**23**), near Bond Street. Over the next 30 years, the building housed the New-York Historical Society, NYU's Medical College, the Lyceum of Natural History (today's New York Academy of Sciences), the YMCA, the exhibition galleries of the National Academy of Design (whose main building was next door at No. 663), and a large meeting room for lectures and other gatherings. Also housed in the National Academy of Design at No. 663 were the New York Athenaeum and the New York Gallery of Fine Arts. Stuyvesant Institute's meeting room became well known in the late 1850s when a splinter group of Democrats habitually convened there rather than at Tammany Hall. (Led by Mayor Fernando Wood, this group, widely considered to be a band of corrupt ward heelers and thugs, had been ousted from Tammany Hall during a reform movement in 1858.) In the 1860s Donaldson's Opera House occupied the premises, concomitant with Broadway's metamorphosis into the city's first general entertainment district.[4]

Gerard Stuyvesant, son of millionaire Nicholas Stuyvesant and a nephew of Peter Gerard Stuyvesant, made 621 Broadway home until his death in 1859. In a dramatic move to forestall a commercial neighbor on the Houston Street corner, Gerard Stuyvesant proposed a deal that St. Thomas' Church couldn't refuse. When the church burned in 1851 and wanted to rebuild further north, Stuyvesant offered to pay $13,000, half the total cost of rebuilding on the same site, if the church would remain there for 20 years. St. Thomas' Church, not as rich as it later became, agreed and didn't move to Fifth Avenue and 53rd Street until 1870. (McKim, Mead & White's landmark 1894 Cable Building occupies the Houston Street corner now, taking the addresses 611–621 Broadway.)

In 1839, the Fifteenth Ward received its ultimate stamp of approval when Mary Mason Jones (fig. 2.4), New York society's reigning grand dame, moved to 734 Broadway (**17**), opposite Waverly Place. Mrs. Jones's first social triumphs had taken place on Broadway, and they included her two sisters, Rebecca and Sarah. They were daughters of the wealthy banker John Mason, and after each girl married, she moved with her family into one of the three connected houses at Nos. 732–736 that their father had given them.

Nicely concealed within the parlor floors of these outwardly unpretentious houses was the most splendid private ballroom in the city, which ran through all three. Though society enjoyed its cotillions, it would have frowned on the

FIG. 2.4 Mary Mason Jones as she appeared during her reign at 734 Broadway. She was Edith Wharton's great-aunt, and the novelist immortalized her as the older, uptown Mrs. Manson Mingott in *The Age of Innocence*. Painting by Thomas Prichard Rossiter, 1852. Courtesy of Mr. and Mrs. Henry L. Pierson.

overt display of extravagance on this scale. But the Mason sisters had an elegant solution. One, two, or all three sections could be opened as circumstances required, and Mary Mason Jones's center house possessed the greatest flexibility for expansion. She had been presiding over balls since her marriage to her father's business associate, Isaac Jones, in 1819. Her sister Rebecca wedded Isaac Jones's cousin, Isaac Colford Jones, and Sarah married the socialite Andrew Gordon Hamersley.

Both John Mason and the Joneses were descended from seventeenth-century colonial families. Mason had been a director of the Bank of New York and was a partner with Isaac Jones in building up Chemical Bank from its small beginnings as a chemical manufacturer with banking privileges. (In the 1990s the more powerful Chemical merged with the Chase Manhattan Bank, keeping Chase's name, and in 2000 the bank merged with J. P. Morgan, adding Morgan's name to Chase.) Together, and through the encouragement of intermarriage between their families, they kept the bank in the hands of Masons and Joneses for decades. In 1831 Mason also became a founder and the first president of the city's first railroad, the New York and Harlem. His real estate holdings included most of the land between Fifth and Park Avenues, from 54th to 63rd Streets, which he bought in 1825 for $1,500. The Jones family also held extensive property. They became known as the "Jones Wood Joneses" for their 132-acre tract of land stretching from Third Avenue to the East River, and from East 66th to 76th Streets. In the 1840s and 1850s, Jones Wood became the focus of municipal attention when the city considered it as the location for its major park. The Joneses opposed the idea, but more important, the Joneses and other social leaders already thickly populating Fifth Avenue were against situating such a premier amenity so far to the east. They exercised their powerful political muscle, and the land that is now Central Park was chosen instead.

The scene at one of Mary Mason Jones's balls was recorded by George Templeton Strong in his diary on December 23, 1845. Strong, an attorney, music patron, and a redoubtable diarist of New York life, was a young man of 25 when he attended this party:

> Well, last night I spent at Mrs. Mary Mason Jones' great ball. Very splendid affair—"the ball of the season," I heard divers bipeds more or less asinine in regard to it. Two houses open—standing supper table—"dazzling array of beauty and fashions." Polka for the first time brought under my inspection. It's a kind of insane Tartar jig performed to a disagreeable music of an uncivilized character.

Everybody was there and I loafed about in a most independent manner and found it less of a bore than I expected. Mrs. Jones, the hostess, is fat but comely; indeed, there's enough of her to supply a small settlement with wives. . . . On the whole, the ballroom, with a waltz raging in the midst of it, was really a showy spectacle. Modern civilization has achieved thus much, that people making fools of themselves do it in an ornamental way.[5]

Complementing its social ascent, Broadway was awarded its chief architectural prize when the vestrymen of the fashionable Grace Church picked the bend at Tenth Street as a replacement for their existing location below Trinity Church at Rector Street. Religion played a critical role in society and the presence of fine churches marked a prestigious neighborhood. In the early 1840s, several key vestrymen had already viewed upper Broadway near Union Square as a desirable spot, and the swerve at East Tenth Street offered a challenging site, for it commanded the whole sweep of the city's most famous street in its two-mile run from downtown. This parcel was part of the land owned by Henry Brevoort, a descendant of one of New Amsterdam's earliest colonial families, whose farm lay just north of the Sailors' Snug Harbor property. In 1843 Grace Church bought a 150-by-140-foot lot (about eight standard lots combined) between Broadway and the Bowery (later Fourth Avenue) for $40,000. (Contrary to lore that Broadway's path was deflected to avoid one of Henry Brevoort's favorite trees, or that he stood with his blunderbuss to prevent his house from being razed to extend Eleventh Street from Broadway to the Bowery, the truth is more prosaic. Broadway was simply angled to run parallel to the Bowery as these streets approached Union Square. The city found no pressing need to extend Eleventh Street east through this relatively narrow strip of land at the expense of a rectory and school for Grace Church.)

The members of Grace Church, who undoubtedly understood the importance of the commission they were about to offer, picked a 24-year-old without any previous commissions named James Renwick Jr., who would later develop into one of America's foremost architects. Apart from the untested young architect's demonstrated flair for design, Grace Church's building committee was interested in his father, James Renwick Sr. James Sr. had married Henry Brevoort's sister, who came into a fortune on Henry's death in 1841 at age 94. Old Henry's vegetable farm was now a real estate bonanza. Yet James Renwick Sr. was not without influence of his own. Son of a wealthy Scottish merchant of New York, he was a distinguished professor of science at Columbia College and a recognized authority in every branch of engineering of his day (a minuscule field compared with today's science). He was also a talented amateur architect and had procured a position for his son that led to James Jr.'s supervision of the construction of the massive distributing reservoir for Croton water being installed at Fifth Avenue and 42nd Street—invaluable experience for the practical aspects of an architect's craft. (John B. Jervis, chief engineer of the Croton water project, designed the notable structure.)

FIG. 2.5 Grace Church with a marble yard occupying the corner lot, 1855. Grace's bells were the likely inspiration for Edgar Allan Poe's poem *The Bells,* written while he was staying at the nearby home of a friend in 1848. Because of cost overruns, Grace's spire was made of wood, which would not be replaced with marble until richer times in 1883. Photograph by Victor Prevost. © Collection of the New-York Historical Society.

The young Renwick's plan for Grace Church called for an English Gothic structure, open yet tightly knit. It was highlighted by a slim, lacy spire, elaborate vaulting and carving, and tracery windows. The entire edifice was sheathed in white marble, and its radiance and movement, encountered at a rare break in the city's uniform grid, immediately created one of the most picturesque vistas in lower Manhattan (fig. 2.5). Quoting George Templeton Strong, David W. Dunlap described Grace Church in *On Broadway,* as follows: "Its architect, James Renwick Jr., knew how to handle so special a site, raising a delicate white tower that seems to float over Broadway and has been known on a wintry sunset to look like a 'pinnacle of alabaster, or a great crystal of rose quartz.'"[6]

After major difficulties with contractors, including trouble over Sing-Sing marble convict workers, Renwick finished the church in the spring of 1846. (Use of this marble had precipitated a riot when it was used on the NYU building 12 years earlier.) The addresses allotted to the entire property ranged from 790 to 802 Broadway (**7**), and the church chose the nice round number of 800 for its own. The final cost of the building was $72,500, 26 percent higher than Renwick's original 1843 estimate. Was the estimate poor? Did unforeseen and unrecoverable expenses occur? Or did Grace Church try to beat in magnificence Richard Upjohn's University Place Presbyterian Church a block away, or Joseph C. Wells's First Presbyterian Church two blocks away on Fifth Avenue? The records have been lost, but in the end Renwick enjoyed a triumph over Upjohn and Wells. Consecrated on March 7, 1846, Grace Church not only won nearly universal acclaim in the press for its beauty but also became the preferred church of the Episcopalians. Front-row pews went for $1,400 per annum, and the church's sexton, Isaac Brown, was their major-domo. (One checked with Brown for the latest scoop before sending out invitations for parties and balls.)

The success of Grace Church launched Renwick's career as an architect, and soon thereafter he was awarded what would be his two most famous commissions. In 1847, he designed the original castle building of the Smithsonian Institution in Washington, D.C., the first of several important projects he undertook in the nation's capital. He later returned to New York to begin work on the Fifth Avenue landmark, St. Patrick's Cathedral, in 1858.

Two less arresting churches were built on Broadway between Waverly and Washington Places. The Unitarian Church of the Messiah (1839) also had a single-towered Gothic design and occupied a two-lot site at No. 728 (**18**), just south of the Mason sisters. A few doors further south, at No. 720 (**19**), a new Baptist congregation erected Hope Chapel in 1847; it was a rather plain structure for its distinguished site near Washington Place.

Across from Grace Church on the northwest corner of Tenth Street stood 787 Broadway (**9**), the resplendent Italianate house of tobacco king Peter Lorillard Jr. Constructed in 1850, the residence fronted 42 feet on the street and showed off a distinctive bowed bay. Lorillard's forebears had been French tobacconists before their and our revolutions, and his father, Peter Abraham Lorillard, made the first American fortune in tobacco. Indeed, it was Peter Abraham's death in 1843 that occasioned the first use in the U.S. press of the term *millionaire* as a description of a vastly wealthy American. Registering polite society's disgust at the prevailing American habit of chewing and spitting in public, Philip Hone rather snidely noted this Lorillard's passing in his diary: "He was a tobacconist, and his memory will be preserved in the annals of New York by the celebrity of 'Lorillard's Snuff and Tobacco.' He led people by the nose for the best part of a century, and made his enormous fortune by giving them that to chew which they could not swallow."[7]

In a step that created a lasting monument to the Lorillards, Peter Jr. added acreage to land that his father had owned in upstate New York, around a lake the Indians called Tucseto (Americanized to "Tuxedo"). Peter Jr. died in 1867, and his son, also named Peter, moved to Fifth Avenue and 36th Street. This Lorillard further extended the rural property to a total of 6,000 acres, and with his friend, the architect Bruce Price, created Tuxedo Park as a residential enclave for the rich in 1886.[8]

Back in 1821, Peter Jr.'s sister married John David Wolfe, a merchant of

German descent whose fortune had been made in the hardware trade. His father, David Wolfe, who started the family business, had been assistant quartermaster in Washington's army. John David Wolfe had retired to a life of philanthropy in 1842, and in 1846 he built a house at 744 Broadway (16), on the southeast corner of Astor Place. While not quite as imposing as his brother-in-law Lorillard's residence, it nonetheless occupied a prime Broadway site.

John David Wolfe's unmarried daughter, Catherine Lorillard Wolfe, became one of the richest women in America through inheritances from both her father and mother. After she came into her fortune in 1872, she devoted her life to philanthropy by giving away more than $4 million to schools, churches, hospitals, missions, and cultural institutions. Grace Church and the Metropolitan Museum of Art were the main beneficiaries of her generosity. As a member of Grace Church, she provided $250,000 for the construction of its chancery and reredos, and left it an endowment of $350,000 upon her death in 1887. Wolfe would be equally generous to the Metropolitan. She was the only woman to subscribe to the nascent museum's first fund drive in 1870, with a donation of $2,500, and upon her death, left 143 oils and watercolors from her own collection to the Metropolitan, as well as an endowment of $200,000 earmarked for the purchasing of contemporary art. The Catherine Lorillard Wolfe Fund, as the Wolfe gift came to be known, was the first self-sufficient bequest the Metropolitan received, and the income from it enabled the museum to buy some of its finest nineteenth-century paintings, including Goya's *The Bullfight,* Daumier's *Don Quixote,* Renoir's *Madame Charpentier and Her Children,* and Winslow Homer's *The Gulf Stream.*

On the west side of Broadway between Waverly Place and Eighth Street (Clinton Place), were Nos. 733–735, the twin granite houses of the shipping magnates Paul Spofford and Thomas Tileston, lifelong friends and business partners. They had come to New York from New England and formed the partnership of Spofford & Tileston in 1818. Here they grew wealthy in ocean shipping during the age of sail and early days of steam, while playing a major role in building up the city's merchant marine industry. In addition, Spofford was on NYU's council and a director of several banks and insurance companies; Tileston was president of the Phoenix Bank.

Before building the two residences on Broadway, the partners had owned twin houses at 502–504 and 522–524 Broadway, and at 37–39 Barclay Street. After 733–735 Broadway (14), they ultimately settled in more grandiose Italianate twin houses at 2–4 East Fourteenth Street on the southeast corner of Fifth Avenue, where they remained until their deaths. Tileston died in 1864, Spofford in 1869, and while their various pairs of houses are long gone, their families share adjoining and matched mausoleums in Green-Wood Cemetery in Brooklyn.

Broadway between Grace Church and Union Square was dominated socially and architecturally by the Roosevelts, the astonishing clan that gave the

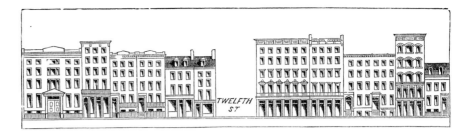

TWELFTH ST

FIG. 2.6 The east side of Broadway from the James J. Roosevelt house (far left) at No. 836 to No. 812 at the far right, 1865. This is one of a set of engravings, covering both sides of Broadway, for David T. Valentine's manuals, which documented city life in the mid-1800s. Broadway was also pictured slightly later by the S. J. Holmes photographic survey of the same stretch from the Battery to Union Square. The fascination with Broadway's evolution continues to this day. Engraver unknown. Author's Collection.

nation two presidents and a first lady (fig. 2.6). Like the Stuyvesants, the Roosevelts had been in the New World since the 1640s. By the early 1800s, the family joined the genteel exodus from downtown to those wealthy pockets on the urban frontier. Two Roosevelt brothers, Cornelius Van Schaack (C. V. S.) and James J. (for Junior), from the Oyster Bay branch of the family, settled above Grace Church on Broadway. C. V. S. was the grandfather of Theodore Roosevelt and the great-grandfather of Eleanor Roosevelt who, in turn, was Theodore's niece and Franklin Delano Roosevelt's wife. Another James, the founder of the Hyde Park branch of the Roosevelts, and the great-grandfather of Franklin, lived for 26 years just off Broadway at 58 Bleecker Street (originally No. 64), on the southeast corner of Crosby Street.

C. V. S. was a shrewd and audacious businessman who made one fortune expanding his father's hardware and glass business, and another by buying up land at distressed prices following the financial Panic of 1837. At the peak of his success in 1844, he bought the best site then available in the city, the southwest corner of Broadway and Fourteenth Street. C. V. S.'s new house at 849 Broadway (1) joined an elegant row being built between Broadway and University Place, on 100-foot-wide Fourteenth Street, with sprawling new Union Square to the north. The main front of his house ran an imposing 65 feet on Broadway; and his home, where Dutch was still (and last) spoken, was the center for the Roosevelt clan in the city.

Whereas C. V. S. was devoted to business, his brother James J. loved law, politics, and society. James J. studied foreign law in England, Holland, and France. While in Paris he met and married the celebrated belle Cornelia Van Ness, daughter of Cornelius Van Ness, a U.S. senator and former governor of Vermont. James J. first held office in New York City's Common Council and later became a member of the state assembly. Just as FDR would surprise and dismay his Republican peers several generations later by becoming a Democrat, James J. departed from the conservative views of his class by backing Andrew Jackson and later, to their shock, the Tammany Hall Democrats. James J.'s pragmatic advocacy won him a seat in the 27th Congress, a judgeship on the Supreme Court of the State of New York, and appointment by President Buchanan to the more exciting position of district attorney for southern New York in 1860 and 1861. His Whig opponent was Philip Hone, who said of James Roosevelt Jr. that he was "the leader of the blackguards, in whose person our poor city is disgraced."[9]

James J.'s house at 836 Broadway (4), midblock between Twelfth and Thirteenth Streets, was not as grand as C. V. S.'s. However, with a 42-foot frontage and a fine Italianate facade, it was the most important house on Broadway between his brother's residence and the Lorillard mansion at Tenth Street. The Roosevelt era in the Fifteenth Ward closed with the passing of C. V. S. in 1871 and James J. in 1875, but they were loyal residents of Broadway to the end, long after fashion had moved on to Fifth Avenue.

In the 1850s, 839 Broadway (2), at the southern end of C. V. S.'s block on the corner of Thirteenth Street, was home to the Bryan Gallery, one of the few public art galleries in which important European paintings could be seen. Thomas Jefferson Bryan was a wealthy and erudite Philadelphian who inherited an ample fortune and devoted his life to the study of art. After graduating from Harvard in 1823, he spent many years in Europe, where he became well known as a connoisseur and collector. He also developed a considerable skill in restoring paintings, discovering some of his most highly prized acquisitions through the careful cleaning of dingy and worm-eaten canvases. In the early 1850s, he sailed to New York with hundreds of paintings, which he intended to put on public display.

Bryan had amassed one of the largest art collections in America, partly because of the political turmoil in Europe. As *The World* put it in an 1878 article on the gallery, "Mr. Bryan was fortunate enough to have been a resident of Paris during the memorable revolutions of 1830 and 1848, periods rich with spoil for the art collector."[10] Bryan had hoped that the strength of his holdings, which included many examples by Italian, French, and Northern European masters, could kindle a widespread enthusiasm for art among his countrymen. As for the collection itself, he saw it as the nucleus of a national gallery. But after a number of years of disappointing attendance and a growing concern that his leased space was a firetrap, Bryan lent his collection for exhibition at the Cooper Union school. On a visit to its gallery one day, Bryan reportedly discovered the venerable Peter Cooper pointing his umbrella dangerously close to a portrait of a burgomaster by Rembrandt (which has since proved to be neither a burgomaster nor by Rembrandt) and angrily removed his treasures from the school's premises. In 1867, he gave 381 of his paintings to the New-York Historical Society—too early, alas, for the Metropolitan Museum of Art, whose founding was three years in the future and which could have used them.

Although C. V. S. Roosevelt possessed the ideal residential site, the most imposing and architecturally appealing house on all of Broadway was the financial titan Samuel Ward's Greek Revival mansion on the northeast corner of Broadway and Bond Street (20). As early as 1831, when many lots on Broadway were still undeveloped, Ward commissioned Alexander Jackson Davis to design a large house, complete with a cupola and a marble art gallery running along its Broadway side (fig. 2.7). Adjacent to fine Bond Street townhouses, some of which had risen in the 1820s, the colossal 70-foot-wide house was set

FIG. 2.7 Samuel Ward's Greek Revival mansion on the northeast corner of Bond Street and Broadway, shortly before its demolition in 1872. This house and grounds, modest compared to later city mansions, nevertheless set a new standard for abodes of the wealthy. Photograph by Rockwood. Courtesy of John Winthrop Aldrich.

back from the street and had a large side yard extending to Jones Alley. This not only increased the already dramatic effect of extravagant space but also shifted the entrance from Broadway, where it would have faced the stables of a Broadway stage line.

As the head of the leading banking house of Prime, Ward, King, & Co., Ward was the most influential financier in America, the J. Pierpont Morgan of his day. In addition to wealth, he had a rich birthright: his grandfather was the patriot Samuel Ward, who had been the colonial governor of Rhode Island, and his father was the Revolutionary War veteran, Lieutenant Colonel Samuel Ward. Banker Samuel Ward, who built the house, died in 1839, but he and his wife, Julia Rush Cutler Ward, had seven children who grew up there. Two of them would make names for themselves. Their son, the versatile fourth Samuel Ward, was a banker, scholar, adventurer, social striver (he married an Astor), Capitol Hill lobbyist extraordinaire and, some say, scoundrel. He presided over the failure of the family firm and went through his relatives' estates, including those left in trust for his sisters. On the untimely death of young Emily Astor, Sam Ward married a New Orleans woman unacceptable to New York society, and the public took little more note of him. In contrast, the name of Julia and Samuel Ward's other outstanding child, the celebrated writer and suffrage leader Julia Ward Howe, was assured its place in history when her inspirational Civil War poem, *The Battle Hymn of the Republic*, was set to the tune of "John Brown's Body." In 1872 the Ward house was razed for the Brooks Brothers store, which took the Broadway address of No. 670.

Hotels soon followed the upper-class migration to the Fifteenth Ward, as "location, location, location" was as accurate a real estate mantra for success then as it is today. Accordingly, Broadway was the natural choice, and what better spot than Mary Mason Jones territory near Waverly Place? Matthew Morgan, a rich banker who had come to New York from New Orleans, would accept nothing less than Broadway. In partnership with New York merchant Hickson W. Field, Morgan bought nearly the whole block fronting Broadway between Waverly and Washington Places. In 1843, at 721 Broadway (15), he erected the New York Hotel, the ward's first, and brought over Jean-Baptiste Monot from France to run the restaurant. Morgan optimistically wrote in a letter to a New York friend that anyone wishing to hobnob with New York society as it was then constituted would find his establishment, remote as it was from the urban center, "much preferable to the hotels in the lower part of Broadway, now almost inaccessible to any species of carriage except the omnibus."[11]

The building's plain brick facade fit in nicely with many of the houses around it. What it lacked in flamboyance, it made up for in size—it was five stories high and covered most of the block. The New York Hotel also sported the obligatory classical porch for its main entrance. This feature had been introduced in the early 1830s by Boston's Tremont Hotel and New York's Astor House, and its presence signified that the establishment concerned was a grand hotel. No longer glorified inns, these hotels offered such new amenities as interior plumbing on each floor, bellboys, French chefs, and individual room keys.

The New York Hotel was an unqualified success. Former president John Quincy Adams appeared at a dinner for 300 people soon after the hotel opened in 1844, and many other dignitaries went on to patronize the place. It also succeeded as a kind of guesthouse for the neighborhood's reigning families. One guest millionaire, Joshua Jones, who was Mary Mason Jones's brother-in-law and a cousin of Edith Wharton's grandfather, had a record tenancy, living there as a near recluse for 40 years. Although he was well-off financially, during his tenancy at the hotel Jones evolved into a miser who refused to pay for wood fires in his rooms. After a walk on a freezing winter night (he traveled everywhere on foot), Joshua Jones returned to his unheated suite and came down with pneumonia. He died on March 14, 1888, leaving more than $7 million in land and shares in Chemical Bank. Edith Wharton, who was born Edith Newbold Jones, inherited about $120,000 (equal today to roughly $2.25 million after taxes) from this estate, and the money gave her the security and independence that marked the beginning of her courageous voyage toward personal autonomy and professional authorship.

Private dining rooms also made their appearance at the New York Hotel. Although these were commonplace in England's better hotels, American hoteliers were proud of their big communal dining rooms, generally second only to their lobbies in opulence. The social critic Nathaniel P. Willis was quick to jump on the New York Hotel's new dining feature, calling it "directly opposed to American ideals of democracy" and warning that it "encouraged the spread of dangerous blue-blood habits."[12] Nevertheless, the hotel's popularity soared, particularly among Southern gentry. So preferred was it by this group that many in the city believed the rendezvous to be a nest of spies and Southern sympathizers during the Civil War. Although this was never proved, when a Confederate arsonist group attacked the city's major hotels and other important buildings during the final days of the war, the New York Hotel was spared. The hotel survived this challenge to its reputation as well and prospered almost until its demise in 1893, when it fell to the loft-building invasion then in full swing.

New York was maturing into one of the great cities of the modern world and, with a World's Fair coming to town in 1853, the construction of hotels crescendoed. Nineteen went up on Broadway alone between 1850 and 1854, and all of them were luxurious. In 1852 the New York Hotel finally got some competition when the La Farge House was built three blocks south on Broadway. Its owner, Jean-Frédéric de la Farge, who Anglicized his name to John La Farge (he was the father of the painter, muralist, and stained glass designer John La Farge), had served in Napoleon's army. One of the soldiers sent to quell the slave insurrection in Santo Domingo, the elder La Farge was captured in an ambush and held prisoner there for three years. After this harrowing ordeal, he managed to take refuge aboard a ship bound for Philadelphia. From there he made a seafaring fortune that he invested in real estate, from plantations in Louisiana to virgin lands in upper New York State. Finally settling in New York City, he married and moved to Washington Place, near Washington Square, in 1843. There, perhaps inspired by the phenomenal success of the New York Hotel down the block, La Farge bought Broadway lots for his own establishment.

La Farge had a superb property: 150 feet on the west side of Broadway, through to Mercer Street, and slightly north of the prestigious Stuyvesant Institute (21/22). It faced Bond Street and was near Samuel Ward's enormous mansion. A young developer named A. N. Tripler had just finished erecting a large, opulent music hall and theater, Tripler Hall (21) (fig. 2.8), which occupied La Farge's property on the Mercer Street side and had an entrance passage to 679 Broadway. Tripler's had originally been built for the Swedish soprano Jenny Lind's triumphant New York debut in 1850, but it was not completed in time. She later sang there, and in 1852, memorial services for James Fenimore Cooper were held in the hall. Daniel Webster organized the event, and Washington Irving and William Cullen Bryant, who had been Cooper's intimate friends, delivered the eulogies.

La Farge was savvy enough to hire a first-rate architect to enhance his property. At 671 Broadway, James Renwick designed a six-story hotel that opened in 1852 (22). Clad in pearly white marble, La Farge House was an example of the voguish Italianate style that Renwick was employing so confidently in a spate of hotel building that had begun with the distinguished Clarendon

FIG. 2.8 Metropolitan Hall (formerly Tripler's), an 1853 engraving from *Putnam's* showing how the theater looked before it burned down in 1854. Engraver unknown. Author's Collection.

(1850–51) on the southeast corner of Fourth Avenue and Eighteenth Street. La Farge House, along with Tripler (renamed Metropolitan) Hall, was destroyed by fire in 1854. *Putnam's* mourned the loss of the latter in its February 1854 issue, calling the music hall "the most beautiful and spacious place of popular recreation in New York . . . which was unrivaled for its extent and splendor by any concert room in the world."[13] La Farge rebuilt the hotel and the hall in the same style but made them larger. (Tripler was no longer involved.) He also had the hall's entrance incorporated into the structure of the reconstructed hotel.

During their run, La Farge House and its music hall constituted an important cultural center in this part of the city. The Winter Garden, as the hall was called in its later years, showcased the famed Shakespearean actor Edwin Booth during the 1864–65 season. His record of over 100 consecutive performances of *Hamlet* was made there, and as the Civil War approached, a dramatization of Harriet Beecher Stowe's *Uncle Tom's Cabin* played there (and at two other theaters) to packed houses. (On November 25, 1864, the night of the Confederate arson attack, Edwin Booth was appearing in *Julius Caesar* with his brothers, Junius Brutus and John Wilkes, who assassinated Abraham Lincoln the following April.) The second La Farge House was gutted by fire in 1869.

While La Farge House was being built, another hotel, the St. Denis (fig. 2.9), was nearing completion opposite Grace Church at 799 Broadway, on the southwest corner of East Eleventh Street (8). This beauty was also designed by Renwick in the Italianate style, but it was profusely ornamented with terra cotta. Its site near the church ensured its success. In 1880, the

St. Denis added a large extension along Eleventh Street, more than doubling its size, to handle increased patronage. It survives as an office building, but the terra-cotta detailing unfortunately has been removed.

In 1870, the Grand Central Hotel was constructed from the shell of the La Farge House and occupied an additional lot, resulting in a 200-foot frontage on Broadway. Its elevators and added height—149 feet in all—made the Grand Central one of the city's first skyscrapers. Although its record for height was soon eclipsed by the Domestic Sewing Machine Building and others, the hotel lasted more than a century, avoiding demolition until 1973, after part of it collapsed.

Many smaller hotels dotted Broadway between Houston and Fourteenth Streets, some created out of the houses of departing families. For example, in 1853 Spofford and Tileston's twin houses became the Astor Place Hotel, one of the most exclusive in its time. Another hotel, the Coleman House at 645–647 Broadway near Bleecker Street (**24**), which survives as an office building, had a cellar restaurant of tremendous cultural importance in the 1850s. This was Pfaff's, where Walt Whitman and the city's bohemian community thrived (figs. 2.10 and 2.11).

No plaque proclaims the existence of this group, a direct antecedent of the Beat poets a century later, nor points out the role of this Rabelaisian circle of colorful nonconformists who helped sustain Whitman during a grim period in his life. Charles Ignatius Pfaff, who opened his tavern in 1855, was a congenial German Swiss, stout and open-handed, "[h]is big head crowned with short and bristling hair and lit up by a silent yet jovial smile."[14] His cellar, if a little dingy and seedy, served excellent beers, fine wines, and delicious coffee,

FIG. 2.10 *(top)* Pfaffians depicted as a licentious bunch in a satirical scene from the February 1864 *New-York Illustrated News*. The behavior is exaggerated, but the physical setting and dress are accurate for the tavern and its period. The gentleman facing the viewers at right is undoubtedly Edgar Allan Poe. Although Poe, who died in 1849, could never have raised a glass at Pfaff's, which opened its doors in 1855, he was the group's bohemian literary patron saint. Engraver unknown. Author's Collection.

FIG. 2.11 *(bottom)* Washington's Birthday parade moving up Broadway to Union Square on February 23, 1861, with the Coleman House at left and Grace Church at upper right. George Templeton Strong wrote that the anniversary was "celebrated with greater emphasis than ever before, at least in my day," as the Civil War loomed and Washington's union was about to be torn apart. Lincoln had arrived in the city amid cheering throngs three days earlier on his way to the capital, and Fort Sumter was under siege by that April. Pfaffians, including Walt Whitman, could well be part of the crowd at the lower left, who are standing just outside the saloon's cellar entrance. Photographer unknown. Author's Collection.

and the kitchen was known for its cheese, cakes, eggs, fish, German pancakes, and sweetbreads. Off the main room in Pfaff's, in the sidewalk vaults (extensions of cellars beyond the building line) was a long table reserved for a coterie of like-minded but most peculiar inhabitants. Charles Pfaff was charmed by the unusual patrons he attracted and enjoyed extending hospitality to the new and different. His regulars—or Pfaffians, as they came to be known—chafed against the restrictions of a prim and rigid society, inaugurating a downtown tradition that lasts to this day.

The Pfaffians gathered informally under the auspices of two flamboyant leaders, Henry Clapp and Ada Clare. Clapp was a bearded, pipe-smoking journalist who had fled the strictures of his native New England to become the founder and editor of the *Saturday Press,* an iconoclastic publication that established newspapers did their best to ignore. He accepted the title "King of Bohemia," which the Pfaffians had jokingly given him in answer to outsiders' queries about their scene. Clare, 22 years Clapp's junior, was the daughter of a wealthy Charleston planter. Her real name was Ada McElhenney, but after her parents died, she changed it to Ada Clare, after the orphaned character in Dickens's *Bleak House.* Clapp was in Paris at about the same time as Clare, and they had separately returned to New York from sojourns in the Latin Quarter, where they imbibed the heady message of Henri Murger's *Scènes de la vie de Bohème.* Their infatuation with the irregular life of the artist was evident in the reports both wrote for the New York press; back at home, each was ready to spread the gospel of bohemianism to other discontented souls. Clapp settled in at Pfaff's first, making it a regular rendezvous for high-spirited writers, actors, and artists and even, for a time, the future French premier Georges Clemenceau.

As a frequent contributor to various journals, Clapp had friends in the local press who happily touted his and his fellow Pfaffians' eccentricities. The *New York Leader* described Clapp as "a queer fellow—a character. He is a born Yankee; speaks French like a native; plays poker like a Western man; drinks like a fish; smokes like a Dutchman; is as full of dainty conceits as a Spanish or Italian poet; is as rough in his manners as a Russian or a Russian bear. His writings are as original as original sin."[15]

Not all of the newspapers were so accommodating. In January of 1858, the *New York Times* sneered: "It would be better to cultivate a familiarity with any kind of coarse and honest art, or any sort of regular employment, than to become refined and artistic only to fall into the company of Bohemians. They are seductive in their ways, and they hold the finest sentiments, and have a distinctive aversion of anything that is low or mean, or common or inelegant. Still, the Bohemian cannot be called a useful member of society, and it is not an encouraging sign for us that the tribe has become so numerous among us as to form a distinct and recognizable class who do not object to being called by that name."[16]

Indeed, such outbursts of condescending stuffiness as this spurred Clapp to start his weekly as America's first bohemian paper in 1858. In 1859 Clare joined Clapp's *Saturday Press,* writing a racy column that offered a mix of opinions and "confessions." Her magnetism, audacity, and beauty soon elevated her to the rank of "Queen of Bohemia." As Clapp's consort (in name only), Clare presided over the parties and dinners staged for sundry Pfaffians and participated in the poetry-writing contests and intellectual discussions that sometimes lasted until dawn. As one of the supremely independent women of her day, she had already shocked brownstone rectitude with the flaunting of her affairs and the birth of a "fatherless" child. Clare's

further defiance of convention—besides keeping late hours, she smoked cigarettes in public, wore her hair short, and parted it on the side instead of the obligatory mid-Victorian middle—was small change.

Drenched in disreputable glamour, from its headquarters in Pfaff's cellar the *Saturday Press* became New York's liveliest literary publication. Many American writers of note, including Horace Greeley and William Dean Howells, were contributors, despite the slim chance of ever getting paid. Howells explained that the group around the journal was considered bohemian because it was against any "existing form of respectability." Walt Whitman's poetry, then considered an affront to respectability, was first published by Clapp when very few others would have dared.[17]

Whitman had been a journalist in Manhattan and Brooklyn, and for 15 years had been producing scraps of poetry (fig. 2.12). By 1855 he had collected them into the first edition of his epochal *Leaves of Grass*. Ralph Waldo Emerson had given Whitman's stunningly original work such glowing praise in a personal letter that—although piqued at the poet's opportunism when Whitman reproduced Emerson's review for promotion—the Sage of Concord stood godfather to *Leaves of Grass*. In *Two Vaults*, which was included in the 1860 edition of *Leaves of Grass*, Whitman brilliantly evokes the tavern's carefree camaraderie: "Laugh on laughers! / Drink on drinkers! / Bandy and jest! / Toss the theme from one to another." In other lines, though, death hovers among the merrymakers, and Whitman seems to allude to the intensifying conflict over slavery and the threat of war on the horizon:

> —The vault at Pfaff's where the drinkers and laughers meet to eat and drink and carouse
> While on the walk immediately overhead pass the myriad feet of Broadway
> As the dead in their graves are underfoot hidden . . .[18]

In 1865, Clapp scored another coup when the *Saturday Press* marked Mark Twain's literary debut by publishing his short story *Jim Smiley and His Jumping Frog* (later titled *The Celebrated Jumping Frog of Calaveras County*), two years before the humorist's first collection of stories appeared.

The Pfaff circle didn't survive past the mid-1860s. In 1864 Ada Clare went to California, and Whitman left New York to attend the wounded in the Civil War. Clare and Clapp died in the 1870s, he from drink and she from the effects of a rabid dog's bite, and their exploits slipped into obscurity. But Whitman never forgot the Pfaffians, and he continued to pay tribute to what Henry

Clapp did for his career. In his final years, Whitman told his friend and amanuensis Horace Traubel:

> Henry [Clapp] in another environment might have loomed up as a central influence . . . he had abilities way out of common. . . . Henry was in our sense a pioneer, breaking ground before the public was ready to settle . . . he seems to be forgotten. . . . Somebody some day will tell that story to our literary historians, who will thenceforth see that Henry cannot be skipped, for the [*Saturday*] *Press* cut a significant figure in the periodical literature of its time. Henry Clapp stepped out from the crowd of hooters—was my friend, a much needed ally at that time . . . He did the honorable with me every time. I have often said to you that my own history could not be written with Henry left out. I mean it—that is not an extravagant statement.[19]

Only a few, of course, sought and enjoyed the bohemian combination of rarified and raucous behavior at Pfaff's. Fulfilling the need for other forms of entertainment, theaters and public rooms featuring the best talent in the country sprouted beside the Broadway hotels. Actress and theater manager Laura Keene, who had leased La Farge's rebuilt hall after the fire, opened her own place, Laura Keene's Varieties (later the Olympic) at 624 Broadway (**27**), a little above Houston Street, in November of 1856. She more than held her own in a field of strong, actor-led companies, including those under Lester Wallack (from whom Keene broke), Edwin Booth, Dion Boucicault, and William Mitchell. These stock companies presented their well-tested plays locally and on tour, and Laura Keene was on the stage of Ford's Theater touring in *Our American Cousin* on the night that Lincoln was assassinated.

Up at Washington Place, Hope Chapel had moved on in 1853, a new Broadway front for offices was built (**19**), and the former church space became the Academy of Minstrels in 1856. Nineteenth-century minstrelsy consisted of a burlesque of black spirituals and plantation songs. This original American music became hugely popular, particularly through the songs of Stephen Foster, the prolific American songwriter who left a rich legacy of tunes, including "Oh Susanna!," "Beautiful Dreamer," and "My Old Kentucky Home." In 1866, the minstrel team of Kelly & Leon took over the space and expanded performances into an early form of vaudeville. They burlesqued opera, offered African-inflected opéra bouffe, and generally lampooned stage and other public celebrities. Edwin Kelly was a fine tenor, and Francis Leon put his very frail body and rich falsetto singing to hilarious use by impersonating the famous prima donnas of the day.

Further north, one Allen Dodworth, who billed himself as a "Professor of Music and Teacher of Dancing," followed his wealthy clients from the downtown precincts they had once inhabited, and opened a dancing academy in a new building immediately north of the Grace Church rectory in 1851. Dodworth Hall, at 806–808 Broadway (**6**), was a four-story brownstone, two lots wide and built in the Italianate style that complemented nearby residences. In

FIG. 2.13 The Gibson Building, which housed Wallack's Theater in the 1870s, at the northeast corner of Broadway and Eleventh Street. Architect Thomas R. Jackson's giant window arcades and eye-catching corner, with an oriel window topped with a niche, enlivened Broadway with a dramatic structure befitting the fare inside. Photographer unknown. Author's Collection.

1854 Dodworth added lectures and concerts to his bill—including composer-pianist Louis Moreau Gottschalk's triumphant performance there in 1855—and provided high-toned entertainment there until his move to Fifth Avenue and 26th Street in 1861. While still under the Dodworth name, the hall descended during the 1860s to broader amusements of the dime-museum and burlesque variety.

The impresario Lester Wallack made the biggest splash in 1860 with his new theater at 844 Broadway (3) on the northeast corner of East Thirteenth Street—smack-dab in the middle of Roosevelt land (fig. 2.13). Wallack's high reputation, the building's ornate design by the influential Thomas R. Jackson (the official city architect), and the fact that it eliminated a warren of stables, made the theater a welcome addition to the neighborhood. Throughout the 1860s, Wallack's theater staged fare that favorably compared with the offerings of London's Drury Lane and Paris's Comédie Française.

While Wallack's new theater was rising, the dry-goods magnate Alexander T. Stewart was creating an even more impressive structure. His new uptown emporium, begun in late 1859 and planned for the full block south of Grace Church (10), was a super-scaled Venetian palazzo erected in white-painted cast iron. It housed New York's first great department store (fig. 2.14), which carried no identifying sign but was known simply as "Stewart's." John Kellum, the architect who designed it, had worked earlier in cast iron with Gamaliel King, the Brooklyn architect who designed Borough Hall. Stewart's store was Kellum's first commission as an independent architect after splitting from King, and it was a masterpiece. It opened onto a portion of the block and took nearly ten years to finish because of a holdout on the Broadway and Ninth Street corner. (The art dealer Michael Knoedler, whose eponymous firm exists today, had moved his business to 772 Broadway (11) at Ninth Street in 1859 and refused to budge until his ten-year lease was up.) When it was completed and opened its doors to the public, Stewart's store at 784 Broadway was

a marvel to behold. Inside, a 48-by-80-foot gallery soared upward, past tiers of open floors, to a domed ceiling, and shoppers couldn't resist the airy interior or its wares. On an average day in 1872, 15,000 people went to Stewart's, spending a total of $60,000, or close to $900,000 today.

Department stores were new to shoppers, and Stewart's was one of the earliest. Taking advantage of far better production and distribution facilities for merchandise, entrepreneurs like Stewart and Macy created palaces for retailing in New York. These were mass-market distributors of goods ranging from furniture, jewelry, and glassware to books, toys, shoes, foodstuffs, and especially clothing. They became the late-nineteenth-century commercial symbol of every aspiring city, and Stewart's stupendous emporium befitted New York's rank at the top.

Stores had been introduced much earlier on this part of Broadway—the ground floors of the New York Hotel and other hotels were lined with them. But Stewart's was something thumpingly new, and soon many other merchants wanted to be near it (fig. 2.15). Early among them was John Daniell, a colonel in New York's Seventh Regiment, who in 1861 opened a ribbon and silk shop at No. 757, on the northwest corner of Broadway and Eighth Street (**13**). Over the next 40 years Daniell expanded into 50 dry-goods departments sprinkled throughout ten adjoining buildings, wrapping around the block from Eighth to Ninth Streets. Shops like Daniell's satisfied an insatiable demand for expensive women's clothing. A fashionable lady in the 1860s might require more than 40 costly hoopskirted gowns, plus accessories, to appear to advantage during a New York season.

Among the later-arriving retail merchants was F. A. O. Schwarz, who opened his first toy store in 1870, between Eighth and Ninth Streets at 765 Broadway (12), moving to Fourteenth Street in 1880. Another famous firm, the top-ranking men's clothiers, Brooks Brothers, bought Samuel Ward's Greek Revival mansion at Bond Street and Broadway and razed it to make way for their new flagship store, modeled on an Italian Renaissance palazzo, in 1874. The firm moved further north in 1884, but the building survives as an interesting reminder that this area was once the city's midtown. Above Stewart's at Nos. 801–803 on the northwest corner of Eleventh Street (5), James McCreery built his large cast-iron dry goods store in 1868. He, too, used John Kellum, who designed a 225-foot facade on Eleventh Street that surpassed even Stewart's Broadway front in length. McCreery's name is forgotten, but his store remains as one of the cast-iron gems of Broadway. Looking past the marvelous array of white Corinthian columns and arches of McCreery's at today's hustle and bustle on Broadway, you can still sense the excitement that shoppers felt more than a century ago.

ASTOR AND LAFAYETTE PLACES John Jacob Astor, a Croesus without peer in America, whose wealth rivaled that of the Rothschilds, also lived on Broadway. But in the 1820s, the city saw greater promise for a large property Astor

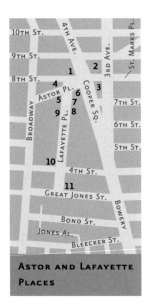

owned near where the Bowery and the then-projected extension of Broadway came together—a place known as Vauxhall Gardens since 1805. (Today it comprises the northern section of NoHo, bounded by Broadway, Astor Place, the Bowery, and Great Jones Street.) Named after the famous London pleasure grounds, Vauxhall Gardens was a resort for New Yorkers run by Joseph Delacroix. He was one of several entrepreneurs who saw a profit in creating beautiful walkways among plantings and statuary, and purveying light refreshments and such simple pleasures as musical performances and fireworks displays, at a time when parks and squares were scarce. Delacroix leased the land from Astor in 1805, and although later reduced in size by new construction, the gardens remained a popular spot for half a century.

A small theater on the Vauxhall grounds featured members of the Park Theater troupe, which in one production included the actor-parents of Edgar Allan Poe. Much later—in the 1840s—the theater was leased by P. T. Barnum. Also in the 1840s, William H. Disbrow opened a riding school on a large plot near the north end of the gardens at 408 Bowery (6). The equestrian training provided by Disbrow complemented Dodworth's dancing school in teaching these essentials to the young ladies and gentlemen of the ward.

Seeking greater income from the land on which Vauxhall Gardens stood, the city decided to convert part of the property to tax-paying residential lots and had 100-foot Lafayette Place (later Lafayette Street) run through it in 1826. Named for the illustrious French statesman and Revolutionary War general who was then visiting the country, it was as wide as Fifth and the other big new avenues that were yet undeveloped. Lined with trees, Lafayette Place ran between a piece of Stuyvesant's farm road on the north, renamed Astor Place, to Great Jones Street on the south.

Between 1830 and 1833, the builder Seth Geer seized the opportunity to construct the most magnificent terrace yet, the marble Colonnade Row (first named La Grange Terrace for Lafayette's country home), at 31–47 Lafayette Place (9) (fig. 2.16). William Backhouse Astor, John Jacob's son and principal heir, built his large Greek Revival residence across the street at No. 32 (8). It was a little larger than the Ward house at Broadway and Bond Street, but not as imposing. Dorothea Astor, John Jacob's second daughter, had eloped during the War of 1812 with a dashing young officer, Colonel Walter Langdon. Though he came from an eminent New Hampshire family, Langdon was not wealthy enough to suit John Jacob. Astor later forgave the couple and gave them an Italianate mansion at 59 Lafayette Place (5), on the commanding corner of Astor Place, and an 800-acre estate in the Hudson River village of Hyde Park. Laura, another of John Jacob's daughters, lived at 45 Colonnade Row with her husband, Franklin H. Delano, the heir to a whale oil fortune. Franklin's brother Warren, a Colonnade Row neighbor at No. 39 who made another fortune in the China trade, was Franklin Delano Roosevelt's maternal grandfather. With Astors leading the way, Lafayette Place speedily filled up with fine homes, churches, and moneyed residents.

FIG. 2.16 Colonnade Row as it appeared in "New York Daguerrotyped," *Putnam's Monthly,* 1853. The spire (left) surmounts the Middle Dutch Church on the corner of Lafayette Place and Fourth Street. Photographer unknown. Engraved by Richardson & Cox. Author's Collection.

The China trade was the extremely lucrative source of many Fifteenth Ward fortunes, and New York commerce with China was already nearly a half-century old when Warren Delano arrived in Canton in the 1830s. Silk and tea were the chief Chinese goods, for which the Americans primarily traded silver and furs, with an occasional cargo of ginseng, which grew wild along parts of the Hudson River and which the Chinese considered an aphrodisiac. A single return trip carrying tea could be profitable enough to cover the cost of building the ship.

Spires of three denominations graced Astor's fiefdom. St. Bartholomew's Episcopal Church, now a historic landmark on Park Avenue at 51st Street, began modestly at the northeast corner of Lafayette Place and Great Jones Street in 1835 (**11**). At a cost of $24,550 for 3¾ lots, the price was comparable to what land sold for around Washington Square, although corner lots on Broadway fetched appreciably more. A block above, on the northwest corner of East Fourth Street (**10**), the Middle Dutch Church (Reformed Collegiate variety) moved from its downtown site where it had been organized by Peter Minuit in 1628. The new church on Lafayette Place, built in 1839, was a Greek Revival masterpiece by the architect Isaiah Rogers, who had designed the Astor House hotel six years before. Ranged across the front were eight stupendous columns—granite monoliths, 20 feet high and 3 feet in diameter, each costing an astounding $3,000. Yet the former Murray Street Presbyterian Church occupied the ideal site at the head of Lafayette Place (**1**). This Georgian church designed by John McComb, one of the two architects of City Hall, had first been built facing the grounds of Columbia College. There, the church won acclaim for its influential pastor, John M. Mason, whose rousing sermons enthralled many of the city's wealthy merchant families of Scottish descent. Following Mason's death and the commercialization of its neighborhood, the church was lovingly dismantled and rebuilt, stone by stone, at Astor Place in 1842.

Homes and churches were soon joined by cultural institutions, led by the Astor Place Opera House. Following its introduction at the Park Theater in 1825, attending expensively staged Italian opera had become a status symbol among old and rich families of the city. But at the National Theater, the house that succeeded the Park Theater and had been specifically built for Italian opera, attendance was weak, and it was not rebuilt after being destroyed by fire in 1841. Nevertheless, in 1845 a number of wealthy men were once again willing to open their purses.

Banker and real estate developer Matthew Morgan of the pioneering New

York Hotel was the initiator. With partners James Colles and James Foster, he
negotiated with Peter Gerard Stuyvesant and John Jacob Astor for a favorable
land lease in the fashionable new area near Fourteenth Street. Astor's offer was
accepted, and Morgan received a triangular plot at the intersection of Astor
Place and East Eighth Street (**4**), across the street from Dorothea Astor Langdon's home. Ground was broken in 1847. The architect selected was Isaiah
Rogers, who chose a restrained Greek Revival idiom rather than the more ornate and majestically columnar designs he had favored for the Middle Dutch
Church and the Merchants' Exchange (1842) on Wall Street (fig. 2.17). Inside,
exclaimed reporter and social commentator George G. Foster, "its white and
gilt open lattice-work, the richness of the crimson velvet sofas and chairs, the
luxurious hangings of the private boxes, and the flood of gas-light shed from
the magnificent chandelier and numerous other points about the house, furnish a *coup d'oeil* of beauty it would be difficult to surpass."[20]

At first the new Astor Place Opera House was a smashing success, but as
time went on, this house fared no better than the previous one, and attendance
slackened. The playhouse expanded its range of dramatic productions, and
British star William C. Macready was engaged to appear during the 1848–49
season, a choice that proved disastrous. James Gordon Bennett's popular *Herald* had already criticized the Astor Place Opera House as the headquarters of
the city's Anglophilic aristocracy, and Macready himself had a long-standing
and well-publicized feud with the American actor Edwin Forrest, a more
bombastic player whose style was beloved by the working classes. The dime

novelist and aspiring political party leader Ned Buntline had long used the pages of his sensational weekly, *Ned Buntline's Own,* to fuel the resentments of the impoverished Irish immigrants in the city's teeming Sixth Ward by dwelling on Macready's scheduled appearance at Astor Place. In May of 1849, after five years of accusations and sabotaged performances, and with some help from Irish ward bosses, the actors' quarrel reached its climax.

On May 7 Macready appeared at Astor Place as Macbeth. Forrest was playing the same part at the huge new Broadway Theater a mile downtown, on the edge of the Sixth Ward. Rotten fruit and even chairs were thrown at Macready during his opening night performance. On the second night, May 10 (Forrest was playing Spartacus), miscreants were escorted out, but a large crowd of hooligans began bombarding the opera house with goose egg–sized cobblestones from the street. Units of the Seventh Regiment stationed there after the first night opened fire, first over their heads and then into the belligerent throng. When the shooting was over, 21 rioters and bystanders had been killed.

The city was shaken by the loss of life and the depth of anger displayed by immigrants toward the rich. News of the 1848 social upheavals in Europe was fresh, and events around the Astor Place disturbance uncomfortably smacked of class warfare. Dubbed the "Massacre Opera House" and the "Upper Row House of Disaster Place," the Astor Place Opera House never fully recovered from its association with death and the angry mob.[21]

A larger opera house, the Academy of Music, was built in 1854 just northeast of the Fifteenth Ward at Fourteenth Street and Irving Place. With growing financial support from wealthy music lovers and status seekers, opera finally possessed a stable foothold in the city. The New York Philharmonic, the country's oldest orchestra, found a home there, too, after moving uptown from the Apollo Rooms at Canal and Broadway where it had been founded in 1842. This new house joined the Mercantile Library, Stuyvesant Institute, Tripler Hall, the National Academy of Design, Bryan Gallery, and NYU in what would grow to become the largest and most influential cultural center in mid-nineteenth-century America.

Key to that cultural growth was the founding of libraries, and the Mercantile Library was an important addition to Astor Place. It had been founded in 1820 for the benefit of merchants' clerks. Its early success in reaching its goals attracted Philip Hone, who became a major patron and participant in erecting Clinton Hall, down at Beekman and Nassau Streets, to house the library's expanding collection of books. In need of more space by 1850, the library bought the ill-fated Astor Place Opera House at auction for $150,000. After spending another $115,000 for extensive remodeling, the library opened as Clinton Hall in 1854. Still in existence (and now on East 47th Street), the Mercantile Library is the second oldest lending library in New York. (The oldest library in the city is the New York Society Library, which was organized in 1700; it moved to University Place, between Twelfth and Thirteenth Streets, in 1855.)

FIG. 2.18 The Astor Library, in its first location, ca. 1860s. The first two sections were designed by Alexander Saeltzer and Griffith Thomas—Saeltzer's original section is the one with the awnings. William B. Astor's large but staid house sits just beyond on Lafayette Place. Photographer unknown. Author's Collection.

By far the largest and most prestigious library was the Astor Library—the core of the monumental New York Public Library of today. John Jacob Astor died in 1848, leaving $400,000 to establish a city library, as he had been urged to do years earlier by Washington Irving and former Harvard librarian Joseph Green Cogswell. Although considered a paltry sum by the press at the time (given Astor's estimated worth of $20 million to $30 million), his heirs made substantial donations of their own to the library. With the original bequest, the first wing was erected immediately north of William B. Astor's residence at 34–36 Lafayette Place (**7**) and opened in 1854 (fig. 2.18). Its 100,000 books exceeded Harvard's 72,000 volumes and the Library of Congress's 50,000. In 1859 William B. Astor added the central hall, giving, in all, $550,000 to the library. His son, John Jacob Astor, grandson of the founder, in turn sponsored the northern wing in 1881, through gifts exceeding $800,000. The total ensemble, resembling a Florentine palazzo, was initiated by Alexander Saeltzer, the architect who designed the Academy of Music. Saeltzer's original building was expanded north by two architects, Griffith Thomas and Thomas Stent, who each copied Saeltzer's design, Stent adding a small attic to the center section. This original Astor library survives as the Joseph Papp Public Theater, a Romanesque Revival glory lighting up Lafayette Street. In the 1850s, the Astor, Mercantile, and Society Libraries housed the largest collection of books in the nation.

Two immense buildings of the 1850s—the Bible House and Cooper Union—completed New York's center of culture around Broadway and Astor Place. Finished in 1853 for $300,000, the enormous Bible House (**2**), which occupied three-quarters of an acre, had a muted Italianate design with brick facades. Built for the offices and presses of the American Bible Society, it also contained 50 stores and offices rented primarily to benevolent societies, mak-

ing it the center of charitable and reform movements for the city and state. Especially notable among the nonsectarian groups housed there was the Association for Improving the Condition of the Poor (AICP). This was a powerful umbrella organization with many charitable spin-offs, including an early model tenement for blacks (1855) between Elizabeth and Mott near Canal Street. Another important Bible House group was the Prison Association. It was chartered by the state to aid those awaiting trial and those released from prison, and also to collect statistics and bring the best available knowledge to bear on the administration of justice. Some of the city's most powerful businessmen led these groups. For instance, James Brown, head of the eminent New York banking house Brown Brothers, was president of the AICP, while hardware magnate John D. Wolfe was president of the Prison Association.

Another charity of city, state, and, later, national importance was the Children's Aid Society. It was founded in 1853 by the young minister Charles Loring Brace, and its headquarters was an office on the second floor of the Astor Place Opera House (4). Brace was a visionary pioneer in caring for the needs of homeless children, mainly by establishing local lodging houses and vocational training, and also by finding foster homes for them in the Midwest. His program was a valuable alternative to institutional care in orphanages, houses of refuge, and asylums. Brace's Children's Aid Society, the AICP, and the Prison Association were but three in a large and unrivaled array of charitable institutions in the city that appeared "on the same scale as our businesses," boasted *Putnam's* in 1853.[22]

Peter Cooper's munificent gift of a people's college, the tuition-free Cooper Union (fig. 2.19), was the other important edifice at Astor Place (3). (It still stands as a university and a tribute to its founder.) Cooper was in the process of accumulating his first fortune by making most of the glue used in America when he began assembling lots for his school in 1825. By 1853, when the cornerstone was laid, he had grown far wealthier through the manufacture of iron, and planned for the pioneering use of structural iron beams for fire-retardant buildings. After a delay—because Cooper's Trenton Iron Works first had to roll out iron to support the heavy presses in Harper Brothers' new Franklin Square plant, and then the U.S. Assay Office on Wall Street—Cooper Union for the Advancement of Science and Art was formally inaugurated on November 2, 1859. In the end, Cooper had spent nearly $700,000 on this wonderful gift to the city, and its architect, Frederick Peterson, complemented Saeltzer's Astor Library with an even more imposing palace in brownstone—it covered the full block south of Bible House. The prominent window arcades of Peterson's design for Cooper Union were an indigenous contribution prompted by those found on the city's large utilitarian buildings, and a likely inspiration for their continued use in the commercial structures that began to dominate Astor Place as the century progressed. Like Bible House, Cooper Union rented out stores and offices—the American Institute, for the development of American industries, and the American Geographical Society were early tenants. In February 1860, Abraham Lincoln delivered his epochal "Right makes might" speech in the Great Hall of Cooper Union, helping to transform his image in the Northern press from that of a hayseed lawyer to one of an ascendant statesman with the intelligence, moral strength, and courage to resolve the country's longtime conflict over slavery.

William B. Astor moved to Fifth Avenue near 35th Street in 1872, after the death of his wife Margaret, and in that same year St. Bartholomew's left Lafayette Place for uptown. In 1875 the massive seven-story printing house of Lange, Little & Company replaced the Langdon mansion at Astor Place, presaging the influx of businesses to come and society's exodus uptown.

While the Astor presence dominated Lafayette Place, and the Delanos and other prominent families lived there, no other residential enclave came close to Broadway's historic cachet with the city's elite in the first half of the nineteenth century. Broadway was the big sea; however, some preferred to be big fish in the smaller inlets of Lafayette Place, Bond, and Great Jones Streets, and other exclusive parts of the ward.

BOND AND GREAT JONES STREETS Bond Street (fig. 2.20) got an early jump on development in the 1820s from the enterprising Charles W. Sandford, an attorney by profession, a spit-and-polish general in the militia (he later commanded the troops at the Astor Place riot), and a trailblazing but ill-starred real estate developer. Fresh from lining newly created Canal Street with houses, erecting the Lafayette Amphitheater (which featured spectacular equestrian acts) near Canal and Laurens Streets, and constructing the Mount Pitt Circus on Grand Street, he took on Bond Street. It had been named after the posh street in London by Samuel Jones, a notable New York jurist (un-

FIG. 2.20 View east on Bond Street at the time of the Harvey Burdell murder at No. 31 (with the crowd on the stoop), February 1857. Except for some trees removed by the artist to better show the curiosity seekers, the street appears much as it was originally developed. Engraving by H. W. Copcutt for *Frank Leslie's Illustrated Newspaper*. Author's Collection.

BOND AND GREAT JONES STREETS

related to the Jones Wood Joneses) who had owned the land. Sandford furnished most of 70-foot-wide Bond Street with some of the finest houses yet seen in the city, but he was mortgaged to the hilt, and financial ruin followed. His Lafayette Amphitheater burned to the ground, audiences for his circus proved scarce, and buyers didn't rush to buy his Bond Street houses until after the payments to his creditors were due. Nevertheless, it was General Sandford who made Bond Street shine as the first acclaimed street in the Fifteenth Ward, predating the ascendancy of Broadway there by a decade. Two trees planted in front of each house made Bond verdant with foliage in season, encouraging profuse tree plantings throughout the rest of the ward.

The financier Sam Ward (5) was not the only illustrious owner who lived on Bond Street and conferred society's blessing upon it in the 1820s and 1830s. Across the street from Ward, at 1 Bond Street, lived the celebrated Dr. John W. Francis (7), an authority on obstetrics and family doctor to the city's wealthiest residents. Number 5 (8) was first the home, in 1829, of Albert Gallatin, Secretary of the Treasury under Presidents Jefferson and Madison, and minister to France under Madison and Monroe. Next at No. 5 lived Winfield Scott, then a major general in the army, who became one of the country's most distinguished soldiers and a Whig candidate for the presidency. William Edgar Howland, of the gigantic shipping enterprise Howland & Aspinwall, lived at several Bond Street addresses in the 1840s. Gideon Lee, who made a fortune as a leather merchant and was mayor of the city in 1833–34, occupied No. 12 (6), where he entertained such notables as President Andrew Jackson on an official visit to the city.

Bond Street's social cachet was further enhanced when Madame Antoinette Teisseire Brugière, who preceded Mary Mason Jones as New York's reigning grande dame, and her family moved into 48 Bond Street (11) in 1833. Her husband, Charles, was a French aristocrat who had fled first the French and then the Haitian revolutions before founding a dry-goods fortune in America. In the 1820s their home at 30 Broadway, at the north end of Bowling Green, was the social center of New York. Antoinette Brugière's 1825 reception for the Garcia troupe introduced Italian opera to the city, but her sensational costume ball in 1829—a first in New York—set the standard for lavish, French-inspired parties for the rest of the century. Also in the 1830s, 36 Bond Street (**10**) had been taken by the rich merchant Abraham Schermerhorn, whose daughter Caroline would become the dictatorial queen of New York society during the Gilded Age. She came from a Dutch ship-chandler family, of a far superior line to the fur-trading Astors, the family she married into in 1853. As the wife of William Backhouse Astor's son William, Caroline Schermerhorn Astor controlled who was in and who was out of society—that is, access to her circle. "The Four Hundred," that phrase connoting the acme of social exclusivity, was coined by her confrere and factotum, Ward McAllister, and in the 1880s and 1890s Caroline Astor gained an implacable fame that even in this age of meteoric celebrity still resounds.

In the 1850s, Bond Street was eclipsed in desirability by Fifth Avenue, as was every other prime area in the city. Its quick slide into commercial use came from increased trade on Broadway, tawdry businesses, and the spread of rowdy gangs over the Bowery. Lurid press coverage of a ghastly murder on the block in 1857 didn't help.

In January 1857 Dr. Harvey Burdell was found face down in a pool of blood, strangled and mutilated in the consulting rooms of his office at 31 Bond Street (**9**). There was no sign of a robbery. Burdell owned the building and also lived there, renting out some of the rooms to boarders. His live-in housekeeper, Emma Cunningham, a 36-year-old widow, was an immediate suspect, as was another boarder, John Eckel, her presumed lover and accomplice. Over the ensuing months, the city reveled in the crime as the press had a field day publishing every salacious detail.

There was the botched investigation by an inept coroner, who flagrantly accused Cunningham and Eckel on scant evidence and ignored the male friends, husbands, brothers, and fathers of a number of women with whom Burdell evidently had assignations in his dental office. The media got a boost in readership, notably the young *New York Times* (founded in 1851), which used its first big crime story, including the offer of a $5,000 reward, to increase circulation. The political repercussions of the ensuing criminal trial temporarily toppled the district attorney, "Elegant Oakey" Hall—a rising star whose nickname came from his impeccable sartorial style. Hall lost the prosecution's case against Cunningham and Eckel, and consequently his job. (He later became mayor of New York City, only to be booted out of office as a Tweed crony in the "Ring" scandal involving massive municipal corruption.) All of these events were reported in words and engraved illustrations, including a purported image from the autopsy of Burdell's heart punctured with stab wounds. The continuing farce surrounding Emma Cunningham, who claimed to be Burdell's wife,

FIG. 2.21 Great Jones Street, looking southeast from Broadway, ca. 1850. Ex-mayor Philip Hone's residence occupied the right-hand corner behind the trees, and the opposite corner house (left) belonged to the banker Charles Handy Russell. Artist unknown. Engraving by J. & H. Orr. © Collection of the New-York Historical Society.

FIG. 2.22 6 Great Jones Street, site of the great Schermerhorn ball in 1854. Engraving from the *Schermerhorn Genealogy and Family Chronicles*. Artist and engraver unknown. Author's Collection.

yet displayed another woman's baby as her own in a failed attempt to claim Burdell's estate, ended in September 1857, with P. T. Barnum exhibiting "THE BOGUS BURDELL BABY" in his Broadway museum. As for the crime, the murderer was never found, and the case remains unsolved to this day.

Great Jones Street (fig. 2.21) never had the panache of its sister Bond Street—nearly half of its southern side toward the Bowery was given over to a string of stables—but three households gave it a high degree of respectability. Philip Hone purchased the southeast corner at Broadway (3) in 1836 for his new home at 1 Great Jones Street. The millionaire shipping tycoon Charles Handy Russell lived across the street at No. 2, on the northeast corner of Broadway (1). Charles and his brother William were running a prosperous

FIG. 2.23 Victoria Claflin Woodhull, ca. 1870. Photographer unknown. Courtesy of Lois Beachy Underhill and the Holland-Martin Family Archives.

importing business when Charles wed Catherine Howland and thus gained entrée into the top circles of New York business and finance. She was the eldest daughter of Samuel Shaw Howland, who cofounded the Howland & Aspinwall company. After his marriage, Charles helped establish the powerful Bank of Commerce in 1839 to restore confidence after the 1837 panic, and became a director of major railroads and shipping lines. He also worked to create Central Park and was a park commissioner for 13 years. But the street's most affluent residents were Peter Schermerhorn and his wife Sarah (née Jones). Peter was the older brother of Abraham Schermerhorn of Bond Street, and Sarah was a cousin of Mary Mason Jones's husband, Isaac. Peter's tract along the East River, mostly made up of Sarah's holdings, was part of the Jones Wood involved in the Central Park controversy.

Peter Schermerhorn's mansion at 6 Great Jones Street (2) was built in 1842 (fig. 2.22). Superbly sited, it occupied the northwest corner of Great Jones Street and Lafayette Place, across from St. Bartholomew's Church. It was there that Peter's son, William Colford Schermerhorn, and his new wife, the former Annie Laight Cottenet, mounted a social event of unprecedented splendor. In 1854, Mrs. Schermerhorn, determined to become Manhattan's ruling hostess, sent out 600 invitations to the city's elite, notifying guests that costumes of the court of Versailles were de rigueur. On the night of the ball, the house's decorations and the servants' attire imitated what might be found among the entourage of Louis XV. A smashing success, the party introduced the German cotillion, a ritual dance at subsequent balls for the next 50 years. The city had been the scene of many fancy social assemblies before 1854, but the Schermerhorn affair substantially raised the stakes for anyone wanting to make social history by giving New York's most extravagant ball.

Great Jones Street lost its allure for the elite about the same time Bond Street did, but in 1868 it attracted two women whose reputations would have nothing to do with their social status. The reformer Victoria Woodhull (fig. 2.23) and her sister and colleague, Tennie, moved into No. 17 (4) and over the next few years showed that they were way ahead of their time, and ours, too. Victoria used men, most famously Commodore Cornelius Vanderbilt, at least as adroitly as men used her. She lit a fire under the suffrage movement and worked tirelessly for equal rights; she fought the larger issue of hypocrisy by skewering (with cause) Henry Ward Beecher, the foremost minister of the age, for his clandestine adulteries; she was the first woman to address a congressional committee (in January 1871) and was a serious candidate for presi-

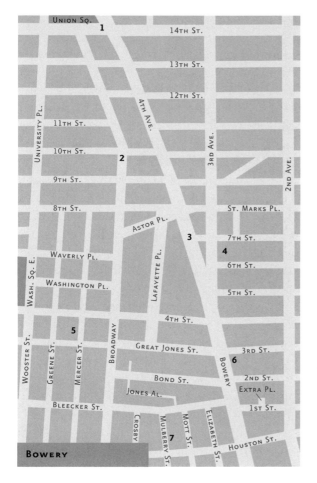

dent in 1872. One of Woodhull's biographers, Lois Beachy Underhill, has contextualized her as a character in Whitman's epic of America: "It has taken a Walt Whitman to understand Woodhull. She came out of the landscape he had peopled in *Leaves of Grass;* she had the same protean energies—a child of 'nature' in the 'swarming vortex of life'—that had been 1870s New York. She had given his 'object lesson to the whole world,' his 'prophecy of the future.'"[23]

Woodhull was a latecomer to Great Jones Street, which, with Bond and Lafayette Place, would soon decline precipitously into streets of trade. They typified the short life of many elegant enclaves that were too close to the main arteries of the city's commerce. Only the unusual, spacious widths of Astor Place, Lafayette, Bond, and Great Jones hint at their once grand residential status.

BOWERY Forming the eastern boundary of the Fifteenth Ward was the Bowery, an ancient commercial thoroughfare derived from an Indian trail. Its name came from the Dutch *bowerij,* or farms, which covered both sides of the road in the 1600s. Throughout the colonial period and for years afterward, the Bowery was the main and virtually the only road north connecting the small town at Manhattan's tip with the rest of the continent. Colonial postmaster Benjamin Franklin, then working for George III, ordered the installation of milestones along the Bowery in 1769, marking the post-rider route to Boston. Paul Revere took that route from Boston in late 1773 and 1774 when he had to deliver urgent dispatches to the patriots in New York. It served both British and American troops during the war, and when the British evacuated Manhattan via the Battery in 1783, George Washington and his soldiers traveled down the Bowery, where they were greeted by throngs of cheering people near a clearing known as Bowery Village. This outpost consisted of a blacksmith shop, a tavern, and a few meager houses, and it was situated about where the Bowery intersects East Seventh Street today (**3**). Below Seventh Street, the Bowery is a prodigal 120 feet in width (fig. 2.24). There, the Stuyvesant and other Dutch farms began, and the road was roomy enough for herds of cattle and wagon trains to coexist as they drove south toward the city.

Even though public art was scarce in mid-nineteenth-century New York, Washington's reclaiming of New York from the British was commemorated on July 4, 1856, by the unveiling of the city's first important outdoor sculpture (**1**) (fig. 2.25). A noble equestrian bronze statue of Washington by the

neoclassical sculptor Henry Kirke Brown was placed on a small island in the middle of the Bowery where it flows into Union Square (roughly seven blocks from where Washington actually met the welcoming crowds). The work is considered to be Brown's most memorable, and it was influential in the extreme; modeled on *Marcus Aurelius,* the most famous equestrian statue surviving from classical antiquity, it had a determining impact on what form public statuary would take in the United States for the next three decades. The *Equestrian Statue of George Washington* was a collaboration between Brown and his student, John Quincy Adams Ward. Ward had apprenticed with Brown for seven years, and after his toil on the Washington statue (in recognition of his apprentice's contribution, Brown generously inscribed Ward's name on the statue next to his own), he was experienced enough to begin an independent career as an artist. Ward would soon become one of the most sought-after sculptors of his day and a leader in his profession; today New Yorkers know him best for his own statue of Washington in front of Federal Hall and *The Indian Hunter* in Central Park.

Originally, Brown and Ward's Washington statue was decorously oriented northwest rather than south, the route Washington had actually taken. The monument was moved in 1930 in conjunction with the bicentennial events commemorating Washington's birth and turned from north to south. Its installation at the southern end of Union Square corrects the direction, if not the site, and it is far better lit by sunlight from the front than it was from behind.

By 1832, when the Fifteenth Ward was created, Tompkins Market had been established in 1830 between Sixth and Seventh Streets (**4**) on the east side of the Bowery, and the city's first railroad—the New York and Harlem—had begun running on the Bowery. Just as the aristocratic precincts of Broadway seemed reserved for the Roosevelts and Joneses, the lower Bowery was becoming a magnet for working-class shopping and entertainment. Toward the upper Bowery near the Fifteenth Ward, the entire region to the east was filling with immigrants, particularly Germans fleeing famine and political unrest in the 1840s.

By the 1850s, this Little Germany, or Kleindeutschland, dominated the Bowery:

> Kleindeutschland boasted thousands of beer halls, saloons, wine gardens, concert halls, club rooms, and other places where wine and beer were sold. . . . "on the Bowery you can count three dozen in the space of a hundred paces, often three in one house: a basement, a store and a saloon; or *Lokal,* being up on the first floor." Here an immigrant could meet his friends and relax, away from the crowded tenements. The "basements with friendly service" catered to the rougher elements and to single men looking for easy girls—or outright prostitutes. These basements provided crude but gaudy quarters for crude but gaudy amusements.[24]

Near Astor Place, the popularity of the Tompkins Market, which had become one of the city's major food markets, justified better quarters. At the same time, the Seventh Regiment's prominent friends swayed the city after the Astor Place riot to build a new armory closer by. Saving money, the city obliged with a combined market and armory building on the existing market site. The market had been named for Daniel D. Tompkins, a four-term governor of New York in the early 1800s. Architect Thomas R. Jackson's new cast-iron Tompkins Market Armory opened in 1860, and its window arcades beautifully complemented those of nearby Cooper Union. The Seventh Regiment's facilities were on the second and third floors, and the market, with its cornucopia of foods, occupied the ground level. In addition to basic groceries, shoppers could purchase fancier prepared foods. Thomas F. De Voe, a butcher and a historian of city markets, described the scene in 1862:

> Under the stairway are located stands Nos. 43 and 45, kept by two Frenchmen, (F. A. Bailly and J. G. Torrilhon,) who keep, besides pork in every conceivable form, boned turkeys, capons, larded bird-game, *filet de boeuf, &c.,* many of which are cooked ready "for parties, breakfasts, dinners, or suppers, cold or warm."
>
> Then, on the eastern side of the same stairway, on stands Nos. 46, 48, and 50, are found L. Bonnard & Co., displaying numerous canisters, containing "Alimentary Preserves"—such as beef, mutton, veal, poultry, game, fish, &c., besides vegetables, truffles, fruits, and the celebrated *pates de foie gras,* or large *geese-livers.*[25]

After its new headquarters opened, the Seventh Regiment was hardly in residence when its soldiers and officers departed for the Civil War in 1861, only to be hastily called back to New York in 1863. Before the smoke had cleared at Gettysburg, they were needed to put down draft riots that had terrorized the city for days. The rioting was triggered by the first draft call of the Civil War, which the city's workingmen, who couldn't afford a substitute or pay the $300 exemption fee, considered to be highly unfair. The incipient draft also fueled the fear among whites of job loss to emancipated blacks. Meanwhile, Fernando Wood and his brother Ben, both Democratic congressmen at the time, were publishing their rabidly anti-Lincoln *Daily News,* a popular blue-collar paper filled with proslavery and anti-Union talk. Just days before the riot, pro-Confederacy governor Horatio Seymore counseled city Democrats in a Fourth of July speech that Lincoln's "bloody" emancipation and conscription policies justified mob violence in response. White laborers, most of them Irish immigrants, took to the streets for five days of bloody insurgency.[26]

What began on July 13 as an attempt to disrupt the draft quickly swelled into a general assault, in many sections of the city, by armed mobs against local institutions, members of Lincoln's Republican Party, and black New Yorkers. By July 16, five Union army regiments had been called back from the front and, aided by militia and police, were fighting pitched battles in the streets, using artillery to destroy the rioter's barricades. The rioting was suppressed on July 17, 1863, and the draft resumed; New York City, whose loyalty had been faltering, stayed behind the war effort. But at least 105 people had been killed, making these riots the most violent public disturbance in American history.

The Fifteenth Ward escaped the death and destruction suffered by the rest of the city. Republican mayor George Opdyke's home at 79 Fifth Avenue (Sixteenth Street) was a focus of mob violence, but the many Republican supporters of Lincoln in the Fifteenth Ward were spared. The new police headquarters on Mulberry Street was another major target, and gangs of rioters heading toward it on July 15 were stopped by a large contingent of police at Broadway and Amity Street. It was an early victory against the rioters, demonstrating the administration's resolve to quell the disturbance. Large concentrations of blacks occupied the wards south of the Fifteenth, and the much smaller group of blacks in the Fifteenth (about 800) avoided most of the wrath of the mob. The proximity of police headquarters was a likely deterrent, although blacks had been attacked southwest of the Fifteenth Ward at Bleecker and Carmine Streets on July 15, and the police had to fight off a mob at Bleecker and Thompson Streets on July 17.

A booming economy following the Civil War bettered the lives of all New Yorkers, especially those of common laborers. By 1870, according to George J. Lankevich's *American Metropolis,* with a population of 942,292 (16 percent over that in 1860), the city's industrial production had risen to more than twice what it had been in 1860, and in the same period the assessed value of city property doubled. "In 1871, its harbor handled 71 percent of the total value of all U.S. imports and exports combined, an all-time high."[27] Although an abundance of jobs on factory floors, construction sites, and the docks helped bring the Irish into the mainstream, Irish discontent resurfaced in the bloody "Orange Riots," which rocked the city in 1870–71. This time the enmity was between Catholic and Protestant Irish immigrants, and again the Seventh Regiment and other militia units were called out to suppress the civil disturbance. One skirmish involved a battle among the police, militia, and protesting Irish people in the middle of Broadway near Grace Church and Stewart's (2), chief haunts of New York's high society. At least 62 people lost their lives in these riots.

By the 1870s the regiment had outgrown its facilities in the Tompkins Market building, and its many socially prominent members wanted an armory in an uptown location. They acquired from the city a full block at Park Avenue and 66th Street for the construction of a building, and after it was completed in 1879, the troops left the Tompkins Market Armory for the redbrick fortress they still inhabit today.

Historically, the Bowery was the city's main north-south route and, having become the boundary between rich and poor wards, was a natural location for police and militia facilities. In 1863, three years after the Seventh Regiment had been ensconced in the Tompkins Market, the city's new marble-fronted police headquarters was built at 300 Mulberry Street (7), a little north of Houston Street and midway between Broadway and the Bowery. Theodore Roosevelt was police commissioner there from 1895 to 1897, before he went into politics and became president in 1901. Following population growth,

police protection for the Fifteenth Ward was intensified in 1845, with the assignment of 14 men from the city's police force. For 15 years they shared space with Volunteer Fire Company No. 4 in a former stable on Mercer Street between Amity and Fourth Streets. In 1860, a handsome station house was erected at 251 Mercer Street (5), and the police force there was 125 strong.

Savings banks also found locations on ward boundaries advantageous. Freed from particular ward associations, more people became customers, and boundary roads like the Bowery made the banks more accessible. In 1875 the exceptionally fine Dry Dock Savings Bank building was erected among the nondescript buildings on the Bowery at Third Street (6) (fig. 2.26). This building, by the architect Leopold Eidlitz, was the third location of the bank, which had started out near the East River shipyards south of Fourteenth Street. Alvin F. Harlow's *Old Bowery Days* describes it as "Gothic with the Czech-Slovakian touch of the Pulvethurm Powder Tower of the architect's native city [Prague]."[28] It moved west to the Bowery ward boundary in search of a broader concentration of working-class depositors. Three years later an el went up in front of it and most of the aging buildings on the entire length of the Bowery became a jumble of shops, eateries, bars, flophouses, and cheap entertainments. Originally, the el tracks were laid in the street bordering the sidewalk. In 1916, new express and local tracks were built, together covering the entire roadbed, hastening the Bowery's decline. Today, the entire section bounded by Broadway, Astor Place, the Bowery, and including the eastern part of Bleecker Street is called NoHo (for *No*rth of *Ho*uston), and the area is resurgent with artists' lofts and trendy stores and restaurants.

Bird's-eye view northeast from the roof of the NYU building on Washington Square, 1859. The spire of Grace Church (center) on Broadway rises above a sea of Greek Revival townhouses. To the right of Grace are the twin spires of St. George's Church on Stuyvesant Square. At the center-right edge of the view stands the crenellated tower of the Mercer Street Presbyterian Church, and to the left of the tower one can see the first cast-iron panels of A. T. Stewart's department store on Broadway being erected. The townhouses in the foreground are on Waverly Place at Greene Street. Photograph by Langenheim Brothers. Author's Collection.

: : : : : **3**

SURROUNDING THE SQUARE

1832–1878

WHILE **B**ROADWAY, **L**AFAYETTE **P**LACE, **G**REAT **J**ONES **S**TREET, **B**OND Street, and Washington Square itself blossomed as the first fashionable locales in the Fifteenth Ward, its other streets—those west of Broadway—also contributed to its growth as the center of affluence and culture in mid-nineteenth-century New York. A tour of the ward continues through the older streets south of Washington Square—*Houston, Bleecker, Amity,* and *Fourth*—and the even older extended streets of *Wooster, Laurens, Thompson, Sullivan,* and *Mac-Dougal.* The focus then switches to *Sixth Avenue,* the busy market street; the elite enclaves of *Waverly, Washington,* and *University Places; Fourteenth Street,* the splendid northern boundary of the ward (and Greenwich Village) and later rialto; and the *Lower Fifth Avenue* historic district. (Numbers in boldface type refer to bold numerals on the corresponding sectional maps.)

HOUSTON, **B**LEECKER, **A**MITY, AND **F**OURTH **S**TREETS One could hardly guess from the multilane truck route Houston Street has become that it was once a narrow residential street. Back in the early 1800s, Houston was the most northern in a progression of east-west streets built north of Canal Street according to the pre-1811 50-foot standard. Its namesake was William Houstoun, Georgia's delegate to the Continental Congress and the son-in-law of Nicholas Bayard III, through whose farm the street ran. (The second *u* was inexplicably dropped from the street name sometime after 1811, and the first syllable is pronounced like *house,* never like the city in Texas.) Houston Street first became attractive to developers when St. Thomas' Church (**22;** see Houston map) and the Reformed Dutch Church (**20**) bought lots there in the 1820s. Then, in 1832, with the northern stretches of the urban frontier nearing Fourteenth Street, Houston Street became the southern boundary of the new Fifteenth Ward. By the time the Third Presbyterian Church was built on the southwest corner of Thompson and Houston Streets (**19**) a year later, the street was lined with many elegant homes.

One early resident, who lived at 26 West Houston Street on the northwest corner of Mercer Street (**21**), was Charles King, president of Columbia University from 1849 to 1864. His father was Rufus King, a member of the Continental Congress from Massachusetts in 1786, and afterward an ambassador to Britain and a U.S. senator from New York. Charles's older brother John became governor of New York, and his younger brother James was a partner in Sam Ward's banking firm. In 1808 Charles had joined the shipping firm of Archibald Gracie, a leading merchant who was a close associate of his father and Alexander Hamilton. (Today, the summer place Gracie erected on the East River is the official residence of the city's mayors.) Charles King married Gracie's daughter Eliza and, after her early death, was remarried to a daughter of banker Nicholas Low, who owned Houston Street property further west

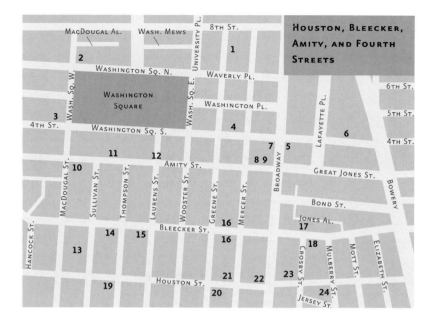

HOUSTON, BLEECKER, AMITY, AND FOURTH STREETS

between MacDougal and Sullivan Streets (**13**). Charles then became a writer, speaker, and influential editor of the *New York American,* first a Federalist (like Hamilton, Rufus King was a Federalist) and later a Whig newspaper.

In addition to fine churches and residences, Houston Street attracted the Abbott Institute, an exclusive girls' school, in 1845. Located east of Broadway on the southwest corner of Mulberry Street (**24**), it was run by Gorham D. Abbott with two of his brothers. The Abbotts hailed from New England and were a well-known family of writers of stories for the young. Their academy was a pioneer in college-level education for young women. After his brothers left the enterprise, Gorham Abbott moved the school to Union Square in the late 1840s, when it became known as the Springler Institute. The original school, plus a new adjoining building to the west (33 and 39 East Houston Street), became a Catholic convent and girls' school run by the Sisters of Mercy.

This stretch of East Houston Street gained notoriety after the opening of Harry Hill's saloon at No. 26, near Broadway (**23**), in 1854. A few years later Hill added a dance floor and musicians to create a concert saloon, as nightclubs were then known (fig. 3.1). Hill, a short, stocky, muscular man, had been a champion wrestler and remained a denizen of the sports world. His friends among professional sportsmen and gamblers were frequent visitors, as were politicians, criminals, and prostitutes. Hill boasted that judges, lawyers, merchants, doctors, and other professional men came as well. Indeed, Hill's catered to a mix of high and low types—unusual for the times—all kept respectable by his strict rules of behavior and willingness to toss troublemakers out into the street. The other saloons and dives joining Hill's on Houston and nearby streets were not nearly so scrupulous, and by 1865 the area had suffered

FIG. 3.1 Harry Hill's proto-nightclub, in an engraving from Matthew Hale Smith's *New York in Sunshine and Shadow* (1868). Hill's was an irregular cluster of two-story buildings on the northwest corner of Houston and Crosby Streets. In later years Hill added a boxing ring, and his place gained fame as the sporting center of the country. Engraver unknown. Author's Collection.

a steep decline. The rector of St. Thomas' Church at Houston and Broadway described it in that year as "the center of the worst neighborhood in this city, the most degraded and the most surrendered to the purpose of crime."[1] Nevertheless, both Harry Hill and the Sisters of Mercy held out until the mid-1880s, when Houston Street became lined with commercial buildings and tenements.

Bleecker Street, the next street above Houston, got its name from the merchant Anthony L. Bleecker, who was of old Dutch stock and heir to the family's 20-acre farm that once covered the street's eastern section. James Roosevelt's substantial Federal-style residence, built in 1821 on the southeast corner of Crosby Street—which, amazingly, still stands (**18**)—was the pioneering settlement that set the social tone for Bleecker Street. James, Franklin Delano Roosevelt's great-grandfather, had moved in with his new wife (his third), Harriet, sister of the shipping magnates Gardiner and Samuel Howland. One of the earliest "uptown" houses of worship, a Presbyterian church, chose in 1825 a site on Bleecker at the head of Crosby Street (**17**), diagonally opposite the Roosevelt residence. Soon afterward, Bleecker Street's 60-foot width caught the attention of several developers, who built three splendid block-long terrace rows between 1827 and 1830, creating stiff competition with Bond Street, Washington Square, and even Broadway.

The first and finest of these 200-foot blockfronts was built by Isaac G. Pearson, right on the heels of Washington Square's Fourth Street row. Pearson erected two elegant granite rows, both with front yards, opposite each other on the block between Greene and Mercer Streets (**16**), one short block

FIG. 3.2 LeRoy Place, south
side of Bleecker Street between
Mercer (left) and Greene
Streets, drawn by A. J. Davis for
Fay's Views of New York (1831).
The block did not last long,
with the eastern three houses
(left) replaced by the early
1870s and the rest demolished
for business buildings by the
early 1880s. © Collection of the
New-York Historical Society.

from Broadway (fig. 3.2). For the first time in a New York row, the appearance of a single palatial winged dwelling was created. The effect was achieved by making the two central houses on the southern side taller, and extending them out a few feet from the others. These two also had bigger raised entrances and lantern-like roof projections.

Pearson secured even more exclusivity for his houses by getting the city to rename the block LeRoy Place, honoring the early alderman and prominent international trader Jacob LeRoy. LeRoy Place's roster of elite residents, which included Catherine Clinton and Gerard Beekman, was another catalyst for Bleecker Street's success as a prime residential street. Catherine Clinton, widow of Governor De Witt Clinton and dowager queen of Saratoga society, resided on the Mercer Street corner of the southern row. Beekman, who lived near the Greene Street end, was related, through the marriages of his colonial Dutch forebears, to half of the 50 or so historic New York families recognized today. (Beekman Place and Beekman Street honor his ancestry.)

Further west on Bleecker Street were two other grand blockfronts, Carroll Place and Depau Row. Erected three and four years, respectively, after LeRoy Place, they kept the social and real estate hopes of Bleecker Street alive. Handsome rows were by that time sprouting up in all the prime neighborhoods. The success of the Fourth Street row and LeRoy Place, together with rising wealth and confidence, had kicked off a new level of residential display.

Carroll Place, named in honor of Charles Carroll, the last surviving signer of the Declaration of Independence, covered both sides of Bleecker between Laurens and Thompson Streets (15). It was built in 1831 by the developer Thomas E. Davis, whose real estate speculation became a boon to Fifth Avenue in 1840. Carroll Place was generally unexceptional, although the houses on the north blockfront were unusual in that they were nearly 29 feet wide, instead of the standard 25 feet, and had small front yards and roof balustrades. These houses were larger because the northern block had been divided into seven lots, as opposed to the eight per block of LeRoy Place.

William Ward, a tea merchant and the brother of Samuel Ward, had the northeast corner at Thompson Street, today 153 Bleecker. (William also owned Hamilton Grange, which had been the Hudson River country estate of Alexander Hamilton.) In 1833, James Fenimore Cooper and his family moved into Carroll Place, a few doors to the east of Ward. The Coopers had just returned from Europe, and Mrs. Cooper pronounced the house "too magnificent for our simple French tastes." Despite Mrs. Cooper's suspiciously self-deprecating comment, this imposing group was nevertheless the least innovative of the new terraces, with a discordant (to purists, anyway) mixture of then-current Federal and Greek Revival styles.[2]

Far more interesting was Depau Row, the southern blockfront of Bleecker west of Thompson Street (14), put up in 1829–30. It was named for and built by Francis Depau, who had married Sylvie de Grasse, a daughter of the French nobleman, Admiral de Grasse, an American ally during the Revolutionary War. (De Grasse's fleet defeated the British fleet stationed at the mouth of the Chesapeake on September 5–7, 1781, sealing off Cornwallis from any hope of resupply or escape. Surrender at Yorktown followed on October 19.) Depau grew rich by establishing the first packet ship route to France, from New York to Le Havre, and he and his wife were residents of their own row. Constructed in the Federal style by the architect-builder Samuel Dunbar, the row had only six houses on the 200-foot block. There was a 50-foot-wide house at each end and four standard 25-foot-wide houses in the center. All were unified by their identical height, a seamless finish, and common detailing, including a long ornamental iron verandah—the first in the city—extending across all six fronts.

One of the big corner houses was taken by department store magnate Alexander T. Stewart, and the other by the visionary surgeon and physician Valentine Mott, the president of the New York Academy of Medicine, a champion of the poor, and a foe of political corruption. A man of advanced scientific understanding, Mott dared to espouse the use of cadavers in surgical instruction, a practice then considered immoral. Medical dissections were illegal in New York City until 1854, 11 years before Mott's death in 1865.

Depau Row's social luster sparkled most brightly in the 1841–42 season when Dr. Mott and his wife threw a grand fete for French royalty. Although the city had held a magnificent public celebration in Washington Square honoring the revolution against the Bourbon restoration in 1830, 24-year-old Ferdinand, Prince de Joinville, third son of Louis Philippe, was visiting America, and the Motts' entertainment culminated his tour in September 1841. Mrs. Louisa Dunmore Mott was a friend of the prince's mother, Queen Amélie, and Mrs. Mott, robed in ruby-colored satin richly veined in gold and set off by a diamond corsage and tiara, was hostess to the young prince and 300 select guests. Society's enduring fascination with European aristocracy was proven once again.

Amid all this fabulous socializing, care for the plight of the lower and

FIG. 3.3 The Bank for Savings on Bleecker at the head of Crosby Street, ca. 1860s. Designed in the Italianate style to resemble a Renaissance church, this edifice symbolized philanthropy and commercial clout, with its abundant small deposits available for huge public works. Photographer unknown. Author's Collection.

middle classes coalesced with a momentous scheme to generate funds for hugely expensive public works. Spurred by New York's commercial interests to build the Erie Canal, a new kind of institution, the Bank for Savings, was created. Established in 1819, it was the state's oldest savings bank and the second oldest in the country. The Bank for Savings encouraged saving by both skilled and unskilled workers at a time when other banks dealt only with merchants, and it paid five percent interest. The Bank for Savings used the deposits to help finance municipal developments, particularly the colossal Erie Canal and Croton water projects, at a time when merchant banks and wealthy individuals considered these massive works too risky. By the 1850s, under astute leadership by the city's old-money and business elite—former mayor Philip Hone was its president from 1841 until his death in 1851—the Bank for Savings had succeeded mightily in its combined philanthropic and commercial endeavors and planned to move uptown from its quarters on Chambers Street. In 1856 the Bank for Savings opened its imposing new Italianate-style building, replacing the Bleecker Street Presbyterian Church facing Crosby Street (17) (fig. 3.3).

Its presence, though, indicated an early decline for all of Bleecker Street east of Broadway. In the following year, 1857, James Roosevelt's widow, Harriet (Franklin's great-grandmother), moved upstate to Hyde Park, and her home opposite the bank was converted into the New York Infirmary for Women and Children, a pioneer in employing female doctors. In addition to these changes, a slum was growing northward to Bleecker Street along Crosby, Mulberry, Mott, and Elizabeth Streets from the notorious crime-ridden Five-Points area below Canal Street. West of Broadway, despite the unparalleled opulence of the stretch of houses there, Bleecker Street's residential luster would not outlast the 1850s, either.

FIG. 3.4 15 Amity, the large central building, from a watercolor by Abram S. Hosier. Poe briefly resided here before he moved to 195 East Broadway. Artist and patriot John Trumbull also lived in this elegant boardinghouse in the 1840s. Courtesy of the Morgan Library.

In fact, the era's arbiters of taste were declaring that the place for fashionable abodes was *above* Bleecker as early as 1854. By then, the street, from the Bowery to Sixth Avenue, was already becoming "*par excellence,* the street of Boarding-Houses" and a thriving artists' community, as one writer described it in 1857.[3] Today Bleecker Street's name still resonates for its later evolution into a colorful Italian neighborhood and bohemian quarter.

Although only 50 feet wide, Amity Street, now East and West Third Street, absorbed some prestige from its neighbors—Great Jones Street, which was Amity's continuation to the east; Fourth Street and Washington Square above it; and Bleecker Street below. Modest Federal houses lined most of the street, and these were the sort of buildings in which Edgar Allan Poe had rooms in the mid-1840s (**9**) (fig. 3.4). In 1845, several months after creating a sensation with the publication of *The Raven* and finding success as a culture critic on the *Broadway Journal,* Poe and his young wife and mother-in-law moved from a boardinghouse at 195 East Broadway to larger quarters on the north side of Amity between Sullivan and Thompson Streets (now 85 West Third Street) (**11**). Number 85 was a three-story boardinghouse that had once been a substantial private home. Poe must have been pleased about residing only one short block from the square and in the center of the city's most privileged ward because he characterized the area as one of the city's "most fashionable quarters." Indeed, there were a number of large and elegant houses on Amity Street itself, near John Ireland's double-width residence at No. 61, at the head of Laurens Street (**12**). Irelands had once owned the entire block.[4]

Two churches were built in the early 1830s on Amity Street: a Baptist church, which occupied part of an old Baptist burial ground on the northeast corner of Mercer (**8**), and the Episcopal St. Clement's Church near Mac-Dougal (**10**). They served the religious and social needs of their well-to-do parishioners for some 15 years before their street's prominence declined. Later, two charities occupied modest houses on the block east of Mercer Street. Number 21 Amity (**9**) was briefly rented in 1860 by the Ladies' Christian Association of the City of New York, as a home for "virtuous" young women who were dependent on their own resources. Two years later the association, a forerunner of the YWCA, moved to Fourteenth Street, and then to 26 and 27 Washington Square North (**2**) in 1868. Number 23 (**9**) was rented in 1867 by a group of Episcopal Church members for their Midnight Mission. Their goal was to save women from prostitution, which flourished near the theater and hotel district on Broadway. The mission moved to 260 Greene Street, near Eighth Street (1), in 1870.

Fourth Street, west of Washington Square, contained some dwellings as handsome as those on the square. In 1859, a Methodist Episcopal congregation commissioned Gamaliel King to design a marble church in an early Romanesque Revival style on the north side of Fourth Street, just west of Mac-Dougal (3). East of the square, unpretentious two-story Federal-style houses built in the 1820s predominated as Fourth Street approached Broadway. Then, in 1851, the small but luxurious Waverly Hotel was built at 697 Broadway, on the southwest corner at Fourth Street (7), and residents considered it a local improvement over the old structures that had occupied the city's outskirts. In the 1840s, Cornelius Vanderbilt's stables and a modest office were built on the north side of Fourth Street between Greene and Mercer Streets (4); they were attached to his new residence on Washington Place. Across Broadway, another of the unsightly coal yards that dotted the city marred the street (5), but as Fourth Street approached Lafayette Place, it again possessed handsome townhouses fit for wealthy residents.

One such plutocrat, the merchant Seabury Tredwell, bought a fine residence on Fourth Street slightly east of Lafayette Place in 1833 (6). The house, built a year earlier and attributed to Minard Lafever, possessed both Greek Revival and Federal elements, and it was similar in appearance to the Carroll Place terrace dwellings on Bleecker Street.

Unlike any mansion on Bleecker, the entire Tredwell house, including its lofty rooms and extravagant furnishings, has survived intact, thanks to the longevity of Gertrude Tredwell, one of Seabury's unmarried daughters. In 1933, she died at the age of 93 in the same damask-draped four-poster bed in which she had been born. Miraculously, a distant Tredwell relative continued to preserve it after Gertrude's death, and the house's many loving friends over the decades have turned it into a wonderful museum named the Old Merchant's House. In the genteel world of the Tredwells, possession of good things meant that there was no need to replace them, and no one ever did. The family's gleaming silver and gilded china, crimson silk hangings, richly grained mahogany furniture, marble mantelpieces, and intricately patterned lace all remain on display at 29 East Fourth Street.

MERCER, GREENE, WOOSTER, LAURENS, THOMPSON, SULLIVAN, AND MACDOUGAL STREETS West of Broadway, the 50-foot-wide north-south streets that extended from the southern wards never had much of a chance with the upscale residents of the Fifteenth Ward, despite the illustriousness of the namesakes they honored. As were Crosby, Mulberry, Mott, and Elizabeth Streets east of Broadway, the streets named for Revolutionary War generals were escape routes from the crowded wards of the lower city. Even before the establishment of the Fifteenth Ward, these north-south streets were filled, up

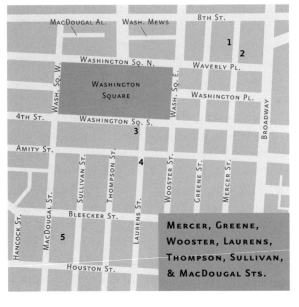

MERCER, GREENE, WOOSTER, LAURENS, THOMPSON, SULLIVAN, & MACDOUGAL STS.

to Fourth Street, with the shanties and ordinary houses, many of them wooden, of tradespeople and artisans who traditionally lived on the cheaper outskirts of the growing city.

The same rich residents who built their fancy homes on east-west Houston, Bleecker, Amity, and Fourth Streets also located their stables among the working-class dwellings on the north-south streets, making those locations even more undesirable and sharpening the contrast between them and the east-west streets. As might have been expected, the popularity of Houston and the other east-west streets soon waned. By the 1850s, wealthy residents had grown tired of the long stretches of shoddy streets just around the corner from their mansions, and so they headed for better quarters. By the mid-1860s, most of the expensive private homes on Bleecker Street had become boardinghouses; a city survey showed that more than one-third of them contained shops and other small service businesses on their ground floors.

A few pockets of fine residences did exist, however, on some of the north-south streets. At the top of this short list was Neilson Place, the renamed section of Mercer Street between Waverly Place and East Eighth Street. Its namesake was William Neilson, an early merchant and insurance industry magnate whose country house once stood there. His niece, Helena, remembered being taken there in 1826 to watch the fireworks display celebrating the opening of the Washington Military Parade Ground.

In 1834 a new Presbyterian congregation commissioned James Dakin, fresh from working on NYU's new building, to design a church on the western side of the street (1). Dakin designed a single-towered Gothic Revival building in the style of a typical English parish church, an artistic addition to the neighborhood (fig. 3.5). Only six houses were erected across the street from the church on this short and exclusive block; the largest of these belonged to Edward Renshaw Jones (2). Another member of the tribe of the Jones Wood Joneses, he was brother-in-law to Mary Mason Jones and the paternal grandfather of Edith Wharton.

By far the longest-lasting group of townhouses in this part of the ward survives as the MacDougal-Sullivan Gardens Historic District (5). The block, bounded by MacDougal, Sullivan, Houston, and Bleecker Streets, had once belonged to Nicholas Low, the banker and political figure in post–Revolutionary War New York, whose daughter became the second wife of Charles King. Low's heirs erected fine Greek Revival rows there in the late 1840s, and instead of selling them, they kept them as investments and rented them

FIG. 3.5 The Mercer Street Presbyterian Church, ca. 1866. Something of the serenity of the upper reaches of Mercer Street can be seen here. Photograph by George Stacy. Author's Collection.

out on long-term leases, even as Italian immigrants crowded into the area in the 1890s. By 1920, the houses were still relatively intact when William Sloane Coffin, heir to the W. & J. Sloane furniture company, bought the block to develop and improve it.

Coffin's idea was to convert the deteriorated old houses into competitively priced apartments for middle-class New Yorkers, and he sold the houses on Houston and Bleecker Streets to pay for the modernization. The front entrances were drastically altered, but the individual back yards were combined into a common garden that makes this group of houses one of the city's most delightful residential complexes to this day.

Another ambitious row of houses once lined both sides of the upper block of Laurens Street below Amity Street (**4**). (Laurens is now La Guardia Place; the blocks north of Houston were renamed for the city's most unforgettable mayor in 1967.) Some of these houses were built by John Ireland in the 1830s as suitable company for him and for his mansion facing down Laurens Street. For added class, this stretch of Laurens was optimistically rechristened Amity Place in the 1840s, but the Irelands had moved away, and residential bliss was short-lived. Laurens Street was cut through the block to West Fourth Street in 1869, destroying Ireland's enclave. Ireland's son and heir, however, immediately returned to a new Washington Square house on the western corner of the Laurens Street extension (**3**). This helped preserve property values in the vicinity until the late 1870s, when an el line finally clobbered Laurens and Amity Streets. Many owners north of the square were appalled by the Laurens Street extension, believing that easier access to the square would encourage criminals to prey upon its tonier precincts. George Templeton Strong fumed that "Rotten Row" would now infect Fifth Avenue. His use of the English locution (London had its own Rotten Row) was apt, as he was referring to three disreputable blocks of Laurens just above Canal Street (now West Broadway) that were home to a string of cheap brothels and a dangerous gang of cutthroats.[5]

Laurens, Thompson, and Sullivan Streets were connected to Fifth Avenue in the first redesign of Washington Square (fig. 3.6). By 1870 Frederick Law Olmsted's landscaping ideas prevailed, and his associates laid out the square with picturesque curvilinear plots of grass, paths, and flower beds. Wood and iron benches replaced the few small stone benches that had been installed ear-

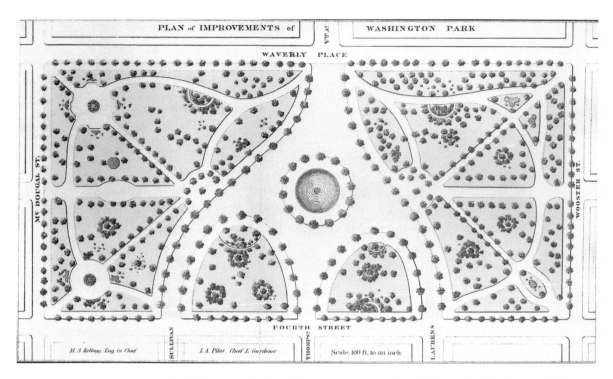

FIG. 3.6 The redesigned Washington Square, with its major connections of Fifth Avenue to the streets south of it, ca. 1870. As mechanized traffic grew with the burgeoning city, the design became an increasing blight on the neighborhood until community activism forced traffic out of the square in the 1960s. Rendering by C. L. Spangenberg. Author's Collection.

lier. The square's iron fence was removed and shipped off to Reservoir Square (later named Bryant Park), and a wooden bandstand was erected in Washington Square's western section. The square's new configuration prevailed for nearly a century, but Olmsted's amenities couldn't prevent its ultimate transformation into one of the city's major traffic arteries.

SIXTH AVENUE Whereas the Bowery had begun as a Dutch farm road, Sixth Avenue (the Fifteenth Ward's western boundary) was one of the city's brand-new 100-foot thoroughfares. West of the avenue lay the original Greenwich Village, today's West Village, whose growth from settlements on the Hudson River was spurred by those fleeing the yellow fever epidemics between 1797 and 1822. (That area, in the city's Ninth Ward, was already old when the Fifteenth Ward, today's Greenwich Village, was created.) The West Village's earlier patchwork of short and narrow streets stood in stark contrast to the spacious streets and avenues of the Commissioners' Plan, which nicely let the old streets be. Many fine houses were built on these older streets, some equal in splendor to those in the Fifteenth Ward. Sixth Avenue separated the quaint streets and little houses to its west from the princely new townhouses, terraces, and mansions to its east—and does so still.

Prominent property owners like the Rogers and Rhinelander families complained that the Tompkins Market was too far away from their real estate developments, and in 1831 pressured the city for a comparable food depot on Sixth Avenue. The next year a triangular piece of land on Sixth Avenue between Greenwich Avenue and Tenth Street was purchased (4). Wooden sheds were erected, and the Jefferson Market, named after Thomas Jefferson, opened in January 1833. A police station, court, jail, militia drill room, fire-

SIXTH AVENUE

house, fire watchtower, well, and pipe shop were soon added to the property. Well water was pumped to a reservoir on high ground near Third Avenue and Thirteenth Street, which fed fire hydrants on the major streets and avenues south of 21st Street and to within a few blocks of the Hudson and East Rivers. Luck and timing made this collection of services a civic-center satellite of City Hall (fig. 3.7).

So successful was the Jefferson Market complex that by 1870 the Albany legislature considered replacing the increasingly dilapidated wooden structures with a new municipal building on the site. Timing was bad, however; the Tweed machine had been involved in the project, and the first attempt was a casualty of the scandal. By 1873, all the city had to show for its $150,000 investment was a pile of rotting building materials. In 1874, the newly formed City Prison Commission hired the well-known architect Frederick Clarke Withers to draw up plans. At the time, Albany wanted to relieve the city's depressed economy with a big construction project, and Withers was eager to use the ample funds authorized by the state. With the revived municipal building proposal, the neighborhood was again lucky, this time exceedingly so. Withers produced a stunning masterpiece of High Victorian Gothic design, bristling with turrets and crowned by a tower with a steep pyramidal roof (fig. 3.8). He expertly integrated ornament with a facade treatment that used horizontal bands of red brick and limestone to stress surface continuity, resulting in a vigorously cohesive whole. (Not all observers agreed, and the effect was sometimes referred to derisively as the "Lean Bacon Style.") The idiom of the Jefferson Market Courthouse was new to New York, although it had been used for important public buildings in Britain since the 1850s. Architects loved it, but many citizens simply didn't know what to make of its ornate features.

Others found the building much too good for its humble Sixth Avenue environment. The *New York Times* called it "a jewel in a swine's snout," and in 1885, the courthouse was voted one of the ten most beautiful buildings in America. Critics even wondered if Tweed had somehow managed to return to power, suspecting that the structure was a graft-producing boondoggle that needed investigation. Despite the widespread approval it had once received, "Old Jeff," as it is affectionately called today, barely escaped demolition in the late 1950s. Now officially a national historic landmark, it has been a salient feature of the neighborhood since the day it was built.[6]

Another outstanding building on Sixth Avenue was the Greenwich Savings Bank, on the southwest corner of Waverly Place (**5**). This Italianate structure was erected in the 1850s, lending some early architectural distinction to the avenue. (An apartment house, Nos. 375–379, now occupies the site.) Two churches also gave the avenue some dignity. One was an Episcopal church built opposite Amity Street in 1843; the reconstructed site is now No. 323, a movie theater (**8**) occupying the shell of a former church decorator's studio. The other, St. Joseph's (Catholic) Church, was built in 1834 at today's Nos. 363–369 on the northwest corner of Washington Place (then Barrow Street) (**6**).

Occupying a restrained and charming Greek Revival building, St. Joseph's is still an active parish today. When it was erected to serve the area's Irish servants and laborers, it was a lonely outpost of Catholicism in the then overwhelmingly Protestant city. (There were only two other Catholic churches in the city at that time.) Thirty years later, it was still a lonely outpost, as immigrants had not yet made substantial inroads into the Ninth or Fifteenth Wards.

Old saloons predated the fine bank and churches on Sixth Avenue, and the

FIG. 3.9 (top) The Woodbine, as reproduced in *Frank Leslie's Illustrated News*, 1878. Engraver unknown. Author's Collection.

FIG. 3.10 (bottom) The Woodbine's interior, 1863. A few of the patrons are wearing the colorful dress uniforms of several Union army units. Painting by E. D. Hawthorne. © Collection of the New-York Historical Society.

Grapevine and Woodbine, between Eleventh and Thirteenth Streets, were among the better known in their day. Back when stagecoaches ran only up to the Jefferson Market, and Sixth Avenue ended at Thirteenth Street, folks left the noise and bustle of the town to take the country air at these and other watering holes at the urban edge.

The more famous and fashionable was the Woodbine, in a fine dormered brick building at No. 501 on the southwest corner of Thirteenth Street (**1**) (fig. 3.9). In addition to drinks and conviviality, this men-only saloon (this was the rule in establishments catering to the wealthy) featured an art collection of some merit. Among the pictures on view were a portrait of Washington attributed to Gilbert Stuart and two works said to be by Hogarth (fig. 3.10). The Woodbine was razed about 1880, but the quaint wooden and once vine-covered Grapevine at No. 458, on the southeast corner of Eleventh Street (**2**),

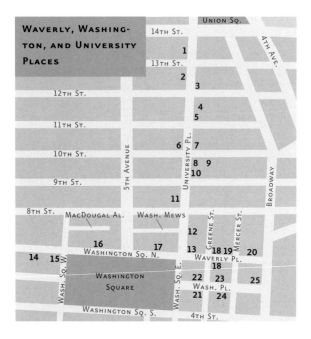

WAVERLY, WASHING-
TON, AND UNIVERSITY
PLACES

lingered on until 1915, when it also fell to progress. Behind the Grapevine site, at 72–76 West Eleventh Street, can be found an even earlier vestige of old Manhattan (**3**). A tiny triangular plot is all that remains of the second cemetery of the Congregation of Shaearith Israel, which established the burial site here in 1805. Some of the original tombstones and a small stone obelisk remained after Eleventh Street was cut through it in 1830.

Another old wooden saloon, down on the southeast corner of Fourth Street at 338 Sixth Avenue, catered to a rougher crowd (**7**). Much later, in the 1910s, when Eugene O'Neill drank there in his Provincetown Players days, it was a dive called the Golden Swan saloon and nicknamed the "Hell Hole." The Golden Swan, like so many other buildings of its time, was demolished in 1927 when the subway was constructed under the avenue.

As did the Bowery, Sixth Avenue suffered the fate of downward mobility when an el was put up along it in 1878. It was a visual scar, as well as a real estate depressant, which lasted until the 1940s.

WAVERLY, WASHINGTON, AND UNIVERSITY PLACES Waverly and Washington Places first appeared on city maps as Sixth and Fifth Streets, respectively, continuing the city's numerical street naming above Fourth Street. But landowners in the area were loath to give up the custom and cachet of commemorative street names, particularly since Bond, Bleecker, and other popular streets had them.

In 1833 owners on Sixth petitioned the city to change their street name to "Waverley" Place to memorialize the recent death of Sir Walter Scott, the revered author whose Waverley novels of Scottish history and legend were international best-sellers. The city granted the change, but a long-uncorrected transcription error in municipal records has left us with "Waverly" (minus the last *e*) as the street's official name. One of the earliest groups of houses in the ward was built on this street when Thomas R. Mercein, a wealthy merchant and former city comptroller, erected a row of nine Federal houses between MacDougal Street and Sixth Avenue (**15**) in 1826. Then came George Rogers's big Federal-style house on the square in 1828 (**16**), and the Row (**17**), which popularized Greek Revival townhouses, in 1831–33. By the late 1830s, Waverly Place was lined from the square to Broadway with elegant Greek Revival residences.

Broadway was still king, but Waverly Place boasted a good number of rich and powerful residents, many of whose homes were wider than those on the square or on Broadway. Some had yards; all were more secluded. James M. and

Stewart Brown of the Brown Brothers banking firm were at Nos. 20 and 21, and George D. and Waldron B. Post were at Nos. 18 and 23 (**18**), respectively. The Posts made their money in pharmaceuticals and were related by marriage to the Browns. The Brown and Post houses were near Greene Street.

George B. Post (1837–1913), a member of the next generation of the Post family, had a considerable impact on New York City. The son of Joel B. and Abby M. Post, he was born on Bleecker Street's Carroll Place. After taking a degree in civil engineering from NYU, he became a star student of the architect Richard Morris Hunt, the first American trained at the École des Beaux-Arts in Paris. A rare individual, both talented and a member of the social elite, Post became an influential and sought-after New York architect and city planner, and the father of the skyscraper. Starting in the late 1860s, Post designed some of the earliest record-breaking tall buildings, such as the headquarters of the Equitable Life Assurance Society on Broadway, the Western Union Telegraph Company building, and the building for the New York World (the first structure taller than Trinity Church's steeple). These buildings were all demolished, but his neoclassical financial colossus, the New York Stock Exchange, with its six 52½-foot-high Corinthian columns and a pediment sculpture by J. Q. A. Ward, as well as his bold, prize-winning, Collegiate-Gothic–style City College campus buildings, are still very much in existence. Another neighborhood Post who later became famous was Emily Price, the daughter of Bruce Price, the architect of Tuxedo Park. When she was 12 the family moved to 12 West Tenth Street, where she was raised according to strict standards of deportment. She married Edwin Post in 1892, but they were divorced in 1905. Faced with the need to supplement her income, Emily Post turned to freelance writing. In 1922 she published the first in a series of best-selling books on etiquette and went on to teach the country manners "according to Emily Post" via a hugely popular syndicated newspaper column and weekly radio program.

Two other commercial fortunes represented on this stretch of Waverly were those of the Haights and the Pearsalls. David L. Haight and his son, David H., made rich by a huge hat and shoe trimmings business they started after the War of 1812, were next-door neighbors at 11 and 13 Waverly Place, near Mercer Street (**19**). Millionaire Thomas C. Pearsall lived one door in from Broadway, at No. 3 (**20**). One of his daughters, Phoebe Pearsall, held out there until 1894, long after her fashionable neighbors fled. Moses Beach, who published lists of the rich in his newspaper, the *Sun,* described the Waverly Place Pearsalls in 1845 when Pearsall's widow, Frances, lived there: "Her husband made money as a Druggist, and realized a princely fortune by investing in real estate. The widow lives in magnificent style in Waverly Place, and supports two or three sons-in-law in good style; and what is more important still, has one or two daughters yet on hand. Her husband was of a Long Island Quaker family, and she the daughter of the rich merchant Thomas Buchanan, deceased."[7]

FIG. 3.11 Anne Charlotte Lynch, the leader of New York's artistic and literary society in the mid-nineteenth century. Portrait by Savinien Edmé Dubourjal, one of her guest artists, ca. 1847. Courtesy of The Metropolitan Museum of Art. Bequest of Vincenzio Botta, 1895 (95.2.3).

One of the most intriguing personalities to live on Waverly Place in the 1840s was not known for her money. Anne Charlotte Lynch, a poet, artist, and teacher of English composition, who lived at No. 116, near Washington Square (14) (fig. 3.11), was an intellectual aristocrat. A tall, slim woman with a gift for bringing people together, she was New York's most charming artistic and literary hostess. At her Saturday night at-homes, often enlivened by guest musicians, she entertained artists and authors of the day. Lynch's artist friends, among them Daniel Huntington, Felix Darley, Frederic E. Church, George Healey, Thomas Rossiter, John Kensett, Charles Eliot, and Thomas Hicks, arranged tableaux vivants at her soirees and drew illustrations for her poems. Many authors were regular guests, including Washington Irving, Poe, Melville, Emerson when he came to town, William Cullen Bryant, Horace Greeley, Margaret Fuller, Lydia M. Child, Frederick Law Olmsted, and Charles Loring Brace. All the writers were expected to read from their works at Lynch's parties, and in this regard Poe was undoubtedly the ideal guest: he recited *The Raven* on more than one occasion, mesmerizing everyone who heard him.

While discussions at Lynch's salon centered on art and literature, social issues were also raised, particularly when Margaret Fuller or Lydia M. Child had the floor. Fuller was a culture critic for Horace Greeley's influential *New York Tribune.* Her 1845 classic, *Women in the Nineteenth Century,* inspired the American feminist movement in the years to come, and her articles for the *Tribune* on a wide range of subjects included prison reform, immigration, prostitution, and slavery. Child was one of the nation's top abolitionists. She was the editor of the *National Anti-Slavery Standard,* the weekly New York newspaper of the American Anti-Slavery Society, which also carried her urban reportage on, among much else, the city's destitute women and children. These radical feminist and antislavery positions and the attacks on society's ills, plus the literary stature of Fuller and Poe, who were the leading critics of the forties, stimulated the culture of the antebellum city and enshrined Lynch's salon as the forerunner of the important New York salons of the 1910s. Lynch married an Italian scholar, Vincenzio Botta, in 1855 and moved uptown to 25 West 37th Street. There she remained hostess to a stream of writers, reformers, painters, sculptors, and musicians until her death from pneumonia in 1891.

The fortunes of Waverly Place and Washington Square North began to change for the worse in the early 1870s. In 1872 the Catholic Sisters of Charity rented 3 Washington Square North for their foundling asylum. To set the building apart from the others on the Row, the sisters had the red brick

FIG. 3.12 Washington Place at the time of Vanderbilt's death, filled with the curious crowd, from *Frank Leslie's Illustrated News*, January 20, 1877. Artist and engraver unknown. Author's Collection.

painted white and the green shutters painted brown, a radical alteration which defaced the Row and which most certainly would have been opposed had anything like today's preservation laws been in place. In the next year, the Greek Revival house at 25 Waverly Place, on the northwest corner of Greene Street, was razed to make way for a small commercial building.

Washington Place was an even more exclusive street, its 70-foot width setting it apart from Waverly Place, Fourth Street, and other 60-foot streets in the standard grid. Matthew Morgan, the force behind the New York Hotel and Astor Place Opera House, was also the major developer of Washington Place. He originally lived at No. 3, next to his business partner, Hickson W. Field, at No. 1 (**25**), but he let his booming hotel take over his house and moved across the street to No. 12. Morgan sold one of his large 44-foot wide lots at 10 Washington Place to Cornelius Vanderbilt (**24**). Vanderbilt, however, did not move to refined Washington Place until 1845. By then he had made enough money to live like a sultan, but he never really fit in, as fashionable society scorned his rough beginnings and coarse manners. It would take another generation and much social maneuvering before his descendants would rise to the top. Nonetheless, as the old commodore lay dying in 1877, a crowd of the curious formed outside on Washington Place (fig. 3.12). Vanderbilt's exploits and entanglements with other titans of business were already legendary; his railroads had transformed the landscape, and his many millions would soon

FIG. 3.13 James I. Jones's residence on the northeast corner of Washington Place (No. 5) and Mercer Street, with a partial view of the Matthew Morgan house at No. 3, ca. 1850, from *Homes in City and Country.* Artist unknown. Author's Collection.

FIG. 3.14 General James I. Jones, sculpted by Thomas Crawford, 1839. Later in life General Jones led the opposition to using the Jones Wood lands for the city's main park, paving the way for today's Central Park. He had earlier been an ally of Philip Hone in creating Washington Square. Photograph by Charles Harbutt. Courtesy of Christopher Morris.

FIG. 3.15 Elizabeth Schermerhorn Jones, ca. 1840. She married James I. Jones in 1838 and turned their residence into a center of society comparable to Mary Mason Jones's home nearby on Broadway. Portrait by C. C. Ingham. Courtesy of Christopher Morris and the Frick Art Reference Library.

FIG. 3.16 View south on University Place from No. 7, 1858. The spaciousness of 75-foot-wide University Place is evident when compared with 50-foot-wide Washington Square East (an extension of Wooster Street) in front of NYU (right). University Place's extra width and link to Union Square made up for its loss of a connection to Broadway. Photograph by George Stacy. Author's Collection.

give his sons enough wealth to rival the Astors. People felt the significance of his passing.

John La Farge, the proprietor of La Farge House, was an early resident of Washington Place. In the 1840s he erected a 32-foot townhouse at No. 22, next to the Reformed Dutch Church on Washington Square (**21**). Henry James Sr. bought a house opposite La Farge's at No. 27 (**22**), near the NYU building, in 1842; one of his famous sons would be born there the following year.

Toward Broadway, at No. 5 on the northeast corner of Mercer Street (**25**), was the most magnificent and unusual residence on the street (fig. 3.13). Built in 1842 for General James I. Jones, of the Jones Wood clan (fig. 3.14), this single house was an extravagant 55 feet wide. It was similar in design to the dwellings of Depau Row but boasted an iron verandah that was even more elaborate than the Depau Row ironwork. Given the beauty of the work and General Jones's reputation and influence, it may well have spurred the use of ornamental ironwork in Gramercy Park and other areas. General Jones's wife, née Elizabeth Schermerhorn (fig. 3.15), was Caroline Astor's older sister, and before Caroline wedded an Astor, Elizabeth's social prestige was second only to that of Mary Mason Jones of Broadway.

Colonel James B. Murray, who had been a pioneering spirit behind Washington Square and the city's first terrace row, returned to the neighborhood in 1851. He bought a Greek Revival residence at 13 Washington Place (**23**), across the street from Morgan and Vanderbilt, and lived there until his death in 1866. For the next 22 years the house remained the Murray family's city residence.

University Place, like Washington Place, was an appendage of Washington Square (fig. 3.16). Mrs. De Witt Clinton moved up from LeRoy Place to a new home at No. 18 on the west side between Eighth and Ninth Streets (**11**).

FIG. 3.17 Mr. and Mrs. James Brown in their opulent living room designed in the French style by the architect Leon Marcotte, late 1850s. A residence typical of the pre–Civil War rich, its plain facade belied the grandeur of its interior. Photography by Mathew Brady. © Collection of the New-York Historical Society.

North of Waverly Place, on the east side, the block's four houses and the Union Theological Seminary continued the Greek Revival theme. The first two houses were 37 feet wide, five feet wider than the largest building in the Row; Philip Hone thought that banker and philanthropist Robert Ray's residence, the second house north of Waverly Place at No. 3, was the best in the city (13). After an elaborate party there in 1834, Hone pronounced the affair "the most brilliant . . . we have seen in a long time" and the house itself "the finest in New York."[8]

The Union Theological Seminary, founded in 1836 and located at 9 University Place from 1838 to 1884, was established for the training of Presbyterian ministers (12). It quickly gained financial security and a distinguished faculty, providing the basis for a greater role in the intellectual life of the city. Like NYU, its presence drew intellectuals to the Washington Square neighborhood. Up the street, Richard Upjohn's Gothic Revival Presbyterian church was erected in brownstone on the southeast corner of Tenth Street in 1845 (8). Its size, spire, and opulence were unsurpassed in the ward until Grace Church outdid it the following year. (Competition among the Episcopalians and Presbyterians, though rarely overt, was keen.)

Upjohn's church was surrounded by three of the finest properties in the neighborhood. Directly behind it on Tenth Street, at 30 University Place, were the mansion and grounds of George Jones, one of Mary Mason Jones's brothers-in-law (9). Across Tenth Street at No. 61, on the northeast corner, William Henry Aspinwall built his mansion in 1845, just as Upjohn's church was rising (7). Aspinwall's firm of Howland & Aspinwall was reaching the zenith of its power as a giant among the shipping merchants whose fast clipper ships ruled the world's seas. Three doors south of the church at No. 41, on the northeast corner of Ninth Street, was the grand residence of James Brown, head of

FIG. 3.18 View northeast on University Place at the Schermerhorn mansion (center) and its New York Society Library neighbor (left) in an evolving business district. Photographer and date unknown. © Museum of the City of New York.

Brown Brothers (**10**) (fig. 3.17). (His cousins and business associates, James M. and Stewart, were the Browns who lived on Waverly Place.) In addition to running a banking firm, James Brown played a role in building the city's maritime industry. He was the principal owner of the Novelty Iron Works, New York's largest builder of iron hulls and engines, and the Collins Line, America's first fleet of transatlantic steamships.

As a courtesy to these powerful neighbors, given the Presbyterian church's more constricted site at the intersection of University Place and Tenth Street, the church's trustees did not order a bell. Upjohn was not pleased; he had provided the space for one and felt that the lack of a bell diminished one of his best works.

Outwardly the University Place houses had little architectural pretension, but the eastern block north of Twelfth Street had two exceptionally fine examples of the new Italianate style—Peter Augustus Schermerhorn's palatial freestanding corner dwelling at No. 101, and the august New York Society Library building at No. 107 (**3**). (In 1872, the Society Library's 50,000 books were available only to its rich subscribers, in contrast to the Mercantile Library's 120,000 volumes and the Astor Library's 135,000 books, which were available to all.) Peter A. Schermerhorn was a son of the elder Peter of Great Jones Street, and *Putnam's* 1854 article on the city's best residences called the younger Schermerhorn's residence "one of our best-proportioned and most correct [Italianate] imitations; more particularly of that modification of it which prevails in Florence" (fig. 3.18).[9]

Famed architect James Renwick lived in a commonplace brick townhouse with Italianate features at 60 University Place, on the northwest corner of Tenth Street (**6**). It seems that Renwick was willing to forgo designing his own

FIG. 3.19 The lower Fifth Avenue neighborhood, with the Phalen house in the foreground on the southwest corner of University Place and Thirteenth Street, ca. 1872. The towers of the Church of the Ascension (left) and First Presbyterian Church (right) dominate the skyline. Photograph by Anthony Brothers. Author's Collection.

home so as to have a place near his in-laws. He had married William H. Aspinwall's eldest daughter, Maria, and the couple took a place directly across the street from where the Aspinwalls lived.

Above Renwick's house, a number of stables and shops were a blight on both sides of University Place and hastened its conversion to commercial use later in the century. Union Court, despite its classy name, was a midblock alley of small wooden tradesmen's houses, taking up most of the eastern end of the block between Eleventh and Twelfth Streets; stables surrounded the Eleventh Street corner (**5**). Things improved a bit when Public School No. 47 for girls was built on the Twelfth Street side (No. 34½) near the corner of University Place in 1856 (**4**). This handsome, still-extant Italianate structure was an early ward school in a new system governed by elected trustees and a central board of education. The Fifteenth Ward's counterpart school for boys was on West Thirteenth Street near Sixth Avenue.

At 120 University Place (**1**), north of Thirteenth Street, lived Frederick de Peyster, a distinguished attorney and descendant of the colonial-era patroons. Most appropriately, he was the longtime president of the Society Library, as the de Peysters were original shareholders in the library in 1772 and supporters ever since.

The wealthy broker James Phalen lived at No. 116, the biggest house on that side of the street (**2**) (fig. 3.19). As Moses Beach, who published lists of the rich, reported in 1845: "[Phalen] is building a fine free stone residence in Union Square. Is a perfect gentleman. During his minority, was with Dana, a lottery dealer of Boston. At his death took his business, spent two or three years in Virginia and Maryland, and made a handsome fortune now invested chiefly in uptown property."[10] One of Phalen's real estate coups had been the purchase of a large plot on the northeast corner at Fourteenth Street and Irving Place, which was initially used as a rope walk and later sold to the builders of the Academy of Music. Phalen left his residence on University Place for the south side of Fourteenth Street between Broadway and University Place, the new center of society in the 1840s. His house on University Place still exists, although the ground floor is given over to a store and the whole building is punctured by exits and fire escapes from its days as a Trotskyist headquarters in the 1930s. Nevertheless, it remains a rare and dim reminder of the old University Place.

FOURTEENTH STREET Even before Fourteenth Street was paved, it was as desirable an address as any in the ward. The first of the sparingly placed 100-foot cross streets in the new grid, its river-to-river setting and 800-foot blocks presented a sensational sweeping vista unmatched by any of the avenues. Three of the four owners of corner houses at Fifth Avenue preferred it and chose address numbers 1 and 2 on Fourteenth Street rather than double-digit Fifth Avenue addresses. By the 1840s even Broadway was outclassed. In 1845, the *Herald* pronounced Fourteenth Street the new center of fashionable New York, and the subsequent rise in real estate values bore out the newspaper's judgment.[11]

At the southeast corner of Fifth Avenue and Fourteenth Street were the paired homes, Nos. 2 and 4, of Tileston and Spofford (**8**), who had previously lived next to each other on Broadway. On the northeast corner at No. 1 (**9**) lived Moses Grinnell (fig. 3.20), whose firm Grinnell, Minturn & Co. equaled Howland & Aspinwall's might in the maritime industry. (Grinnell, Minturn's prize clipper ship *Flying Cloud*'s 1854 record of 89 days and 8 hours from New York to San Francisco was not broken until 135 years later, in 1989, by an America's Cup–type racing yacht unencumbered by cargo.) Across Fifth Avenue at 1 West Fourteenth (**6**) was the earliest of the corner houses, a Greek Revival beauty constructed in 1835 by William Halstead, a prosperous dry goods merchant. The only residence facing Fifth Avenue, at No. 82, was built on the southwest corner in 1847 and owned by Myndert Van Schaick (**7**). Van Schaick, who became rich as an auctioneer in Philip Hone's brother's firm, was a lifesaving supporter of NYU during its early years. He was also the chief ally of Col. James B. Murray in securing city and state approval for the Croton water system; as a state senator, and later, president of the Water Board, he went on to push the massive and complex project to completion.

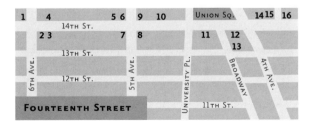

At 11 East Fourteenth Street, midblock toward University Place, stood the

FIG. 3.20 Grinnell residence on the northeast corner of Fifth Avenue and Fourteenth Street, ca. 1862. A partial view (extreme right) of No. 11, the home of Edward Cunard, can be seen. Photograph by Anthony Brothers. Author's Collection.

house of Edward Cunard, the second son of Samuel Cunard, the founder of the great British steamship line (10). Edward had been dispatched as an agent to New York at a crucial time in the city's business history. New York had been first among the maritime powers with its clippers and sailing packets, but in the fledgling age of iron and steam that honor was passing to England. To New York's chagrin, Cunard's hugely successful and superior regular steamship service (twice a month and without a fatality) had first chosen closer Boston as its major American port. With New York's head start in sailing, however, Cunard couldn't attract enough transatlantic business to make Boston pay off commercially, and so Edward switched his line's port of entry and debarkation to New York. Cunard's value to New York and America in concentrating trade at the city's port was immense.

C. V. S. Roosevelt controlled the commanding corner at Fourteenth Street and Broadway. His neighbors on that spectacular Fourteenth Street block included Charles H. Marshall at No. 40, agent for the celebrated Black Ball Line, whose regularly scheduled packet ships first secured New York's port supremacy in the early 1800s; James Phalen at No. 46 from University Place; and at No. 48 Frederick Bronson, son of the enormously rich banker Isaac Bronson and father-in-law of Col. James B. Murray. Whale and fish oil magnate James F. Penniman lived in the largest house on the block (11) at No. 44. (Before the Civil War, these oils were America's prime lubricant and illuminant, and were in high demand as the prewar economy expanded.) George Templeton Strong was amazed at Penniman and the other merchant princes' Brobdingnagian extravagance in interior decoration—a luxury not yet extended to the houses' exterior facades: "One can't make a satisfactory guess at the amount he's [William Aspinwall] invested in rosewood, satin, mirrors, cabinets, and vertu. And they say that Langdon, William B. Astor [both of Lafayette Place] and Penniman go beyond him in display and costliness. . . .

Langdon's arrangements are said to have cost not much less than eighty thousand dollars."[12] (This amount exceeded the *entire cost* of Grace Church, which opened in 1846, the year that Strong made this entry in his diary.)

Built in 1845, Penniman's house and those neighboring it were tastemakers in that they were the first Italianate brownstone row in New York, a style that would soon blanket the rapidly growing city. The house made dining history, too, when it later housed the famous Maison Dorée, a restaurant launched in 1861. Named after a leading Parisian restaurant, it was the first to wrest top culinary honors from Delmonico's. Until then considered the city's best restaurant, Delmonico's was in the process of leasing the Grinnell residence at 1 East Fourteenth Street. To help regain first place, Delmonico's management lured away the Maison Dorée's master chef, Charles Ranhofer, who had formerly been in charge of arrangements for the grand court balls of Napoleon III and Empress Eugénie. Ranhofer reigned at Delmonico's on Fourteenth Street and its successive Fifth Avenue locations uptown for the next 34 years.

West of Fifth Avenue, Fourteenth Street was not as fashionable. Near Fifth Avenue, on the north side, the large Springler–Van Beuren estate had a long, viable, and independent existence as a working agricultural concern. This 22-acre farm had been bought by Henry Springler in 1788. Its farmhouse, which was directly in the path of Fourteenth Street, was later moved north of the street line, and remained there with its gardens and farm animals until 1849, though gradually shrinking in size as lots were sold off and leased.

By the late 1840s houses were rising all around the farm, and two Sixteenth Street neighbors, Col. Herman Thorn and Richard K. Haight, erected Italianate mansions surrounded by generous yards. In 1849–50, Springler's daughter, who then owned the property, decided that she wanted an Italianate mansion of her own (5). It became 21 West Fourteenth Street; 50 feet wide and 70 feet deep, it was situated on over an acre of land. Though she demolished the farmhouse, the old stables and a tiny farm operation were kept so that she could have the freshest milk, eggs, and vegetables for her own table. In 1908, when Springler's great-granddaughter Elizabeth Springler Van Beuren died there, the mansion's little farm had been reduced to about one-half acre but had been in continuous existence since the Dutch colonial era. The *New York Times* noted this enduring city curiosity: "Its [the mansion's] garden is still kept up. Its fine trees give a pleasant shade, and its old-fashioned wooden gate and railings speak of the fashion of a by-gone age. Until a very few years ago it was maintained as a small farm, and the visitor to the city was often brought to see the very last cow which ever browsed in lower Manhattan as it cropped the little stretch of turf."[13] With its stately, lord-of-the-manor mansion and the whiff of the barnyard, the property was a mixed blessing for the street.

Henry James Sr., after trips to London and Paris and travels between New York and Albany, moved his family in 1848 toward the western end of Fourteenth Street at No. 58 (3). Here they would stay until 1855—the most perma-

nent address that his five children would know. In 1853, the Scotch Presbyterian Church erected a building on the north side, across the street from the Jameses (4). Its presence there helped West Fourteenth Street retain a pleasant residential character until 1893, when the church elders moved it to 96th Street and Central Park West. In 1859, Roland Macy established a small store at 204 (today, 524) Sixth Avenue, one door from the southeast corner of Fourteenth Street (2). It grew rapidly into a popular, full-fledged department store, taking over building after building around the Fourteenth Street corner (fig. 3.21), and by the 1870s Macy's was comparable to Stewart's, with departments selling stock other than apparel—books, house furnishings, china, and silverware. During the same decade, Macy's took a leading role in secularizing the American Christmas, first by installing illuminated window displays to signal the beginning of the shopping season, and second by featuring Santa Claus live on the premises.

In 1858, the Palace Garden opened on the northwest corner of Fourteenth Street and Sixth Avenue. Similar in concept to Vauxhall Gardens, it attracted working-class pleasure seekers instead of the genteel set the operators wanted, and it became a favorite gathering place during the day for housemaids and their infant charges.

In 1866, Alexander Saeltzer, architect of the Academy of Music, designed a similar but smaller theater on part of the Palace Garden grounds at 105 West Fourteenth Street, a little west of Sixth Avenue (1). First known as the Theatre Français for its French-language productions, the stage was soon leased to a number of theatrical entrepreneurs. For the average theater patron, on whom success depended, the initial excitement over the French theatrical fare had waned after only a few months.

Although many of the first families who settled on Fourteenth Street still lived there in the early 1870s, its days as an elegant residential street were num-

FIG. 3.22 Architect Griffith Thomas's grand cast-iron Domestic Building, mid-1870s. It was a Union Square and Fourteenth Street landmark for 55 years. Photograph by L. G. Strand. Author's Collection.

bered. By then Broadway, from the Battery to Union Square, had been taken over by trade, and Fourteenth Street was following suit. Then, in 1872, in what amounted to a visual and industrial proclamation of the radical change in neighborhood character, the Domestic Sewing Machine Company erected one of New York's earliest skyscrapers on the site of the Cornelius Roosevelt homestead (fig. 3.22).

Sewing machine and piano manufacturing were two of the city's important industries, and their showrooms and offices proliferated in the Union Square area. Sewing machines (along with available paper patterns and textiles) allowed the average family to own more clothing than even the wealthy had enjoyed several generations earlier, and the machines made by Singer and others spurred the rise of the city's garment industry. Pianos had spread throughout the country as the chief home-entertainment media of the day, and superb instruments made by firms like Steinway & Sons, founded in New York City in 1853, helped establish the city as a center of culture and entertainment. Concerts with top musical stars at Steinway Hall and international piano competitions held with performer antics, cutthroat marketing, and much fanfare promoted the company's pianos and brought fame to New York. Singer's machines were world famous, too, and Isaac Singer built the country's first major international business, becoming the largest manufacturer of sewing machines in the world by 1875.

Even so, the most significant new development from the 1870s was the

FIG. 3.23 Fourteenth Street looking east from Broadway. A chromolithograph by Maerz, "Union Square in Midsummer," from the *New York Mirror*, August 12, 1882, shows many of the theatrical enterprises located on Union Square, with the Union Square Theater flying the American flag (right). Stars of the New York stage surround the view. © Museum of the City of New York.

birth around Union Square of the modern entertainment industry (fig. 3.23). During the quarter century between 1845 and 1870 there had been an explosion in the entertainment in the city. *The Black Crook,* acknowledged as the first American musical, premiered in 1866 at Niblo's Garden on Broadway near Prince Street. Immigrants and migrants from rural areas poured into the city in search of distraction from the drudgery in their daily lives. A concentration of both high- and low-class theaters and music halls had formed on Broadway above Grand Street, and by the early 1870s the northern end of this entertainment district had reached Fourteenth Street.

Spearheading this new activity, the Union Square Theater was built in 1870 at 62 East Fourteenth Street, between Broadway and the Bowery (**12**). First a notable variety house, it much later became a movie theater, and its run in show business lasted more than a century. Further east, two spacious concert-lecture halls had been built near the Academy of Music in the 1860s—Irving Hall at the southwest corner of Irving Place (**15**) and East Fifteenth Street, and Steinway Hall at 109–111 East Fourteenth Street (**14**). These halls and theaters, including the Academy of Music (**16**) and the Theatre Français (**1**), along with Wallack's (**13**) and Broadway entertainments, were the beginnings of a rialto that would flourish around Fourteenth Street and Union Square in the late 1870s. As John W. Frick has described the transition in *New York's First Theatrical Center—The Rialto at Union Square,* theaters, agents, costume and scenery suppliers, photographers, transient lodgings, and other support facilities first coalesced here into the industry for which the city and country re-

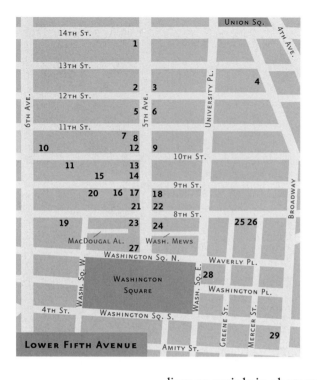

main famous throughout the world. By 1880, Union Square as an entertainment destination was the Times Square of its day.[14]

LOWER FIFTH AVENUE Within all the splendid residential enclaves the city had to offer, there were two ultimate loci of social power in the "old New York" of the 1870s that Edith Wharton knew as a girl. One was Fifth Avenue and the streets that radiated off it between Washington Square and Fourteenth Street—collectively known as "lower Fifth Avenue" or "Washington Square" (fig. 3.24). The other was the burgeoning uptown realm marked by her great-aunt Mary Mason Jones's mansion at Fifth Avenue and 57th Street. Fortunately, most of the Washington Square quarter has been preserved, whereas the bulk of the architectural colossi that graced the world of Mrs. Jones lives on mainly in photographs, books, films, and museums.

Of course, the area that made up Wharton's "old New York" had come into existence several decades before she was born. In the 1830s, the merchant James Boorman, who had been one of the prime movers behind the development of the Row on Washington Square, erected the first block of houses, at 1–7 Fifth Avenue, between Washington Mews and Eighth Street. The corner house on the Mews at No. 1 (**24**) was originally a girls' school that Boorman built for his widowed sister, Esther Smith, to run. The school employed gifted instructors, many from the nearby Union Theological Seminary, and it became academically distinguished under Smith's successor, Lucy Green, who had formerly taught there.

Arguably the school's most famous local product was one of the pupils, the beautiful and vivacious Jennie Jerome. A daughter of the speculator Leonard Jerome, Jennie finished her education in Europe, and in 1873 met Lord Randolph Churchill, the younger son of the Duke of Marlborough. They were married on April 15, 1874, and on November 30, 1874, their eldest son, Winston Leonard Spencer Churchill, was born prematurely in the coatroom of Blenheim Palace.

Lucy Green's brother, Andrew Haswell Green, long a resident of One Fifth Avenue, was an immensely effective advocate of civic improvements in nineteenth-century New York, comparable to Robert Moses in our own time. He was president of the Board of Education and president and comptroller of the Central Park Commission. In 1871, as city comptroller, he tackled the political and fiscal crisis that the embezzlements and kickback schemes of the Tweed Ring had brought upon New York. He played a key role in establishing the New York Public Library, and as a preservationist worked to safeguard

FIG. 3.24 (top) Lower Fifth Avenue, distinguished by its bower of trees, looking north from a little below Eighth Street, ca. 1865. This stretch of the avenue retained its early ambience until the 1920s, when apartment houses replaced most of the private residences. The tower of the Church of the Ascension can be seen rising above the houses to the left. Photograph by Anthony Brothers. Author's Collection.

FIG. 3.25 (bottom) Henry Brevoort's Greek Revival mansion and stable (left) on the northwest corner of Fifth Avenue and Ninth Street, ca. 1895. Photograph by Joy W. Dow. Courtesy of Joy W. Dow Jr.

City Hall, the Palisades, and Niagara Falls. After 1868, Green earned the title of "Father of Greater New York" for his indefatigable work in consolidating the five boroughs into one united city.

It was Henry Brevoort Jr. who gave Fifth Avenue its first show-stopping residence and initial social clout (see fig. 3.26). Brevoort had 41 acres to promote for development in the 1830s, nearly double the size of the Sailors' Snug Harbor estate below or the Springler farm above his land. Washington Square and the Row had been successful in attracting the cream of society, and Brevoort sought to attract wealthy New Yorkers further up Fifth Avenue and to his property. As a leading society figure, Brevoort set a conspicuous example

by building a mansion at 24 Fifth Avenue on the northwest corner of Ninth Street in 1834 (**14**). Modeled after Samuel Ward's new mansion at Bond Street and Broadway, Brevoort's residence carved out a slightly larger plot with a slightly larger house in the same Greek Revival style with a different but equally fine design (fig. 3.25). It was sure to get attention, and it did.

A few years later, William C. Rhinelander built on his family's Washington Square property at the northwest corner of Fifth Avenue (**27**). When Rhinelander's house of worship, the Episcopal Church of the Ascension, burned down on Canal Street in 1839, the congregation selected a new site near him, on the northwest corner of Fifth Avenue and Tenth Street (**12**). Richard Upjohn, who had just designed Rhinelander's house, was hired as architect for the church. His Gothic Revival brownstone was the first church built on Fifth Avenue, and it became a lure to others. Completed in 1841, the church was the focus of national publicity three years later when President John Tyler wed Julia Gardiner there; the event marked the first time that a president married while in office. In the 1880s, the artist John La Farge created masterpieces for the church in a redesign of the interior by the McKim, Mead & White firm. La Farge, who had grown up in the ward and had a studio at 51 West Tenth Street, painted an important mural, *The Ascension,* for the church's chancel and designed two exquisite stained glass windows; all are still extant.

While the church was rising against a backdrop of open fields, Henry Brevoort Jr. and his beautiful wife, Laura (figs. 3.26 and 3.27), a belle from Charleston, decided to stage the grandest private party the city had yet seen—

an extravagant masquerade ball. On February 28, 1840, they opened their home to between 500 and 600 guests. Those invited were "the elite of the country," burbled the *Herald*, which sent a reporter—in costume, of course.

Society coverage was a growing practice at the paper, which filled its front page with the story a few days after the event. Plans of the first and second floors of the Brevoort residence were printed, followed by an item on the host, noting that Brevoort was a lineal descendant of one of the earliest Dutch families in North America, and that his forebears had been successful merchant princes in Holland to boot. Naturally, the *Herald* dispensed news of the house's decor and the costumes worn by the revelers, whose names were not supposed to be mentioned. To satisfy everyone, the reporter resorted to dropped letters, barely disguising the identities in question. Perhaps to assuage its readers, who would never see the inside of the Brevoorts' house, the *Herald* wondered if masquerade balls elicited immoral behavior: "Miss B———y, looked very beautiful in her rich Persian costume; she has long been a beautiful belle; was once engaged to be married to Mr. B———d, then to the celebrated Hon. C———s B———r, Lord Durham's attache, whom she discarded; she made havoc with many hearts at the Ball, but fruitlessly, for on Friday, at noon, she eloped from her father's house in College Place, and married Mr. B———n, of South Carolina, and is now playing the fancy dress character of a married lady, at the Astor House."[15] Readers who kept up with society gossip would know that Miss *Barclay,* daughter of the British consul Anthony Barclay, was one of the Lallah Rookhs (an Indian princess) present, and that her secret amour, Mr. *Burgwyn* came as Feramorz, a Persian prince. (Their costumes were based on characters in a poem of Oriental romance called *Lallah Rookh,* by Thomas Moore, an Irish poet and a friend of Byron's. Moore had an enthusiastic following in the United States for his rhymes set to music, which, according to Ken Emerson's *Doo-da!,* with its influence on Stephen Foster, "laid the foundation for much of American popular song.")[16]

Fifth Avenue had made its debut with Brevoort's gloriously successful ball, and the avenue and its tributary streets began to bloom. New Yorkers would not see anyone attempt a social victory on this scale again until the Schermerhorn ball at 6 Great Jones Street, 14 years later.

Until his death in 1848, Henry Brevoort Jr. continued developing the neighborhood around Lower Fifth Avenue. He created a charming Greek Revival row of eight houses near Fifth Avenue at 14–28 West Eleventh Street—five of them for his daughters (**7**). Later, in 1847–48, he built a smaller four-building Gothic Revival row (10–16 Fifth Avenue) at the northwest corner of Eighth Street (**21**). Brevoort's mansion was demolished in the 1920s to make way for a hotel, but most of the row houses survive.

The large plot immediately north of Brevoort's house, which extended to Tenth Street, lay empty until 1850, when Hart M. Shiff, a merchant and banker from New Orleans, built there (**13**). French-born Shiff hired the archi-

tect Detlef Lienau to design a modest urban chateau—the city's first in this style. When the house was completed in 1852, superbly finished in brick with brownstone trim and sporting New York's only mansard, it was an impressive new addition to the avenue (fig. 3.28).

Four years later, just north of the Church of the Ascension at 40 Fifth Avenue (8), the prominent banker and Central Park commissioner John A. C. Gray built an even more arresting brick and brownstone-trimmed residence that was meant to be the latest word in Parisian elegance. While not on as grand a scale as the Shiff house, its striking high ogee-curved mansard topped with iron cresting hastened the arrival of the French Second Empire style in New York. Architect Calvert Vaux, who was Frederick Law Olmsted's partner in planning Central Park, designed Gray's house. French-inspired architecture would be taken to fantastic levels later in the century, when palatial châteaus for the rich would line upper Fifth Avenue. The Shiff and Gray dwellings were also demolished in the 1920s, replaced by apartment houses.

Meanwhile, James Renwick's architectural practice was not limited to public buildings. Befitting his patrimony—his uncle was, after all, Henry Brevoort Jr.—Renwick began designing houses for the side streets off Fifth Avenue. In 1851, his parents moved to 21 Fifth Avenue (18) on the southeast corner of Ninth Street, into a house that Renwick is thought to have designed (fig. 3.29). One of the most architecturally notable houses in all New York, it was an early example of the Romanesque Revival style, enhanced with handsome ironwork in the front yard fences, stair railings, and parlor floor balconies.

Although this house was demolished in the 1950s, a few examples of Renwick's work in the area remain. West Ninth Street has a superb group of his Italianate townhouses in Nos. 19–23; another group, at Nos. 29–33, has been marred beyond recognition by extensive alterations (**15**). At Nos. 35–39, three more by Renwick were enhanced by beautiful terra-cotta decoration, but these, too, were razed to make way for an apartment house in the 1920s. On West Tenth Street, Nos. 20–38 are a regal terrace of Italianate townhouses, equal to the Row in architectural excellence; they are thought to be by Renwick, although no direct evidence exists for that attribution (**11**).

South of where the senior Renwicks lived, on the northeast corner of Eighth Street, three houses at 9–13 Fifth Avenue (**22**) built for speculation were being run as first-class boardinghouses. Henry James Sr. leased one of them briefly in 1847 before moving to Fourteenth Street. Samuel J. Tilden, a corporate lawyer (he practiced with Andrew Haswell Green), governor of New York in 1874, and the Democratic presidential nominee in the disputed election with Rutherford B. Hayes, lived there early in his career, well before he commissioned his Gothic-style brownstone mansion on Gramercy Park.

By 1854, though, with the Broadway hotel boom in progress, the owners saw greater potential for lodgings and remodeled the houses to create one of Fifth Avenue's first two hotels (fig. 3.30). A relatively small and plain structure at first, it wisely took the "Brevoort" name; later, when two adjoining buildings were incorporated into it, the Brevoort Hotel became Greenwich Village's (West and Central Village's) best place to stay and had a famous run lasting nearly a century. As it grew in popularity and profitability, its facade became more decorative, featuring ornate window heads and an elaborate pediment roof. An apartment building built in the 1950s now covers the full blockfront. Though undistinguished, it, too, adopted the name of "Brevoort" for drawing power. (The avenue's other pioneering hotel, constructed in 1853–54, was the opulent Parisian-style St. Germain at 1 East 22nd Street, which covered the southern part of today's Flatiron Building site.)

Following the Brevoort Hotel's appearance on the avenue in 1854, the next attempt at providing communal living, on a less transient, "apartment-hotel" or "French flats" basis, was the Grosvenor, located at 37 Fifth Avenue on the northeast corner of Tenth Street (**9**). It was built in 1871 by Francis Cottenet, an importer and father-in-law of Peter Augustus Schermerhorn. The Grosvenor occupied Cottenet's former house and yard. Its architect was Detlef Lienau, the designer of the Shiff house across the avenue. Again, he made use of expensive materials and endowed the building with fine detailing

FIG. 3.30 The Brevoort Hotel
as it originally appeared,
ca. 1865. Photograph by
Anthony Brothers. Author's
Collection.

and a modest mansard roof so it would fit in, as best it could, with its Fifth Avenue neighbors. Cottenet, who knew that New York society was extravagantly Anglophilic and suspicious of French living arrangements, took the name "Grosvenor," which was associated with a magnificent London estate and Mayfair's ultra-fashionable Grosvenor Square.

Apartments for fashionable living had *just* become acceptable to New Yorkers after the warm reception for an apartment building designed by Richard Morris Hunt on East Eighteenth Street in 1869. The newspapers praised the Grosvenor's "nest of elegant homes" profusely, as well as its clear understanding of upper-class needs: "the security and comfort of home life, with none of its cares." The hotel's cachet was ensured by its remaining the Cottenet family's city home; they alternated stays there with visits to their Hudson River villa (extant, and also by Lienau) on 65 acres in present-day Ardsley-on-Hudson.[17]

Cottenet's venture inspired William C. Rhinelander to develop three contiguous expensive Fifth Avenue lots, which he had long held vacant, on the southwest corner of Ninth Street (**17**). Between 1874 and 1876, the similarly elegant Parisian-style Berkeley Hotel went up at 18 Fifth Avenue. Rhinelander shrewdly if unimaginatively took the name "Berkeley" from Berkeley Square, another fashionable residential enclave in London. (Both the Grosvenor and Berkeley apartments were razed during the 1920s and 1930s.) Three small apartment buildings (still existing) were built in 1876–77 at 48–50 and 51 West Eighth Street (**19**), upgrading that stable-filled area; in 1876, the Van Schaick home (**1**) at Fourteenth Street was replaced by the Knickerbocker Hotel, since demolished. However, the quarter remained relatively untouched by this first

FIG. 3.31 First Presbyterian's magnificent full blockfront has protected the light and air of this part of the avenue ever since the church was built. Gone since this 1921 photograph are the block of residences (left) and the pair of A. J. Davis townhouses (right) next to the churchyard. Photographer unknown. Courtesy of the First Presbyterian Church, New York City.

early wave of moderate high-rise development, all of which was made possible by one of the most important technological strides ever made in terms of Manhattan's future—the invention of the "safety brake" elevator by Elisha Otis in 1851.

More propitious events in Fifth Avenue's and the Fifteenth Ward's history were the arrivals of the First Presbyterian Church (fig. 3.31) and one of its elders, the millionaire merchant, philanthropist, and bibliophile James Lenox (fig. 3.32). Erected in 1719, First Presbyterian was literally the first Presbyterian church building on Manhattan island. It stood on Wall Street near Broadway and its competitor, Trinity Church. Trinity was destroyed by fire during the Revolution, whereas First Presbyterian served as a barracks for British troops. After the war in 1810, First Presbyterian constructed a beautiful single-spired edifice, derived from English models, that outshone Trinity until Upjohn's Gothic Revival building replaced it in 1846. However, in 1840, as Wall Street became increasingly commercial, the congregation began looking north.

After solving issues involving burial vaults and voting rights, lots were bought for a new church on the west side of Fifth Avenue between Eleventh and Twelfth Streets (5). Fortunately for the church and the neighborhood, the entire blockfront was purchased in 1844 for $52,750. In addition to being a grand site for the church, the full blockfront preserved light and air for a large stretch of the avenue and was a bulwark against commercial invasion from the north around 1900. Architect Joseph C. Wells, one of the founders of the American Institute of Architects, designed the church, which cost $55,000, in the then–de rigueur Gothic Revival mode. Again drawing on English prece-

dents, with its tower copied from the Magdalen tower at Oxford and embellished with quatrefoil tracery, this stately structure overshadowed the Church of the Ascension and was a neighborhood landmark visible for miles. The new First Presbyterian opened in January 1846.

One year later, James Lenox, an elder and principal benefactor of First Presbyterian, moved from 59 Broadway to the northeast corner of Fifth Avenue and Twelfth Street (3). Sole heir to the millions made by his merchant and real estate–investor father, Lenox spent his money liberally, enabling four of his brothers-in-law to take prime Fifth Avenue corner lots from Eleventh to Thirteenth Streets. Lenox's own residence, a Gothic Revival marvel, set a new ward record with 72 feet fronting on Fifth Avenue at No. 53, and 80 feet on Twelfth Street. His total lot, which included a garden on Twelfth Street, extended to 125 feet. It was architecturally integrated with his sister's adjoining house at No. 55 to the north—with the added 50 feet of Fifth Avenue frontage, the two houses together had a palatial appearance heretofore seen only in terrace rows (fig. 3.33).

James Lenox had gone into partnership with his father, Robert, but he left the business for a life in philanthropy and books. He was the founder and major sponsor of Presbyterian Hospital, built on part of his inherited 30-acre Lenox Hill estate, which ran between Fifth and Park Avenues, from 68th to 74th Streets. With books and art filling his Twelfth Street mansion, James Lenox hired one of the country's preeminent Beaux Arts architects, Richard Morris Hunt, to design a library building for his collections at Fifth Avenue and East 70th Street. The library, which was available only to scholars, opened in 1877. This library (whose building was demolished) and the Astor Library on Lafayette Place, augmented by money and books from a trust left by Samuel J. Tilden, merged to form the city's majestic New York Public Library in 1895. Opened to the public in 1911, it is the nation's second largest research library, after the Library of Congress, and one of the eminent libraries of the world.

The only surviving example of lower Fifth Avenue's original grand houses is coal baron Irad Hawley's imposing Italianate residence at 47 Fifth Avenue (6), a little south of Lenox's house. A group of artists and patrons bought the building in 1917 on behalf of their organization, the Salmagundi Club, and retained the interior, which suggests the sense of the luxurious living arrangements enjoyed by lower Fifth Avenue's elite families. Much of the house's exterior deteriorated over the years, but in 1997 the club meticulously restored the facade's original details so that one may again glimpse the architectural

FIG. 3.33 James Lenox's residence on the northeast corner of Fifth Avenue and Twelfth Street, with his sister's adjoining home, ca. 1890s. Photographer unknown. Author's Collection.

elegance of old New York. On the parlor floor the club holds exhibitions that are open to the public.

Number 60 Fifth Avenue, on the northwest corner of Twelfth Street, was the home of Robert B. Minturn, partner in the firm of Grinnell, Minturn & Co. (2). Minturn's was a riches-to-rags-to-even-more-riches story. He was the son of a prosperous shipping merchant, whose firm, like many others, was ruined by the War of 1812. Left nothing upon his father's death in 1818, he entered business life as an office boy in the counting house of a Pine Street merchant. Before he was 21, Minturn had become a partner in the company, and four years later he moved to the shipping and shipbuilding firm of Fish & Grinnell. When that concern dissolved, Minturn partnered with Grinnell to create a business empire that reached every continent with its fleet of New York clippers.

Minturn began hosting his gentlemen-only Thursday night soirées after he moved from Hudson Square to Fifth Avenue in 1847. By then he had become one of the city's most public-spirited and influential businessmen. Here in his new home, leading merchants, public officials, and other movers and shakers discussed the weighty concerns of the day—mainly the city's poor, the creation of a great city park, and the potential breakup of the Union. George Templeton Strong attended one of these gatherings on February 21, 1861, and his diary entry for that date notes that among those assembled were "reputable fogies, ancient and medieval . . . political notabilities . . . great scholars . . . and that florid donkey Alfred Pell [a merchant, not the Alfred S. Pell who helped create Washington Square]." Among the notable men he lists by name are William Aspinwall, Hamilton Fish, George Bancroft (founder of the U.S. Naval Academy), and William M. Evarts (Secretary of State, 1877–81).[18]

Anne Charlotte Lynch transplanted her Waverly Place artistic and literary salon first to 37 West Eighth Street and later to 20 West Ninth Street (20) between 1848 and 1855. Another more scholarly literary gathering was already in full swing on Eighth Street. In the 1840s, while the Brevoorts, Schermerhorns, and Joneses hobnobbed and tried to outdo each other in displays of wealth, Evert Duyckinck was cultivating another sort of guests a short distance away. He was a member of the city's cultural elite and frequented Lynch's soirées. Publisher, editor, author of the periodical *Literary World* and the *Cyclopaedia of American Literature,* and stalwart mentor of other writers, Duyckinck lived at 50 East Eighth Street (then 20 Clinton Place), midway between Greene and Mercer Streets (**26**). His famous "cellar" featured punch parties, Saturday night suppers, and gatherings of artists and writers who convened over brandy and cigars. He made his 18,000-volume collection of books available to writers, most memorably to Herman Melville, who received much of his literary education by reading avidly in Duyckinck's library. Between 1847 and 1850, while he was writing *Mardi, Redburn,* and *White-Jacket,* Melville was a regular guest at Duyckinck's. After he moved away from New York in 1851, he missed the conviviality he had known on Clinton Place, writing to his former host, "I suppose the Knights of the Round Table still assemble over their cigars and punch, and I know that once every week the 'literary World' revolves upon its axis. I should like to hear again the old tinkle of glasses in your basement, and may do so, before many months."[19]

Duyckinck, a Democrat, differed with the Anglophilic Whigs on the direction that literature and art were taking in the United States. Instead of aping English ways, his coterie and its many supporters sought, through a radical branch of the Democratic Party, to create nothing less than a comprehensive nonelitist and independent American culture. One of Duyckinck's main allies during the 1840s was John I. O'Sullivan, whose *Democratic Review,* a national magazine located in New York City, advocated such an indigenous culture. O'Sullivan promoted American authors, including women and budding writers, by publishing work such as Whitman's early short stories. Technological advances in printing in the 1840s permitted the relatively cheap production and distribution of periodicals and books. Duyckinck also strongly supported the city's American Art Union, an organization that encouraged, publicized, and distributed American artists' works, predominately genre paintings and prints. This drive for a national versus a derivative culture effectively ended in the 1850s as the Civil War loomed, and it would not be revived until early in the twentieth century. Duyckinck died in 1878 and bequeathed his books to the Lenox Library, thus eventually enriching the collection of the New York Public Library.

George Palmer Putnam, a member of Duyckinck's circle and a sponsor of the *Literary World,* created his own magazine, *Putnam's Monthly,* launched in January 1853. Putnam was a Whig, encouraged American authors, and produced a far more cosmopolitan periodical that encompassed the literatures of Europe as well. *Putnam's* was the best of America's antebellum magazines, and no less a literary figure than William Makepeace Thackeray declared it the best in the world. It celebrated New York City's culture, and its political essays led to the principles on which Lincoln's 1860 Republican platform was based.

New York's two most high-toned social clubs were also near the square. Two doors from Duyckinck at 46 East Eighth Street (**25**) was the Century Association, whose goal was, according to its constitution, "the cultivation of a taste for letters and the arts and social enjoyment." Founded in 1847 and still flourishing in its midtown location, the Century had a culture-oriented membership that included "publishers, authors, lawyers, artists, judges, and professionals of all sorts, the best names in the metropolis—names familiar as household words in literary, artistic and legal circles," as one historian noted in 1873.[20] By and large, this characterization of the Century's membership obtains today.

The other notable and still-existing social club, the Union, was founded in 1836, and its membership was drawn from the city's oldest Dutch and English families. In the 1850s it was located at 691 Broadway (**29**), between Amity and Fourth Streets.

In addition to the library, reading room, and gallery space offered by the Century Association, local patrons took a direct lead in sustaining the country's first native group of landscape painters—the Hudson River School—and promoted exhibitions and art education that spurred the formation of the Metropolitan Museum of Art. Among the leaders was John Taylor Johnston, a resident of Fifth Avenue and one of the ward's principal art patrons. Johnston was president of two New Jersey railroad lines and the son of John Johnston, the wealthy merchant who had been a primary founder of the Row. The younger Johnston attended New York University and Yale law school, and followed his father in becoming a staunch supporter of NYU by serving on its council and donating money.

From his walks through the makeshift, ill-lighted studios of NYU artists (**28**), Johnston came to cherish art, collecting the work of these and other painters. Sensitive to the plight of the NYU artists, Johnston and his brother, James Boorman Johnston, secured the site of a piano factory on West Tenth Street near Sixth Avenue, and in 1857 commissioned a modern building to serve artists' needs. For an architect, the Johnstons chose Richard Morris Hunt, who had recently moved to New York and was working from a studio in the NYU building.

Hunt designed the classical French-inspired redbrick Studio Building (fig. 3.34), which opened in January 1858 at 51 West Tenth Street (**10**). The first specialized quarters for artists in the city, it contained 25 studios, various small auxiliary rooms, and a large, skylighted two-story exhibition gallery in the center. Bedrooms were attached to some studios for tenants who combined home and workshop. The separations between working and living spaces, as well as the public exhibition space, made building-wide receptions possible. On these occasions artists mingled with critics, patrons, and interested spectators, thereby fanning appreciation of fine art. The opening of the Studio Building did much to cement the ward's claim to be the epicenter of the fledgling New York art world.

Hunt's attractive and functional building had artists waiting to get in. It replaced the NYU building as the center of artistic life in the city and

FIG. 3.34 Richard Morris
Hunt's Studio Building at 51
West Tenth Street near Sixth
Avenue, ca. 1860. Photographer
unknown. Courtesy of the
Avery Architectural and Fine
Arts Library, Columbia Uni-
versity in the City of New York.

remained so for nearly a century. Even Hunt moved his studio there shortly
after the building's opening, and some of the best-known artists of the day
followed. Among the first arrivals were the painters John W. Casilear, John
La Farge, Frederic E. Church, William M. Hart, Sanford Gifford, Jervis
McEntee, Martin Johnson Heade, Emanuel Leutze, and William S. Hasel-
tine. Launt Thompson, sculptor of statuary busts and medallion portraits, was
another early tenant; he would be joined later by Winslow Homer, Ralph
Blakelock, Albert Bierstadt, and William Merritt Chase. It was in the Studio
Building that Hunt, who provided the only professional architectural training
then available in the United States, taught such important architects-to-be as
Frank Furness, Henry Van Brunt, George B. Post, Charles Gambrill, and
William R. Ware.

One year before commissioning the Studio Building, Johnston finished
construction of his own Italianate mansion at 8 Fifth Avenue (**23**), on the
southwest corner of Eighth Street. Clad in a slate-colored stone that turned
so white that nearly everyone assumed it was marble, the residence itself became a de facto center for the arts. With his art collection overflowing at
home, Johnston converted a stable behind his house into a gallery that faced
Eighth Street, and he opened it to the public every Thursday afternoon. It was
one of the finest collections in the city, and included Turner's *Slave Ship,*
Homer's *Prisoners from the Front,* and Frederic Church's *Niagara,* as well as
works by Thomas Cole, John F. Kensett, Asher B. Durand, and the French
academicians.

The Johnston brothers' efforts notwithstanding, many cultural activities
were halted during the Civil War, so that the city's resources could be diverted
toward the assistance of the Union cause. This task was made difficult by the
city's tangled role in the national conflict. Manhattan's financial well-being
had grown increasingly tied to the South. The Port of New York prospered

from the cotton trade, which contributed more than $200 million worth of business annually, and nearly an equal amount of credit to Southerners was outstanding. A number of newspapers, like the *Herald*, and politicians, like Fernando Wood, played on fears of financial ruin and fanned the flames of racial hatred.

Social ties were even stronger than money or Wood's repellent public defense of slavery. According to Will Irwin's history of the Union League, a generation of Southern women had filled the city's most exclusive schools and seminaries. Southern belles were the "glamour girls" of the balls and parties that made up the New York social season, and young Southern men caught the attention of Yankee ladies with their courtly manners and "touch of rakishness." Many marriages linked the slave-holding South with Washington Square and other elite districts. Some of the most prominent members of New York's social clubs were Southern. The aristocratic Union Club had Judah P. Benjamin, who became the Secretary of State and the financial brains of the Confederacy, and John F. Slidell, who became the Confederate commissioner to France. It was not surprising that New York was called a "Copperhead" city when the war began in 1861. Nevertheless, the Fifteenth Ward and the city's businessmen stood behind Lincoln in the presidential elections of 1860 and 1864, when the rest of the city was against him by two-to-one margins.[21]

Robert B. Minturn, John Taylor Johnston, and others in the lower Fifth Avenue enclave played key roles in Lincoln's war effort and the city's cultural development. Henry J. Raymond, for example, who lived at 12 West Ninth Street (**16**), was the founder and first editor of the *New York Times*, chairman of the Republican National Committee, and the man Lincoln called "my lieutenant-general in politics" for his unceasing support of the president. Even the *Herald* came around after publisher James Gordon Bennett received a visit from Albany political kingpin Thurlow Weed, who was a friend and ally of Raymond. Once the war began, the political climate in the North changed to strong support for Lincoln.[22]

Early in the war, the prominent New York clergyman Henry W. Bellows and three eminent physicians initiated the pioneering U.S. Sanitary Commission, devised to ensure medical care for Union soldiers and instruct them in hygienic practices. Bellows was president; Frederick Law Olmsted, the landscape architect of Central Park and author of three books on the antebellum South and the ills of slavery, was executive secretary; and George Templeton Strong was treasurer. The commission's headquarters was located at 823 Broadway, between Twelfth and Thirteenth Streets (**4**). This forerunner of the American Red Cross created the Army Medical Corps, and its members founded the Union League, a New York City social club advocating undivided support of Lincoln and the Union. (The Union League bore no relation to the much older Union Club, which had been founded in 1836.) Its formation came

FIG. 3.35 Military encamping in Washington Square during the 1863 draft riots. Engraving from *Our Police Protectors*, by A. E. Costello, 1884. Other than some rioting along lower Mac-Dougal Street and conflict near police headquarters, the Fifteenth Ward was remarkably free of attacks by the mob. Artist and engraver unknown. Author's Collection.

at a low point in Union fortunes, both in the course of the war and in the outcome of the congressional and gubernatorial elections of 1862.

In March 1863 at a meeting in the chapel of NYU, Robert B. Minturn was chosen as the Union League's first president. The terrible draft riot in the city that summer had only made plainer the worsening Union prospects (fig. 3.35). In the teeth of adversity, the club sponsored black regiments, held a magnificent Metropolitan Fair that generated over a million dollars in proceeds for the sick and wounded, and fought with all its considerable social and political might for Lincoln's reelection in 1864. It carried New York State for Lincoln, as in the city, *only* the Fifteenth Ward voted for him. Similarly focused Union Leagues in other doubtful states like Indiana and Pennsylvania helped sway voters for Lincoln, but it was the fall of Atlanta in September 1864 that clinched the election.

Despite ongoing political struggle and privations due to the war, a group of gentlemen from the Union League Club forged ahead in support of the arts. Aware of the plethora of museums and galleries in European cities, in contrast to New York, and heartened by the overwhelming popularity of the Picture Gallery at the 1864 Metropolitan Fair, this group urged its fellow members a year later to sponsor an art museum for the city. By 1868, the club's committee on art began work to bring about, what club member Professor George Fisk Comfort of Princeton set as the goal: "[a] great museum—one worthy of New York City and of our country—[that] should represent the History of Art in all countries and in all ages, of art both pure and applied." In 1870, they founded the Metropolitan Museum of Art, and the first board of trustees selected John Taylor Johnston as their president. Over the next 15 years, Johnston propelled the museum toward its destiny as the outstanding institution we know today.[23]

By the 1870s, the libraries, schools, galleries, studios, clubs, salons, and other gatherings around Washington Square were at the core of America's cultural energy, and the city could finally be compared with London and Paris. This singular neighborhood continued over the next century to be the nation's preeminent fount of artistic inspiration, when, living up to the example of Whitman's poetry, all the arts gradually broke free from the yoke of convention, erupting in sensational displays of modernity in the 1910s and post–World War II decade. Although forgotten now, this first burst of culture and counterculture in antebellum New York set the stage for future expressions of creativity by awakening the country to accessible literature and art.

During this same postwar period, when the growth of the els and other vast changes were transforming the city, residents of the lower Fifth Avenue neighborhood sensed that vigilance and resistance would be necessary to protect what remained of their Washington Square quarter. Although no protective laws or organizations then existed, a strong sense of community had grown among the area's homes and churches, salons and social clubs. A business and entertainment district was taking over Fourteenth Street, but a first order of business for the neighborhood arose when the square itself became endangered by an attempt to build an armory within its borders.

A number of militia units were seeking new quarters in the 1870s. The New York City Armory Board, pressed to find more city-owned space, proposed part of Washington Square for an armory in 1878. They nearly succeeded, but local property owners, already alarmed by a road that cut through the square and a proposed el that would traverse the square's southern border, put up a fight. They drummed up popular support against the incursion, petitioned the board of aldermen (one list of 7,500 signatories included 200 doctors and many members of the Union and other clubs), and pressured the mayor and the state legislature. Residents sought and received favorable press coverage (fig. 3.36), and they enlisted the support of the New York Academy of Sciences and the New York Academy of Medicine. (The "park as lungs" theory still had currency.)[24] So strong was the opposition to the armory proposal that the state legislature passed a law in June 1878 that expressly prohibited the use of the square in any way other than as a park. However, the road through the square continued to be a sore point as horse-drawn carriages and carts gave way to air-polluting, noisy, and dangerous traffic later on. The spirit of community resistance to discordant change grew steadily from this 1878 event.

(After the city created a department of public parks in 1870, the square's official name became Washington Square Park in 1878. However, these pages will continue to refer to it simply as Washington Square, as did Henry James in his 1881 novel by that name.)

Despite the inroads of traffic, tenements, and business, many descendants of the original families who staked their claim to lower Fifth Avenue remained in the area, some for generations. They loved the neighborhood, they knew they possessed a remarkable and unique heritage—the first of nearly everything that had turned New York into a world-class city—and they were the single most important reason that a large part of the architecture of old New York remains for us to enjoy. Holding on to their mansions and town-houses, these proud and stubborn residents adamantly resisted the waves of commercialism and real estate gigantism soon to come.

The permanent Washington Square Arch from the Judson Hotel tower, 1895. The commercial invasion of the Washington Square district is in full swing. The first generation of business structures fills the skyline. Northeast, to the right of the spire of the University Place Presbyterian Church, architect George B. Post's 14-story office building is nearing completion at Twelfth Street and Broadway (Nos. 817–819). Fifth Avenue remains unaffected. The white Brevoort Hotel sits north of the arch at Eighth Street. Further on, the Berkeley and Grosvenor Hotels rise above the houses, and the tower of the First Presbyterian Church (left) still dominates this stretch of the avenue. Photographer unknown. Author's Collection.

: : : : : **4**

NARROW ESCAPE

1879–1908

N THE FINAL DECADES OF THE NINETEENTH CENTURY, WASHING-ton Square's survival as an elegant residential district was in grave doubt. The fashionable set's eyes were now trained on Central Park and upper Fifth Avenue, leaving the square directly in the path of Manhattan's steamroller development. Following an economic slump in the 1870s, New York real estate had rebounded with the construction of six-story and higher iron-framed buildings. The blocks west of Broadway above Canal Street (part of today's SoHo Cast-Iron Historic District) were ripe for industrial development, and in 1884 a big leap northward was made when a nine-story warehouse rose on the southeast corner of Bleecker and Greene Streets (fig. 4.1). A few years later, tall loft buildings were erected even further north on Waverly and Washington Places. By 1890, many long-established residential areas such as lower Broadway and Hudson Square had been decimated, and in October of that year, a supplement to the authoritative *Real Estate Record and Builder's Guide*, entitled "New Mercantile District," treated the commercialization of Washington Square as a foregone conclusion. To the *Guide* and other observers of the urban scene, the only question was whether tenements or lofts would be first to engulf the area.

Keeping the environs of Washington Square in the public eye was to prove vital to its ability to resist change. Popular interest would be stimulated by favorite restaurants, exotic and creative denizens of the long-running bohemian scene, venerable "old New York" homes and street vistas that were oases of serenity in the rapidly changing city, and notable people, buildings, and events associated with the area. All of this, when highlighted by the press, would create an invincible perception that the neighborhood was worth saving.

By 1879 the press had anointed the whole area around Washington Square as New York's bohemia. In 1879–80, one of the earliest descriptions of this "republic within a republic" appeared in an influential New York magazine, *The Art Journal*. Its five-part series covered the genteel artist milieu found there and the lure of the place for those who wished to experience "a Bohemian life [with] scenes and suggestions which respectability . . . cannot furnish."[1] Illustrations of richly appointed artists' studios accompanied the series. The press also covered the raffish element flourishing around Bleecker Street in the immigrant quarters south of the square. A number of hospitable French and Italian restaurants and boarding houses there became the haunts of a crowd of artists, writers, and other creative people whose lifestyles provided for groundbreaking changes in the arts and society at large.

Wholesale changes had occurred years earlier across the southern part of the ward. East of Laurens Street, French people filled the former houses of the first settlers. By 1879 some 24,000 of them had created a short-lived working class French Quarter between Laurens and Broadway, stretching from Grand

FIG. 4.1 The Cohnfeld Building on the southeast corner of Greene and Bleecker Streets (site of the eastern portion of LeRoy Place), ca. 1885. Photographer unknown. Courtesy of the Alfred Zucker Drawings, The Alexander Architectural Archive, The General Libraries, The University of Texas at Austin.

Street all the way to the southern edge of the square. Although a few Americans, Germans, and Italians lived on these blocks, the majority of the residents were of French ancestry. Newcomers were recent exiles and emissaries of the Commune, a communist insurrection in Paris during 1871, and immigrants exploring their prospects in the city. Despite their poverty and relative insularity (most spoke little English), they introduced many New Yorkers to the joys of café life and French food and wine in picturesque restaurants and shops. Many of the restaurants were dives, but a few of the better ones, like Francis Leroy's Restaurant du Grand Vatel (named after the Prince de Condé's legendary chef, François Vatel, who supposedly committed suicide over the failure of his grand fete for Louis XIV) at 123 Bleecker Street, on the corner of Wooster Street, became well-known attractions of the neighborhood. Scribner's, which had published a novel about bohemian life around Washington Square in 1878, gave the country a vivid description of the French Quarter in the November 1879 issue of *Scribner's Monthly,* accompanied by charming engravings (fig. 4.2).

Although some of the regulars at the new Pfaff's at 653 Broadway, a few doors north of the original spot on Broadway near Bleecker Street, could still

be labeled *bohemian,* unconventional high jinks were in more ready supply around a table or two in the nearby French Quarter restaurants. *Puck* magazine editor, poet, and novelist Henry C. Bunner knew the quarter well and captured the diverting scene at the Restaurant du Grand Vatel in the mid-1880s:

[T]he table-cloths were coarser than the wrappings of Egyptian mummies; there was little to show that the spoons and forks had ever been plated; there was no ceremony among the diners and shirt-sleeves were always *en règle.* And a great bowl of soup was passed around that every guest might help himself, much as it might have been done in the time of the [restaurant's] namesake. But everything was clean, and all things were decent and well-ordered within that respectable resort. Poor French clerks and saving French tradesmen mostly frequented it. Now and then there was a table-full of newspaper men, actors, artists and unclassified Bohemians, who atoned for their uncontrollable noisiness by amusing all the graver patrons of the house with their ready mirth and ephemeral wit, always generally loud enough to be at the service of the whole room.[2]

Toward the end of the century, as houses were torn down and replaced by factories and warehouses, Vatel's closed. Much of the French citizenry moved to the West Side, carving out a new quarter north of 23rd Street.

West of Laurens Street and the French neighborhood, on the blocks of Thompson, Sullivan, and MacDougal Streets, landowners decided to "improve" their holdings by building tenements. All of these dwellings were built after the Tenement Law of 1879, which mandated minimal ventilation and room-size standards for such housing. The conditions were far from ideal—two apartments shared one toilet, and the bathtubs were in the kitchens—but the tenements avoided the worst overcrowding and lack of sanitation that characterized the packed multifamily houses and earlier tenement buildings of the Lower East Side. A number of recently built small factories and stables were scattered among the houses and tenements on all of the streets south of the square, with low-income housing and industrial expansion aimed at precincts east and north of the square. By the 1890s, the Irish, blacks, and a smattering of other groups who had occupied the dwellings in the southern portion of the Fifteenth Ward after the original occupants departed were giving way to waves of Italian immigrants, creating the city's second Little Italy. (Although more than half—54.7 percent—of the Fifteenth Ward's population lived in the tenements south of the square in 1902, this was much less than that in the surrounding and uptown wards, where the tenement population count was closer to the all-Manhattan average of 77.5 percent.) Italians, too,

FIG. 4.3 *(top)* MacDougal Street from West Third Street, looking north at the east side of the street, 1949. Maria's place was the three-story house near the square with the black car in front. Its cellar restaurant, which held Maria's in the 1890s, was, in the 1940s, the Calypso, where writer James Baldwin once worked as a waiter. Photograph by Joseph Roberto. Courtesy of New York University Archives.

FIG. 4.4 *(bottom) "Chicken Night" at Maria's,* drawn by George B. Luks, a regular there, ca. 1896, from *Forty-Odd Years in the Literary Shop,* James L. Ford, 1922. Author's Collection.

brought the delights of café life and cheap but delicious food and wine to the city, as well as colorful saint's day festivals and a pushcart market on Thompson Street.

Of all the new Italian restaurants in the area, Marietta Da Prato's ("Maria's") at 146 MacDougal Street, between West Third and Fourth Streets, was the most popular, especially among better-fixed residents (fig. 4.3). Maria had opened her boardinghouse with a cellar restaurant in 1892, and her chicken nights and spaghetti hours in a convivial atmosphere brought her local fame (fig. 4.4). It wasn't Pfaff's in literary merit—never did Maria's boast a star

like Walt Whitman—but guests contributed music and monologues, poetry and repartee in a kindred devil-may-care spirit. Some regulars, of course, were hangers-on and sight-seekers. One book by a pair of contemporary revelers defined the milieu as "quite two hundred Bohemians in one huge lump, with another lump made up of one hundred more verging Bohemians, Philistines and the curious."[3] After a few years of success, Maria left MacDougal Street for a new place at 82 West Twelfth Street near Sixth Avenue. However, when she had to move again in 1902 because of a new apartment house planned for the site (Nos. 82–84), she went all the way to West 21st Street, leaving most of her old crowd behind.

Another popular Italian restaurant, the Café Bertolotti, opened in 1905 at 85 West Third Street (fig. 4.5) around the corner from the original Maria's. It quickly became a mainstay of the hard-up bohemian artists and lasted into the 1920s. "Proprietor Angelo Bertolotti wore a derby, collected walking canes, and shared an endless supply of anecdotes with patrons," wrote Rick Beard and Jan Seidler Ramirez in *Greenwich Village: Culture and Counterculture*. "Signora Bertolotti, affectionately known as 'Mama,' served a famous lunch of thick minestrone soup, bread and butter, and red wine for fifteen cents, tip included."[4]

In one of the early waves of Italian immigration, Achille La Guardia, a concert musician, arrived in New York with his young wife, Irene, in 1880. At the time, approximately 12,000 poor Italian immigrants lived in wretched circumstances in Manhattan's Five Points section. (The neighborhood, no longer in existence, now makes up part of Chinatown.) Achille, with his musical training and ability to speak several languages, chose not to live among his less advantaged compatriots and took rooms in a boarding house at 177 Sullivan Street, a few doors north of Houston Street. Sullivan Street in 1880 was years away from being an Italian colony, and here, two years later, the La Guardias' second child, Raffaele Enrico, was born. Unable to find enough work in his field, Achille La Guardia enlisted in the U.S. Army as a warrant officer and moved with his family in 1885 to Fort Sully, South Dakota, where he was bandmaster in the Eleventh Infantry Regiment. By the time Raffaele came back to New York in 1907, Sullivan Street had become solidly Italian, part of an immigrant neighborhood he never knew. Today, with the area thoroughly gentrified, a number of descendants of these immigrants remain and nevertheless claim Raffaele La Guardia—who became affectionately known

FIG. 4.6 The statue of Garibaldi, Washington Square's first
statue, 1905. The photographer
is unknown, as are the circumstances of the Christmas
wreath. Sculpture by Giovanni
Turini. © Collection of the New-
York Historical Society.

as Fiorello, or the "Little Flower," during his three terms as mayor—as one of their own.

Italians of all classes proudly contributed sums ranging from five cents to thousands of dollars for a statue in the square of Giuseppe Garibaldi, the Italian patriot and guerrilla general. His series of victories in Sicily and Naples between 1859 and 1862 led to the establishment of Italy as a modern unified nation in 1871. But earlier, between 1851 and 1853, Garibaldi had been a New Yorker, eking out a livelihood making candles while living in a friend's house on Staten Island. After Garibaldi's death in 1882, enthusiasm grew among New York's Italian community for a commemorative monument, and the Italian-born sculptor, Giovanni Turini, who had once served under Garibaldi, was commissioned to make it. Turini's larger-than-life-size bronze statue (nearly nine feet in height) shows the patriot in the act of drawing his sword; installed on the east side of Washington Square, it is mounted on a granite pedestal facing west toward the fountain (fig. 4.6). The sculpture was unveiled on June 5, 1888, amid a colorful celebration in the square, with addresses delivered by Mayor Abram S. Hewitt and distinguished members of the Italian community. Thirty bands played patriotic airs, and the Garibaldi Guard, in red shirts, black scarves, and gray trousers, were joined in the festivities by three French military organizations whose names were a reminder of America's own revolution—Le Fils de '89, the Gardes Lafayette, and the Grenadiers Rochambeau. Garibaldi's statue was the first sculpture to be placed in the

square, and the day was a fitting prelude to the centennial for George Washington the following year.

DePau Row, the once-elegant terrace in the section of Bleecker Street between Thompson and Sullivan Streets, was, in the 1890s, right in the middle
of a changing immigrant neighborhood. It was purchased in 1896 for a housing experiment called Mills House No. 1 (fig. 4.7) by Darius Ogden Mills, a
New York banker, philanthropist, and politician. Mills had the ambitious vision of an affordable yet elegant hotel, grand in scale and facade, for working-
class bachelors who could not afford to live alone or even to board with families. He hired the high-profile architect Ernest Flagg, whose commissions and
model housing plans made news. Flagg designed two 90-by-90-foot, 12-story
wings in Indiana limestone, linked by a glassed-in stairway and crowned by a
bold cornice supported by hefty wrought-iron brackets. Although the bedrooms were tiny, the hotel was equipped with modern sanitary facilities and
boasted lounges, restaurants, and smoking and reading rooms. For such ac-
commodations, Mills took a modest five percent profit, and *Scribner's* proclaimed the hotel "A Palace at Twenty Cents a Night."[5] Mills House No. 1 was
and is an enormous building for the neighborhood. Today, as a residential
condominium conversion renamed the Atrium, at 160 Bleecker Street, it dominates the area around it as emphatically as it did then.

Part of the credit in making Mills House No. 1 a milestone in design should
go directly to Ernest Flagg, whose combination of social and civic roles was unusual. As a cousin by marriage of Cornelius Vanderbilt, he became a Beaux Arts
architect to the rich and powerful, yet he remained a bona fide urban reformer.

In addition to designing beautiful houses, hotels, and office buildings, Flagg planned tenement and apartment house layouts for housing-regulation proposals and for model-tenement construction. When his spectacular 47-story Singer Tower went up in 1908, at 149 Broadway, it was the tallest building in the world. The Singer Tower was wantonly demolished in the 1960s, but Flagg's Beaux Arts skill is still on display in a marvelously inventive firehouse he and W. B. Chambers designed in 1898 at 44 Great Jones Street.

Across Sixth Avenue, and to the south near the Hudson River (today's TriBeCa), another business district was expanding northward toward the square; Trinity Church was converting its Queen's Farm slum district of run-down houses into a commercial quarter. The church's industrial development scheme never generated enough momentum to reach as far as the Fifteenth Ward; one lonely 12-story loft, built in 1907 on Sixth Avenue at 2 Cornelia Street and designed in the then-fashionable Beaux Arts style, is the nearest that this commercial threat came. Today the building, also a residential condominium, appears almost quaint against the distant backdrop of later commercial buildings. At the same time, streetcars and elevated railroads (els) brought clamor to the streets and the threat of commercialization along their routes as they began to crisscross the city.

In 1878, an el was erected to go up Laurens Street and west over Amity Street for its run up Sixth Avenue (fig. 4.8). Elevated railroads were a valiant attempt by the city to alleviate the population crush in the lower wards and promote development of the island's northern reaches. The els were both a blessing and a curse to Washington Square. Though they spewed cinders (until electrification), shook foundations, darkened streets, hurt residential values along their paths, and hastened the exodus of moneyed residents from areas near them, the els succeeded magnificently in their mission and, as a byproduct, aided in preserving the square by reducing the pressure for change in its immediate environs. Els shunted hoards of passengers around the

Fifteenth Ward to and from the business districts in the lower city. They established vast new residential areas on Manhattan's upper west and east sides. Ridership increased from 242,000 in 1872, when the els were first expanding, to an astounding 290 million by 1908 (and a record 374 million in 1921). Yet stops along their routes could also bring potential customers from the entire region to commercial enterprises within the ward. Public transportation—els, streetcars, subways, and, later, cars and buses—thus presented a growing threat to Washington Square, second only to that of encroachment by the business districts themselves.

Horse-drawn streetcars (both trains and streetcars began as horse-drawn carriages on rails) had made their appearance much earlier when tracks were laid on the Bowery in 1832. Though they appeared less onerous than the els, streetcars hurt residential values and hastened commercialization along their routes, especially where multiple lines converged, concentrating passenger traffic. By the 1860s, a number of the ward's streets had been affected. Lines wound their way up Thompson Street and west across Fourth Street, up MacDougal to Eighth Street, and then west to Sixth Avenue. Streetcar lines on Wooster and Greene Streets met on University Place, and Crosby and Bleecker Streets served multiple routes. Houston, Eighth, and Fourteenth Streets became crosstown streetcar routes in the 1870s. In 1885, a horse-drawn omnibus line was started by a private group, the Fifth Avenue Coach Company, to forestall streetcar tracks on Fifth Avenue. Earlier, the department store magnate A. T. Stewart had opposed tracks on Broadway, fearing that streetcar noise and hoi polloi would discourage his carriage trade. After stiff opposition from affected merchants and property owners, Broadway finally got streetcar tracks in 1893. This followed a giant brouhaha in the late 1880s, when the chief promoter, Jacob Sharp, and several aldermen were imprisoned for bribery. Sharp had paid as much as $20,000 (something like $365,000 in today's money) for a single vote in order to get his way over local resistance. In 1907, the Fifth Avenue Coach Company would again provide an innovative solution, this time in the form of green-lacquered gasoline-engine De Dion motor buses from Paris. One of their primary benefits—the elimination of tons of manure from the avenue—went unmentioned by the press.

Fifth Avenue had avoided streetcars, and soon the threat of loft buildings on its side streets diminished. While lofts and tenements were rising to the east and south of the square, the city's main retail center remained anchored at Stewart's store on Broadway between Ninth and Tenth Streets. Avoiding the leasehold property still owned by Sailors' Snug Harbor, the retail trade migrated up Broadway, over Fourteenth Street and up Sixth Avenue. (Today's Ladies' Mile covers part of this stretch.) The garment industry, which had always situated itself close by its retail outlets, commissioned loft buildings on the side streets off Broadway, particularly from Eleventh to Thirteenth Streets, also sidestepping leasehold problems. These commercial buildings stretched almost all the way to Fifth Avenue. Construction stopped only because a large segment of the garment industry moved en masse to Fifth Avenue from Four-teenth to 23rd Streets around 1900. (It was not until the late 1920s that the in-dustry settled into the present Seventh Avenue garment district.)

Meanwhile, the *Real Estate Record and Builder's Guide,* founded in 1868, had helped to rationalize the metropolitan market in real estate with its regular and accurate reports of lot transactions, building costs, mortgage rates, and such. It also published influential analyses, "insider" columns, and editorials. The *Guide's* major 1890 supplement, "New Mercantile District," was perplexed as to why residents of Washington Square chose to resist such "improvements" as loft buildings, and why Sailors' Snug Harbor remained a leasehold obstruc-tion to such development. Not that the *Guide* was oblivious to the square and its history: "It is a very old district as age goes in New York. . . . much the finest of the public squares in the city. . . . known to contain the dwelling places of a larger number of the Four Hundred [wealthiest families] than any other equally limited section of the city." But the *Guide* had seen the future and, more to the point, local residents were not its subscribers or primary advertis-ers. As far as it—and its vested interests—were concerned, progress meant commercialization. As for the Sailors' Snug Harbor trust's leasehold property, the land not only "lay across the passage like a dismantled or sunken ship in a narrow channel" but also had become "an incubus on the neighborhood." The *Guide's* solution: "The trustees should obtain an enabling act from the Legis-lature, if necessary, and the land should be placed on the market and sold." Ever mindful of its developer-builder constituency, the *Guide* even recom-mended that "Greene Street could be extended to the [Union] square, and the improvement would help to relieve a badly-congested traffic."[6]

However, the Sailors' Snug Harbor trust remained financially sound and was established enough to ignore its critics. And did "progress" really mean commercialization of the streets surrounding the square? Several mayors had lived on the Row, and friends and allies of mayors lived in the area. The Epis-copal and Presbyterian rectors had important churches and parishioners lo-cated on or near trust land. So the trust's governing authorities took a wait-and-see stance while its housing stock continued to decay. Eighth Street, long named "Clinton Place" and lined with fine residences, was hit the hardest. As the most convenient streetcar route between the Jefferson and Tompkins Markets, and between el stations on the Sixth, Third, and Second Avenue lines, it soon attracted commercial tenants. By 1900 it had lost its commemo-rative designation, reverting to its original numerical name. Throughout East Eighth Street's long stretch through trust property, nearly every dwelling had been converted to commercial use. At the eastern end of trust property on Eighth Street, John McComb's once-beautiful Georgian church at the head of Lafayette Place had become a theater in 1870, its spire demolished and its facade marred by signs.

Lafayette Place, keystone of the eastern part of the Fifteenth Ward, was itself succumbing to the commercial pressures of the day. On the point of land

FIG. 4.9 The DeVinne Press Building, by Babb, Cook & Willard, photographed shortly after it was erected in 1885. The elegant homes of Lafayette Place (left) and Fourth Street (right) are still in evidence, but the area was doomed as a residential enclave, and today this beautiful Romanesque-style edifice is a beloved NoHo landmark. Photographer unknown. Courtesy of the National Trust for Historic Preservation.

where the Bowery and Lafayette Place came together at Astor Place, a little north of the growing Astor Library, the now-forgotten Brokaw Brothers were building a deluxe men's clothing store. Starting in a ramshackle bunch of houses, they had made a fortune supplying Civil War uniforms to the Union Army, and by 1872 had built a new edifice for their business at the Astor Place intersection. While high-end stores were moving north, Brooks Brothers' move south to nearby Bond Street and Broadway around this time was likely influenced by the emergence of the Brokaws' store. In 1885, toward the southern end of Lafayette Place on the northeast corner of Fourth Street, the massive DeVinne Press building replaced Greek Revival townhouses, underscoring the threat that the printing and publishing trade represented to the architectural fabric of the neighborhood (fig. 4.9). D. Appleton & Co., another important publisher, was already housed in a huge office building that had been erected in 1879 at the eastern end of Bond Street, replacing the houses at Nos. 1–5. By 1900, the fate of the entire section of the ward east of Broadway was irrevocably sealed by what happened to Lafayette Place. Renamed Lafayette Street, this short enclave was extended south to the City Hall area and was promptly turned into a busy, noisy thoroughfare. Lafayette Street was created just as the city's first subway, the IRT, was being built underneath it. Already long established for commercial development, the once-prestigious Great Jones, Bond, and Bleecker Streets were being torn up and reconfigured by the extension. Concurrently, the southern group of nub-end streets below Bleecker—Crosby, Mulberry, Mott, and Elizabeth—had metamorphosed into one of the worst slums in the city.

Of all the structures erected during the commercial invasion, the 13-story Bayard Building (originally known as the Condict Building) at 65 Bleecker Street between Broadway and Lafayette Place was the most daring and notable. Louis Sullivan designed it in 1898 in the distinctive style of the Chicago School, which opposed the vogue for Neoclassicism then spreading through-

out the country. Sullivan's only commission in the city, the Bayard Building soars from its sturdy base, as critic Paul Goldberger wrote, to "one of the richest and most lyrical cornices" in the city, in which a "sextet of angels flies from the tops of the structural columns."[7] As beautiful and different as it was at the time, it had no influence on the direction architecture was then taking in New York (fig. 4.10).

In 1896 John Wanamaker, Philadelphia's leading department store owner, took over A. T. Stewart's emporium. After Stewart died, the successor firm, Hilton-Hughes Co., failed. (This business failure had nothing to do with retail prospects at Ninth Street and Broadway, but rather was the result of supplier and customer boycotts of the company mounted to protest gross mismanagement of Stewart's estate.) Wanamaker leased the entire block south of the original cast-iron store and erected one of the more massive buildings in the city, covering the entire site. Designed by the Chicago architect Daniel H. Burnham in the style of a gargantuan palazzo, it complemented the much smaller original cast-iron store, which had been considered an immense building in its own time. Both larger and taller than the Bayard, Wanamaker's had 14 stories, 32 acres of retail space, a 1,300-seat auditorium, and a huge restaurant, all of which was joined to the original building by a three-tiered "Bridge of Progress." Opening in 1907, Wanamaker's retail operation lasted until the 1950s, and Burnham's building, at 756–770 Broadway, survives.

Macy's, at the southeast corner of Sixth Avenue and Fourteenth Street, had also grown into a large department store, anchoring a strong retail presence on Fourteenth Street until its move north to Herald Square in 1902. Show business, particularly in the form of vaudeville and burlesque shows along Fourteenth Street, helped keep commercial activity alive downtown long after the center of theatrical production shifted at the turn of the century. In 1896, the Mutoscope Company shot its first movies in a studio atop the Roosevelt Building (Edison's advance in film was a bit earlier in New Jersey) on the northwest corner of Broadway and Thirteenth Streets. Seven years later, Paramount Pictures came into being when Adolph Zukor gave up his fur business on Twelfth Street near Broadway and started his Automatic Vaudeville peep-show parlor around the corner on Fourteenth Street. In addition to stores, the peep show's neighbors were dance halls, saloons, and arcades, jammed with immigrants looking for inexpensive thrills. Between 1908 and 1913, D. W. Griffith again made film history in the ward with his pioneering experiments at the Biograph Company, in the former Edward Cunard mansion at 11 East Fourteenth Street. Griffith, whose main studio was in the ballroom of the old mansion, made an estimated 450 films there; he went beyond the mere filming of stage activity to instead make movies that for the first time were considered art. He also directed films outdoors, using the streets of New York, Central Park, and the surrounding towns and countryside, before leaving the Biograph and moving to California in 1913.

A magnet to immigrants and ringed by commercial buildings in a booming real estate market, the Washington Square neighborhood had cause for alarm. In 1880s New York, and in the whole United States, for that matter, historic preservation of a *district* was an unknown concept. Since the 1850s, concern had been raised about individual sites linked to a celebrated person or historic event—Mount Vernon, for example, had been saved by a women's group in the 1850s. The notion that new buildings were likely to be *less* distinguished, interesting, or valuable than what they replaced had no precedent. There wasn't the slightest consciousness in the *Guide*'s 1890 supplement that *anything* of value would be lost by wiping out the entire Washington Square neighborhood. Indeed, "backward," "retarded," and "phenomenal inertia" were the publication's terms for the district, which, it complained, "has been a city of the dead in the heart of a city of the living."[8]

Part of the *Guide*'s lack of concern for older structures surely derived from its fondness for the new commercial buildings; the supplement displayed lavish photographs and engravings, many full-page, of them. Most of the owners of these new loft buildings took pride in how their buildings looked, whether modest or large in size, and many hired talented architects to design them in ornamented styles that are highlights of some of the city's most delightful streetscapes. The very existence of the SoHo Cast Iron and NoHo Historic Districts, and NYU's preservation and reuse of many university-owned lofts, are well-deserved tributes to these nineteenth-century owners

and architects. The aforementioned redbrick DeVinne Press Building (1885) by Babb, Cook & Willard; Appleton & Co.'s former headquarters on Bond Street, an imposing cast-iron Second Empire design (1879) by Stephen D. Hatch; the exuberant Beaux Arts firehouse (1898) by Flagg & Chambers on Great Jones Street; and McKim, Mead & White's Cable Building (1894) on Broadway at Houston Street are all extant and are wonderful examples of the period. Notable, too, are the Bouwerie Lane Theater (1874, originally the Bond Street Savings Bank), an elaborately columned cast-iron beauty by Henry Englebert on Bond Street at the Bowery; the old Puck Building (1885), once home to the publishers of a satirical magazine of the same name, on Lafayette at Houston Street; and Henry J. Hardenbergh's ornate loft building (1888), with its interesting dwarf columns, on Lafayette at Great Jones Street.

Many of the ornate commercial buildings designed by Alfred Zucker, a prominent architect of the period, survive as well. His neoclassical, 150-foot-high NYU Building of 1895, on the east side of the square between Washington and Waverly Places, housed university classrooms and offices on its top three floors, with the American Book Company occupying the lower seven. Its artistically differentiated university floors are a variant of one of Louis XV's twin palaces facing Paris's Place de la Concord, while the more massive columns at the building's base complement the Greek Revival entrances of the Row (fig. 4.11). The 155-foot-high Borgfeldt Building of 1897, a hat factory by Zucker on Wooster Street between Third and Fourth Streets, also features a neoclassical palace top surmounting a stately array of seven-story window arcades.

Although forgotten today, Zucker was the leading architect of the mercantile district so highly touted by the *Guide*. He designed the northern-thrusting, 140-foot-high Cohnfeld Building at Bleecker and Greene Streets (built in 1884–85 and destroyed by fire in 1890); he also created in 1891 a brick, iron, terra-cotta, and stone warehouse that replaced the former James I. Jones residence at 5–7 Washington Place, and many other commercial lofts east and south of the square. Born Alfried Zücker in Germany, he was educated and worked briefly there before emigrating to New York in 1872 at the age of 20. He worked as a bricklayer in the city before finding work in Washington, D.C., which led to a position as a draftsman in the Office of the Supervising Architect of the United States. Then, in 1883, after a stint as the architect in charge of all public buildings in Mississippi, he returned to New York, where, for two decades, he gained prominence throughout the city as the creator of bold, stylistically diverse, large-scale structures, many of which still dot the Washington Square area. In 1904, Zucker sailed with his family to South America, fleeing from creditors, according to press reports. There he found more exciting prospects in Buenos Aires, which was preparing vast improvements, similar to Napoleon III's transformation of Paris, for its 1910 centennial celebration of independence from Spain. In Buenos Aires, as Alfredo Zucker, he designed a number of Beaux Arts hotels.

Not long after the first blockbuster lofts began appearing in the ward, a chain of events began that was to prove of inestimable importance in later efforts to preserve the original character of Washington Square. In 1887, planning began for the centennial anniversary of George Washington's 1789 inauguration: a gala national celebration based in New York City. It promised to be a popular jubilee in an era when patriotic fervor ran high. The Civil War and Reconstruction were over, and the country was on the mend. Idolatry of Washington was also at a high point, kindled by Philadelphia's Independence Day Centennial in 1876 and New York's Evacuation Day Centennial in 1883. For the latter event, a 13-foot-high bronze statue of Washington, by J. Q. A. Ward, with a base by Richard Morris Hunt, was erected in front of Federal Hall on Wall Street. These events were capped by many parades—a rousing form of free public amusement that drew excellent attendance. For the 1889 centennial, a parade through the city was planned for the last two days of the three-day festival, which was to begin on April 29.

Several temporary triumphal arches were suggested for the parade route; two were proposed for Fifth Avenue at Madison Square, where the principal reviewing stand would be located, and one for Front and Wall Streets, the location of the shoreline when Washington had landed there in 1789. However, William Rhinelander Stewart, the grandson of William C. Rhinelander, and a philanthropist, head of the Rhinelander Real Estate Company, and president of the New York State Board of Charities, saw a marvelous opportunity to highlight his threatened neighborhood. Stewart, who lived on Washington Square North, proposed that an arch be placed on Fifth Avenue at the point where it begins at Washington Square and that the parade route be changed to go through it. (The change was from Broadway and over Waverly Place to Fifth Avenue, instead of Broadway and over Fourteenth Street to Fifth.) As an enticement, Stewart assured the city that private funds would pay for the monument. Given the $2,500 price tag, the city readily agreed to the route, and, at Stewart's request, commissioned Stanford White to design a fourth arch.

William Rhinelander Stewart had a tremendous ally in the editor Richard Watson Gilder, one of the foremost cultural leaders of the day. Gilder's publication, *The Century,* was the nation's indisputable magazine of fine taste, snagging contributions by Mark Twain, Ulysses S. Grant, William Dean Howells, Winslow Homer, and Charles Dana Gibson. Gilder lived near Union Square with his wife, the former Helena de Kay, on East Fifteenth Street in a converted stable, which had been extravagantly and elegantly designed for them by their friend, Stanford White. Helena, trained as a painter, was one of the founders of the Art Students League, and the Gilders' home became a center of literary and artistic life. Their Friday evening salon included writers, artists, and theater people, and among the names recorded in their guest book were Matthew Arnold, John Singer Sargent, William James, and Eleanora Duse. White, of course, was a regular at these gatherings. Finding their place too small, the Gilders moved in the fall of 1888 to 55 Clinton Place, later renumbered 13 East Eighth Street. Richard Gilder referred to it as "our new *old* home; for it is one of those old-fashioned New York houses in the neighborhood of Washington Square (just back of the Brevoort) which take in and make immemorially comfortable and at home the newest comer." The Gilders' salon moved with them to Clinton Place. Their daughter, the novelist Rosamond Gilder, remembered a giant wisteria that covered the front facade, "filling the rooms in springtime with the fragrance of its blossoms, and in summer with the coolness of green leaves." Commercial neighbors were still a respectable distance away, and gracious residences near Fifth Avenue, like the Gilders', lasted longer than most. Even before their move to Clinton Place, Richard Watson Gilder, who was as public-spirited as he was influential, was on the centennial planning committee.[9]

When White received the centennial arch commission in 1888, he was working day and night on plans for Madison Square Garden, the giant pleasure palace and landmark of the Gilded Age; he was but 35 years old and had only begun to make a mark on the city. He had shown exceptional talent and promise as an architect with Henry Hobson Richardson of Boston before becoming a partner in the firm of McKim, Mead & White in 1879. Their fame was quickly rising, and White would take it to far greater heights. He had worked on the firm's widely noticed Villard Houses, palatial dwellings worthy of the Medici, on Madison Avenue. On that same street, White had designed as well a château fit for a prince for the jeweler Charles L. Tiffany. There were

also several high-profile Fifth Avenue commercial buildings to White's credit (nearly all since torn down). White had other assets, too. At six feet three inches tall, the red-haired White was physically impressive, and he was club-bable and charismatic to boot. He was already well known to the Sailors' Snug Harbor trust, whose land stood to benefit from the arch. (White had designed the base for the bronze statue of the trust's founder, Robert Richard Randall, which was unveiled on Staten Island in 1884. The statue itself was the work of White's close friend and colleague, the sculptor Augustus Saint-Gaudens.)

Earlier, in 1879, on the square's eastern side, McKim, Mead & Bigelow (Bigelow left the firm in 1879) had erected the Benedick, an apartment house for bachelors named after the resolutely unmarried hero of *Much Ado About Nothing*. It was a beautiful addition to the square. A redbrick building with tiers of distinctive bay windows, the Benedick's construction did away with several small and unsightly dwellings and shops that had long disfigured that side of the square, just south of the Reformed Dutch Church. (The Benedick, shorn of its bay windows, is extant.) White's social life had been centered on the Benedick, where he found congeniality among the artists and their free-wheeling attitudes, before (and after) his marriage in 1884 to the well-born Bessie Smith, of Smithtown, Long Island. His work on the centennial arch would both improve the square and pump up his own career.

The centennial turned out to be as successful an affair as its planners had prophesied, and White's design was a vibrant surprise (fig. 4.12). Set 100 feet north of the square, it spanned Fifth Avenue between the Rhinelander house, where W. C. Rhinelander's two daughters still lived, and the Row. Smaller and more slender than today's permanent arch in the square, it was made of staff (plaster and horsehair) on a wooden frame, with a frieze of garlands and laurel wreaths of papier-mâché, and was crowned with a balustrade and an eight-foot polychromed statue of Washington. Stuffed bald eagles perched on the arch's keystones. Clusters of flags and streamers of bunting completed the primary decorations. Hundreds of Edison's small electric lights (perhaps this was the first use of them in outdoor ornament) outlined the arch in the twilight and evening hours. The *Boston Evening Gazette* reported that the arch had become "one of the chief points of interest in the city, and ragged urchins as well as the rich and great stand gazing upon it in admiration." White's arch had stolen the show, making the other temporary arches seem especially flimsy and cardboard-like in comparison—"architectural shams and monstrosities," according to the *Commercial Advertiser* in its May 10, 1889, issue. White succeeded so brilliantly, in fact, that the public clamored for a permanent arch by him, and a special Committee on the Erection of the Memorial Arch at Washington Square was immediately organized.[10]

William Rhinelander Stewart had collected more than $2,500 from his lower Fifth Avenue, Washington Square, and Waverly Place neighbors for the temporary arch. Presented with the opportunity to redo the arch in stone, he became the committee's treasurer to raise the substantial sum—$150,000—needed for a marble version. As secretary, Richard Watson Gilder was to assist with fund-raising and help promote the project (fig. 4.13). White would place the new arch a short distance inside the square, avoiding the more constricted Fifth Avenue location, and the arch would go up in tandem with fund-raising for it. Thus began a six-year building project, duly reported and encouraged by an appreciative press, whose accounts captured the attention of the entire country. With Gilder's influence, stars of the popular and classical stage were encouraged to give benefit performances, among them the famed Polish pianist Ignacy Paderewski, who raised $4,000. Old rich, new rich, and folks in general contributed to the fund. The Rhinelander heiresses each gave $1,000; John D. Rockefeller contributed $500; the draftsmen in White's firm together gave $130. A truly broad-based public endeavor, it could hardly have come at a better time for the Washington Square neighborhood. The *Guide* nevertheless remained an adamant foe of the square, objecting in 1891 that it would be unwise "to locate the arch in a section of the city that has seen its best days, and that twenty years from now will be changed in character—changed in such a way that no one will visit near it, except those whose personal interest brings them here."[11]

Along with running news of the fund's total, papers kept the growing list of its contributors in front of their readers, who could note the presence of well-known names from the square to Central Park. The years between 1890 and 1895, when the permanent arch was rising, also witnessed the acceleration of residen-

FIG. 4.13 Key figures in this group atop the newly built permanent arch (April 5, 1892) are William Rhinelander Stewart with top hat and light colored trousers, Stanford White with bowler hat and prominent mustache (center, directly to Stewart's right), and Richard Watson Gilder in profile with top hat (standing near Stewart's left, with one bowler-hatted gentleman between them). The other men include those associated with Stewart's business office, employees of the building contractor David H. King, plus several members of the press. In the background above the group are the towers of the old NYU building (left) and the Reformed Dutch Church (right), soon to be demolished. Photographer unknown. © Collection of the New-York Historical Society.

tial palaces being built on upper Fifth Avenue. The Metropolitan Museum of Art was expanding as well, adding an extra dash of cultivation to the avenue. Back in the 1820s and 1830s, Washington Square's prestige had launched Fifth Avenue's success, and in the 1890s the avenue returned the favor. Henry G. Marquand, John Taylor Johnston's successor as president of the Metropolitan and a noted art patron, was the committee president who led the arch project to completion. Richard Morris Hunt, architect of the museum's new Fifth Avenue facade and of a number of Fifth Avenue's châteaus, lived on Washington Square and had chaired the 1889 arch-building committee.

Almost unnoticed in the 1889 centennial euphoria was the installation of the square's second sculpture in 1890 (fig. 4.14). Placed on the west side of the square was a bronze portrait bust of Alexander Lyman Holley, a metallurgist, engineer, inventor, and writer who is regarded as "the father of modern American steel manufacturing" for his role in bringing the Bessemer process for making steel to the United States from Britain. (The Bessemer process drastically reduced the cost of steel production, leading to the widespread use of the metal.) After Holley's death in 1882, the U.S. Institute of Mining Engineers commissioned J. Q. A. Ward to sculpt his portrait; the resulting image is modeled with a powerful gaze and the hint of a smile. The elaborate Beaux

FIG. 4.14 Bust of Alexander Holley and its elaborate limestone pedestal, 1905. Photographer unknown. © Collection of the New-York Historical Society.

Arts–style limestone pedestal on which the work sits was designed by Thomas Hastings, one of the two architects who created the New York Public Library. The commissioners of Central Park declined the offer of a Holley memorial, perhaps because its subject was not sufficiently known. Its placement in Washington Square most surely was at the request of Abram Hewitt, mayor in 1887–88, and his son-in-law Edward Cooper, who had been mayor in 1879–80 and was, at the time, one of the square's most prominent residents. Hewitt, the ironmaster Peter Cooper, and Peter's son Edward had been colleagues of Holley in developing the country's iron and steel industry.

In 1894, Peter Cooper himself was commemorated by Augustus Saint-Gaudens's larger-than-life bronze statue set within a shrine-like niche designed by Stanford White. The collaborative effort is located in a small triangular plot just south of the Cooper Union building where Third Avenue branches off from the Bowery. Far more eyes, however, were on White's second arch for the square.

The new arch was completed in 1895 to an even more sensational reception than that which was accorded the dedication of the first. The structure was 73½ feet high, and major decorative elements from the first arch were repeated in the second. Garlands and wreaths were carved in marble, as were inscriptions and reliefs honoring George Washington, the city and state of New York, and those who conceived and built the monument. Marble eagles perched on the keystones. The one on the north side, by the sculptor Philip Martiny, was so admired that replicas were made for exhibition at the World's Columbian Exposition in 1893. The creative roles played by artist and patron are represented by the female figures in relief on the north spandrels, which were designed by the sculptor Frederick MacMonnies. The women's faces, carved from photographs, were modeled on White's wife, Bessie, who looks east, and Stewart's wife, who looks west toward their house on the square. On the south facade are inscribed words from Washington's first inaugural address: "Let us raise a standard to which the wise and honest can repair. The event is in the hands of God." Originally, White had planned for a large sculptural group surmounting the arch—reminiscent of the quadrigae that crowned the triumphal arches of ancient Rome—but that embellishment was too rich for the committee. The monument, a majestic gateway, was an instant hit and quickly became one of the icons of the city. For White, the arch helped solidify his credentials for civic works and decoration, and its popularity did much to establish the classical ideal as the basis for virtually all commemorative architecture up to World War I. The two existing sculptured figures of

FIG. 4.15 *(top)* Two-page spread from *Frank Leslie's Illustrated Newspaper*, June 22, 1893, showing Stanford White's original sculpture program for the arch with small sculptured groups for the pedestals, as opposed to the large figures of George Washington that were later installed. Drawn by Hughson Hawley. Author's Collection.

FIG. 4.16 *(bottom)* Washington Square Arch as built, with the pedestals awaiting their sculptures, ca. 1910. Stanford White's Judson Church and campanile are visible through the arch. In the foreground is the wrought-iron, Greek Revival fence for No. 13 on the Row. Photograph by McKim, Mead & White. Author's Collection.

Washington facing north and set against the east and west piers are different from the ornamentation that White had intended and were not executed until a decade after his death in 1906 (figs. 4.15 and 4.16).

The impact of White's arch on the neighborhood was felt almost immediately. When the cornerstone was laid during the 1890 Decoration Day (later Memorial Day) celebrations, Joseph Pulitzer's *World* used the occasion to run

FIG. 4.17 *A Winter Wedding—Washington Square* (1897), the square's Gilded Age portrait by Fernand Harvey Lungren. The view is southwest, encompassing the nabobs and stoops of the Row, toward the newly constructed arch glowing in the rosy sunset. Mark Twain coined the term *Gilded Age* in 1873, referring to the shallow materialism of the post–Civil War period, with its booming, freewheeling, and corrupt economy. The term stuck and took new meaning in the 1880s as the period of superextravagance by the American rich, as exemplified by the Astors and Vanderbilts. By the 1890s, public fascination with the millionaires' rituals and rivalries was at its peak. In 1892, the *New York Times* was the first of the city's 16 daily papers to run Caroline Astor's guest list of her "Four Hundred." They were that era's celebrities, and the press had been clamoring for names. By the time of Mrs. Astor's death in 1906, the Gilded Age was over. Muckraking and other exposés, a five-year depression, and scandals in the Astor family had taken their toll both on the wealthy and on the public's perceptions of them. Private Collection. Courtesy of the Berry-Hill Gallery.

a large story on the square and its distinguished history. Most of the article concentrated on living residents and illustrated with engravings the houses of five of the most distinguished people. First in this group, appropriately, was William Rhinelander Stewart's house at 16 Washington Square North. Next, at 32 Washington Square West, originally the grand Alsop residence, was the home of Mrs. Annette Hicks-Lord, whom the *World* described as "famous in both continents for her charming grace as a hostess." Queen Victoria had received her, and Mrs. Hicks-Lord's own commanding presence and splendid receptions had earned her the sobriquet "the Duchess of Washington Square." Former mayor Edward Cooper's double house at the Fifth Avenue end of the Row was also shown. Edward, Peter Cooper's son, had leased the house after the departure of the banker and socialite William Butler Duncan, who had put the two end houses together to form the most opulent residence on the square. Following Cooper's place, Philip Schuyler's house at 18 Washington Square North was illustrated. He was the head of a historic New York family, whose ancestors

included colonial-era Dutch merchants and Revolutionary War patriots. Lastly, Richard Morris Hunt's residence at 2 Washington Square North was featured, the *World* pointing out that the house belonged to Mrs. Hunt, née Catherine Clinton Howland, of the shipping-fortune Howlands. Press coverage of the rich was nearing a peak in 1890 (fig. 4.17).[12]

With timing fortuitous to White's design of the permanent arch, the congregation of the Berean Baptist Church had engaged White in 1883 to design a new building complex at 51–55 Washington Square South, at the southwest corner of Thompson Street (fig. 4.18). It would honor the Baptist minister Adoniram Judson, the country's first internationally known missionary. White combined Early Christian and Italian Renaissance forms and chose a yellowish-brown brick for this structure—a church, tower, and hotel (for income)—evoking, in concert with the square, the beauty of a spacious Italian piazza, or the ancient grandeur of the Roman Forum when viewed from north of the arch. White's total ensemble was an astounding accomplishment, and the square was graced with architectural gems that have given lasting pleasure. The advent of the Judson Church provided additional consolation to the square's residents, who, as the arch was nearing completion, saw the razing for commercial buildings of both the NYU building and the Reformed Dutch Church, the square's previous ornaments.

Refusing to miss a beat in popularizing his neighborhood, the indefatigable William Rhinelander Stewart further cemented the Fifth Avenue connection by associating Washington Square with the next major event, the 1892 Columbus Day quadricentennial. It was the nation's culminating cultural celebration of the nineteenth century. Linkage with the avenue was especially important because Edison's electric-lighting technology had markedly improved, and decorative streetlight fixtures were being planned for Fifth Avenue. They would be introduced during the Columbus Day celebrations, and, when installed, Stewart felt they *must* start at the square. To encourage this city decision, Stewart established a grandstand for the event there, making the square a focal point of the festivities, which included several days of highly orchestrated activities. Stanford White, in charge of the Fifth Avenue decorations, joined in by having the Washington Square Arch elaborately lighted by the Edison Company for spectacular evening and nighttime illuminations.

On October 12, a military parade was the main event, consisting of soldiers, firemen, and members of ethnic and fraternal organizations. Starting from the Battery, the procession moved around Washington Square before starting for the new Columbus Monument at today's Columbus Circle. Among the 65,000 who marched that day were soldiers from every state in the Union. The press claimed that over two million people lined the streets, and that it was the biggest parade in history. Lower Fifth Avenue got its streetlights, plus some fancy traffic signals later created for the avenue, and the square played a role in every subsequent important parade well into the twentieth century. (Part of the reason for the tremendous New York turnout in October 1892 was that Chicago had won the World's Columbian Exposition but delayed it from the starting date of October 12, 1892, so that it could capture a larger number of Exposition-goers during the summer months of 1893.)

In 1893, as the arch was progressing, an article titled "Fifth Avenue" appeared in *The Century*. It chronicled the recent upturn in Washington Square fortunes and the contrast between lower and upper Fifth Avenue. The author was Mariana Griswold Van Rensselaer, the possessor of two historic family names and a resident of 9 West Tenth Street. Van Rensselaer's parents had both been raised on the Row; recently widowed, she had returned to the old neighborhood to pursue a rewarding career as a writer and architecture critic, the latter then an extremely rare professional specialty for a woman. The article Van Rensselaer wrote explained that lower-avenue folk had something the upper Fifth Avenue folks did not:

> They [streets between the square and Fourteenth Street] are not the fashionable streets they were in my childhood; but "good people" still live in them, and the number is now increasing again year by year, desecrated dwellings being restored within and without, and a belief steadily gaining ground that, whatever may be happening a little farther up the avenue, this quarter mile stretch will remain a "good residence neighborhood." We who live in this part of New York recognize its inconvenience as regards visiting many of our friends, and enjoying Central Park when the buds begin to swell. But we maintain its exceptional convenience in almost every other respect, we are proud of the aroma of fifty years' antiquity which we breathe, and we delight to maintain that this is the only part of New York, outside the tenement districts, where a "neighborhood feeling" exists. Sometimes, down here, we even call upon a newly established neighbor whom we know only by name. Perhaps, up near the Park, you do not do this, because people with such nice names are not so apt to settle near you.[13]

Despite Van Rensselaer's inference that the flora of Central Park was an amenity lacking in Washington Square, the district—in striking contrast to uptown's barren streets—was actually an oasis lush with trees. Street trees were a nuisance in areas of building activity and street widenings, and many were killed by the soft-coal furnace fumes and gas leaks that fouled the air at the time. But the city's refusal to plant trees because of a few difficulties with them denied its inhabitants a basic urban amenity. It hadn't always been so. In fact, street trees had once been treasured by the city council, but around 1900 even such stalwarts as Frederick Law Olmsted and the *New York Times* had turned against them. In 1894, Olmsted advised against planting trees on Madison Avenue because he said that they wouldn't survive. The *New York Times* went further, railing against the idea of keeping or planting trees. Trees couldn't live on the city's streets, sunlight was the best disinfectant, and planting shade trees in tenement districts might even raise the infant mortality rate, the paper warned in an amazingly cockeyed 1903 editorial. This blast came at a time when every visionary writing about the future of cities—for example, Edward Bellamy in his classic *Looking Backward: 2000–1887* (1888)—had "broad streets shaded by trees" at the top of his or her list. Indeed, they still do. What trees were planted in Manhattan during this disgraceful interlude had to be managed through private initiatives, of which there were many, until the Parks Department finally took it as its mandate in the 1930s.

Within a decade of Mariana Van Rensselaer's report on the rejuvenated neighborhood north of the square, the commercial threat to it virtually ceased. So strong had the opposition to "improvement" become that the latest crop of millionaire residents took to buying up parcels of land near them when they sensed a potential sell-out to commercial interests. Wealthy antiquarian print collector Thomas F. Eno, who owned the former Shiff mansion at 31 Fifth Avenue, bought adjoining lots. So did Thomas Fortune Ryan, a ruthless and incredibly shrewd financier who accumulated one of the largest fortunes in the country. He originally purchased 60 Fifth Avenue, the old Minturn residence on the northwest corner of Twelfth Street, and then bought adjacent property, plus the large former Lenox parcel across the avenue, for protection. (Ryan loaned the former Lenox residence to the Institute of Musical Art, which later became the Juilliard School of Music.) The *New York Times* published these developments on July 30, 1905, announcing that the danger had faded: "The prospect that the lower end of Fifth Avenue will keep its present residential character has been greatly improved within the last two or three years. Whatever possibility there may have been that the neighborhood would be claimed for business is materially less than it was then."[14]

There was also at the time an attempt by the cultural elite to ratify tradition and confirm the country's prosperity via a flowering of more conservative strains within the arts in New York—a cultural confluence known as the American Renaissance. The Columbus Day quadricentennial turned out to be a defining moment for the fine arts in America, as a panorama of classical architecture prevailed on the fairgrounds in Chicago. As New York Central Railroad president Chauncey Depew put it at the fair's opening, "New York stands to the rest of the continent as Florence did to Europe in the fifteenth century." Richard Morris Hunt's Administration Building for the White City echoed Brunelleschi's great dome for the cathedral in Florence, the first architectural masterpiece of the Italian Renaissance, and McKim, Mead & White's vast New York State Pavilion was patterned on the Villa Medici in Rome. "This is the greatest meeting of artists since the fifteenth century," exclaimed Augustus Saint-Gaudens, one of the fair's top sculptors.[15] (The country's three leading sculptors—Saint-Gaudens, J. Q. A. Ward, and Daniel Chester French—had all studied in Italy.)

Chicago's postponed World's Columbian Exposition opened in 1893, winning international renown for its array of classical buildings, fountains, and sculpture set among gardens, parks, and a lagoon. This "White City," clad in plaster and lath, was designed by some of the country's best architects and artists, many of whom, including Hunt, George B. Post, and the firm of McKim, Mead & White, were New Yorkers. Although the Exposition buildings were temporary structures, the idealized, dream-world city was stunningly beautiful and inspiring. Soon, an idea crystallized among politicians, businessmen, philanthropists, and artists that *both* an artistic dimension to cities and the improvement of living conditions were important. By the early years of the twentieth century, cities in the United States and Europe had grown astronomically, and the older urban cores were rotting. Nearly all American cities had been laid out on a grid, with few of the amenities that had been on such proud and lavish display in Chicago. When the arch was built in Washington Square, there was no monument like it in the city. The Statue of Liberty stood majestically in New York Harbor, of course, and a number of other sculptures occupied plinths at key spots in the city. Yet no important monument or building commanded views on the city's streets as they did, for example, in Pierre Charles L'Enfant's Washington, D.C. Grace Church, at the bend in Broadway, remained the best visual treat in the city's oppressive gridiron plan, otherwise so lacking in public amenities and spatial variety. (Churches at the head of Wall Street and Lafayette Place were two more limited examples of visual anchorage.) White's arch was the first monument to beautify the city's grid, a distinctive and early example of how art could transform a city's streets.

Many movements, commissions, and associations arose in the years after 1900 to address problems in the urban environment. Chief among those inspired by art was the City Beautiful movement. It had the practical benefit of initiating the first urban planning efforts in big cities but, overall, was a grand utopian attempt to upgrade transportation and cure the drab monotony of the grid by carving out of it radial streets, circles, and squares. New intersections would be focal points for monuments, fountains, and stately buildings. Though well-intentioned, the scheme ignored the needs of old neighborhoods that would be destroyed by the new diagonal streets. In New York City, the movement took form in the City Improvement Commission of 1904, which formulated a plan published in 1907. One feature of the plan, extending Christopher Street to Union Square, would have killed the best blocks in the ward, but the plan fell through when the gross impracticability of implementing it within the existing urban fabric became clear. (Haussmann had accomplished this feat in Paris but had gutted and then *rebuilt* the affected areas.)

One of the lasting organizations to come out of this period was the Municipal Art Society (MAS), which had been founded in the World's Columbian Exposition year of 1893, with Richard Morris Hunt as its first president and Richard Watson Gilder as one of its directors. Concerned with installing public art and beautifying the city, its work and influence benefited the Washington Square district over the years, particularly in regard to the future issue of zoning. Another group was the Washington Square Association, established in 1906.

The Washington Square Association was, in effect, made necessary by the city's laissez-faire attitude toward commercial development, which had permitted three long-simmering issues to come to a boil by 1906. One continued threat involved the urban merchants' desire to bring New Jersey shoppers into Manhattan by high-speed rail rather than by ferries. In the late 1870s, one early promoter shook up the neighborhood by proposing a tunnel under the Hudson River ending at Morton Street, that would be connected further by tunnel to a large terminal under Washington Square. Engineering failures, primitive technology, and insufficient financing doomed that plan. However, lobbying for a Hudson River tunnel resumed in the 1880s with a plan that would continue a tunnel under Washington Square and up University Place to connect with Grand Central Terminal. Intermediate stations could pop up anywhere along the route, with one at Ninth or Tenth Streets and University Place, arguably because of proximity to A. T. Stewart's and other stores on Broadway. Funds ran out on that scheme, too.

However, in 1904, with Wanamaker's gargantuan addition to Stewart's underway, the danger peaked. A tunnel was to be built under Christopher Street to Sixth Avenue (one link in today's PATH system), and Wanamaker wanted it extended east across Ninth Street to his store. The city and other merchants would presumably benefit because the tunnel would continue as far east as Second Avenue. Stations along the way at all the north-south avenues would provide connections to surface links at those points. That meant a station was also planned for Fifth Avenue, with commercial growth around it soon to follow. Because these plans would slash the heart of the district, the neighborhood citizens who would later establish the Washington Square Association stopped the crosstown extension. Thanks to their opposition, the tunnel extension was kept to a route north under Sixth Avenue, with stations from Ninth up to 33rd Streets.

The neighborhood group couldn't have stopped the tunnel at Sixth Avenue without luck and two powerful but inadvertent allies—the MAS and the Department of Trade and Transportation. As it happened, in that crucial year of 1904, the MAS had extended its mandate into subway planning, and part of its proposal included the installation of crosstown subways under all the major east-west streets. But the municipal Department of Trade and Transportation, which, at the time, rivaled the Chamber of Commerce in influence over city policies, was opposed and stopped it. As efficient as the MAS's idea seemed, the Department of Trade and Transportation believed the crosstown routes would cause an upheaval in real estate values. As shortsighted as that opposition may have been, the Washington Square group latched onto it and got the Ninth Street route killed as well. It didn't hurt that George B. McClellan Jr., was then mayor (1904–9). McClellan lived on the Row and had spent part of his youth on the square when his father, the Civil War general and Democratic presidential candidate in 1864, had taken the Alsop mansion (prior to Mrs. Hicks-Lord's tenancy) as his city residence. Later, in 1915, subway service (the BMT) began operating under Broadway in the district, and its station at Eighth Street (and Wanamaker's) is the closest it got to the square.

Another threat during Mayor McClellan's term of office had roots stretching back to the 1830s when the Fifteenth Ward was founded. Front yards had first appeared around Washington Square, and yards on part of the public street had set Fifth Avenue on its path to fame. Now, the Common Council resolution permitting these 15-foot encroachments required their removal if the city deemed it necessary, but after more than two generations these extensions seemed like an unconditional right to their owners. From the square to Central Park, the avenue was lined not only with yards, sculpture, plantings, and fences, but more substantial architectural elements like stoops, bay windows, porches, and porticoes, many of them quite elaborate. Their existence became increasingly threatened as traffic increased and wider roadways were needed.

Rumblings about removing the front yards had been heard in the Common Council as early as the 1860s, but by 1906 the traffic situation had become intolerable, and Mayor McClellan acted. He ordered the widening of the Fifth Avenue roadway from Washington Square to 42nd Street. Sidewalks were to be cut back, allowing for two more lanes of traffic, and encroachments were to be removed to maintain sidewalk space. It wasn't easy. Wrote McClellan: "Of course I was obliged to fight for it, not only in the courts against property owners affected, but also Tammany Hall, for the borough president had been in the habit of exacting illegal fees for the maintenance of sidewalk encroachments."[16]

The Washington Square Association once again came to the rescue by obtaining an exemption from the removal order for the lower Fifth Avenue blocks. It used the same basic argument that had originally won permission for encroachment, namely, that this residential stretch of the avenue ending at the square was far less used than the rest, and therefore the existing roadway width was quite adequate. Unwittingly and condescendingly buttressing the association's argument, a *New York Times* editorial in December 1906 spoke of Washington Square and Gramercy Park as backwaters in the modern city: "[T]he trucks are never there, the cabbies don't go through, the streetcars aren't so very neighborly, and there is an air of sequestration that impresses one with an air of desertedness pervading." These areas were, the paper continued, "quaint and curious corners of the old town. . . . but few frequent them from choice, and there they lie, cloistered in between the bulwarks of bustling business, majestic in their apparent idleness, relics of a splendid past, when the elite rode in chaises and the Sunday afternoon promenade was taken with flouncy parasols and tall walking staffs."[17] (The *Times* had only recently moved from its own downtown backwater in 1904 to a handsome new tower at 1 Times Square.)

The third problem facing the Washington Square Association involved University Place, a residential enclave much like lower Fifth Avenue. Since it was connected directly to Union Square, linked by many streets to Broadway a block away, and already diminished by streetcar routes, how long could it remain residential? Nonetheless, the 1880s had been kind to the street, and the association and local residents were determined to keep out further commercial interests. A French hotelier named Jean-Baptiste Martin had cobbled together three adjoining houses on the southeast corner of Ninth Street in 1883 for his Café Martin, a combination hotel-restaurant that had a reputation as one of the best eateries in the city. Capitalizing on the thriving French quarter a few blocks to the south, Martin attracted cooks, waiters, and customers from the area, making French food, wines, and atmosphere his trademarks. Its table d'hôte ran around a dollar, double the price of what second-tier restaurants like the Restaurant du Grand Vatel or Maria's commanded. By 1902 Raymond Orteig, Martin's headwaiter, had taken over for Martin, who had gone on to create a more opulent restaurant on Madison Square. Orteig rechristened the Ninth Street place the Lafayette, and further enhanced the café's Left Bank personality, keeping it a neighborhood favorite. Orteig kept abreast of news of the brasseries of Paris for exciting additions to his menu at the Lafayette, and offered foreign newspapers, checkers and chess, cards, and dominos for his café regulars.

Also in 1883, the Albert Hotel opened on the southeast corner of Eleventh Street and University Place (fig. 4.19). This was a new building designed by the up-and-coming architect Henry Hardenbergh, who was simultaneously working on his famous Dakota apartment house at 72nd Street and Central Park West. Hardenbergh chose bright red brick and white stone for the Albert's facades, to which he deftly added rounded balconies alternating with squared ones, iron balconies intermingling with stone balustrades, and fanciful ornamentation. Delicately carved shells and leaves, pendants and car-

FIG. 4.19 The Albert Hotel around 1890. Photograph by W. W. Silver. © Collection of the New-York Historical Society.

touches, Corinthian colonnettes and geometrical forms, and even a few neo-Gothic monster masks were applied with the mastery of composition that brought him fame. It was—and is—a wonderful addition to the neighborhood.

Developments around University Place in the 1890s indicated that little time remained before a commercial onslaught. By 1896, the loft-building invasion on University Place had produced NYU's replacement on the square at Waverly Place, and the headquarters of Merck & Co., the pharmaceutical firm, on the southeast corner of Eighth Street, both designed by Alfred Zucker. Later, a large six-story loft for the clothing manufacturer Simon Sterns & Co. replaced six houses on the southwest corner of Ninth Street and University. Following a short break, loft building picked up again in 1905 with the Empire Realty Corporation's 11-story monolith, which covered most of the east blockfront between Eleventh and Twelfth Streets. Seemingly the battle had been lost. In June 1905, the *New York Times* reported optimism in real estate circles about the commercialization of University Place and, even more distressing to the Association, Sailors' Snug Harbor trust's decision to assist commercial expansion on their extensive property, which included the imminent demise of Orteig's Lafayette Hotel and restaurant for a loft building.[18]

Persuasion by the Washington Square Association was a factor in keeping the Society Library, whose key directors and members were local stalwarts, on

University Place, where it remained until 1937. Upjohn's Presbyterian Church also remained, albeit with a dwindling number of parishioners. The Lafayette held its own and even grew in popularity, as the Sailors' Snug Harbor trust rethought its real estate development policy. These weren't the only holdouts on the street, but they may well have been crucial in eventually turning the tide. Commercialization of University Place continued, slowed down by World War I, until the 1920s, when, *mirabile dictu,* loft buildings, and, unfortunately, Upjohn's church, were demolished to make way for apartment houses. Other lofts have been converted to residential use today, making University Place once again a delightful residential street.

During the 1880s and 1890s, apartment houses—rather than lofts and tenements—began to take hold in the neighborhood west of University Place. The Benedick was joined on the square by the Washington, a large brick apartment house erected in 1884 on the southwest corner of Washington Square West and Waverly Place. The Washington View Apartments, a modestly sized brick building on the southwest corner of MacDougal and West Fourth Streets, followed in 1889. Construction near the square was relatively rare, but the elegant, small-scale, Beaux Arts–inspired apartment house was put up at 82–86 Washington Place West in 1903. One of the tenants was the novelist Willa Cather, who lived there from 1908 to 1913 when she was managing editor of *McClure's,* the muckraking journal. She previously roomed at 60 Washington Square South. Numbers 27 and 28 Washington Square North, the two westernmost houses, were replaced by a handsome granite and buff-colored brick building. This structure was the Richmond Hill, an apartment house with a secret.

It was built in 1898 by the Chisholm family, owners of land west of the Rhinelanders on Washington Square North. (Both the Chisholms and the Rhinelanders had married into the original landowning John Rogers family.) Already fearing that the square was destined to house businesses, the Chisholms had been shaken by the construction of a printing plant built in 1890–91 at 171–173 MacDougal Street across from their property. Though she watched the parade of lofts taking over the east side of the square with horror, Mary A. Chisholm (née Rogers), ever protective of her family's real estate investments in the changing city, had the Richmond Hill built as a "swing" building. Designed with peculiar apartment layouts with long interior corridors to accommodate a large service elevator in the rear, the structure could pass as an apartment house yet, because of the elevator, could be easily made into lofts with a loading dock on MacDougal Alley. Converting the Richmond Hill into lofts was a comfortable option for the Chisholms, but they never had to exercise it.

Midblock, at 20 Washington Square North, the Rogers' 1828 Federal-style house had been remodeled in 1880 into a ritzy four-unit apartment house. Henry J. Hardenbergh was in charge of the renovation for the Rogers estate, tastefully integrating it with the rest of the block. East of Fifth Avenue, 3

FIG. 4.20 Gonfarone's hotel and restaurant, 1914. The factory (left) on MacDougal Street, a stone's throw from the square, although small in scale and highly ornamented in the Romanesque style by James Renwick's successor firm, was, nonetheless, an early (1891) omen of the neighborhood's potential conversion to a business district. Earlier, the 1870s apartment house (right), built in the stable-strewn western block of the street, had given hope that the section would remain residential. Photograph by W. J. Roege. © Collection of the New-York Historical Society.

Washington Square North, previously used as a foundling asylum, was converted into a studio building in 1884. Made taller by a few feet and lengthened to reach Washington Mews, it had a fashionable new Queen Anne facade. The design marked a defiant break with the Row's existing architecture, but restrained design and use of compatible facade materials—brick, stone, and terra cotta—softened its impact. The stylish newcomer didn't raise an eyebrow at the time.

Following the commercial onslaught, physical changes in the Fifteenth Ward at the turn of the nineteenth century were mild, and the neighborhood character cherished by Mariana Van Rensselaer and many others grew stronger under the aegis of the Washington Square Association. Eighth Street had become the Main Street of the neighborhood, home to its best hotels and restaurants. Raymond Orteig, who very successfully ran the Lafayette, also took over the older Brevoort in 1902, and both became long-running favorites for the French colony and more affluent bohemians. Of the two, the Brevoort was the fancier spot, with an upstairs formal dining room and ballroom for its wealthy and aristocratic guests, and for when one made it big with his or her play or book.

West of Fifth Avenue, Gonfarone's restaurant-hotel occupied the southwest corner of MacDougal and Eighth Streets, just a few blocks north of the Italian community below the square (fig. 4.20). In 1894 Catherine Gazetta Gonfarone, a widow, had first established a small restaurant in the corner house, and later in the 1890s, she expanded into adjoining houses with the help of her talented restaurant manager, Anacleto Sermolino. At first only Italians ate at Gonfarone's, but soon impecunious American writers and artists in the neighborhood discovered it, making it their favorite. MacDougal Alley, just around the corner, was evolving into an artists' colony second only to the Tenth Street Studio Building in importance, and soon established painters and sculptors, who brought their friends and patrons, made Gonfarone's their first choice for eating, too. Music was added: a piano, violin, and cello trio, plus a singer, played arias from operas, potpourris from operettas, popular canzone, and Italian folk songs. Within a decade, the place's reputation for good, inexpensive Italian food and festive musical entertainment was bringing crowds to MacDougal and Eighth Streets, where Gonfarone's had expanded into five houses around the corner.

Near Fifth Avenue at 3–5 West Eighth Street, the modern Marlton Hotel was erected in 1900. At eight stories, the handsome fireproof (though not by today's standards) brick building towered over the surrounding dwellings. While it never remotely achieved the panache of the much older hotels, it touted its "Absolutely Fireproof" quarters in contrast to its wood-beamed Lafayette, Brevoort, and Gonfarone neighbors, whose facades had begun to sprout fire escapes. Other developments on West Eighth Street were mainly residential. Further west toward Sixth Avenue at Nos. 53 and 55, two five- and six-story apartment houses were built in the 1890s. But the notable event on West Eighth Street was that the germ of an arts center was being established there.

In 1907, Gertrude Vanderbilt Whitney, the future founder of the Whitney Museum of American Art, leased a stable at 19 MacDougal Alley and had it remodeled into a studio. A budding sculptor, she was drawn to the area for the congenial community of sculptors already working there. Among them was Daniel Chester French, the creator of the *Seated Lincoln* for the Lincoln Memorial, *Alma Mater* at Columbia University, and four female figures for the U.S. Customs House, among many other monuments. (French, at the time, was a central figure in New York's cultural affairs; not only were his sculptures all over the city, but he was an influential advisor to the Metropolitan Museum of Art.) Whitney trained as a sculptor under James Earle Fraser, another leading sculptor of the day, who was also a resident of the Alley. After establishing his studio at 17 MacDougal Alley, French bought the house fronting it (12 West Eighth Street), which he rented out to fellow artists. French's house later became one of the four Whitney purchased on Eighth Street to form the original Whitney Museum, which was founded in 1930 and opened to the public a year later. Both Whitney and French lent immense prestige to the Washington Square district—Whitney, initially, for her nonpareil social prominence.

Little change occurred in the neighborhood above Eighth Street, and, surprisingly, what changes there were added to the charm. A good example can be found on West Ninth Street near Sixth Avenue, where two delightful brick Queen Anne–style apartment houses—the Portsmouth at Nos. 38–44, and the Hampshire at Nos. 46–50—were built in 1882–83. These fashionable elevator buildings, with their cast-iron entrance porches and restrained six-story

FIG. 4.21 Henry Siegel's new Fourteenth Street store with its own el station connection directly into its second floor sales rooms, ca. 1906. In 2000, the main corner building underwent conversion to a posh apartment condominium, as the entire stretch of Fourteenth Street to Fifth Avenue again became residential. Photograph by Hall. © Collection of the New-York Historical Society.

heights, fit remarkably well with their townhouse neighbors. Ida Tarbell, the muckraking journalist, magazine editor, biographer, and historian best known for her exposé of John D. Rockefeller, lived at No. 40 from 1901 to 1908.

At the northern end of the district, East Fourteenth Street was becoming lined with high-rise commercial buildings as tall business structures replaced houses with storefronts. On West Fourteenth Street the Knickerbocker apartment house on the southwest corner of Fifth Avenue was converted to offices in 1888. The real sea change, however, came with R. H. Macy's move in 1902.

A phenomenal success, Macy's had outgrown its store at the southeast corner of Sixth Avenue and Fourteenth Street, and wanted to expand into new facilities there. The store tried to make a deal with the Chisholms and Rhinelanders, who owned the land. Unable to do so, the business moved but kept the old place empty to prevent occupation by a new commercial tenant, thereby forcing customers to come to Macy's sprawling new emporium 20 blocks north at 34th Street. Most of Macy's Fourteenth Street leases were scheduled to run out in 1903, except for one in effect until 1913. Henry Siegel, whose mammoth Siegel & Cooper department store was a competitor, wanted to capitalize on the value of the old Macy's location and protect his own store's downtown location at Nineteenth Street and Sixth Avenue. So Siegel put a squeeze play on Macy's. Through an intermediary, he paid $125,000 more than Macy's had offered for a small but key plot on the prime

34th Street corner of Macy's planned store. Siegel gained control of the property and pledged to sell it to Macy's, but *only* if Macy's would relinquish the old store leases early. His move didn't work. Macy's Palladian wedding-cake of a store, by architects De Lemos & Cordes, still has a slice taken out of it from Siegel's holdout, and Siegel's store on the old Macy's site, built after most of the leases expired, still stands (fig. 4.21). Macy's at 34th Street had defined the new shopping arena, and Fourteenth Street never regained its former retail luster and entered a period of slow decline.

Ironically, this downturn spared the residential blocks to the south from the commercialization that was overtaking other parts of the ward. Though Thirteenth Street, as Fourteenth's back door, succumbed to business, on Twelfth Street, where the super-rich financier Thomas Fortune Ryan was holding out, new construction was strictly residential. The Ardea, a ten-story apartment house at 31–33 West Twelfth Street, had been built in two stages between the mid-1890s and 1901 and dominated the block. This distinguished structure, with a dark facade of brick and brownstone lyrically set off by delicate ironwork balconies, was commissioned by George A. Hearn. (Hearn is a variation of the name Heron, and the ardea bird is a magnificent type of heron.) He was a retailer, art collector, and Metropolitan Museum of Art trustee, and built the Ardea to house executives of his giant Hearn Brothers' department store on the block north between Thirteenth and Fourteenth Streets. Hearn's father had founded the business in the 1820s and moved it to 30 West Fourteenth Street in 1879. There the family expanded it, with growing success, into 19 connected buildings and one of the city's once-proud emporiums.

Next door to the Ardea at No. 29, the small Ardsley House had been constructed in 1889–90 as a hotel. Near Sixth Avenue, Nos. 82 and 84 (formerly home to Maria's second restaurant) were replaced by an apartment house. East Eleventh Street, near Fifth Avenue, had two modest hotels, the nine-story Alabama (1902) and the smaller Van Rensselaer (1901), put up at Nos. 13–15 and 17–19, respectively. Nearly all of the remaining neighborhood additions west of University Place and below Thirteenth Street were houses or apartments.

Adjoining the Van Rensselaer at 21 East Eleventh Street was the residence of Mary Cadwalader Jones, who married into the Jones Wood Joneses and was a pillar of New York society until her death in 1935 (fig. 4.22). She was the sister-in-law and friend of Edith Wharton, and a confidante of Henry James, who found her home "the great good place" full of warmth and welcome during his many unhappy times in New York.[19] Her daughter, the prominent

FIG. 4.23 43 Fifth Avenue, ca. 1910. Photograph by Platinarchrome Co. Postcard courtesy of Andrew Alpern.

landscape architect Beatrix Jones Farrand, was a founding member of the American Society of Landscape Architects. Her many distinguished clients included the Rockefellers, the Morgans, and the White House; the grounds of Dumbarton Oaks in Washington, D.C., constitute her finest surviving work. Farrand maintained her headquarters at East Eleventh Street until her move to California in 1929; her New York office remained in the house until it was sold in 1935.

On Fifth Avenue, Appleton's new book publishing headquarters claimed the northwest corner of Thirteenth Street in 1895. Happily, though, the signal event for that part of the avenue was the erection of a grandly conceived 11-story apartment house at No. 43, on the northeast corner of Eleventh Street, in 1905. On the site of James Donaldson's 50-foot-wide home, architect Henry Anderson designed a Beaux Arts extravaganza. Clad in ornate stone and brickwork, it had a regal doorway flanked by pairs of two-story-high Ionic columns; tiers of Parisian-style wrought-iron balconies rose to a soaring mansard roof ringed with handsome brick chimneys. Known by its address, No. 43, the building had two ten-room suites per floor and was a towering presence on lower Fifth Avenue until the 1920s, when other apartment houses lined up north and south of it (fig. 4.23).

Down the avenue at No. 12, one of four Gothic-style townhouses was razed for another Beaux Arts apartment house, the Rhinelander (1903), by architect Louis Korn. The Rhinelander's nine stories and 25-foot width presented less visual impact than that of No. 43 or the Marlton Hotel; indeed, it was an understated newcomer, which today seems charming and quaint. Several nearby

residences by Henry Hardenbergh had earlier enlivened the avenue. He designed a pair of attached dwellings, built in 1883–84, on what had been the lawns between the Brevoort and Shiff mansions. They were vaguely Romanesque Revival in feeling. The house he remodeled at 3 Fifth Avenue in 1888 smacked more of the one-upmanship in townhouse building taking place elsewhere in the city. Its elegant two-story bay window, distinctive window treatment, and mansard roof presented a marked contrast to the building's sedate neighbors.

In 1901, No. 3 became the residence of philanthropist Annie Leary, a papal countess (fig. 4.24). Her father, James Leary, had been a business associate of John Jacob Astor. He sold Astor hats and bought Astor's beaver pelts for his Broadway hat shop, where toppers were big business. Annie loved society, parties, jewelry, opulent furnishings, and costly clothes; her arrival at No. 3 boosted social interest in the neighborhood, as had Thomas Fortune Ryan's purchase of 60 Fifth Avenue in the same year. Countess Leary, however, moved to her new palace at 1032 Fifth Avenue in 1904, and No. 3 began a new life as the A Club, a housing cooperative founded by some of the city's most radical freethinkers.

The A Club was one of a number of activist groups in the Washington Square district that captured national attention around the turn of the century. They began to flout convention and to write about the dark side of the prevailing good times.

Many people in the nation were caught up in the intellectual ferment of the day, as the cost of the country's glittering prosperity to impoverished laborers and immigrants was made shockingly evident through exposés by crusading journalists. Citizens learned in pungent detail about the stench of the stockyards, the shame of the big-city political machines, the corruption of the Senate, the evil works of the trusts and insurance companies, and the tragic plight of the urban poor. *McClure's* magazine, the premier forum for the muckrakers, attracted national attention with investigative articles by Lincoln Steffens and Ida Tarbell. Steffens's "Shame of the Cities" series, which ran during 1902–3, drew critical attention to his cause and made his reputation as a critic of municipal government. In 1890, his friendly rival Jacob Riis had first published *How the Other Half Lives,* the epochal photographic and reportorial documentation of the unspeakable conditions within the city's tenements. Riis had gained the ear and support of police commissioner Theodore Roosevelt, whose headquarters' back door on Mott Street, just above Houston, faced the Barracks, one of the worst of the hovels (fig. 4.25).

FIG. 4.25 The Barracks (center) from the back door of police headquarters. The view is north to Bleecker Street, ca. 1900. Photograph by Jacob Riis. © Museum of the City of New York.

The A Club, which had set up cooperative housing in Countess Leary's former home in 1905, was named when one of them said, "Oh, just call it a club." The newspapers called it the Anarchist Club and predicted that alphabet-letter clubs B, C, and D would follow in turn. There were about 18 members, including writers, painters, lawyers, clergy, and settlement workers—"everybody a Liberal, if not a Radical—and all for labor and the Arts," wrote socialist, feminist, and pacifist member Mary Heaton Vorse.[20] Mark Twain, then a nearby neighbor at 21 Fifth Avenue, was a frequent visitor. He found the club a congenial place to smoke his cigars and spin his tales. Many other intellectuals and artists stopped in, and one, the writer Maxim Gorky, who was in New York in 1905 raising money for Russian revolutionaries, brought notoriety and press coverage to the new group of intellectual bohemians through a most effective medium: scandal.

The Gorky contretemps arose from the fact that the famous author was traveling with a woman who was not his wife—one Madame Andreieva, an actress. Czar Nicholas II's agents leaked this story to the American newspapers, inciting them to stir up a scandal about their supposed illicit relationship. Gorky wasn't the first Russian revolutionary to come for fund-raising, and he had been warmly received when he landed in the city, but the sex angle was juicy and the press jumped on it. Polite society ran for cover, and reputable hotels refused to accept the couple. After the neighboring Brevoort Hotel and Rhinelander Apartments also rejected them, some members of the A Club stepped forward to put the couple up. The A Club's support for Gorky was an early assault on convention, supplying more than just talk or a stinging article.

Lower Fifth Avenue became host to another attack on convention in 1907 when the rector of the Church of the Ascension, the Rev. Percy Stickney Grant, founded the Public Forum at the church. Free discussions on any serious subject were encouraged, and taboos were broken when the forum included topics like birth control, race relations, and whether or not Christ

FIG. 4.26 Church of the Ascension mural by John La Farge, architectural details by Stanford White, sculpture by Louis Saint-Gaudens, and mosaics by D. Maitland Armstrong, 1884–88. The entire interior of the building constitutes a masterpiece of the American Renaissance. Photograph by and courtesy of Scott Hyde.

was a socialist. Occasionally, police were called from the Mercer Street station to eject unruly debaters who became too abusive toward the guest speaker of the evening. This and the revolt kicked off by the A Club grew and found new expression in 1913 at two legendary gatherings—Mabel Dodge's salon at 23 Fifth Avenue and the Liberal Club at 137 MacDougal Street.

By the time of the 1893 Columbus Day fair, the Hudson River School of American landscape painters had largely given up native landscapes and genre scenes for allegorical compositions inspired by the Renaissance. Manhattan already seemed like a modern-day version of fifteenth-century Florence or Rome, marked by collaborative work of artists, craftsmen, and architects on the city's mansions, public buildings, and monuments (fig. 4.26). Parallels inescapably were drawn between American business tycoons and the merchant princes of the Italian city-states, and the classical style took firm hold on both artist and patron. The style set (some, including Louis Sullivan, said "set back") the standard for American architecture until the 1920s.

Clusters of artists could be found in the Benedick on Washington Square and in studios at 3 Washington Square North and MacDougal Alley; individual studios abounded elsewhere in the neighborhood. Several clubs for artists and their friends flourished too, notably the exclusive Salmagundi Club then at 14 West Twelfth Street and the Tile Club at 58½ West Tenth Street. Of the two, the Tile Club was a little cozier. Located in a secluded artist's studio behind the house at No. 58, it was close to the Tenth Street Studio Building and

FIG. 4.27 William Merritt
Chase, by James Carroll Beck-
with, 1881–82. Courtesy of the
Indianapolis Museum of Art,
Gift of the Artist.

attracted some of its residents. Stanford White and several of his friends took
to painting tiles there—hence the club's name. Augustus Saint-Gaudens,
Winslow Homer, and William Merritt Chase became members, and they
gathered "in the evenings to talk, smoke, eat oysters with hock or mallards
with Burgundy, dispute each other's ideas and criticize each other's paintings."
However, the Studio Building at 51 West Tenth Street remained the largest
and most influential community of artists in the nineteenth-century city, and
never more so than after Chase's arrival in 1878.[21]

Chase had been part of the new trend in art training, for those who could
afford it, of studying in the Paris or Munich academies and imbibing the instruction and experience found there. Chase studied at the Royal Academy in
Munich, which rivaled Paris at the time as a mecca of art instruction. He en-
rolled with its best teachers, as only the more gifted students could do. There,
he learned to apply bravura brushwork to exotic subjects, his style emulating
the palette and compositions of Hals and Velázquez. After six years, when he
had become skilled enough to sell his work and have it exhibited in the United
States, he returned to New York. Before leaving Europe, he began buying
antiques for his anticipated studio. Chase brought home not only his art

FIG. 4.28 William Merritt
Chase, *Tenth Street Studio,*
ca. 1880–85. In addition to the
swan, Chase had other stuffed
birds, including two ibises, a
pelican, and a raven decorating
his studio. Courtesy of the
Carnegie Museum of Art, Pittsburgh; Purchase 17.22.

training but also the German studio system, in which larger-than-life painter-teachers set up elaborate studios where they held absolute sway.

On the streets of New York Chase was a conspicuous sight, dressed in the height of fashion with spats, a topper, and a scarf drawn through a jeweled ring, and walking a sleek Russian greyhound. Despite giving the appearance of a dandy, Chase was a brilliant teacher, a born communicator, and a hard-working artist (fig. 4.27). He was also upbeat and gregarious, similar to Stanford White in manner and effect. Chase created a studio complex, modeled on the richly decorated ateliers of European artists, that was strewn with bric-a-brac and antiques, and hung with Venetian drapes, tapestries, rugs, paintings, and bizarre objects (fig. 4.28). Japanese masks, a Zulu war shield, and a stuffed swan—tethered upside down with wings flung open as in Dutch bounty paintings—were some of the objects that did double duty as wall decoration and painting props. In this exotic-looking lair, sporting a fez and assisted by a manservant dressed as a Nubian prince, Chase was the epitome of haute bohemianism. And it was all put to dazzling effect as Chase's marketing tool.

Since the 1860s, artists working in the Studio Building had opened their studios to the public for group shows, and they and their famous guests frequently made the news. Frederic E. Church and Albert Bierstadt, celebrated exemplars of the Hudson River School, were particularly adept showmen, especially when it came to promoting their gigantic panoramic landscapes. As early as 1859 Church exhibited his *Heart of the Andes,* hiring a press agent to publicize the event. The picture attracted 12,000 visitors who paid an admission of 25 cents, and police were required to handle the crowds lined up on Tenth Street waiting to get in.

Chase brought new meaning to art marketing. In 1879 he purchased the building's central, originally communal, double-height gallery for his major

studio, making it his personal showplace. This chamber, as well as his two smaller rooms, all decorated to the hilt, were increasingly featured in magazines and newspapers, stoking Chase's reputation as an artist, connoisseur, and teacher. He used his studio for classes, exhibitions, meetings, dinners, balls, and costume parties—all in the service of his sales. Occasionally, his parties captured outside attention. One gathering in 1890 featured a performance by the Spanish dancer Carmencita before about 75 society guests, after which Chase painted her portrait.

Studio Building artists were all men, but in the 1890s women were gaining slightly more prominence in the male-dominated worlds of art and literature (the Academy of Arts and Letters didn't admit women members until 1926), and successful women artists, sculptors, and architects had studios near Washington Square. *Godey's Magazine,* which had long guided the feminine aspirations of most well-to-do homes, in 1895–96 ran a series of articles (with photographs) on these studios, the first of their kind. The country's first organization of women artists and writers, the Pen and Brush, was formed in 1892 when painter-sisters Janet and Mary Lewis invited a group of eight writers and three other artists to their Chelsea studio. Ida Tarbell became the third president of the growing club in 1913, serving for 30 years. In 1923, Pen and Brush bought the 1848 townhouse at 16 East Tenth Street, where it remains today with 300 members. Like the Salmagundi Club, its main rooms are open to the public so that, in addition to attending free exhibits and lectures, visitors at the Pen and Brush can view the luxurious quarters that even the side streets off Fifth Avenue once possessed.

Late in 1905, a magazine named itself the *Bohemian* and started running pieces by accomplished writers and artists on the worlds of art, theater, music, and journalism—circles that were popularly understood to be bohemian. It improved in size, illustrations, and general tone, and in 1907 the magazine spotlighted the many New York restaurants in its domain. Noting the amazing multitude of good and inexpensive restaurants around Washington Square, the article, "When New York Dines à la Bohème," gave another geographic outline of this foremost bohemia: "In the Italian quarter, down around Bleecker Street and all through the Washington Square district." Such writings helped the country at large to become aware of the area (fig. 4.29).[22]

With the respectable visibility of Chase, the notorious living arrangements of Gorky, the fractious meetings of the Public Forum, and decades of writers' fascination with the area, the Washington Square neighborhood was becoming established by the press and its own history as the national center of art and unconventional artistic life. These siren attractions drew creative people and freethinkers from all over the country. Their exotic lifestyles fascinated the public, and the many writers and journalists among them kept alive the image of Washington Square as a quarter to be cherished. Saving the neighborhood, however, would be a long-fought battle.

Among the movements initiated or reignited around 1900, a tiny cult of historic preservationists were jolted when more and more old landmarks became endangered. In 1893, City Hall, which had been created principally by the architect John McComb Jr., narrowly escaped being razed for a new municipal building. In 1901, five of the nine houses of Colonnade Row on Lafayette Place were shamelessly demolished for a Wanamaker warehouse. The Morris-Jumel Mansion and Fraunces Tavern, sites of George Washington's Revolutionary War adventures, were threatened in 1903, and they, too, barely escaped. In 1908, St. John's Chapel, built opposite Hudson Square in 1803 and considered McComb's masterpiece, fell. The truncated remains of McComb's lesser but once beautiful church at Astor Place had recently been reduced to rubble for Wanamaker's addition. Trinity Church, owner of St. John's, was no friend to the past; the institution's eyes were fixed on its lucrative loft-building plans and shedding the embarrassing "slumlord" label it had acquired from the scandalously ill-kept acres of houses it owned on the west side between modern-day Fulton and Christopher Streets. The church had let these structures deteriorate into tenements and brothels.

Again, Washington Square got lucky. St. John's imminent demise created an uproar in 1908, *just* at the time another big public blowout was being planned—the next year's 15-day Hudson-Fulton celebration, the focus of which was to be the history of New York. Shops and department stores took up Old New York as their marketing theme, and the Metropolitan mounted its first exhibit of early American painting and decorative arts, drawing throngs of visitors. Best of all for the Washington Square neighborhood, "The Great Historical Pageant" and the festival's other two parades would terminate in the square. In that same year of 1908, quite a different sort of art exhibit was on display at the small Macbeth gallery on Fifth Avenue at 40th Street. The rebellious group of American painters showcased there would soon bring a crescendo of national attention to the bohemia centered on Washington Square.

MacDougal Street looking north to Eighth Street, from West Third under the el, ca. 1918. MacDougal Street, as well as many other downtown places and personalities, were photographed by Jessie Tarbox Beals during the heyday of the pre–World War I bohemia. Beals turned her shots, like the one above, into postcards with hand-lettered inscriptions, which helped promote Greenwich Village to the rest of the country. The tallest structure (center right) was the Hotel Holley (named for the statue in the square) on Washington Square West. It and its neighbors have all been replaced by apartment houses, the el is gone, and the once grand residences housing the Provincetown Playhouse have been remodeled, but most of this stretch looks pretty much as it did in 1918. The dormered houses at the left were built from 1829 to 1831. Washington Square's trees can be seen at the right edge. Photograph by Jessie Tarbox Beals. Courtesy of the Alexander Alland Collection. © Collection of the New-York Historical Society.

: : : : : **5**

BOHEMIA U.S.A.

1908–1920

ON THE WINTRY NIGHT OF JANUARY 23, 1917, SIX MERRYMAKERS clambered up the narrow interior staircase of the Washington Square Arch to throw a party (fig. 5.1). Equipped with Chinese lanterns, red balloons, cap pistols, food, thermos bottles filled with tea, and hot water bags for seats, the six had gained access from an unlocked metal door at the base. Atop the arch they kindled a fire in an iron bean pot and ate, sipped tea, and chatted until dawn. Tea had been chosen for its ceremonial role at the Boston Tea Party, and cap pistols discharged into the cold night air punctuated their revolution. The evening's climax came when the group declared Washington Square a free and sovereign republic, independent of uptown.

The six secessionists included two well-known artists: John Sloan, one of the dissenting painters who had bearded the reigning National Academy of Design with a separate exhibition in 1908 (the Academy had choked on the group's gritty urban realism), and Marcel Duchamp, king of the New York Dada movement. Both Sloan and Duchamp were in league with others in developing the Society of Independent Artists, an enterprise designed to create a market for new art by holding its own exhibitions. It was in the first of these showings in April 1917 that Duchamp drastically tested his own group's admissions policy (any submission by a member was acceptable) by entering his upside-down porcelain urinal that he titled *Fountain* and signed "R. Mutt." The work was refused.

Despite the high jinks, the artists' need for independence was real—independence from the straitjacket of conformity imposed by such leading art institutions as the National Academy of Design, the Metropolitan Museum of Art, and the Academy of Arts and Letters. A resolution put before the third institution in 1908 perfectly summed up the stance of these organizations:

> The National Institute [American Academy] of Arts and Letters in its long established office of upholder of Taste and Beauty in Arts and Letters in America, welcomes the approach of a return to the standards made sacred by tradition and by the genius of the great periods of the past.
>
> The National Institute feels that the time has arrived to distinguish the good from the bad in the Arts, and to urge those who have loved the literature and painting that are accepted by the winnowing hand of time to turn away from the Falsehoods of this period and again to embrace only the genuine expressions of man's genius.
>
> And the National Academy calls upon all those who write or speak on this essential subject of our culture as a nation, to ask their hearts to join in abhorrence of the offences, and to insist on the integrity of our arts.[1]

What better locus of resistance could be found for a declaration of independence than the Washington Square Arch? It commemorated the founding of

revolutionary America as a new country, and by 1917 it stood in the heart of the neighborhood where a sizzling new modernism had taken root.

John Sloan and his painter-friends William Glackens, George Luks, and Everett Shinn had worked as artist-reporters for several Philadelphia newspapers before following their charismatic leader and art teacher, Robert Henri, to New York in the early 1900s. These five were the core of The Eight, the group that would make history with its breakaway exhibition in 1908. At the time, the prevailing taste, smugly fostered by the National Academy, ran to hackneyed landscapes, insipid portraits, and sentimental narrative paintings derived from classical sources. Instead, drawing on their newspaper experience and influenced by Walt Whitman's belief that *everything* was fit subject matter for poetry, Henri's group painted such subjects as tenement life in immigrant neighborhoods, the urban riverfront, coal deliveries on snowy streets, the Staten Island ferry, street urchins and old people, sporting events, bar interiors, the theater, and scenes in the public parks and squares (fig. 5.2).

Henri (fig. 5.3), who had studied at the Pennsylvania Academy of the Fine Arts (then the country's best art school) and later in Paris, was elected a full member of the National Academy in 1906. Even though he served as a juror for the spring annual in 1907, he was unable to prevent the exclusion of his younger colleagues from it. Outraged that American academicians and collectors found Italian poverty picturesque but scorned depictions of it in New York as being vulgar, Henri planned a dramatic show of independence. To the original group of Sloan, Glackens, Luks, and Shinn, Henri added three more like-minded but stylistically different American painters: Symbolist Arthur B. Davies, Impressionist Ernest Lawson, and Post-impressionist Maurice B. Prendergast.

Henri's group secured the Macbeth Gallery, located in a small commercial building at 450 Fifth Avenue (at 40th Street) near the New York Public Library, from a sympathetic dealer, William Macbeth, for an exhibition opening on February 3, 1908. The *Evening Sun* ran an editorial in January that dubbed them "The Eight," and praised and justified their decision. On February 2, the

FIG. 5.2 William Glackens, *Washington Square*, 1913. Glackens's drawing exaggerated the crowded conditions, but overuse and poor maintenance of the square was a problem at the time. Digital image © The Museum of Modern Art / Licensed by SCALA / Art Resource, NY.

FIG. 5.3 Painter, teacher, and firebrand Robert Henri, 1907. Photograph by Gertrude Käsebier. Courtesy of the Delaware Art Museum.

day before the opening, the *New York World* featured in its Sunday supplement a full page of photographs of the artists and their work. The article began, "Not to be outdone by Paris or London, New York is having an art war all its own." Public interest had been aroused. On Monday, from nine in the morning until six in the evening, Macbeth reported that a "steady stream of people was pouring into the gallery, at a rate of 300 an hour at one point." The Eight had made their point magnificently. Even though the economy was bad that year, seven paintings were sold during the two-week run. Gertrude Vanderbilt Whitney (fig. 5.4) bought four of them, and her largesse would be felt by these and other artists in the coming years. John Sloan recalled that her purchase of such pictures was "almost as revolutionary as painting them."[2]

Macbeth's and other galleries were located uptown, in close proximity to their wealthy customers, but the home of The Eight was clustered around Washington Square. Five of them—Sloan, Glackens, Shinn, Lawson, and Prendergast—moved to or had studios there. Sloan and Glackens lived there until the 1930s, and Shinn, the youngest of The Eight, remained in the neighborhood until his death in 1958.

A month before The Eight mounted their sensational show at the Macbeth Galleries, a smaller and quieter exhibition at Alfred Stieglitz's 291 Fifth Avenue ("291") gallery signaled an epochal change in American art. Stieglitz, like Henri, was a charismatic leader, and both were inspired by Walt Whitman, whose individuality and fearlessness in breaking taboos made him the most influential creative spirit of the era. Like Whitman, Stieglitz and Henri believed in art unhobbled by convention and found the whole realm of urban

humanity vital to their work. But whereas Henri was a westerner who wore a ten-gallon hat and whose buccaneering father had shot and killed an opponent in a card game, Stieglitz was the bourgeois son of a successful Hoboken businessman. Only in their opposition to the fin-de-siècle art establishment were Stieglitz and Henri associated.

By 1911 Stieglitz had introduced America to Cézanne, Matisse, and Picasso. The gallery quickly attracted a handful of artists who understood Fauvism, Expressionism, and Cubism, such as Marsden Hartley, Arthur Dove, John Marin, Abraham Walkowitz, and Max Weber, and it became a haven for modernists in a country completely unprepared for this strange brand of art. Stieglitz's sumptuous photography magazine, *Camera Work*, also evolved into a valuable, though limited, distribution source for the European and New York avant-garde's new discoveries.

Although Realism was, and remains, a strong strain in American art, the country's future vanguard grew from Stieglitz and his circle, rather than Henri's. One of Stieglitz's important contributions to American modernism was the salon he made of his gallery, where classes, talents, disciplines, and even nationalities could cross-pollinate. Two other contemporary New York salons, those of Mabel Dodge and Walter and Louise Arensberg, were also cultural crossroads. All three salons blossomed during those crucial times when American modernists most needed support.

Back at the square, Mabel Dodge (fig. 5.5) took a quite different route from Stieglitz to hosting an avant-garde salon, but her gatherings at 23 Fifth Avenue between 1913 and 1917 sparked interplay between different types of people to an astounding and unprecedented degree. She later described the "Socialists, Trade-Unionists, Anarchists, Suffragists, Poets, Lawyers, Murderers, 'Old Friends,' Psychoanalysts, I.W.W.'s, Single Taxers, Birth Controlists, Newspapermen, Artists, Modern-Artists, Clubwomen, Women's-place-is-in-the-home Women, Clergymen, and just plain men" who showed up in evening attire, jewels, sandals, and work clothes.[3] Other images recalled by Dodge and her visitors—of Harlem jazz entertainers, an experimental peyote party, and Isadora Duncan's modern dances—give some idea of her catholic-

ity of interests. In fact, she exemplified the essential difference between her times and earlier modern eras by her willingness to abandon stultifying convention and to embrace whatever was new.

Born Mabel Ganson in 1879 to a wealthy family in Buffalo, New York, she rejected the constricted life of a Victorian society matron in favor of the intellectual and social freedom advocated by other cultural radicals of her day. After her first husband, Karl Evans, died in an accident, the Ganson family sent Mabel and her two-and-a-half-year-old son to Paris. En route she met Edwin Dodge, an architect from a rich Boston family; she married him in Paris in 1905 and set about making the new life of her dreams in Florence. For the next eight years there, she refurbished a Renaissance villa and surrounded herself with exquisite furnishings and intellectually stimulating people. Among her illustrious friends were the American expatriates Gertrude and Leo Stein, whom Mabel also visited in Paris, and Bernard Berenson. The Steins were avatars of modernism in the arts and literature, and leaders in purchasing works of the European avant-garde painters and sculptors, and Berenson was on his way to becoming world-renowned as a connoisseur of Renaissance art and an arbiter of taste. In Florence, presaging things to come, Mabel had these lines by Walt Whitman embossed in purple and silver as the seal on her stationery: "If I contradict myself, well, then, I contradict myself."[4]

By 1912, Mabel Dodge had tired of the Florentine world and returned to settle in Manhattan. She picked a large apartment in a staid brick house at 23 Fifth Avenue, on the northeast corner of Ninth Street, near Washington Square and the heartland of America's bohemia. Edwin Dodge was soon sent packing, and, with her son off to school, she began the life for which she would be remembered. The house where Dodge landed belonged to General Daniel Sickles, a crusty old Civil War veteran who had shot his wife's admirer in 1859, survived the trial, and lost a leg in the Battle of Gettysburg. He occupied the first floor, while Mabel's apartment was above him on the parlor floor. Here Mabel established a refuge from convention.

Although she had neither sparkling wit, nor profound wisdom, nor dazzling beauty, she did have great wealth. In any case, there was something about Mabel Dodge that drove men to distraction. According to her friend, the writer Lincoln Steffens, what made Dodge so attractive was her elusive but compelling personality, which mingled the sophistication of "[Mme] Récamier" with aspects of a "waif, Venus's fly-trap, muse, and even sorceress." Some of her intimates believed she was able to generate psychic phenomena, haunt houses, and project "forms and sounds of abysmal woe." "When she

isn't shining," Steffens said, "she's a wet, cold, cloudy day," referring to her power to communicate misery.[5] Once, rebuffing the painter Andrew Dasberg's advances, she suggested sublimating his sexual desires in painting. He did so, gaining public notice for three abstract portraits of her. The critic of the *New York World* described the apparent effect the withholding muse had on her worshipper: "In her presence he seems to feel like a torso stripped of skin and palpitating in roast beef flavors of deep red and shining white; away from her his thrill collapses and the torso is jammed, twisted and flattened as if a motor car has run over it. . . . One of the sequences [displays] the unfolding of the torso and the exposure of the artist's heart in blossom as a tulip, with an amethyst shining in place of the navel. . . . The third dedication is entitled 'Absence of Mabel Dodge' and is the most perfect portrayal that can be imagined of mental, moral and physical smash."[6]

Dodge's passionate love at the time was the recent Harvard graduate and firebrand journalist John Reed (fig. 5.6), who lived in rooms above Lincoln Steffens at 42 Washington Square South. In 1913 Dodge had assisted Reed in dramatizing the Paterson, New Jersey, silk-workers' strike in a grand pageant staged in Madison Square Garden. It was one of the most unusual cultural events in American history, uniting the labor of anarchists, socialists, philanthropists, painters, and poets. As described by Lois Palken Rudnick, one of Dodge's biographers, the pageant was part of her immersion "in the spirit of her times, supporting, writing, and speaking about the various causes that promised to liberate her and her fellow men and women from the spiritual and psychological shackles of the past. She became [an honorary] vice-president of the Association of Artists and Sculptors that sponsored the Armory Show;

a member of the advisory board and contributor of *The Masses,* the leading left-wing journal of the day; a supporter of the Women's Peace Party; and one of the early popularizers of Freudian psychology in a weekly column she wrote for the Hearst papers."[7]

Above all, though, Mabel Dodge's salon unforgettably demonstrated an essential aspect of a great city and of what it would take for New York to supersede Paris as the world's capital of culture: to be a receptive center of cosmopolitans. When New York City again welcomed the internationalism of its culture in the 1930s and 1940s, and was creating a world-class art of its own, world leadership came with it.

By 1913, Stieglitz, Dodge, Henri, and a number of others in the fledgling American modernist movement recognized the importance of understanding and embracing the new currents in European painting so that American art could draw on the best of native and foreign sources. New schools and movements were almost entirely ignored by dealers, collectors, and museums before 1913, and continued ignorance would keep American art languishing in the retarded provincialism that had pretty much been its lot since the founding of the colonies. Several forward-looking painters in Henri's 1910 Independents show felt that the avant-garde work of *both* American *and* foreign painters should be exhibited together, and began planning for such an event on a larger scale. They formed the Association of American Painters and Sculptors, which was expanded to comprise 25 people—including artists from both Henri's and Stieglitz's circles—whose major role was to stage the Armory Show of 1913. (This International Exhibition of Modern Art was nicknamed for its location in the Sixty-Ninth Regiment Armory at 25th Street and Lexington Avenue.) In 1912 the group chose Arthur B. Davies, one of The Eight, as president. Davies astonished all but a few close confederates by becoming a phenomenally effective fund-raiser and administrator, and an outspoken champion of the most radical European art. The resulting Armory Show, which turned out to be a milestone in the history of art and the most important art event ever held in America, opened on February 17, 1913.

Arch-conspirator Duchamp, whose *Nude Descending a Staircase* (fig. 5.7) had stolen the show, left wartime France and followed word of his Armory Show success to Manhattan in 1915. There he met Walter Arensberg, who had fallen in love with Duchamp's work, and became a central figure at the gatherings hosted by Walter and his wife, Louise, in their Upper West Side duplex apartment at 33 West 67th Street. Their salon was a successor to Mabel Dodge's and an uptown extension of the Washington Square bohemian community. The principal significance of the Arensberg salon was its hospitality to the influx of French artists who arrived in New York during World War I. From 1915 to 1921, Walter and Louise Arensberg brought France—the source of twentieth-century modernism—and America together, with incalculable effect on both the major poets and major visual artists of the era.

Although the Arensberg salon was uptown, the main source of its intel-

FIG. 5.7 Marcel Duchamp, *Nude Descending a Staircase, No. 2,* 1912. © Artists Rights Society (ARS), New York / ADAGP, Paris / Estate of Marcel Duchamp. Courtesy of the Philadelphia Museum of Art: The Louise and Walter Arensberg Collection, 1950.

lectual strength was found in the precincts of Washington Square. Duchamp, the star of the coterie, had his own lodgings on West 67th Street subsidized by the Arensbergs, but he socialized in the Brevoort's café and restaurant, and satisfied his obsession with chess at Frank Marshall's chess club, then at 146 West Fourth Street (the number later changed to 148). Marshall's club, the informal precursor of the Marshall Chess Club, was across the street from Polly's and over the Pepper Pot restaurant (fig. 5.8). It also attracted Arensberg, Alfred Kreymborg, and Man Ray, all enthusiastic players, although not as fanatical as Duchamp. Man Ray, Duchamp's friend and soul mate among New York Dadaists, lived and worked at 47 West Eighth Street. Duchamp's friends Albert Gleizes and Joseph Stella, who were also among the Arensbergs' favorite artists, took up residence in the Brevoort to be among the French contingent there. The 1917 Independents show (where Duchamp's porcelain urinal made such a commotion) was planned in the Arensberg apartment, but it depended heavily on downtown artists. William Glackens was briefly the society's first president; in its first months the job fell to John Sloan, who kept the exhibitions going as an annual event and held office until 1944. Among the Arensberg salon's Village poets were Kreymborg and Mina Loy. Both had published their poetry with Walter Arensberg in *Rogue,* and both were associated with members of the Liberal Club. Their dramatic works were performed on MacDougal Street by the Provincetown Players. Even the salon's chief

musical figure, the movie star–handsome composer Edgard Varèse, lived in the Brevoort and was a celebrity in its café.

Indeed, these lively additions to the émigré French community socialized more in the Brevoort than anywhere else, and they kicked off the hostelry's 40-plus years as one of the city's more permanent centers of creative life. As a comfortable headquarters and a foil to the more intellectual Arensberg, Dodge, and Stieglitz salons, Raymond Orteig's Brevoort hotel and café were a fabled rendezvous for activists and thinkers of all stripes, particularly if they were French. Hutchins Hapgood, a prolific journalist whose social mobility ranged from the Harvard Club to Lower East Side bars, wrote: "The [pre-WWI] Brevoort, of course, under French management, was a bubbling and sparkling place; every expressive personality in the city seemed to get there first or last. Artists, poets, journalists, sociologists, suffragists, anarchists, feminists: everybody who was, even in a small degree, differentiated from the inexpressive mass, and in all the stages of genial intoxication."[8]

A few modern artists who could afford this bit of transplanted Paris made it their home. Varèse, who had emigrated to Manhattan in 1915, was the most important because of his wide contacts among the European avant-garde. Varèse had known some of the geniuses in the music world of his day— among them Claude Debussy, Richard Strauss, Ferruccio Busoni, and Erik Satie—and had, he said, "been rather more closely associated with painters, poets, architects, and scientists than musicians." The list of Varèse's Paris friends and acquaintances included Pablo Picasso, M. M. Hugué Manolo, André Derain, Raoul Dufy, Guillaume Apollinaire, Fernand Léger, Amedeo

FIG. 5.9 John Sloan, "Caught Red-Handed," from *The Masses*, July 1914. Sloan's cover followed the shooting and torching of worker's tents in Rockefeller's Colorado coal fields. With his Bible tossed aside, the quaking J. D. Rockefeller Jr. is shown trying to wash the blood from his hands before the angry mob breaks down the door. Courtesy of the Delaware Art Museum.

Modigliani, Gleizes, Robert and Sonia Delaunay, Max Jacob, and Jean Cocteau. Varèse's room in the Brevoort had a door to the lodgings of his new American friend, the Paris-trained sculptor Jo Davidson. Although of a bohemian temperament, Davidson was a friend of Mabel Dodge and Gertrude Vanderbilt Whitney, and tycoons like Andrew Mellon and John D. Rockefeller paid him large sums to create portrait busts of themselves. Davidson thrived in both milieus—the world of arts and letters and the whirl of society dinner parties—where "his jovial vitality, his bold black eyes and virile beard, as well as his gifts as a raconteur" made him a particular favorite.[9]

Among the little publications and mainstream press at the time, *The Masses*, whose editorial offices were located near Washington Square, stood out as a new kind of magazine (fig. 5.9). Originally founded in 1911 downtown on Nassau Street, it had become a combination of radical bible and talent showcase, unlike any other magazine before or since. *The Masses'* large-format (13½ × 10½-inch) pages were filled with drawings that appeared as individual statements independent of the text. Its articles, shocking for the time, advocated free love, divorce, birth control, toleration for homosexuals, sexual satisfaction for women, and complete racial equality. More provocative than even the written contents of the magazine were the stunning rough-realist crayon drawings in the tradition of the French lithographer and cartoonist Honoré Daumier. A martyr to free expression, he had been jailed in 1832 for his political caricatures, and his style stood in ebullient contrast to the finished techniques preferred by academic and mainstream magazine illustrators. Daumier's technique gave *The Masses* its distinctive look. John Sloan, George Bellows, Stuart Davis, Boardman Robinson, and other artists who used this

FIG. 5.10 Left to right: Crystal Eastman, Art Young, Max Eastman, Morris Hilquist, *The Masses'* attorney, C. Merrill Rogers Jr., *The Masses'* later business manager, and Floyd Dell. In addition to denying use of the mail, a federal grand jury indicted (under the Espionage Act) on November 21, 1917, seven of *The Masses'* staff, including Max Eastman, Young, Rogers, and Dell, for opposing the war effort. They were tried in 1918, facing 20-year prison terms, and the government lost the case. The group is standing outside the since-demolished U.S. Courthouse and Post Office building that once occupied the southern end of City Hall Park. The indictment occasioned this press photograph by the International Film Service. Courtesy of the National Archives.

drawing style also searched the slums for simple, genuine subjects; their crayons sketched immigrants and blacks, peddlers and prostitutes, street urchins and bums.

A direct heir to the muckrakers, *The Masses* expanded exposés in dozens of new directions. Two favorite targets of the articles and cartoons were the puritanical avenger Anthony Comstock, the head of the New York Society for the Prevention of Vice, and organized religion, which was depicted as a complacent tool of capitalistic forces. Beyond irreverent assaults on the establishment, *The Masses* was a nondoctrinaire and good-humored political magazine committed to what it called the "liberation" of the working class. It espoused socialism and Marxism as panaceas at a time when gross abuses perpetrated by employers were routinely and conspicuously ignored by the press. Both *The Masses* editor Max Eastman and frequent contributor John Reed wrote scathing accounts of actions against the International Workers of the World (IWW) strikes in Lawrence, Massachusetts, and Paterson, New Jersey, and of the deaths of 11 children and 2 women when guards shot into and set fire to the strikers' tents in John D. Rockefeller's Ludlow, Colorado, coal fields.

Max Eastman (fig. 5.10) had been a brilliant young philosophy instructor at Columbia University and a campaigner for women's rights when he was asked in 1912 to revive *The Masses* from a dull version of itself that had recently folded. Its contributors—the artists John Sloan, Art Young, Charles A. and Alice Beach Winter, and Maurice Becker, and the writers Louis Untermeyer, Mary Heaton Vorse, Ellis O. Jones, Horatio Winslow, and Inez Haynes Gilmore—made Eastman a job offer. Arriving in a letter written with a paintbrush on a torn-off scrap of drawing paper, it said, "You are elected editor of *The Masses*. No pay." Tall, handsome, and very persuasive, Eastman was a much-needed dynamo for the enterprise. He convinced millionaires like Mrs. O. H. P. Belmont, copper king Adolph Lewisohn, and the publisher E. W. Scripps to support the magazine despite its radical political goals; he also induced the wealthy young businessman Berkeley Tobey to be its business manager. Tobey wound up spending his modest inheritance paying *The Masses'* printing costs. In 1913, Eastman moved *The Masses'* offices uptown, first to Fourteenth Street between Fifth and Sixth Avenues, and then, finally, to 91 Greenwich Avenue. John Reed and Floyd Dell (see fig. 5.10), a bohemian poet, playwright, and feminist from Chicago, joined the staff in 1913. With Dell as managing editor and Eastman at the top, *The Masses* was off on a rollicking five-year run as a beacon for America's avant-garde. It reached some 20,000 subscribers across the country before the federal government shut it down in December 1917 under the provisions of the Espionage Act, drafted in the wake of America's entry into World War I in April of that year (see fig. 5.10).[10]

Eastman and Dell in particular made *The Masses* a sounding board for women's rights during the critical period when the nation's suffragists were struggling to win the vote. The modern women's movement had begun in the 1850s, had peaked after the Civil War in the 1870s with the advent of Victoria Woodhull and of the Woman's Christian Temperance Union (antialcohol, prosuffrage), and in 1908 sought a wide reservoir of strength with its first Fifth Avenue parade. As the *New York Times* reflected on suffragist progress in a 1929 article on Fifth Avenue parades, "At first a few hundred self-martyred pioneers [marched]—women and a few men—grimly determined to face jeers and stones if need be. Then, presently, more bands and buoyancy, yellow ribbons, saucy signs, as youth, too came marching. And suddenly, in 1917, Fifth Avenue for miles was full of women—actresses, teachers, tenement mothers, stenographers, college girls, waitresses—50,000 of them, out to win."[11]

Labor Day parades—one of the big four, along with those on Memorial Day, the Fourth of July, and Saint Patrick's Day—were swelled by a strong suffragist contingent in 1912 following the tragic Triangle Shirtwaist fire (fig. 5.11). To this day, the catastrophe remains the worst factory fire in the city's history. On March 11, 1911, 146 garment workers died horribly in the Triangle Shirtwaist Company's sweatshop just off Washington Square. Occupying the

FIG. 5.11 Firefighters using pitifully inadequate equipment to quell the blaze in the Triangle Shirtwaist Company's top three floors, 1911. Poor and dangerous working conditions were prevalent in all of the era's loft buildings. Photographer unknown. Courtesy of Brown Brothers.

FIG. 5.12 Women march in the city's Labor Day parade rally in Washington Square to proclaim their rights as workers and citizens, 1912. Photographer unknown. Courtesy of Brown Brothers.

top three of ten floors in a loft building at the northwest corner of Washington Place and Greene Street, 500 employees, mostly Jewish female immigrants between the ages of 13 and 23, worked under terrible conditions. To keep the workers at their sewing machines, the proprietors locked the doors to the exits. There were no sprinklers, means of escape were inadequate even for those able to force the doors open, and the fire department's hoses, ladders, and nets couldn't cope with flames on such high floors. The fire shocked the

FIG. 5.13 Max Eastman with his wife, Ida Rauh, a lawyer, actress, sculptor, poet, birth control advocate, labor agitator, and mother. The couple married in 1911 but scandalously kept their separate unmarried names on their apartment mailbox. Photographer and date unknown. From the Collection of Yvette Eastman.

city and roused support for women's rights in the workplace, as well as for changes in fire and building codes (fig. 5.12).

Strong and courageous women affiliated with *The Masses* gave the Washington Square rebellion a wholly new character. Crystal Eastman, Max's older sister, a suffragist on the national stage, was also a journalist, a social and peace activist, and a lawyer (see fig. 5.10). She helped draft labor reform legislation, and in 1917, she and Roger Baldwin founded the Civil Liberties Bureau, the precursor of the American Civil Liberties Union, to defend conscientious objectors. Max Eastman's wife, Ida Rauh (fig. 5.13) had been Crystal's roommate while Crystal was attending NYU law school, and Ida, too, lived in the worlds of both the social reformer and the literati. Crystal and Max Eastman and Ida Rauh assisted Margaret Sanger in her valiant fight to make birth control and information about it available to all. It was at Mabel Dodge's lower Fifth Avenue salon that Sanger had learned of the pioneering research in the range of sexual expression, birth control, and free and frank sexuality by the British psychologist Henry Havelock Ellis. Sanger went to jail in 1917 for distributing contraceptives to immigrant women behind the curtained windows of a Brooklyn tenement storefront—the country's first birth-control clinic. A year earlier, Ida Rauh had been arrested in Union Square for testing convention, in the age of Comstockery, by distributing birth-control pamphlets.

Another staunch supporter of women's rights who was later to become world-famous was Dorothy Day, who as a young reporter was Dell's assistant on *The Masses* in 1917. She was then living a sexually free life and drinking with the rough crowd at the Golden Swan (known to regulars as the Hell Hole, a raffish barroom in an old wooden building on the southeast corner of Sixth Avenue and Fourth Street). Day subsequently became one of the militant suffragists who were imprisoned in Washington for demonstrating and went on a successful hunger strike to get themselves accorded the rights of political prisoners. She later became a legendary advocate for social justice and a tireless worker for the poor. (In 1997, Day was proposed for sainthood by John Cardinal O'Connor, the Roman Catholic Archbishop of New York.)

According to Dell, the woman most responsible for giving the Washington Square rebellion its unique character, "whose gay laughter was heard around the world," was the ardent feminist Henrietta Rodman (fig. 5.14).[12] Dell, who had met Henrietta Rodman shortly upon his arrival from Chicago in 1913, summed up Rodman's free spirit thus: "[She] had an extraordinary gift for stirring things up. Incredibly naïve, preposterously reckless, believing wist-

fully in beauty and goodness, a Candide in petticoats and sandals, she was laughed at a good deal and loved very much indeed, and followed loyally by her friends into new schemes for the betterment of the world."[13]

Rodman successfully challenged the city's board of education for its glaringly unequal treatment of men and women teachers (neither marriage nor children were permitted for women); publicized and made an issue of daycare, one of the strongest barriers to women's equality in the workplace; and formed the Liberal Club on MacDougal Street, which brought Manhattan's activists and intelligentsia together. She, too, forcefully exemplified the new modernism by disregarding convention and accepting the new, and it was Rodman's crusade for dress reform that caught on quickly with independent-minded women. They soon adopted her look—loose-fitting sack gowns, brown socks, sandals, and no hats over their bobbed hair—giving the streets of the Washington Square quarter their most distinctive visual appearance, and further piquing the interest of the press.

After and partially inspired by the 1913 Armory Show, more and more articles appeared in the Sunday supplements of the New York papers on the strange creatures who had produced those works and the milieu from whence they came. In 1914 the *Morning Telegraph* carried one of the earliest of these pieces, "The New Washington Square," which neatly laid out the district with the names and places of its major sites—the Washington Square Bookshop, Polly's restaurant, the Washington Square Players, the Liberal Club, the Washington Square Gallery, the offices of *The Masses*—plus a list of the "riff raff," or "famous unknowns" who made it their home or haunt. In essence, the article was the first Baedeker to the nation's premier bohemia. It was written by Walter Arensberg's friend, Kreymborg, who described himself as one of those "unknowns" and as a "bum." In his introduction, Kreymborg recognized, and was the first to do so in print, that an important cultural gap was being filled:

> Until very recently there never was, here in our own New York, a common ground for at least the display of one's [creative] wares. Which moreover, is the fundamental reason why New York lags so far behind its European sisters, whether in art or propaganda production. New York has and has had its coteries and cliques, its Mouquins and Joels and Café Boulevards and Monopoles, and this that and t'other; but never one district or domicile where a democratic effort, whether conscious or no, has ever been made to centralize the output of poet, sculptor, feminists, madmen, etc. The rumblings are here at last. Not definite rumblings, not the rumblings of a united, co-operative, mutually helpful society or machine of beings, but the rumble of this man here and that man there who has something to say, and who has at last sensed what smells like the market-place-to-be. These rumblings and the tendency toward that potentiality, I like to call—be it fancy, or conceit or what not—the New Washington Square.[14]

Kreymborg's list included a small sampling from Rodman's Liberal Club, the salons of Dodge, Stieglitz, and the Arensbergs, and the Henri and Stieglitz circles of painters. For the most part he said they were just anonymous "dreamers and schemers," each fighting his or her "own particular battle, just as much, for example, as the Liberal Club." Astoundingly for the times, almost a third of those who made Kreymborg's list were women. (Of the 122 men and women named, 34 writers and poets comprised the largest group; 18 were involved with the theater, dance, and the musical stage; 16 were artists; 13 were social activists; 10 were press people; 4 worked at Polly's restaurant; 4 were lawyers; and 22 were linked to other professions and interests.)

On the heels of Kreymborg's article, a piece in the *New York Tribune* asked six "well-known persons" why they lived in the "seductive" district (the Washington Square district and West Village). Everett Shinn, Max Eastman, Mary Heaton Vorse, the author Leroy Scott, and the playwrights George Middleton and Thompson Buchanan expressed the same general views. Eastman's words still resonate today:

> I live in Greenwich Village [at the time, at 206½ West Thirteenth Street] for the same reason that a trout houses in quiet water near the rifts. I want to be very close to that exciting current of life and business that flows north and south on the main avenues. I want to be able to rush into it for pleasure or profit on a moment's notice. But I don't want to live right in it, because I can't stand the strain. And so I seek out the little low-roofed cove you call Greenwich Village, where only an occasional backwater eddy of the main stream reaches me, and I live in complete quietness, with air and sunshine that I couldn't find elsewhere on Manhattan Island south of Riverside Drive. I love the big city, but I love the village too—and here, in a way, I have both.[15]

In 1914, several of the independent rumblings that Kreymborg sensed came together in a row of four brownstones just below the square at 133–139 MacDougal Street. This area also had been the haunt of nonconformists since the 1890s, with Maria's restaurant across the street at No. 146 and the Café Bertolotti around the corner at 85 West Third Street. The loudest noise came from Henrietta Rodman's Liberal Club, numbering about 100 members, which had been the pioneer settler.

Rents were cheap in the run-down houses when Rodman located the club's quarters in rooms at No. 137 in 1913. She let the space on alternate Saturdays to the Heterodoxy Club, a powerful feminist organization. (The membership of the group, whose goals went far beyond acquiring the vote, included Mabel Dodge, Henrietta Rodman, Crystal Eastman, and Ida Rauh.) Occupying two parlor-floor rooms, the club had two chief attractions—an upright electric pianola and a big fireplace. Furnishings were simple, with only a few tables and some wooden chairs scattered about. In addition to weekly lectures and symposia covering intellectual subjects and the latest fashions, dancing enlivened the scene. On Friday nights people paid a quarter for wine and the opportunity to dance such daringly modern arrivals as the turkey trot, from San Francisco, and the tango, from the new French dance competitions, to the player piano.

Dancing also helped pay the bills. In 1914, the Liberal Club received financial help and its members could revel on a larger scale after Floyd Dell organized masquerades inspired by the popular Left Bank tradition of Quatres-Arts balls. Ticket sales raised money for *The Masses* and the Liberal Club, and the dances were widely advertised. Provocative posters by Village artists for these events, featuring, for example, a gleefully naked girl astride a green faun, and a nude tossed over the shoulder of a bereted artist, triggered such libidinal fantasies that Webster Hall, the site of the affair, was jammed. (Webster Hall, a former community center at 119 East Eleventh Street, was the site of many subsequent balls.) Harry Kemp, the era's well-known tramp poet, came to the first Liberal Club ball dressed as the Assyrian King Ashurbanipal. Curious uptowners were drawn to these bohemian spectacles in droves.

Soon after the Liberal Club found quarters, Polly Holladay (fig. 5.15) and her lover, Hippolyte Havel, opened their quintessentially bohemian restaurant, an immediate neighborhood favorite, in the basement of 137 MacDougal Street. The Boni brothers' venturesome bookstore for modern literature (also known as the Washington Square Bookshop) opened in No. 135 next door. In 1914, too, a group in the Liberal Club, named the Washington Square Players, consisting of Albert Boni, Ida Rauh, Lawrence Langner (an attorney and theater buff), and Philip Moeller (a playwright and director) were making plans to convert No. 139 into a theater for American plays. The cultural core of the district had come to life.

Polly Holladay, wrote Floyd Dell, "came from the staid town of Evanston, Illinois, and looked very madonna-like, presided with benignant serenity over

the wild and noisy hoard of young people who began to collect in her restaurant, seeing to it that these truants and orphans were properly fed." (A good meal there could be had for 20 cents.) Havel, her partner in this enterprise, was a Czech immigrant. A fiery-tempered, mischievous little man with a shock of unruly black hair, he had a generally disheveled appearance that belied his intellectual background as a responsible journalist and anarchist philosopher. According to his journalist friend Hutchins Hapgood, Havel could easily greet you with a "How do you do?" but he might just as well exclaim, "Excuse me for a minute—I see a damned fool over there and I want to go and kiss him." Havel's jealous rages over Holladay's numerous affairs eventually doomed the relationship. In 1915, with a new partner, George H. Baker, Polly moved her increasingly popular restaurant to 79 Washington Place West; in 1916, she moved it to 147 West Fourth Street, where it stayed until 1918 (fig. 5.16). Many restaurants appropriated her idea for atmosphere. The spare, Windsor-chair knockoffs and communal wooden tables that were standard apparatus for Holladay restaurants became de rigueur for other bohemian establishments.[16]

One important fallout from the Armory Show was the establishment of more galleries devoted to exhibiting the modern art introduced to the country in 1913. One of the earliest (1914) and most important of these was Robert J. Coady's Washington Square Gallery, featured in Kreymborg's article as one of his major "rumblings." Located at 46 Washington Square South, in a shabby house on the Fourth Street row, visitors could find "characteristic Picassos, . . . Braque and Gris and Léger, as well as examples of Matisse and lesser big men

FIG. 5.16 Polly's restaurant at 147 West Fourth Street, ca. 1917. Mike, the waiter, stands center. George Baker, Polly's restaurant manager, stands to the right. He is talking to the actress Renée La Coste, who is wearing a beret. Photograph by Jessie Tarbox Beals. Courtesy of the Schlesinger Library, Radcliffe Institute, Harvard University.

like Derain and [Vlaminck]. And then there is the father of all children, Rousseau!" Visitors could also find Coady, the pugnacious, redheaded Irishman for whom the city itself was the most fascinating display of modern art. He and his short-lived magazine, *The Soil,* revolutionized the meaning of art and blurred the difference between highbrow and lowbrow. To Coady, American art was "young, robust, energetic, naïve, immature, daring, and big spirited. Active in every conceivable field." Art could be many things beyond the narrow confines of the National Academy: the skyscraper, steel plants, bridges, Indian beadwork, ragtime, syncopation, the cakewalk, football, Coney Island, railroad signals, boxers, cigar store Indians, Prospect Park, and the zoo were some of the things he named. Coady's influence was felt long after he died of pneumonia at age 39 in 1921, and his call to erase distinctions between the fine and popular arts echoes in our own time on both sides of the continuing debate over what constitutes art.[17]

In a tiny room in the rear of 46 Washington Square South, one Guido Bruno had an office. He was an odd mixture of litterateur and carnival shill who had emigrated from Czechoslovakia in 1906. Bruno, whose real name was Curt Josef Kisch, promoted free expression. His early literary accomplishments included the publication of little magazines in which modernist writers and artists appeared, but his later journals increasingly tended toward the hawking of bohemian exotica. By 1915 Bruno had acquired the top floor of the decrepit two-story wooden building at 58 Washington Square South, on the southeast corner of Thompson Street (fig. 5.17). The place was already an

eyesore with garish Coca-Cola signs on the first floor when Bruno added giant placards between the windows of the second, advertising "Bruno's Garret" to the sightseers on the Fifth Avenue Coach's buses, whose station in Washington Square lay directly opposite his premises. Another large sign running the width of the structure shouted, "Greenwich Village." This was a thumb-in-your-eye insult to the Washington Square Association, which had been fighting, albeit unsuccessfully, to abolish outdoor advertising in the city. Bruno's signage even bothered his bohemian neighbors. Eventually, Bruno ran afoul of the law over his publication of an "indecent" booklet that Kreymborg wrote about a prostitute and her pickup, and had to relinquish No. 58 in the fall of 1916. Nevertheless, before Bruno left the building, he had roped in enough visitors to prove to a pack of succeeding entrepreneurs that bohemia was profitable.

Early in 1917, "Mother" Grace Godwin became the next proprietor to take over the garret at No. 58. Her unconventional eatery owed its inspiration to Bruno's demonstration that downtown atmosphere could be packaged for profit, though she rejected his giant placards in favor of smaller and more discrete advertisements; the décor was pure Polly Holladay. Word quickly spread, wrote Jan Seidler Ramirez in *Greenwich Village: Culture and Counterculture*, that diners "could observe aspiring local painters scratching graffiti on the restaurant's walls, or rub elbows with impoverished poets and budding Bolsheviks." Adding to the drama of dining, "the philosophically inclined proprietress made a practice of engaging customers in 'soul chats' while inveigling them to purchase the painted cigarette cases that her cherubic daughter Nancy peddled from table to table." Grace Godwin's Garret, as her place was known, was the most visible, as it was the end of the bus lines on Washington Square, but many other restaurants were already successfully trading on the square's radical chic.[18]

The Little Book of Greenwich Village, a 1918 tourist guide to the area around Washington Square, spotlighted the current crop of top "Restaurants and

Tearooms": Grace Godwin's Garret at 58 Washington Square South; The Green Gate at 11 East Eighth Street; The Hearthstone at 174 West Fourth Street; Ye Pig & Whistle Inn across the street at 175 West Fourth; Gonfarone at 179 MacDougal Street (the Brevoort and Lafayette, with equally notable restaurants, were listed under "Hotels"); the Mad Hatter at 150 West Fourth; the Samovar at 148 West Fourth; Three Steps Down at 19 West Eighth Street; the Dragon Fly (over the Samovar); and Puss In Boots at 57 West Tenth. (Polly's was then moving to Sheridan Square.)[19]

A list of the guide's secondary places, that is, those not rating a descriptive blurb, had addresses dotting the quarter from Eleventh to Bleecker Street:

Black Cat, 557 West Broadway (between Bleecker and West Third Streets)
Broad's Chop House, 53 West Third Street
The Checker Box, 18 Barrow Street
The Crumperie, 6½ Sheridan Square
Enrico & Plagieri, 64 West Eleventh Street (Italian restaurant founded by ex-Gonfarone waiter, Enrico Fasani)
French Pastry Shop, 144 Sixth Avenue (at Eleventh Street)
Galotti's, 64 West Tenth Street (Italian restaurant founded by ex-Gonfarone waiter, Peter Galotti)
The Green Witch, 49 East Tenth Street
Greenwich Village Mill, 47 West Third Street
Joan's Dancing. Tea, 54 Sixth Avenue (at Washington Place)
The Red Lion, 233 Thompson Street
Renganeschi, 139 West Tenth Street
The Russian Tea Room, 239 West Fourth Street
The Silhouette Shop, 144 West Fourth Street
The Village Kitchen, 53 Greenwich Avenue

One spot, the Hell Hole (fig. 5.18), didn't make the guide's lists, which were geared more to Fifth Avenue Coach riders than to the bohemians the booklet touted. As the Golden Swan, it had been a favorite of the notorious Irish waterfront gang known as the Hudson Dusters when the bohemian crowd discovered it around 1910. Tom Wallace, its Irish proprietor, who avoided the headaches of garbage disposal by keeping a pig in the cellar, shunted the Dusters off to a back room when he saw a chance for a better-paying clientele. Because of its connection with the underworld and late-night truck drivers, the place never closed, and artists and writers congregated there when the Brevoort café shut up for the night. It was Eugene O'Neill's favorite drinking spot in his Provincetown theater days, and several people he met there served as the basis for characters in *The Iceman Cometh.* John Sloan has left an etching and Charles Demuth a watercolor of the gamy old barroom (fig. 5.19). Mary Heaton Vorse probably best described why it wasn't included in *The Little Book of Greenwich Village.* It had, she wrote, a

"smoky quality about it. Something at once alive and deadly . . . sinister. It was as if the combined soul of New York flowed underground and this was one of its vents."[20]

By 1918 the Fifth Avenue Coach Company was even running a regular column titled "Bohemian Excursions" in its complimentary magazine, *From a Fifth Avenue Bus,* which it distributed to an annual ridership numbering over one million. Readers could find endorsements of and directions to a selection of local establishments (presumably included for a fee). The tourist trade had taken firm hold, and the eastern geographic boundary of Greenwich Village had migrated from its historic limit at Sixth Avenue over to University Place.

Meanwhile, Ida Rauh's drama group, the Washington Square Players, ran into problems with the city's fire and building inspectors while planning to convert 139 MacDougal Street into a theater. As a result they were forced to lease an existing theater uptown. (This troupe later became the Theatre Guild.) However, events during the summer of 1915 in Provincetown, Massa-

FIG. 5.20 The Provincetown Players' stage at 39 MacDougal in November 1916. Among those preparing the set for the first play, Eugene O'Neill's *Bound East for Cardiff,* are O'Neill (on ladder), Hippolyte Havel (seated), and George Cram Cook (far right). Photographer unknown. © Museum of the City of New York.

chusetts, led the following year to a theater at No. 139, featuring the ground-breaking plays of Eugene O'Neill.

Mary Heaton Vorse and her family had a small vacation house and fishing wharf in Provincetown that, by 1915, had become the summer headquarters for a group of the Washington Square rebels. Sitting around a driftwood fire one evening, Vorse and her husband, Joe O'Brien, the Hutchins Hapgoods, the Wilber Daniel Steeles, and George Cram Cook and his wife, Susan Glaspell, cursed the trite and uninspired fare on the Broadway stage and decided to put on works of their own. Nearly all of the friends were writers, and, as it happened, Hapgood's wife, Neith Boyce, had written a play called *Constancy,* which poked fun at the recently failed romance between Mabel Dodge and John Reed. Cook and Glaspell had also written *Suppressed Desires,* satirizing the Freudian gospel then emanating from Dodge's salon and the Liberal Club. After they tried out these one-acts in the Hapgoods' cottage, Vorse let the writers-turned-actors use her wharf for their plays. The Provincetown Players theater was born.

George Cram Cook (fig. 5.20) became the moving spirit behind the players, both in their wharf theater the following summer and at 139 MacDougal Street that fall. Cook was a Midwesterner who had been a novelist, poet, critic, sculptor, farmer, and college professor, but most of all he dreamed of a new kind of theater. He felt that ancient Athens had proved that a unified culture could exist in which the commonplace and artistic worlds were united, and that this unity of life and art was most evident in the Athenian theater. In Provincetown, looking for new plays in the summer of 1916, Cook learned that the then-unknown Eugene O'Neill was also staying there with a box of unproduced plays, and O'Neill was quickly invited to address the players.

O'Neill chose one of his sea plays, *Bound East for Cardiff*. After this tale of the crew of the tramp steamer Glencairn was read to the group, Glaspell wrote, "Then we knew what we were for."[21] No time was lost in producing the play in the wharf theater. It was O'Neill's first production on any stage. With no plot and with dialogue more like that found in a novel than in a conventional playwright's script, the play was an atmospheric piece without precedent in the American theater. The audience was thrilled, and the wharf shook with applause.

After the season ended, Cook, brimming with excitement that his vision of a new Athens might be realized, moved the Provincetown Players to Mac-Dougal Street. He planned to avoid problems with city inspectors by keeping the theater as a subscription-based private club, a ploy that worked for only one season. Cook then moved the theater to better facilities at No. 133, previously a residence, a storehouse, a stable, and a bottling works. (The theater exists today after a 1942 remodeling, inside and out, of the houses at Nos. 133–139.) Plays continued to be put on by the Provincetown group, with O'Neill as their star writer and Cook handling every conceivable production problem, from 1916 until 1920, when the playwright's growing fame propelled him into larger Broadway theaters. Cook was the first to stage O'Neill's *The Emperor Jones,* and he even had an expensive dome for better lighting constructed at No. 133 before the play moved to Broadway in 1920. *The Emperor Jones,* an expressionistic one-act play about a black porter who imagines himself a king, was the work that made O'Neill's reputation. It was also the most memorable and successful play ever produced by the Provincetown Players. But Cook, who had given O'Neill a stage when no one else would, found stardom in O'Neill, but not for satisfaction for himself. After another season, when the uncomfortable and tiny 185-seat MacDougal Street playhouse was no longer the amateur theater of Cook's dreams, he and Glaspell sailed for Greece in 1922. His theater, though, became famous as the most important place where American drama was established as a serious art form.

During Cook's years with the Provincetown Players, he encouraged participation by artists in all fields in his hope for a true synthesis of expression. He succeeded in involving many of the Village writers and artists, including some notable ones, as playwrights and set and costume designers, but with mixed results. The budding poet Edna St. Vincent Millay, for example, found modest success as both an actress and a playwright, while the novelist Theodore Dreiser's one drama bombed. His play, a study of degeneracy, lost $1,500 and alienated Cook's supporters. Only O'Neill, the chief and most prolific member of Cook's troupe, had any formal theatrical training.

Albert and Charles Boni's Washington Square Bookshop, next door to the Provincetown Players at 135 MacDougal Street, was Kreymborg's fondest "rumbling." The brothers had published Kreymborg's first modern poetry magazine, *The Glebe,* and their shop was named first in "The New Washington Square":

Washington Square reads books. But Washington Square does not read the books you and I read—Chambers or Booth Tarkington or Graustark McCutcheon or Rex Beach. Washington Square reads Strindberg and Nietzsche and Dostoevsky and Whitman and Masefield and Wedekind and the rest of the modern bombshells. . . . So Washington Square goes to the Washington Square Bookshop, or, as it is more popularly known, the Boni's. . . . Albert is the favorite with the men clientele, Charles with the ladies, which is in rapport with the ethics that the world of Washington Square approves, where the woman is the equal, if not the superior, of the man.[22]

Kreymborg named some more modern authors found on the brothers' shelves, most of them recognizable today: "Chekhov, Wells, Maeterlinck, Emma Goldman, Shaw, Andreyev, Synge, Schnitzler, Frank Harris, Sudermann, Wolzogen, Tagore, Carpenter, Hauptmann, H. James and W. James, Ellen Key, Wilde, Traubel, Noguchi, and the latest of the latest, Lord Dunsany." In addition to hard-to-find books, the shop was "a happy combination of library and bookshop," a publisher of books and magazines, and "a programme of entertainments, such as poetry and play readings and exhibitions and soirees toward keeping the shop open evenings." In 1917 the Bonis dissolved their operation when Albert decided to pursue his true love, book publishing. Albert teamed up with Horace B. Liveright to form Boni & Liveright, one of the most adventurous publishing houses of the 1920s and 1930s.[23]

Fortunately for Washington Square readers, the same year that the Bonis closed their shop, Egmont Arens opened an excellent bookstore at 17 West Eighth Street (fig. 5.21). Arens's shop was on the parlor floor of a house very much like its MacDougal Street predecessor, and Arens kept the same blister-globe chandeliers and book-filled tables that had made the old shop so likeable. Arens's place wasn't a center for creative enterprise the way the Bonis' store was, but the shelves were stocked with an equally impressive selection of books and magazines. On the magazine rack just inside the door, one could find representatives of the new movements in American art, thought, and lit-

FIG. 5.22 Margaret Anderson, ca. 1920. Anderson appears considerably less scruffy for this sitting than in contemporary accounts of her on the streets of the Village. Photographer unknown. Courtesy of the University of Wisconsin–Milwaukee Archives.

erature—*The New Republic, The Nation, The Freeman, The Dial, The Little Review, Vanity Fair, Modern School,* and *Plowshare*—periodicals hard to find elsewhere, and certainly not all in one place. The Arens bookshop remained Washington Square's favorite during the 1920s for browsing, and even purchasing books when the price could be afforded by those less well off. A long tradition of Eighth Street bookshops began here at No. 17, and, despite the disappearance of dozens of quirky independent book vendors in the neighborhood, two booksellers can still be found on the street.

Of all the magazines displayed on the rack of Arens's shop, the most famous and best, by 1920, was *The Little Review.* The remarkable couple that owned and produced it, Margaret C. Anderson (fig. 5.22) and her lover, Jane Heap, lived in the top-floor apartment at 27 West Eighth Street. Anderson, the founder of the magazine, was a beautiful and vivacious young woman who had rebelled against her prosperous Midwestern family life and was searching for one "[b]eautiful as no life had ever been." In college she read such writers as Henry Havelock Ellis, Dostoevsky, Shelley, Keats, and Swinburne, and developed a passion for conversation. Believing that the most stimulating exchanges took place only among artists, she moved in 1906 to Chicago, then the center of mid-American intellectual ferment. She worked as a book reviewer and as a literary editor on the Chicago papers, and gained a practical knowledge of the printing room after she joined the staff of *The Dial.* (Originally based in Chicago, *The Dial* moved to New York in 1918.) By 1914 Anderson was ready for her own monthly magazine and founded *The Little Review,* which was grounded in her conviction that "people who make Art are more interesting than those who don't; that they have a special illumination about life; and that this illumination is the subject-matter of all inspired conversation; that one might as well be dead as to live outside this radiance."[24]

In 1916 Anderson found an ideal partner for her venture in Jane Heap, whom she considered "the world's best talker." Heap became Anderson's valued assistant, and the pair moved *The Little Review* from Chicago to California. Their stay was brief. In September 1916, Anderson produced its most famous issue: 64 pages of blank paper accompanied by the statement that since *The Little Review* would publish nothing second-rate, it preferred to publish nothing. So early in 1917 they brought the monthly to New York, and, with the crucial assistance of Ezra Pound as their new European editor, Anderson displayed real genius for picking the best writers of her time. Soon T. S. Eliot and Wyndham Lewis appeared in Anderson and Heap's journal for the first time, along with William Butler Yeats. Works by Hart Crane and Ford Madox Ford followed, as did selections from an earlier contributor, William Carlos Williams, and much of Pound's own work. Then, in March 1918, when Anderson and Heap moved in at 27 West Eighth Street, Anderson achieved her ultimate coup—she serialized James Joyce's *Ulysses* in *The Little Review,* marking the novel's first publication anywhere, although the serialization was stopped before it was complete.[25]

Pound had sent Anderson the manuscript, and when she read it, she exclaimed, "This is the most beautiful thing we'll ever have! We'll print it if it's the last effort of our lives."[26] *Ulysses* had been too hot a potato for even the Bloomsbury group to touch, but Anderson forged ahead alone. During the three years it ran—a period of the Comstock laws plus rampant xenophobia inflamed by the war and rising communism—the U.S. Post Office burned four issues for alleged obscenity. Joyce's masterpiece was decried or ignored by virtually everyone, except for a few experimental writers and self-styled guardians of morality.

On October 4, 1920, the Society for the Suppression of Vice served the Washington Square Bookshop with papers. The complaint cited the sale of the July-August issue of the *Review,* which contained the Gerty MacDowell episode. Anderson and Heap were tried in the Court of Special Sessions, found guilty, and fined $100. Hundreds of sympathizers turned out to support them in court, and they were defended by the eminent New York lawyer John Quinn. A financial backer of *The Little Review* and a friend of Pound and Joyce, Quinn was also an art patron, collector, and militant advocate of the avant-garde. He got the two women off lightly, but not one New York newspaper spoke out in support of either *The Little Review* or James Joyce. (Later, Joyce was charged with writing pornography, and it was not until 1933 that it was legal to sell *Ulysses* in the United States.)

While the Washington Square cultural rebellion was underway during the 1908–20 period, other battles were being fought for the physical protection of the quarter. In 1909, reminiscent of the 1878 armory proposal, the city sought to install a courthouse in the square; however, the neighborhood's protectors had become strong enough to force the city, without much ado, to find a site elsewhere. Although the threat of commercialization had nearly ceased, the continued growth of the metropolis and transportation demands kept it alive. The square lay squeezed between lofts on Broadway and factories on the waterfront. Seventh Avenue had been extended south through the West Village, and the widening of Varick Street threatened another industrial invasion. Garment factory lofts on Fifth Avenue, though, were the most immediate menace, poised for expansion south toward Washington Square. In 1909, members of the Washington Square Association were appalled when the superwealthy Thomas Fortune Ryan, at 60 Fifth Avenue, stopped holding out, opting instead to move to 858 Fifth Avenue (at 67th Street). Two years later came the inevitable, when a monstrously tall loft rose on the northeast corner

of Twelfth Street on property that Ryan had previously held for protection (fig. 5.23).

Fortunately, help was on the way—but not without a bizarre twist that could have proved disastrous. Fifth Avenue retailers also had become alarmed by the encroachment of the tall factory lofts into their tony precincts above 23rd Street, and they appealed to Mayor William J. Gaynor for help. In 1910 the mayor floated his own harebrained scheme to relieve the related problem of congestion with a new avenue running parallel midway between Fifth and Sixth Avenues north of Eighth Street. This would have cut a 100-foot-wide swath through the best remaining blocks in the Washington Square district, but the Fifth Avenue Association had its own nightmare scenario: loss of fashion's crown to Gaynor's upstart street.

The Fifth Avenue Association turned instead to the powerful and sympathetic Manhattan borough president, George McAneny, who first attacked the tall loft problem with a proposal to restrict building height. Tall buildings were not just a problem for Fifth Avenue. Whole sections in the Wall Street financial district were becoming sunless canyons, and the 18-story St. Regis (1904) and 19-story Gotham (1905), across-the-street neighbors at 55th Street and Fifth Avenue, had proved that even luxury hotels could be offensive sun blockers. Growing concern about tall buildings led to the wider proposition for controlled land use—namely, the separation of residential and business districts—and the concept of zoning was born. In 1914 the New York State Legislature granted New York City the right to impose zoning, and the first

zoning law in the country passed the city's Board of Estimate on July 25, 1916. The Washington Square Association had been meeting with the city administration throughout the period and saw to it after 1916 that zoning was used to protect its prime residential streets.

With zoning laws effectively ensured by the end of 1915, the Sailors' Snug Harbor trust could comfortably announce a policy change, and in January 1916 the Washington Square neighborhood got the good news. At the annual meeting of the 310-member Washington Square Association held in the First Presbyterian Church, the trust described its intent to build housing instead of lofts on its property and its desire to drive out commercial businesses from its holdings. Noting "the artists who are making Washington Square one of their favorite centres," the trust outlined plans for rebuilding housing on the south side of Eighth Street between Fifth Avenue and University Place (fig. 5.24).[27] Behind that, studios would replace stables on the north side of Washington Mews. Work proceeded at once, and the trust's housing experiment in the heart of the district proved a success. According to the *AIA Guide to New York City*, the remodeled Eighth Street houses are "[a] set of brick houses made picturesque by the addition of bold decorative eaves, brickwork inlaid in a stucco ground, and bits of wrought ironwork. A stage set, symbolic of the 'village' of a bohemian artist." Today they stand as one of the most charming and unique streetscapes that we have in the city.

Although the *Tribune* had noted renewed interest in Washington Square and the general West Village area in 1914, and a number of tumbledown houses and stables had earlier been remodeled, this development by the Sailors' Snug Harbor trust on Eighth Street was the catalyst that brought a resurgence in value to the area. By the summer of 1917, the Sunday real estate section of the *New York Times* was reporting increased demand for apartments near the square, with units being snapped up as soon as they became available. One agent had 500 applicants from "Riverside Drive, Park Avenue, upper Fifth Avenue, and other localities" waiting for apartments near the square, and the leading real estate operator in the district, Vincent Pepe, declared, "The Sailors' Snug Harbor apartment development in [East] Eighth Street has turned, as if by magic, a dingy neighborhood into a delightful residential block, and apartments rent there from $1,200 [per year] upward."[28]

As the neighborhood continued to improve, though, its chief architectural ornament, the Washington Square Arch, remained incomplete. Frederick MacMonnies, one of the sculptors originally hired for the commission, had proposed two ensembles of Washington-related figures in high relief, set as "bouquets" against the two piers. However, MacMonnies had gone to France, which made communication difficult. Then, after Stanford White's murder by a man who suspected White of romantic involvement with his wife, and the deaths of other key members of the arch committee, the sculpture program lapsed. William Rhinelander Stewart revived the project in 1912, and the committee chose two distinguished local sculptors to complete the work, Hermon MacNeil and Alexander Stirling Calder (the father of the avant-garde maker of mobiles and stabiles, Alexander Calder). The neoclassical idea of bouquets was abandoned for simpler and larger images of Washington: MacNeil's showed the man as general of the revolutionary armies, at about 40 years of age, and Calder's represented him as president and statesman, at about 60 years old. MacNeil completed his figure and relief by 1916; Calder finished his sculpture in time for its dedication on February 22, 1918, Washington's birthday.

The completion of the sculpture for the arch was not the only event in the late teens that called attention to Washington Square. Shortly after America entered World War I, the war commissioners of the Allies—which then included czarist Russia and Japan—were entertained by gala receptions in the city during the spring and summer of 1917, and the arch was successively draped with their national decorations (fig. 5.25). The occasion dramatically underscored the centrality of New York City in helping the old-world powers in preserving their civilizations. In 1918, shortly after the armistice was declared, Fifth Avenue was festively lined with flags and officially anointed as the Avenue of the Allies. After the war ended the following year, the returning troops marched through the arch and up Fifth Avenue in a city overwhelmed with gratitude; in 1920 Washington Square received a commemora-

tive flagpole and base designed by the firm of McKim, Mead & White. Initially installed in the center of the view through the arch, the memorial has
since moved slightly southeast of it (fig. 5.26).

By 1920 Washington Square and its environs, now fully anointed as
"Greenwich Village," had been indelibly etched in the national psyche as Bohemia, U.S.A., the magnet for all of the country's free creative spirits. But
World War I, Comstockery, and the country's first red scare, which lasted
from 1914 to 1924, put a heavy damper on the original rebellion, and many in
the vanguard moved on. In 1918, 101 members of the IWW membership were
tried and convicted under the Espionage Act, including their leader, Bill Haywood, who had frequented Mabel Dodge's salon. Haywood and a number of
the others who were convicted jumped bail and boarded a ship to Russia. Eugene V. Debs, the labor leader and head of the American Socialist party, was
sentenced to ten years in jail for a speech he had made; he was pardoned in
1921. During the Palmer Raids of 1919 (named for U.S. Attorney General
Mitchell Palmer), mass raids and arrests of communists and anarchists were
commonplace occurrences throughout the land. As the result of one roundup,
Emma Goldman and 248 other aliens were put aboard a ship in December
1920 for deportation to the Soviet Union. Many creative people were sickened
by the excessive persecution and the trend toward intolerance that they saw
developing. In response, they left for Europe.

Most of the people in the forefront of Washington Square's vanguard
movements chose to become émigrés, changed the direction of their creativ-

ity, or passed away. Mabel Dodge went to Taos, New Mexico, where she founded an art colony. There she married Tony Luhan, a Pueblo Indian, and became an early fighter for the rights of Native Americans. Stieglitz closed 291 and concentrated on photography and promoting the career of painter Georgia O'Keeffe, whom he would marry in 1924. The Arensbergs moved to California in 1922. Coady transferred his gallery uptown to 489 Fifth Avenue to be near other art showrooms, but he died shortly thereafter in 1921. Cook and Glaspell lived in Greece until Cook's death in 1924, while Ida Rauh, divorced from Max Eastman, became known as the "Duse of MacDougal Street" for her exuberant acting with the Provincetown Players. Margaret Anderson moved to Paris but not before she published, in the spring of 1922, a landmark of art criticism—"Aesthetic Meditation on Painting" by Guillaume Apollinaire. Both Duchamp and Man Ray had decamped for Paris in 1921. A year before, John Reed died of typhus in Moscow and was buried there. Henrietta Rodman died at the age of 45 from a brain tumor in 1923. Crystal Eastman married and moved to England; her brother, Max, went to have a look at Soviet Russia but returned and later resided at 8 West Thirteenth Street from 1944 until his death in 1969. Dell remained a Village resident and concentrated on his writing, and Polly's restaurant relocated to Sheridan Square, catering more and more to the tourists than to Holladay's bohemian friends. Gertrude Vanderbilt Whitney's Studio Club for artists took over the 147 West Fourth Street building that Polly vacated in June 1918.

The Whitney and its artists kept the flame of creativity burning brightly around Washington Square. Louise Norton, one of the spirits behind *Rogue,* left Allen Norton, married Edgard Varèse, and bought a house in the MacDougal-

Sullivan Gardens block at 188 Sullivan Street. The couple lived there until Varèse's death in 1965. The Provincetown Playhouse and the Washington Square Bookshop remained hangouts for new generations of nonconformists, as did the beloved Brevoort and Lafayette hotels, which survived into the 1950s. Gertrude Vanderbilt Whitney's rebel enterprises—the Whitney Studio, the Whitney Studio Club, the Whitney Studio Galleries, and the Whitney Museum of American Art—grew from their modest start in her MacDougal Alley studio into one of the country's premier art institutions. Moreover, for nearly four decades beginning in 1914, the heiress and her assistant, Juliana Force, sustained a needy brood of artists on Eighth Street. (The Whitney Museum moved uptown in 1953.)

From the twenties through the forties, which encompassed a mighty boom and bust followed by World War II, another contingent of painters centered around Eighth Street and Washington Square were creating a new sensation in art. This group became known as the New York School; after their rise, the city would never again languish in the backwaters of international culture.

Red Grooms, *The Cedar Bar*, 1986. An artist's interpretation of the renowned bar and the New York School milieu in the 1950s. This nondescript bar on University Place between Eighth and Ninth Streets became the chief hangout of the New York School crowd in the 1940s and 1950s—the heyday of Abstract Expressionism. As the artist-habitués became famous, the place metamorphosed into a tourist attraction. Jackson Pollock is the large figure (center-right) with a striped T-shirt, and Willem de Kooning stands (far left) wearing a long coat and a hat. The tall man standing under the "BUD" sign to the right of de Kooning is Harold Rosenberg, one of the art critics whose advocacy helped promote the group of painters, especially de Kooning. © Red Grooms / Artists Rights Society (ARS), New York. Photograph by Bruce M. White. Courtesy of the Princeton University Art Museum.

: : : : : **6**

HOME OF THE NEW YORK SCHOOL

1921–1950

ROM THE 1920S THROUGH THE 1940S, THE POPULATION OF THE
Washington Square district changed dramatically. Although a group of New
York's social elite remained until the 1930s, and some even later, most of their
single-family homes were subdivided into flats, and most of the new apartment houses were designed with much smaller one- and two-bedroom units.
New residents were mainly upper-middle-class, professional people, including many young married couples. They enjoyed the convenient location and
Village atmosphere with its informality, its cultural heritage, and, for some, its
bohemian associations.

While its demographics were shifting, the environs of the square became
a huge tourist attraction, beginning a long-running love-hate relationship between residents and visitors. Busloads of tourists had been arriving since
World War I, and as tourism grew Village hangouts expanded and multiplied
to cater to the visitors (fig. 6.1). In 1935, the city formed the New York Convention and Visitors Bureau to build tourism into a major industry. New York
was a boomtown for servicemen on leave during World War II, and the
overflow from Times Square came down to Washington Square. Tourist volume mushroomed both during the war and after and increased the popularity
of the Village during the postwar years as a nice place to live. The neighborhood was proud of the visitors' attention, and local businesses prospered, but
residents feared the honky-tonk aspects of becoming a tourist mecca.

A large contingent of artists remained in the neighborhood. They occupied rooms in the dilapidated houses and tenements southwest of Washington Square, in the increasingly decrepit housing and loft stock of the Sailors'
Snug Harbor trust property east of Fifth Avenue, and in the aging commercial structures around Fourteenth Street. These cheap flats were home to one
group of artists, collectively known as the New York School, whose abstract
painting and sculpture were responsible for an upheaval in the art world and a
shift of the center of modern art from Paris to New York. During the same
30-year period, the neighborhood that supported these artists managed to
survive, relatively unscathed, several turbulent events—the 1920s real estate
boom, the transformation of Sixth Avenue, the 1930s Depression, and the
post–World War II redevelopment-driven recovery with its first urban renewal battles.

The Roaring Twenties got off to a sputtering start in New York City. In
1919, soldiers flooding home from World War I found the arms and shipbuilding plants shut down and the local economy in turmoil. Private builders
refused to pay the new, higher wartime wages, and New Yorkers suffered from
overcrowding and unemployment. By 1921, however, with housing and office
space in dwindling supply, the most intensive construction boom in the city's
history was underway. Spurred on by tax exemptions and reduced restrictions

FIG. 6.1 Tour buses in Washington Square from *Leslie's Illustrated Weekly,* August 21, 1921. Drawing by Walter Jack Duncan. Author's Collection.

on investments in housing by insurance companies, residential construction took off first, with dwelling units added at an unprecedented rate: from 32,000 new units going up in 1921 to a record—still unbroken—of 107,185 in 1927. Also by 1921, automobiles, trucks, and buses were congesting the city's streets, and Model Ts clogged the radial roads leading to the countryside on weekends. Motor vehicle registrations in New York City more than doubled between 1920 and 1926, jumping from 223,000 to 573,000 in those six years. Both traffic demands and real estate development would continue to press heavily on the neighborhood of Washington Square, with plans for a new route through the square and new housing blocks replacing venerable old buildings.

One drag on the economy that lasted from 1920 to 1933 was Prohibition. The Volstead Act had taken effect on January 17, 1920, crippling legitimate restaurant and hotel business, and fostering the rise of thousands of illegal speakeasies, dives, and liquor-peddling drugstores (fig. 6.2). Estimates of their peak number ranged from 32,000 to 100,000. Although Prohibition was a joke to most of urban America—and a complete absurdity in New York City—many restaurants closed. In the Village, Gonfarone's shut its doors, but the Brevoort and Lafayette, though reduced to serving booze out of coffee cups, held on.

By the 1920s all New Yorkers, including the rich, had fully accepted apartment house living. Parcel after parcel on Fifth Avenue and other prime streets, most of them 100 feet wide, were sold to developers for tall apartment structures, typically 15 stories, each 10 feet high. Tenements, then a city building type that included apartment houses, could rise no higher. Other commercial structures, such as office buildings and hotels, could be constructed to unlimited height, incorporating setbacks mandated by the 1916 zoning law. Many tenants, however, wanted the excitement of high-rise living, and the real es-

FIG. 6.2 Joseph W. Golinkin, *Speako de Luxe*, 1933, a high-end speakeasy at 19 Washington Square North run by Barney Gallant, a nightclub impresario and Village character. © Museum of the City of New York.

tate industry obliged with a new addition to the skyline—skyscraper apartment-hotels.

Apartment-hotels were a fiction made necessary by the city's Building Department definition of *any* apartment house as a "tenement," from the worst multifamily hovel in a slum district to the most opulent Fifth Avenue spread staffed by servants and fit for royalty. Apartment houses could be built higher than the maximum for tenements only if they maintained the key difference between hotel and tenement—that they were commercial buildings with no cooking permitted in hotel rooms. So apartment-hotels, which were in truth high-rise apartment houses, had ground floor restaurants with room service, and kitchen-like "serving halls" inserted in the apartments to get around the regulations. After the Multiple Dwelling Law of 1929 was passed, partly as a result of this sham, cooking was permitted to occupants of apartment-hotels, and the serving-hall ruse was no longer necessary. The earliest soaring apartment houses were apartment-hotels: first, the 34-story Hotel Shelton went up in 1924 at Lexington Avenue and 49th Street, and then, in 1925, the spectacularly tall 42-story Ritz Tower was erected at Park Avenue and 57th Street.

As the skyscrapers became a part of the Manhattan streetscape, the mansions of the Joneses, Astors, and Vanderbilts on upper Fifth Avenue were being torn down, and lower Fifth Avenue and Washington Square also witnessed the wholesale demolition of their original residences. The first to fall, in 1921, were the houses at 23–27 Fifth Avenue. Number 23, the former home of General Sickles and Mabel Dodge, was replaced by the large, 13-story redbrick apartment house known as 25 Fifth Avenue. The Rhinelander mansion and its two neighbors to the west (14–16 Washington Square North) were the next to be destroyed for a small-scale apartment house erected on their sites in

FIG. 6.3 Washington Square West in the 1930s. Three of the four apartment houses pay obeisance to the Judson Church campanile with sensitively designed water-tower enclosures. Photographer unknown. Courtesy of Brown Brothers.

1922. The addition was sympathetic because it incorporated part of the original facades in its neo–Greek Revival design, which was only five stories high with a roof balustrade that matched that of No. 13 on the Row across Fifth Avenue, and because it replaced an Italianate house at No. 16 that was not in harmony with the rest.

Washington Square's first high-rise apartment house was erected in 1925 on the site of the old Alsop residence at 25 Washington Square West, on the northwest corner of Washington Place (fig. 6.3). By 1931, three more 15- and 16-story apartment houses lined the west side of the square, and a lone 16-story apartment house was erected in 1927 on the south side, at 71 Washington Square, between Laurens and Wooster Streets. Earlier in the 1920s, the south side of the square, already the victim of a long history of disfigurements, suffered another blow—the Washington Square Garage. The apartment building at No. 71 stood adjacent to this automobile parking garage, a six-story industrial structure with large factory-style windows, one lot from Wooster Street. A similar and still existing garage was also built in the 1920s on University Place, on the west block between Twelfth and Thirteenth Streets. Both were built to be in close proximity to the enormous Wanamaker department store on Broadway, which was drawing an increasing number of shoppers in cars.

Stylistically, all of the new apartment houses were tightly constrained by two factors: building laws affecting height (with zoning setback requirements after 1929) and the developers' desire to make every square inch profitable. These concerns, plus the city's reversal on encroachment rights for stoops, bays, porches, and so on, which had been permitted to intrude onto the sidewalk area, left no physical room for the exuberant, high-relief ornamentation that had characterized previous Beaux Arts buildings. Apartment house architects, faced with these restrictions, produced brick- and stone-clad boxes embellished with low-relief, picturesque details drawn from a wide variety of periods and styles—Renaissance, Gothic, Federal, Beaux Arts, and more. Art Deco, which appeared after 1925, relied on vertical emphasis, multicolored materials, patterned brickwork, and abstract geometric and organic ornament. Only two tall Art Deco apartment houses were erected in the area, and they were completed by 1931: 14 Washington Place by Schwartz & Gross, and 59 West Twelfth Street by Emery Roth, the latter the more artfully conceived of the two.

Emery Roth was one of a handful of talented architects—who also included Rosario Candela, Schwartz & Gross, and J. E. R. Carpenter—that devised the texture of New York's cityscape in the 1920s and 1930s. These architects' work, taken together, gave the city its mood and sense of place, which a number of today's architects are striving to recreate. Roth's designs, along with other fine 1920s buildings on lower Fifth Avenue and its side streets, form a rich ensemble that lends that ambience to one of today's most delightful New York neighborhoods. Roth is best known for his romantic twin-towered San Remo and El Dorado apartment buildings on Central Park West, as well as for the Ritz Tower; the Washington Square district is fortunate to have a number of his creations.

His 14-story purplish-brick structure at 39 Fifth Avenue, which opened in 1922, is notable for its multicolored terra-cotta loggias executed in an eclectic Venetian Gothicism. Down the avenue at No. 24, the site of the Brevoort mansion and grounds, is Roth's 16-story Fifth Avenue Hotel, which was completed in 1926. Its two-story base is clad in limestone, and the massive superstructure is covered with two shades of buff brick to create a pleasing surface. A contemporary newspaper called the hotel a "fine expression of the Italian Renaissance developed in stone, marble and polychrome terra-cotta." One University Place, designed by Roth in 1929, occupies the northeast corner of University and Waverly Places, and dominates the northeast view from Washington Square. It rises from the pavement as sheer masonry cliffs of brown brick, topped by an Italian campanile–style water tower echoing the Judson Church tower across the square. Further up University Place, on the southeast corner of East Tenth Street, Upjohn's church and rectory were replaced by Roth's 12-story Devonshire House of 1928. Strongly influenced by Spanish and Moorish precedents (despite its fancy English name), the structure's unusual variegated brick and stone, colored in deep shades of brown, tan, and red with additional green tones, were selected for their capacity to reflect light.[1]

Roth's most dramatic design for the district, a grand apartment house for Washington Square, was never executed, an unfortunate casualty of the deteriorating economic condition in the early 1930s. It was slated for land that covered, except for one lot on Third Street, the full block between Thompson Street and La Guardia Place, from the square to Third Street. In 1927 the plot

FIG. 6.4 Emery Roth's winged fantasy apartment house for the full block of Washington Square South between West Broadway and Thompson Street, early 1930s. The Great Depression killed the plan. Artist unknown. Courtesy of Emery Roth & Sons.

had been the first choice for the site of the new Museum of the City of New York, which was built instead on city-owned property at 103rd Street and Fifth Avenue. The Washington Square scheme had been promoted by the banker and museum board member James Speyer, who subsequently purchased the parcel for Roth's fantasy. This conjectural building had a striking central tower reminiscent of the "Flash Gordon" finial towers of Roth's El Dorado, with four giant apartment wings radiating from it (fig. 6.4). Conceived as a premier residence, the proposed extravaganza might have spurred the southern portion of the square's evolution into an elegant residential district. Instead, the area became the principal target of New York University's expansion plans in the 1950s. (Roth's two 12-story wings facing the square would have been relatively massive sun blockers but would have been kinder to the square than future developments there.)[2]

Commanding the western side of lower Fifth Avenue, between the Church of the Ascension and the First Presbyterian Church, was a large cooperative apartment building, 40 Fifth Avenue. Built in 1929 on the eve of the Depression, it replaced the residences at Nos. 40–44. Architects Van Wart & Wein designed an elegant 15-story neo-Georgian redbrick and stone edifice, crowned with a Georgian-inspired church belfry, in perfect counterpoint to the Gothic Revival church towers of its neighbors. Known simply by its address, it barely escaped falling into receivership in the early 1930s but thereafter became—and still is—one of the best residences in the Washington Square district.

One of No. 40's first residents, Judge Joseph F. Crater, gave the building unwanted notoriety when he mysteriously disappeared without a trace in 1930. Governor Franklin D. Roosevelt had appointed him to the State Supreme Court in April 1930. After dinner at a midtown Manhattan restaurant on August 6, he stepped into a cab with about $5,000 in his wallet, waved goodbye to a friend, and vanished. An investigation hinted at corruption in his Cayuga Democratic Club, closely associated with Tammany Hall. Crater was never found and what happened to him still remains a mystery. His was one of the most famous disappearances in American history, and "paging Judge Crater" jokes can still be found in the press and on the stand-up circuit.

The 21-story, redbrick and stone apartment house at 51 Fifth Avenue was also built just before the 1929 crash. It had one of New York's most illustrious citizens in residence, the former governor and the 1928 Democratic presidential candidate Alfred (Al) E. Smith, who had just lost the election to Herbert Hoover. Smith was then the president of the group that planned and constructed the Empire State Building in a period of tremendous excitement over the race to build the tallest skyscraper. The Chrysler Building had just beaten the Bank of the Manhattan Company's skyscraper on Wall Street, and the 102-story Empire State Building, finished in 1931, would top them all until the 1970s. Smith guided the enterprise to completion under budget and then through difficult financial times (it was known as the "Empty State Building" throughout the 1930s) to eventual leasing success after World War II. Built on the rise of Murray Hill at Fifth Avenue and 34th Street, as yet unblocked by other giant structures, it is the world's most famous skyscraper, an icon of the city, and a magnificent visual landmark dominating the skyline north of Washington Square.

Only one lower Fifth Avenue plot fell to business use in the 1920s when the eight-story Macmillan Building was erected in 1925, replacing 60 and 62 Fifth Avenue at the northwest corner of Twelfth Street, property once owned by Thomas Fortune Ryan. A stripped classical design by the architects Carrère & Hastings and Shreve & Lamb (the precursor firm to Shreve, Lamb & Harmon, which was responsible for the Empire State Building), the new structure was actually meant to be the base for a much taller edifice to be built by the publisher Macmillan when needed. It remains, without the addition, as the headquarters of the Forbes publishing company. Twelfth Street still acts as a barrier between residential Fifth Avenue and trade from the north.

Over on University Place, a turnaround was in progress. The street was a commercial backwater when the Sailors' Snug Harbor trust, with the help of more sympathetic zoning, spurred new residential interest with its East Eighth Street and Washington Mews development in 1915. After the war, in 1919, the trust hired a Beaux Arts–trained architect, Harvey Wiley Corbett, to continue residential construction on its Manhattan property. Corbett had previously designed office buildings, churches, municipal facilities, and memorials, and this trust commission was his first foray into apartment-house design.

On the site that formerly held the financier James Brown's mansion at the northeast corner of University Place and Ninth Street, a commercial building was razed to make way for Corbett's pleasant ten-story building, sheathed in tan brick and frosted with picturesque Spanish Renaissance details, including tiers of wrought-iron Juliet balconies. It opened in 1923, occupying 41–43 University Place, but the building is now numbered and known as 29 East Ninth Street. Using many of the design principles employed for the University Place apartment house, Corbett went on to redo much of the long block between East Ninth and Tenth Streets, from University Place to Broadway: 33–45 East Ninth Street in 1925 and 38–58 East Tenth Street in 1928. His success was soon followed by other major residential construction in the area.

In 1926, in addition to Emery Roth's One University Place and Devonshire House, a 12-story redbrick apartment house replaced an office building covering the entire west blockfront between East Ninth and Tenth Streets. Another, similar in height and design, replaced three more business structures on the northwest corner of East Tenth Street, and in 1929, a 12-story apartment house of brown, gold, red, and orange brick rose on what had been the site of the Schermerhorn mansion on the northeast corner of East Twelfth Street. The Albert Hotel, which at the turn of the century had added a 12-story Beaux Arts section on University Place, joined the 1920s boom with a six-story annex in redbrick and stone on the northeast corner of East Tenth Street. These warm masonry apartment buildings of the 1920s completely changed the character of University Place from a dingy commercial street to a cozy corner of the Village; conversion of the remaining commercial buildings to apartment dwellings continues today (fig. 6.5).

On Broadway, only two new buildings were erected in the district during the 1920s. At the northwest corner of East Tenth Street, diagonally across from Wanamaker's flourishing enterprise, the 16-story Brittany Hotel was built in 1928–29 by the architectural firm of Farrar & Watmough. Its redbrick facades with 40-pane casement windows and neo-Gothic terra-cotta detailing complemented both Grace Church across the street and the recently built apartment houses on University Place. Up Broadway, at the southwest corner of Fourteenth Street facing Union Square, Emery Roth's 23-story Union Building was also built in 1928–29. A mediocre work, the stark buff-brick office tower replaced the landmark cast-iron Domestic Sewing Machine Building of 1872, a particularly unfortunate development considering the site's prominent location.

Of all the neighborhood changes in the 1920s, by far the most spectacular was the building of the 27-story skyscraper apartment-hotel known as One Fifth Avenue. It was designed by Harvey Wiley Corbett of Helmle, Corbett & Harrison in 1927, the banner year of the Roaring Twenties—Babe Ruth slammed 60 homers, Ford introduced the Model A, *The Jazz Singer* electrified movie audiences with its talking and singing, 268 productions opened on Broadway, and Lindbergh flew across the Atlantic. The hotel replaced the

venerable houses running from 1 to 7 Fifth Avenue between Washington
Mews and East Eighth Street. The land belonged to the Sailors' Snug Harbor
trust, and the developer, Joseph Siegel, probably picked Corbett to satisfy the
trustees and calm nearby residents; Corbett was, after all, already a proven success in the neighborhood.

While One Fifth Avenue was under construction, Lindbergh's flight
earned the proprietor of one of its neighbors, the Brevoort Hotel, a place in
aviation history. In 1919, Raymond Orteig, an aviation enthusiast, offered
$25,000 to the first pilot who could fly solo across the Atlantic. Before Charles
Lindbergh took his chance on winning the money, other men tried but failed
to complete the flight, and some died in the attempt. Orteig eventually re-
gretted the idea of the prize because of the lives lost, but after Lindbergh's triumphant return from Paris and the ticker-tape parade in Manhattan, Orteig
gave the Lone Eagle a grand reception at the Brevoort on June 16, 1927. There,
with Orville Wright in attendance, Lindbergh received his prize.

In less talented hands One Fifth Avenue might have been a fiasco, but
Corbett designed a romantic tower that rose to acclaim, even though it dominated the whole environs of Washington Square (fig. 6.6). Designed in the
same eclectic mode employed by Roth and others, the building was graced
with subtle Greek- and Gothic-inspired detailing consistent with that of

nearby houses and churches. However, the scale and height of the structure
(One Fifth Avenue was the tallest building between City Hall Park and Madison Square until the 1960s), as well as its sensitive site, required creative massing of the upper stories that would soar alone above its neighbors. Corbett's
solution has a base, a middle, and then a series of setback masses capped by a
tower, with each section possessing a different significance depending on one's
distance from the structure. A singular combination of materials was chosen
to integrate these parts, creating a masterpiece of contextual design.

To passersby, the four-story limestone and granite base is the "building"
most commonly experienced. Its facade maintains the wall plane, and its fenestration and profile are a continuation of the adjacent East Eighth Street row
that had been the Sailors' Snug Harbor trust's 1915 residential development.
Limestone panels extending up another story referred to both the stairwell
towers of the Eighth Street row and the neighboring five-story Brevoort Hotel. Corbett took other cues from nearby buildings. At the corners he placed
dentil courses that repeated those on the cornice of the John Taylor Johnston
mansion across Fifth Avenue. Corbett connected these courses with a row of
pointed arches echoing the strong Gothic Revival details on the houses diagonally opposite One Fifth, between Eighth and Ninth Streets, and on the two
Gothic Revival churches further up the avenue. His rows of Juliet balconies,
read horizontally, picked up the roof balustrades of the Washington Square
North buildings when viewed from the square. In addition, Corbett's decorative iron window guards on the ground floor provided a visual continuity with

the iron fences that lined properties up and across the avenue when One Fifth was built.

Two large doorways facing Fifth Avenue comprise the base's primary ornamentation. Their massive granite frames and moldings hint at the Washington Square Arch, and the doorway lanterns with quatrefoil motifs are a link to those on the nearby Church of the Ascension. Inside, a grand, double-height lobby (extremely rare in New York) featuring monumental Doric columns forms a temple-like interior befitting the architectural importance of the building.

From a longer street perspective, particularly looking down Fifth Avenue to the square, the midsection of the building becomes prominent, its sixteenth-floor setback corresponding to the cornice line of the neighboring apartment houses. Here, Corbett used buff-gray brick with vertical accents in white, black, and brown. He reached back to the ancient technique of trompe l'oeil painting, using these colored bricks to simulate Greek pilasters and Gothic buttresses for the major decoration of the section—thus transforming a brick box into a marvel of subtle architectural illusion.

Gothic effects predominate. Chamfered corners provide some relief from the middle section's box-like form and cleverly create the impression of turrets guarding the corners of the building. These decorations become real turrets with crenellated parapets above the sixteenth floor. Below, the dentil courses and vertical stripes of white or black brick headers outline the faux turrets. Half-panels of limestone at the point where they abut the turret edges enhance the effect by making it appear that part of the panel is hidden by a real wall projection. Extending the motif, Corbett's next illusion was one he had successfully used in his 1916 Bush Terminal Building tower on West 42nd Street—vertical stripes of white (sunshine) and black (shadow) bricks, laid together to simulate angled buttress projections from the facade. At the parapet level, these trompe l'oeil buttresses terminate in pointed black and white terra-cotta extensions to enhance their three-dimensional quality, although some of them continue upward a full story as brick piers, appearing to turn into flying buttresses. Near the top, high-relief terra-cotta and brick battlements line the roof. Real gargoyle waterspouts placed at the sixteenth-floor setback clinch the effects.

Corbett's interesting and subtle deployment of window tiers as pilasters, complete with bases and capitals, were in total harmony with the area's Greek Revival heritage. For the pilaster shaft, each window spandrel was made to look like a projecting panel. The effect was achieved by putting a two-inch slate windowsill and a vertical stripe of black brick on one side to create the illusion of a shadow. A white grout line on the other side of the spandrel, coupled with brown brick for the spandrel area, endows the entire tier with the faint suggestion of being a raised pilaster shaft. This faux shaft rises to a parapet, where it is crowned with a real capital composed of a small pair of slightly projecting blind brick arches and a coping-stone abacus. On the primary north, south, and west faces of the building, the Juliet balconies and limestone decoration form the bases of the trompe l'oeil pilasters. On the back (the eastern side) of the building, these pilasters extend upward over large windowless areas of the facade. Above the twenty-third-floor setback, the north and south turret-like sections on the east face each have a single faux pilaster. Here Corbett achieves the projecting-shaft effect by using brown brick and by defining the southern edge of each shaft with a stripe of white bricks, simulating a real pilaster edge lighted by the sun in the northern hemisphere.

The massing of the setbacks and tower section above the sixteenth floor offers a different view to the observer. Set among the neighborhood's low-scale buildings, One Fifth's tower evokes memories of a European town cathedral, a mountaintop castle, or a lighthouse on a cliff, or even visions of Count Dracula. This resemblance was more pronounced in the early decades of One Fifth's existence, when it had working lights, or "eyes," atop its chimney. (Damaged by lightning, they were removed in the early 1960s.)

One Fifth opened on January 1, 1928. Although there were some scattered expressions of nostalgia for the original buildings, it was almost universally acclaimed as a wonderful addition to the cityscape. The critic H. I. Brock wrote later that year:

> With the sun shining on the big upstanding thing and touching it up with pale yellow against a blue sky that not all the modern invasion of coal smoke can keep it from being our occasional canopy; with the same sun warming the old red bricks; we have an entirely new and very handsome spectacle down in this heart of the city's elder and outgrown fashion. Another fine view is that at night, with the mass looming steeply against the stars or against the scudding clouds revealed by the city's upward glare. Enormous and theatrical the dark bulk seems from the cobbled way of the Mews below, bordered with little houses which once were the stables of the rich folk who set the measured pace of that elder fashion, and in which now rules the *new* fashion of Bohemianism *de luxe*.[3]

Brock was so taken with One Fifth that he put a drawing of it on the cover of his 1929 chronicle of the city, *New York Is Like This*. Even before construction was finished it became a subject for artists, and the building has remained so ever since. The view over the arch from the square has been photographed so often and has appeared on so many postcards that in iconic value it joins the Statue of Liberty, the Empire State Building, the Brooklyn Bridge, and a handful of other notable sights in defining the city. With the addition of the Two Fifth Avenue and Brevoort apartment houses in the 1950s, some of the historical references to One Fifth's architectural details are gone, and coal smoke has obscured the trompe l'oeil additions, but surprisingly much remains visible and intact after 70-plus years of sitting in the maelstrom of Manhattan's development.

At the time Corbett designed One Fifth, he was well aware of the Art Deco style permeating the decorative arts and architecture. He proved this, perhaps for the benefit of his students at Columbia University, as one commentator suggested, by simultaneously designing a sister building to One Fifth—the Master Apartments at 103rd Street and Riverside Drive. This apartment house, with about the same overall dimensions and massing as One Fifth, is pure Art Deco without a trace of historical reference and is a fascinating building in its own right. Art Deco, though, was one of several breakaway architectural movements in the 1920s—like de Stijl in Holland, Constructivism in Russia, the Bauhaus in Germany—that would lead to the dominant International Style, with its stark simplicity, after World War II.

Ads for rentals at One Fifth, in the fledgling *New Yorker* magazine and elsewhere, played up its location in the midst of the city's foremost cultural center. One Fifth hovered over both the working-artist quarters in MacDougal Alley and the haute-bohemian studios of Washington Mews (fig. 6.7). It also stood on the corner of Eighth Street, the main street of the burgeoning artists' community. Close by were two of the best spots for seeing the leading developments in American and European art in the 1920s: Albert E. Gallatin's Gallery of Living Art and Gertrude Vanderbilt Whitney's Studio and Club. A block away from One Fifth, in December 1927, Gallatin opened his gallery in NYU's building off the northeast corner of Washington Square. Gallatin, an NYU trustee, was the great-grandson of Albert Gallatin, an NYU founder and a cabinet officer in the Jefferson and Madison administrations. The free-admission gallery featured a changing exhibition of Gallatin's collection of paintings by European modernists, most famously his landmark works by Pablo Picasso, Fernand Léger, Joan Miró, Giorgio di Chirico, Henri Matisse, Piet Mondrian, and Georges Braque. Gallatin's gallery was the first public art institution to be readily accessible to both artists and the general public, staying open in the evenings as late as nine or ten o'clock. Vanguard artists haunted Gallatin's collection; among the regulars were the future giants of the New York School—Arshile Gorky, Philip Guston, Hans Hofmann, Jackson Pollock, and Willem de Kooning.

In 1923 Whitney had moved the Whitney Studio Club to 10 West Eighth Street next door to her Studio galleries at No. 8 from its original quarters on West Fourth Street. These spaces were the nucleus of the Whitney Museum of American Art, which would be founded in 1930. The core group of exhibitors, most of them realist painters and representational sculptors—John Sloan, Jo Davidson, Jerome Meyers, Joseph Stella, Guy Pène du Bois, Rockwell Kent, Edward Hopper, William Glackens, Stuart Davis, Robert Laurent, Charles Demuth, and Maurice Prendergast—were joined in the mid-1920s by a younger generation. Among the newer Whitney Club members were Gaston Lachaise, Reuben Nakian, John Flannagan, George Ault, Yasuo Kuniyoshi, Isabel Bishop, and Reginald Marsh.

Further down at 52 West Eighth Street, the International Style in architecture made an eye-popping appearance in Manhattan when the Film Guild Cinema, designed by Frederick Kiesler, was erected there in 1929 (fig. 6.8).

(It was later renamed the 8th Street Playhouse.) Kiesler, a Romanian-born avant-garde architect, painter, designer, and poet had been part of the de Stijl group when his theater designs were exhibited in the Paris Exposition of Arts Décoratifs of 1925. Visiting the exposition was Jane Heap, still an editor of *The Little Review*, who was impressed with Kiesler's work. She wrote to Manhattan's Theatre Guild to help her magazine's efforts to bring Kiesler's exhibition to New York with the architect as its director. He accepted an invitation under the combined sponsorship of the Theatre Guild, the Provincetown Players, and the Greenwich Village Theater (on Sheridan Square), and moved to New York City in 1926.

Soon after setting up his studio, Kiesler was approached by Simeon Gould, who was planning the first theater dedicated to film. Movies were on the point of becoming talkies, and Gould envisioned a new kind of house that did away with the proscenium-arch stage used for theatrical productions. Opening to praise in 1929 on a site previously occupied by stables, Kiesler's 485-seat theater featured a dramatic interior with a round cat's-eye screen, and a striking

Mondrian-like grid for a facade that was unlike anything else in the city. The venture floundered financially in the worsening economy, and the building was sold and altered, but it remained a beloved local movie house for the next 60 years. Today it's a video rental store.

In 1931 the neighborhood and the city got another early taste of the International Style before the construction industry virtually closed down during the Depression. A group of Columbia professors with new ideas for invigorating higher education had banded together to establish a less hidebound institution of their own in 1918. Their appropriately named New School building went up at 66 West Twelfth Street where four townhouses once stood (fig. 6.9). (Originally called the New School for Social Research, its official name today is New School University.) Joseph Urban, a Viennese-trained architect and stage designer who had created some of the jazziest theaters and sets of the twenties, including Ziegfeld's Theater and Follies, was the founders' choice for their school in late 1929. Urban's Bauhaus-style design, containing a stunning oval theater that exemplified his talents, survives.

The school also was able to secure the talents of two vigorous artists, Thomas Hart Benton and José Clemente Orozco, to paint murals for the boardroom and cafeteria. Benton's series of ten paintings, showing a dynamic America at work in the industrial belts and the agricultural heartland, is considered to be his masterpiece; it celebrates and satirizes our mores and customs. Orozco, one of the painters at the forefront of the Mexican mural movement, created five panels with scenes of scientists, artists, laborers, soldiers, and peasants of all races combining forces against social and political oppression. The New School sold the Benton murals in 1984 for $3.4 million to the Equitable Life Assurance Society, which displays them in the lobby of its midtown building at 1290 Sixth Avenue. The Orozcos remain in their original location in the New School; the institution itself, although no longer a shocking visual presence on the street, continues to thrive and expand.

The New School, which would later gain enormous cultural significance because of its brilliant teachers drawn from talented émigrés escaping the worsening conditions in Europe, had been built near Sixth Avenue, where elevated trains still ran, for easy access by its students. Sixth Avenue provided convenient transportation to other parts of the city, and its local bars and cafeterias would become important in the rise of the New York School artists. Development along this major city artery in the 1920s and 1930s had a substantial impact on the future of the entire Washington Square district.

Mass transit was also important to the Jefferson Market Courthouse and the jail on Tenth Street, whose penal facilities for women had become appallingly overcrowded. To alleviate the deplorable conditions, the city hired Sloan & Robertson to design a new jail to be called the Women's House of Detention (fig. 6.10). The architects complied with a stylish 13-story structure covering the old jail and market-building site in 1931. It could have passed for a fine Art Deco apartment house, although the interior sported the latest in jail-

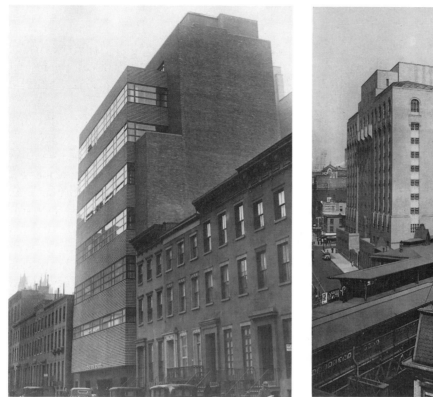

FIG. 6.9 (left) The New
FIG. 6.9 (left) The New
School shortly after its erection,
ca. 1931. It and Kiesler's Playhouse were pioneers in the
trend toward International
Style architecture in the city.
Photographer unknown. Courtesy of Underwood Archive.

FIG. 6.10 (right) Women's
House of Detention, ca. 1933.
The structure crowded the
Jefferson Market Court House;
the Eighth Street el stop
and the Alden Hotel are in the
foreground. Photographer
unknown. Courtesy of the New
York Public Library.

house technology. The prison overshadowed the Jefferson Market Courthouse building until 1976, when the prison was razed to make way for the public garden that is there today.

Earlier in the flush 1920s, the city had planned to replace the Sixth Avenue
el with a subway and also build another subway along Eighth Avenue. Part of
the Eighth Avenue line would run under Greenwich Avenue to join the Sixth
Avenue subway at a huge new multilevel underground station at Sixth Avenue
and West Fourth Street. Massive demolition of buildings and consequent dis-
location of people were imperative to bring about such a huge reconfiguration
of the transit system. Even though earlier street extensions, such as those
involving Lafayette Street and Seventh and Sixth Avenues, had been rudely
disruptive to those affected, the community had not yet been jolted enough by
the ill effects of gargantuan public works projects to complain. In the latest extension of Sixth Avenue to Canal Street, which commenced in 1924, 165 buildings were truncated or torn down and 10,000 tenants evicted.

There was no public outcry when hundreds more buildings were razed on
the east side of Sixth Avenue and the south side of Houston Street. (The station and its side-by-side local and express tracks required the extra width. The
cost of demolishing homes and businesses was less than the money required
for the much deeper cuts needed to accommodate local-over-express tracks,
such as the ones on the Lexington Avenue lines.) Stanford White's Cable
Building at Broadway and the Puck Building at Crosby Street were mercifully
spared, as the steamroller otherwise ruthlessly demolished Houston Street all

the way to the East River. Sixth Avenue later recovered with new buildings and a delightful series of mini-parks on its destroyed eastside lots below Eighth Street. Houston Street, though, became a multilane east-west thoroughfare, with a strip of excess land south of the roadway. That strip became a Hooverville, covered with the tents and shacks of the homeless during the Depression.

One positive result of the Sixth Avenue extension was the reclaiming of the Minetta Lane–Minetta Street section (the Minettas) of the Village for moderate-income housing (fig. 6.11). This piece of land at the southwestern corner of the Fifteenth Ward had been built up in the 1820s with modest homes for working people of small means. But by 1900 it had deteriorated into one of the worst slums in the city, and the local settlement house, Greenwich House, began lobbying the city for its clearance. Mary K. Simkhovitch, an influential charity matron, ran Greenwich House, and her campaign attracted realtors and moral enforcers eager to disperse the "unsavory crowd," which allegedly included prostitutes and some 2,000 blacks. They wanted the buildings razed for the Sixth Avenue extension to include all of the Minetta-area houses as well.[4]

However, Vincent Pepe, a local realtor with an office close to the Minettas at 40 Washington Square South, had other plans. Observing the recent success of the MacDougal-Sullivan Gardens project a little to the south, as well as the residential development northeast of the square promoted by the Sailors' Snug Harbor trust, in 1925–26 he sponsored the remodeling of a core group of 13 of the century-old Minetta dwellings into modern apartments. This venture was a success, too, and with other properties on the street and lane reclaimed, the Minettas have been preserved as a quaint bit of old New York.

While Pepe was at work on the Minettas, Columbia University was acquiring the full block between Sullivan and MacDougal Streets, from Washington Square South to West Third Street, for a future law school. In 1924,

while holding the property, Columbia renovated the remains of the once-elegant, marble-fronted Fourth Street row, from Nos. 43 through 47, with a sensitive design that helped preserve the low-rise picturesque quality of the neighborhood southwest of the square. One of the first tenants in the remodeled houses, occupying a small studio at No. 47 in 1925, was the 21-year-old painter Arshile Gorky. He had come to New York via Turkish Armenia, Providence, Rhode Island, and Boston; he would later emerge as one of the most respected artists of the New York School and become a seminal influence on the generation immediately behind him. (In the early 1930s Gorky moved to 36 Union Square.)

As the Depression in New York reached its nadir in 1932, the plight of the city's numerous unemployed artists became desperate. The market for artworks had plummeted, decorative work on public and private projects virtually ceased, and the success of the camera and radio had devastated opportunities for magazine and newspaper illustrators. Relief for artists, from both governmental and private initiatives, began in that terrible year. New York's governor, Franklin Delano Roosevelt, authorized a special work-relief program for New York artists through the sponsorship of art classes. This program provided work for artist-teachers and free instruction for young artists who couldn't have afforded it otherwise, but only about 100 artists benefited from this early relief. Far more important was the beginning of the biannual (spring and fall) Washington Square Outdoor Art Exhibit in the spring of 1932 (fig. 6.12). It was organized by the Artists' Aid Committee, a prestigious

FIG. 6.13 Joseph Delaney, *Jackson Pollock*, 1932. Pollock took part in the first Washington Square outdoor show. Chalk on paper, 10″ × 7¼″. Courtesy of Stephen Naifeh and Gregory White Smith and the Estate of Joseph Delaney.

private group headed by Vernon C. Porter, director of the Riverside Museum. The committee consisted of Gertrude Vanderbilt Whitney; Juliana Force, director of the Whitney Museum of American Art; Herbert E. Winlock and Bryson Burroughs, director and curator of paintings, respectively, of the Metropolitan Museum of Art; William Henry Fox, director of the Brooklyn Museum; Alfred H. Barr Jr., director of the Museum of Modern Art; and Edward G. Steinert, secretary of the Washington Square Association. The show provided a forum for selling works of art and finding work. By the show's third run, reported the *New York Times* in the spring of 1933, 500 exhibiting artists had sold 486 pieces for a total of $4,158, and had received commissions for commercial work and portraits of pets. According to the *New York Times*'s "Gallery-Goer's Week" column of May 7, 1933, the Washington Square event deserved to be visited every bit as much as the other galleries around town:

> On the south side of Washington Square[,] Art came back to its ancient bohemian dwelling with such gusto that it overflowed into side streets, north, south, and west. Near the square you may find three adjacent artists, one of whom will do your profile portrait in pencil for as little as 50 cents; his next neighbor in the sidewalk show is asking $150 for some bright oils and smooth watercolors; the third indicates by a hand-lettered sign that suggestions of barter instead of cash will not fall on unheeding ears. . . . For some of these devotees of art the open-air show is a grim necessity; for some it is a lark. There is every variety of work. And the whole sprawling, effervescent show is something you must not miss.[5]

MacDougal Alley was one of the streets on the exhibition itinerary, and in the initial show of 1932 a visitor could have seen 21-year-old Jackson Pollock's work there in the artist's first public showing (fig. 6.13). His early representational pictures, going for five to ten dollars apiece, all went unsold. Born in Cody, Wyoming, Pollock had come to New York in 1930 from Los Angeles. His now legendary and brilliant trajectory in art—from an apprenticeship based on Picasso, Miró, Wassily Kandinsky, Hofmann, Surrealism, and the Mexican muralists to an apogee of shocking originality in design by dripping, pouring, and spattering paint on the canvas—was key in making New York the center of world art. In the 1930s, though, Pollock, Gorky, and their cadre of pioneering peers needed work relief, and they soon received it on an unprecedented scale.

Roosevelt, elected president in 1931, and Fiorello La Guardia, elected mayor in 1933, proved to be a godsend to the city and its artistic community.

FIG. 6.14 Streetcar tracks being taken up on West Eighth Street by WPA workers, 1936. These federal projects were a boon to the local artist community during the Depression. WPA Photograph. Federal Art Project. Courtesy of the New York Public Library.

Both were sympathetic to the idea that artists, as well as writers, actors, and musicians—all hit hard by the Depression—were as deserving of assistance as other productive workers, and they created relief systems for them over considerable opposition by conservatives (fig. 6.14). Roosevelt and the Democratic congress controlled the relief funds, and La Guardia, although Republican, proved to be a magnificently effective advocate for all of New York City's distressed people. By 1936, writes George J. Lankevich in *American Metropolis,* he had "so successfully played the bureaucratic and personal game" that one-seventh of all WPA spending was allocated to his city (with one-twentieth of the country's population). "[I]t was this infusion of funding that lifted New York out of the Depression."[6]

New York artists benefited from the unexpected federal largess. By 1936 Pollock and his fellow artists earned $23.86 a week for unsupervised work, at a time when saleswomen in a five-and-dime store earned $10.80 for a 50-hour week. Many other unskilled workers made as little as seven dollars a week, and professional men were encamped in public parks and sleeping in the subways. Unintentionally and amazingly, the Federal Art Project of the WPA also created a fraternity among these highly individualistic and competitive artists. With a reduced need for part-time work, artists spent time with one another in WPA offices, on the job, at the Artists Union (a lobbying group), and in lofts and cheap cafeterias. Indeed, the camaraderie and shared experience among the Abstract Expressionists was considered by some an informal graduate program in art. Most of the artists who would become the trailblazers of Abstract Expressionism, such as Gorky, Pollock, de Kooning, William Baziotes, Mark Rothko, Adolph Gottlieb, and Guston, could de-

FIG. **6.15** The Whitney Museum of American Art, shortly after its opening, 1931. It was a dramatic addition to the streetscape. The tame architectural combination of modern and historical details, however, lacked the shock value and the flagrantly anticontextual quality of the Kiesler building down the block, or of Joseph Urban's New School on West Twelfth Street. Nevertheless, it initiated the principle that the architecture of contemporary art museums should reflect the same creative energy as the works inside. WPA Photograph. Federal Art Project. Courtesy of NYC Municipal Archives.

vote their energies to art with little distraction because the WPA temporarily freed them from financial anxiety.

Although the WPA hired them as artists, the New York School was as yet unappreciated by the established art world and virtually unknown outside of it. These artists exhibited in the Washington Square Outdoor Art Exhibit or in a sprinkling of galleries, if they showed their work at all. Generally they served as their own viewers, critics, and teachers. A few professional affiliations that included these artists, such as the American Abstract Artists group, put on their own shows and valiantly fought for exhibitions in galleries and museums, with limited success. Not until the 1950s, when the market for their art began to take off, did the New York School artists branch out from their loose-knit community that for 20 years had been centered on Eighth Street, between Sixth Avenue and the Bowery. Their studios and haunts were on or near Eighth Street, where rents were low for century-old rundown housing, particularly on East Eighth Street, which had been ravaged by commercial activity. The sale of a painting for a typical price of $50, a rare event for the group, could pay the monthly rent for a single artist, leaving $15 for art supplies and meals.

In 1931, the Whitney Museum opened at 8–14 West Eighth Street. In designing the Whitney Museum (fig. 6.15), the architectural firm of Miller & Noel was forced to retain the upper floors as they were on account of the fenestration of the original Eighth Street houses, but they had to deal with several problems in order to do so. Their renovation scheme centered on integrating the discordant facades, but No. 14's windows were set on too divergent a level to be accommodated, so only the exteriors of Nos. 8, 10, and 12 could be included in the refurbishment. *New York 1930* describes the solution. They unified the outsides of those three houses by sheathing them with a salmon-pink stucco "set off by plain white stone lintels and sills. The color was inspired by the buildings of Marrakesh, the 'Rose City' of Morocco." A pair of strong band courses further integrates the design elements: the lower one, with vertical grooves, separates the rather unadorned upper sections from the heavily ornamented ground floor. "Fluted white marble columns flank the aluminum and red Numidian marble main entrance," while a white metal eagle in bas-relief crouches protectively above, "announcing the museum's American theme."[7] A geometric-patterned sidewalk installed in front and spanning the length of the new facade served as an apt welcome for the enterprise. (It was restored in 2001.)

FIG. **6.16** Edward Hopper, *Roofs, Washington Square*, 1926. Hopper's painting of the Row's rooftops. Hopper's style is one of exceptional clarity and one with instantly recognizable subject matter simplified and distanced just enough that the abstract pattern of shapes and color in a painting stand on an equal visual footing with the subject matter at hand. Courtesy of the Carnegie Museum of Art, Pittsburgh; Bequest of Mr. and Mrs. James H. Beal.

While the Metropolitan Museum of Art specialized in the art of the past, and the Museum of Modern Art (MoMA), founded in 1929, then equated modernism with European art, the Whitney was a citadel of American realism. This genre fit nicely with the national mood of introspection and the cultural xenophobia common during the Depression, and it was also the kind of art looked on most favorably by the WPA art projects. American artists from both the Robert Henri and Alfred Stieglitz camps found a home at the Whitney, but the budding local avant-garde remained outsiders until after World War II.

Edward Hopper, a Whitney artist and the quintessential Realist painter of twentieth-century America, lived and worked in the studio building at 3 Washington Square North for more than 40 years. He had first learned to paint under Henri. Then, after studying briefly in Paris and visiting other parts of Europe between 1906 and 1910, he refined his own distinct style (fig. 6.16). Hopper's images capture a certain look and feel of America, in the city, country, and seaside. Using the play of strong, sometimes searing light on the myriad fascinating complexities and contrasts in the urban fabric, particularly New York's, or showing the stark sunlit contrast between nature and manmade objects (a solitary house, a row of buildings, a gas pump, or a lighthouse), his scenes are frozen in time. They haunt the viewer's imagination. Hopper supported himself as an illustrator until the mid-1920s, when his paintings began to sell. His canvases became popular and influential in the early 1930s. An avid moviegoer himself, Hopper, more than any other American artist, has inspired generations of illustrators, photographers, and particularly filmmakers with his work. Alfred Hitchcock's *Psycho* (1960), Terrence Malick's *Days of Heaven* (1978), and Herbert Ross's *Pennies from Heaven* (1981) are a few of the films influenced by Hopper.

By the mid-1930s, the feisty realist painter Thomas Hart Benton had be-

come one of the country's most celebrated artists. Benton, a resident of 10 East Eighth Street (part of the row remodeled in 1915), had received an amazing amount of attention in newspapers and magazines for his important mural cycles for the New School (1930), the Whitney Museum (1932), and the State of Indiana (1933). His fame reached even loftier heights when *Time* ran his self-portrait on its December 24, 1934, cover. Benton, originally from Missouri, left for a teaching position at the Kansas City Art Institute soon afterward, but he continued to be influential for the rest of the decade (fig. 6.17). Teaching in New York, he had already instructed Jackson Pollock, who would become his most famous student.

Benton, like Hopper, had studied in Paris (he lived in France from 1908 to 1911) and imbibed the heady brew of early modernism. Moving to New York in 1912, he painted, designed movie sets, and taught. In 1927 he began teaching at the Art Students League, where Charles Pollock, Jackson's older brother, was studying. Jackson followed Charles as a Benton pupil in 1930, while his teacher was in the middle of the New School mural commission. Benton regarded Jackson as a friend as well as a student, often sharing his home and meals with the young painter at his apartment on Hudson Street near Abington Square. (Benton and his family moved to Eighth Street after the artist attained some material success in 1933.) In Benton's course, "Life Composition, Painting and Drawing," Pollock learned how to draw the human figure and how to analyze reproductions of late Renaissance and Baroque paintings, breaking down the images into cubes, volumes, and linear movements. One of Benton's biographers, Henry Adams, referring to Pollock's later abstract work, claims that "thanks to Pollock, Benton had the pleasure of knowing that his compositional theories would play a central role in the ongoing development of modern art."[8]

Indeed, Pollock's early representational work looked like Benton's, and critics have also noted Benton's influence on Pollock's early abstract paintings. In later years Pollock denied Benton's impact on his mature work, and Benton insisted that the only thing he taught Pollock was how to drink a fifth a day. Despite these public denials there was a deeper and mutually affecting relationship between the two painters that went beyond Benton's artistic influence on Pollock. According to Adams, Pollock imitated "Benton's western persona, his macho posturing, his gruffness toward women, [and] his chauvinistic Americanism."[9]

In 1935, the year Benton left New York, Jackson Pollock moved into the fifth-floor walkup apartment just vacated by his brother Charles at 46 East Eighth Street, between Greene and Mercer Streets. The rent was $35 per month, which he shared with another brother, Sande, until 1942, when Jackson's lover, the painter Lee Krasner, moved in. At the time, the Sailors' Snug Harbor trust was demolishing the old houses on the southern blocks east of University Place in anticipation of improved economic conditions for new construction. No. 46 was an exception. This once fine residence, home to the Century Association in the mid-1800s, lasted, with its neighbor at No. 44, until the current apartment house at Nos. 44–58 was built in 1950. Five years before the building was torn down, Pollock and Krasner married and moved to Springs, Long Island, but during his ten-year stay on Eighth Street in the 1930s and 1940s, it became a hotbed of Abstract Expressionist activity. Pollock's work changed radically, starting him on the path to a renown far surpassing Benton's.

West of the Whitney Museum, 52 West Eighth Street was a bastion of support for Abstract Expressionism. Here was the studio school founded by Hans Hofmann, who trained many young artists in the basics of painting techniques and brought to them a deep appreciation of the new European art movements. Born in Munich in 1880, Hofmann had lived in Paris from 1904 to 1914, where he was a student alongside Matisse and became friendly with Picasso and other important Fauves and Cubists. In 1915 he established in Munich his own school, which was modeled on the one Matisse had opened in Paris.

By 1930 Hofmann's reputation had grown, and he was invited to the University of California at Berkeley as a guest professor. With the rise of Hitler in his native country, Hofmann decided to stay in the United States and accepted a teaching position at the Art Students League in New York. Feeling uncomfortable with the strong realist tradition there, he opened his own school downtown, first temporarily at 52 West Ninth Street in 1936, and then at 52 West Eighth Street from 1938 to 1958. His teaching studio was in a room at the front of the third floor of the 8th Street Playhouse, an appropriate setting for Hofmann's brand of art. Although the dozen or so major figures of the New York School never studied with Hofmann (when his classes began, they were nearly all in their middle 20s and early 30s, well past the age of apprenticeship), his school was an important art center that constantly drew visi-

FIG. 6.18 Sixth Avenue looking east on Eighth Street, Main Street of the New York School, showing the Waldorf Cafeteria (lower right), 1954. Photographer unknown. Courtesy of Hulton Archive / Getty Images.

tors. Hofmann's evening sessions, during which he offered impromptu lectures, were attended by neighborhood artists, who would then move on to continue their discussions at the Waldorf Cafeteria, situated around the corner at 394 Sixth Avenue. (Hofmann became Pollock and Krasner's next-door neighbor in the early 1940s when he and his wife moved into the top-floor apartment at 44 East Eighth Street.)

Although informal, the Waldorf Cafeteria was the first clubhouse of the New York School, where, "among the 'Village bums, delinquents, and cops,' artists could smoke, drink coffee, . . . and table-hop from argument to argument" (fig. 6.18). Some called it "the Waxworks" because of the eerie pallor its lighting cast on the patrons.[10] Built in 1942 as one in a chain, the cafeteria occupied a one-story commercial building, one door south of the Eighth Street corner, on land that had been cleared for the West Fourth Street subway station. It provided just the kind of nondescript place that the artists preferred for their social gatherings—there was nothing to attract outsiders. Better and cheaper food could be found at nearby restaurants, like Romany Marie's, which in the 1930s was located at 42 West Eighth Street. The proprietor was a colorful character who had been operating restaurants since before World War I, and she was a favorite of painters like John Sloan and Stuart Davis. Another inexpensive eatery was the Jumble Shop at 28 West Eighth, on the corner of MacDougal Street; it had murals painted by artists in exchange for meal credits, and the rear of the building had been the sculptor James Earle Fraser's studio on MacDougal Alley.

In addition to the Hofmann School the area was dotted with places involved with new art techniques and developments. Pollock, for instance, had studied sculpture in 1932 at Greenwich House in the early state relief program. Around the same time, he gained lithography experience at Theodore Wahl's

FIG. 6.19 East Eighth Street from the southeast corner of Greene Street, showing Nos. 35 and 39 (center with fire escape), ca. 1939. This was the epicenter of the New York School in the 1950s. The foreground sign marks the site location (block and lot number). Photographer unknown. Courtesy of NYC Municipal Archives.

printing workshop on Minetta Lane. In 1936, Pollock worked several months in David Alfaro Siqueiros's workshop at 5 West Fourteenth Street, learning how to use an airbrush and Duco paint, a commercial lacquer used on cars and for spraying large surfaces. Here Pollock also experimented with producing an image by placing a canvas on the floor and spattering on it paint from a stick, anticipating his later methods. (The three leading Mexican muralists, Orozco, Siqueiros, and Diego Rivera, were then all working in the United States.) Later in the 1940s, Pollock worked in Stanley William Hayter's Atelier 17 at 43 East Eighth Street, diagonally across from his apartment building, making prints and engravings. (The name "Atelier 17" came from Hayter's previous studio in Paris, which was at 17 rue Campagne Première.)

As the New York School artists' ideas coalesced into their distinctive styles, they organized more serious gatherings than cafeteria, restaurant, and studio chats. In 1948, William Baziotes, David Hare, Robert Motherwell, and Mark Rothko founded a school in a studio at 35 East Eighth Street, later simply dubbed Studio 35 (fig. 6.19). Barnett Newman joined a little later and, with Motherwell, set up a series of Friday evening lectures by advanced artists on such topics as subject matter, finish, titles, self-expression, community relations, museum patronage, and public awareness. The school closed in 1949 because of financial difficulties, and the studio was taken over by three professors from NYU's School of Art Education who used it to provide studio and exhibition space for their students. In 1949, two doors east at 39 West Eighth, another group of artists formed the Club—no one could come up with a better name. It grew out of the Hofmann School and Waldorf Cafeteria discussions, took in the original Studio 35 group, and through the 1950s remained the focal point of Abstract Expressionist activities. Members invited various speakers to participate, widening the range of lecture topics to include philosophy, social criticism, music, and literature. There were also parties in honor of artists who were having one-person shows or who were visiting from abroad, and for other creative figures, such as Dylan Thomas, on the occasion of his first trip to America.

After hours, or when the Club was not open, or just when a drink would help, the Cedar Street Bar (or the Cedars, as it was familiarly known) around the corner on University Place functioned as an unofficial Club annex. It occupied a corner of an old garment-maker's loft building and was another thoroughly drab and undistinguished hangout of the type preferred by the New York School crowd. Inside, the smoke-filled long room had a bar to one side, brass-studded leatherette booths, and slightly peeling, waiting-room green walls. The unambitious décor included some English sporting prints (the personal taste of one of the bar's operators), a couple of small fluorescent beer signs, stacked liquor bottles, and an unreliable wall clock. In the 1940s, mainly artists and their friends and students drank there with other neighborhood regulars. It was the kind of place where you could fall down drunk, hold a conversation, or even punch someone if a real or perceived insult called for it. Pollock, de Kooning, Franz Kline, Guston, and David Smith were legendary drinkers there. The poverty and raucous camaraderie found at the Cedars evoked the *vie de bohème* of the Village's past, piquing the interest of outsiders. It was Pollock, however, who was the bar's top star, and it was Pollock whose drunken antics in the early and mid-1950s would bring notoriety to the Cedars during its heyday.

If the New York School artists were invisible to the art establishment in the early 1940s, they were equally invisible to the average neighborhood resident or visitor. Indeed, despite the sometimes raucous goings-on in the Cedars and the Club, Eighth Street was regarded by many as a pleasant Main Street. "Present day Villagers come to Eighth Street to shop and window shop, to saunter, buy a paper, run into friends, stop for a cup of coffee," said *The Greenwich Village Guide,* a 1947 book put out by the *Villager,* the staid, local weekly paper.[11] Readers of the *Villager* could find notices of cake sales, weddings, births and deaths, recipes, business news, press releases, a column by a cat, and an occasional bit of excitement, such as in 1943, when it proudly reported Eleanor Roosevelt's leasing of an apartment at 29 Washington Square West in preparation for her husband's retirement after his term in office. Earlier, the local paper had been the *Quill,* which maintained some of the verve and irreverence of the district's pre–World War I bohemia in its gossipy items on local establishments and people, but it died along with the exuberance of the 1920s.

The novelist, philosopher, and feminist Simone de Beauvoir, however, saw

something more in Eighth Street. She was a guest at the Brevoort Hotel in 1947 and wrote that the whole neighborhood of the hotel was like a piece of her native Paris (fig. 6.20):

[O]n Eighth Street, it's moderately lively: you can stroll there as you stroll on the rue Bonaparte or the rue de Seine. I'm beginning to know the little shops one by one. There are many small bookstores where they sell rare books, antique shops, and jewelry stores whose display windows are full of embossed silver and turquoise from Santa Fe. Here, you find treasures worthy of good days at the flea market: antique taffetas, cloaks, and odd blouses and dresses of the sort the women artists of Montparnasse used to like unearthing near the Porte de Clignancourt, not long ago. There are also wide studded belts, whimsical sandals, rugs, jackets, and woven skirts from Mexico or Guatemala. It would be impossible to find these colorful and vividly beautiful objects in any uptown store. If I'm tired of walking, I sit down on one of the sunny benches in Washington Square: there are elderly women wistfully warming themselves, workers taking a rest, students—no doubt from the nearby university—studying or yawning. One can read as peacefully here as in the Luxembourg Gardens.[12]

Beauvoir didn't spot the New York School scene on Eighth Street during her brief stay in the city, but she did visit Peggy Guggenheim's daring gallery on 57th Street where Beauvoir found that "among the Americans, abstract painting seems to have the place of honor."[13]

Peggy Guggenheim was what the New York School needed most in the 1940s—an angel as their earlier peers had found in Gertrude Vanderbilt Whitney. This new patron of the avant-garde was the daughter of a copper-mining heir and a niece of Solomon R. Guggenheim, the collector whose Museum of Non-Objective Painting (later the Solomon R. Guggenheim Museum) had opened in 1939. Bored with her pampered life amid New York's Jewish upper crust, she fled to Europe in 1920 at the age of 22. Later in London, under no less a mentor than Marcel Duchamp, Guggenheim learned about Cubism, Surrealism, and abstract art, and she began collecting for a gallery there. After England entered the war, Guggenheim sailed with her belongings to New York early in 1941. She arrived with an entourage of fellow refugees, including the Surrealist painter, Max Ernst, with whom she shared a brief and tumultuous marriage. In 1942 she asked Frederick Kiesler to design the space for "Art of this Century," a combination museum and commercial gallery that would display her collection as well as exhibitions of European and American art. The installation, on the seventh floor of a building at 30 West 57th Street, was a knockout. "The only trouble," Guggenheim considered, "was that the décor rivaled the pictures."[14] (A gallery for Surrealism had lighting that alternately

spotlighted one side of the room and then the other at three-and-a-half-second intervals, as well as concave walls with pictures extended on wooden arms.) Works by European masters like Jean Arp, di Chirico, Alberto Giacometti, and Picasso were shown side by side with emerging New York School talents, including Pollock, de Kooning, Motherwell, Baziotes, Rothko, Gottlieb, and Clyfford Still. Guggenheim thus gave most of the Americans their first break (fig. 6.21).

The art establishment remained unimpressed, and it was to take the efforts of a young New York writer, Clement Greenberg, to turn critical opinion around and put New York on the cultural map. Greenberg, who had a degree in English literature from Syracuse University, began work as a salesman in his father's necktie firm. When the Depression put a crimp in the business, he began freelance writing and soon found he could make a living at it. By the late 1930s, he had shown enough talent to join the staff of the *Partisan Review*, which was just starting out as one of the "little" magazines publishing highbrow literature and opinion, independent of the Stalinist and Trotskyist politics then enveloping New York's intellectual circles. Greenberg also felt that he might become an artist and attended Hofmann's lectures during the 1938–39 school year. This education, together with the heated conversations among the writers and editors of the *Partisan Review*, provided him with a strong background for his later art criticism.

During the 1940s, Greenberg immersed himself in the artists' milieu around Eighth Street. In 1941 he met Krasner and Pollock on Eighth Street on the way to the studio of an artist whose work they had heard about but not seen. Greenberg joined them, thus beginning a long practice of studio visits in which his famous eye picked out the work of nearly all of the major mem-

FIG. **6.22** Lee Krasner Pollock,
Clement Greenberg, Helen
Frankenthaler, and Jackson
Pollock at Eddie Condon's jazz
club, 1951. Condon's was
located on West Third Street in
one of the buildings razed for
NYU's Bobst Library. When in
town, the Pollocks often stayed
with their artist-friend Alfonso
Ossorio at 9 MacDougal
Alley. Photographer unknown.
Courtesy of the John Gruen
Papers 1952–1993, Archives of
American Art, Smithsonian
Institution.

bers of the New York School (fig. 6.22). He frequented the Club and the
Cedars, and also dropped by the area jazz clubs like Eddie Condon's at 47 West
Third Street, the Open Door at 57 West Third, and the Five Spot at 5 Cooper
Square (between Fourth and Fifth Streets on the Bowery). Many artists pa-
tronized these as well.

By the late 1940s, Greenberg had moved into an apartment at 90 Bank
Street in the West Village. He was writing in *The Nation,* in which he had re-
viewed Peggy Guggenheim's shows, and in the *Partisan Review.* Between October 1947 and March 1948 he published three major articles in the *Partisan
Review* and in *Horizon,* a British cultural monthly, which were notable for
their trenchant advocacy of Abstract Expressionism and which captured the
mass media's attention. Within two months of the first article, *Time* scorn-
fully reported Greenberg's pronouncements in a one-column article entitled
"The Best?" Interest had been piqued, as *Time* and *Life* were then at their pinnacle of power in moving public opinion. Seven months after Greenberg's last
article, *Life* convened a round table among the art-world bigwigs to "clarify
the strange art of today." Ten months after that, on August 8, 1949, *Life* hit
the newsstands with a feature story on Pollock and a banner headline that
read "JACKSON POLLOCK—Is He the Greatest Living Painter in the United
States?" By asking the question, *Life* answered it.[15]

The setting was the cold war. America's young Central Intelligence
Agency (CIA), seeking to avoid controversy yet counter Soviet propaganda
and its state-controlled socialist-realism brand of art, began providing munificent covert support for Abstract Expressionism and other free-enterprise
achievements from America's vanguard. Working through Nelson A. Rockefeller, an early cold warrior whose personal fiefdom was MoMA, the agency
may have influenced Henry Luce, *Time/Life*'s chief and a MoMA trustee, in
running *Life*'s 1949 spread on Pollock. Also, MoMA's European exhibitions
and promotion of New York School artists in the 1950s, secretly bankrolled by
the CIA, surely boosted prospects for these artists and America's leadership in

the arts. Nevertheless, as Frances Stonor Saunders has recently concluded in her outstandingly researched book, *The Cultural Cold War: The CIA and the World of Arts and Letters:* "Abstract Expressionism, like jazz, was—is—a creative phenomenon existing independently and even, yes, triumphantly, apart from the political use which was made of it."[16]

Although Pollock had snared most of the limelight in 1949, Willem de Kooning was a close second in the Abstract Expressionist movement. Born in Holland, de Kooning had studied at the Rotterdam Academy of Fine Arts in the 1920s. Dreaming of America as the land of opportunity, he worked his way over on a steamer in 1926 and jumped ship in New York. While making a living at odd jobs, de Kooning frequented Village galleries and cafeterias, where he met Arshile Gorky, who became his friend and advisor. In the 1930s, while his style began evolving toward abstraction, de Kooning joined the New Deal mural program. He began exhibiting in group shows in the 1940s and was given his first one-person show at the Charles Egan Gallery in 1948. This exposure brought him increasing attention; Greenberg hailed de Kooning as "one of the four or five most important painters in the country."[17]

Pollock and de Kooning remained friendly rivals in the Club and the Cedars, but with Pollock's infrequent visits, de Kooning gained prominence. (After 1945, Pollock lived on the eastern end of Long Island, returning to Manhattan one day a week for alcoholism-related psychiatric treatment.) De Kooning developed a strong following among the New York School artists and a growing band of young admirers. His studio at 85 Fourth Avenue, near Eleventh Street, was only a short distance away from the action on Eighth Street. By the time of Pollock's death in 1956 from a car accident while driving drunk, de Kooning's reputation as a preeminent New York School painter was equal to Pollock's.

During the years when the ascendancy of Abstract Expressionism was solidifying the cultural supremacy of New York City—and the United States—a new center of creative bohemian life was forming. The San Remo bar, on the northwest corner of Bleecker and MacDougal Streets, was its unofficial headquarters. Congregating in the San Remo in the late 1940s, Allen Ginsberg biographer Barry Miles writes, "were James Agee, Larry Rivers, Paul Goodman, John Cage, Merce Cunningham, Chester Kallman, and virtually everyone connected with Judith Malina and Julian Beck's newly launched Living Theater."[18] By 1950, Ginsberg, whose poetry would ignite a fierce public reaction, was a weekend regular. He was often joined by Jack Kerouac and Gregory Corso, making the "Remo" the chief hangout of the Beat Generation, a label originated by Jack Kerouac that probably first appeared in writing in a 1952 article in the *New York Times* by John Clellon Holmes. Joining the Beats at the Remo in the early 1950s was a less inflammatory group of vanguard poets, since called the New York School of poetry. Its charter members included Frank O'Hara, John Ashbery, Kenneth Koch, and James Schuyler.

Frank O'Hara, the star of the group, was a curator at MoMA and often could be found among the artists at the Cedars.

Partisan Review occupied space in the Bible House at 45 Astor Place, near Union Square, then the center of local communist activity. Under communist dogma—Moscow had condemned modern art in 1932—if art did not glorify the worker and the state in realist terms, it was frivolous at best and, at worst, could be dangerous to the cause. The communists also hated bourgeois intellectuals, which the *Partisan Review* represented. Mary McCarthy, one of the brightest young literary lights in New York, was a founding member of the *Partisan Review* and was usually in the midst of the passionate editorial disagreements. Reminiscing about her early working life there, she wrote: "This whole region [around Union Square] was Communist territory; 'they' were everywhere—in the streets, in the cafeterias; nearly every derelict building contained at least one of their front groups or publications. Later when the magazine [*Partisan Review*] moved to the old Bible House on Astor Place, *The New Masses* [a communist magazine] had offices on the same floor, and meeting '*them*' in the elevator, riding down in silence, enduring their cold scrutiny, was a prospect often joked about but dreaded."[19]

Hitler had also condemned modern art and thought, causing many writers, painters, musicians, composers, and philosophers to flee Europe. New York City was a major beneficiary of the flow of exiled émigré talent. The New School created a university in exile in which many of the European intellectuals could teach, and their legacy endures in the fields of art and architecture. In 1942 the whole contingent of Surrealists settled mostly in or near the Washington Square district, where they powerfully influenced the direction of art in the New York School. (André Breton, their leader, lived in the West Village near Abington Square.) Gorky, Pollock, Motherwell, Baziotes, Rothko, Gottlieb, and Still had all gone through a Surrealist phase in their development. The Jumble Shop on Eighth Street became the chief haunt of the French writers and painters.

Beyond its role as a haven for those seeking freedom, the New School was a potent force for modernism in all of the major arts. The school hosted some of the most significant vanguard music and dance performances of the period and offered the first college courses on modern music, art, and architecture taught by such notable instructors as Berenice Abbott (on photography), John Martin, Doris Humphrey, and Martha Graham (on modern dance). (Graham's studio and troupe headquarters were nearby in a loft at 66 Fifth Avenue.) Art lectures were delivered by two of the world's most distinguished connoisseurs and critics—Leo Stein and Meyer Schapiro. In the realm of the new currents in painting, it was Schapiro, the galvanic teacher, multidisciplinary critic and historian, and eminent intellectual who, in league with the New York School artists, did the most to legitimize abstract art in art-historical and broader cultural terms.

Just when so many European talents were migrating to New York, Mabel Dodge Luhan (then a 60-year-old grandmother and married to Tony Luhan, a Pueblo Indian) returned to the city from Taos, New Mexico, in January 1940, with an eye to restarting her salon. Sure that there were "youngish people who crave[d] something more satisfying than café society," she hoped to attract a crowd similar to the one that swarmed around her in 1913.[20] Her former quarters at 23 Fifth Avenue having long been replaced by an apartment house, she chose a suite in the tower of One Fifth Avenue with views of her old neighborhood and the midtown skyline. At the time, One Fifth was especially known as the residence of stage and screen stars, with Boris Karloff, Sylvia Sidney, Judith Anderson, Guthrie McClintic, Frances Farmer, and Xavier Cugat all making the hotel their New York headquarters. The British Consul also had a suite there and was visited by the Duke and Duchess of Windsor when they were in town. Downstairs, the #1 Bar had become immensely popular after Prohibition ended in 1933. With its dueling pianos, the supper club was a launching pad for new talent; Bob Hope and Louis B. Mayer discovered a young singer named Dorothy Lamour there. However, for Mabel Dodge Luhan, the city's intelligentsia had moved too far from what she had known in terms of artistic trends, concern with communism, and pending war in Europe, and she soon returned to Taos.

By 1950, New York City had supplanted Paris as the capital of Western culture. As the historian Thomas Bender has written, "Instead of being a province of Paris, or even an imitation of Paris, New York in the 1940s became Paris. And the assimilation of the culture of Paris was crucially important for what happened in New York. The music, art, and dance that had been created in Paris from 1900 to the mid-1930s—unlike the increasingly nationalistic music of Germany or the intensely Russian Imperial Ballet at St. Petersburg—was of mobile character, capable of extension and vernacular expression."[21]

In addition to the culture shift, two other events in 1939 and 1945 confirmed America's dominance on the world stage. At the 1939–40 World's Fair held in New York City, America showed its industrial superiority to the world by proselytizing for a brighter future through its technological innovation. RCA unveiled its advances in television broadcasting on opening day, with FDR becoming the first U.S. president to appear on the tube. General Motors' Futurama Pavilion, showing America's landscape transformed by highways and cars, was the runaway hit of the fair. After World War II, the selection of New York as the home of the United Nations in 1945 was further confirmation that the metropolis had been transformed into the world's capital city.

Progress, however, revived old fears for the future of Washington Square as a bulwark against the very thing that had enthralled 1939 fairgoers: the vision of a nation—and city—dominated by automobiles and the network of roads needed to sustain them. La Guardia had used the bulk of the Depression-era federal funds for huge construction projects. In addition to a com-

prehensive subway system and the most extensive public housing program in the country, a vast network of highways connected Manhattan to the other boroughs and New Jersey. "By 1940," *American Metropolis* reported, "there were more miles of nonintersecting highways in New York than in the next five largest American cities combined. . . . three major bridges (the Triborough, the Whitestone, and the Henry Hudson) and at least one hundred smaller ones were completed." The Queens-Midtown tunnel opened in 1940.[22]

Driving the need for better transportation were the city's population growth and its manufacturing vitality. By 1950, the city's population—almost eight million—made it larger "than forty-five of the forty-eight United States and far surpassing in size many of the original members of the United Nations." Garment manufacturing "had been New York's greatest industry since before the Civil War," and in 1950, garment manufacturing "provided more jobs to more workers than did the autos of Detroit or the steel of Pittsburgh." "[F]orty percent of the country's freight passed through the city each year."[23] Even before that, when La Guardia was 18 months into his first term, the square's place in the center of downtown Manhattan was threatened again, this time by Parks Commissioner Robert Moses.

Among La Guardia's superb choices for commissioners, Moses (fig. 6.23) was the most qualified, bringing his worldwide prominence as a planner and builder to the new administration. He had built the state's park system, including the magnificent parks and parkways that opened up Long Island to the masses, and by 1934 he began his 34-year career as New York City's development czar with the reorganization of the municipal parks department and the construction of 60 new parks. Moses, brilliant and phenomenally effective, would go on to command over $20 billion in construction projects. In 1935 he sought to turn Washington Square into a traffic circle, and he gave short

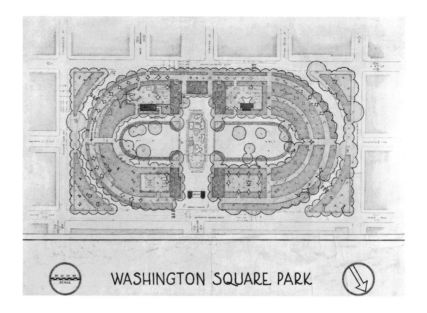

WASHINGTON SQUARE PARK

FIG. 6.24 Plan of Moses's
Bathmat proposal, 1935. This
glorified traffic circle sparked a
30-year fight over traffic in
the square. Artist unknown.
Courtesy of the NYC Department
of Parks and Recreation.

shrift to those who opposed him. This sarcastic attack on the preservationists, from a letter to Charles C. Burlingham, the aged former president of the New York bar and the politician who had critically helped La Guardia get elected, is vintage Moses:

> I realize that in the process of rebuilding south of Washington Square there would be cries of anguish from those who are honestly convinced that the Sistine Madonna was painted in the basement of one of the old buildings there not presently occupied by a cabaret or speakeasy, that Michangelo's David was fashioned in a garret in the same neighborhood, that Poe's Raven, Don Marquis' Archie the Cockroach, and Malory's Morte D'Arthur were penned in barber shops, spaghetti works and shoeshine parlors in the purlieus of Greenwich Village, and that anyone who lays hands on these sacred landmarks will be executed if he has not already been struck down by a bolt from heaven.[24]

The secret in dealing with Moses, it turned out, was to wear him down, forcing his attention toward projects in which he could make progress.

Beginning in 1935, Moses floated a new plan to convert the square into an oval roadway serving as a bus turnaround and north-south route for automobile traffic (fig. 6.24). This proposal, later called the *Bathmat plan* because of the shape that the traffic pattern would take, shook up the community and elicited a letter of opposition from the Washington Square Association. The scheme lay dormant until 1939, when Moses became heavily involved in the city's housing development plans. These plans targeted, in part, large areas directly south of the square and relied on the approval of the Bathmat plan, which would connect Fifth Avenue to the land slated for development. Also by then, many in the Washington Square Association had begun feeling that to facilitate rehabilitation south of the square, which they considered to be a slum district, the creation of the Bathmat might be a good trade-off to make the housing project economically feasible.

FIG. 6.25 Lower Fifth Avenue at the start of the outdoor dining season, looking south from Longchamps, ca. 1939. Photographer unknown. Courtesy of Hulton Archive / Getty Images.

In a close vote of 19 to 18 in the association's executive committee, the group came out in support of Moses's plan, which badly split the association's membership. A committee in opposition quickly formed, and it collected thousands of signatures against the plan. The Bathmat's foes publicized powerful arguments against it—the safety of NYU's 32,000 students, mothers with small children, and older children unaccompanied by adults would be compromised. A resident of Washington Square South complained in the *New York Times:* "What is the matter with the Park Commissioner? Does he not know what Washington Square stands for? Would he put bowling alleys in the Parthenon, a swimming tank on Bunker Hill or a gymnasium in the Lincoln Memorial?"[25] Stanley Isaacs, the Manhattan borough president, who had recently fought Moses's Brooklyn-Battery bridge proposal, was instrumental in stopping the Bathmat plan. Then the war intervened, and the issue of traffic within the square was put on hold until the 1950s.

In the mild real estate recovery prior to World War II, three significant new buildings arrived in the Washington Square neighborhood, two of them on Fifth Avenue. In 1938, the Schrafft's restaurant chain opened its monumental modernist outpost on the southeast corner of Thirteenth Street at 61 Fifth, sporting a distinctive curved facade to make it more visible from a distance. Schrafft's competitor, Longchamps, had just installed one of its glittery restaurants in the ground floor of the loft building on the northeast corner of Twelfth Street (fig. 6.25). Both chains were attempting to attract a middle-class audience by purveying a taste of the sophisticated dash of New York's café-society haunts like the Stork Club and El Morocco. A year later, the Berkeley Hotel at 20 Fifth Avenue was razed for a fine 16-story redbrick apartment house, known as No. 20. With a mixture of Gothic and Greek Revival decoration, it fit in comfortably with its older neighbors. The third new development was Eighth Street's second movie house, the 590-seat Art Theater, which was erected in 1940 at 36 East Eighth Street. It was designed by the theater architect Thomas Lamb in an unexciting modernist mode, and large light-gray glazed tiles were used for the required sheer-facade look made de rigueur by the International Style. (It acquired a new facade in 1999.) The Art Theater joined the 8th Street Playhouse in making Eighth Street the place to see the best foreign and American films and revivals.

Also in 1939, the Sailors' Snug Harbor trust wanted to replace most of the Row east of Fifth Avenue with a tall apartment house. The trust's move was an indication of the woeful lack of preservation interest then present in the city. However, the Municipal Art Society, whose membership included Harvey Wiley Corbett, successfully argued for a smaller apartment house. The new building kept the historic shell of the houses at 7–13 Washington Square North and raised the roofline only slightly to accommodate full-height top-floor rooms in place of the original cramped servants' quarters. Although most of the interiors were destroyed in the remodeling, at least the basic character of the terrace was left intact. As part of the trust's overall development, a quaint row of small-scale houses was constructed in the gardens of the grand houses. The row of ten two-story residences faced the south side of the Washington Mews, and the houses were designed in a style complementing the remodeled stables opposite on the north side.

In January 1945, during the waning months of the war, the Washington Square Association was aghast to learn that Joseph Siegel, the builder of One Fifth Avenue, was planning to put up a twin-towered skyscraper apartment house covering the entire west blockfront between Washington Square and Eighth Street. For this massive 35-story structure, more than twice the size of One Fifth and facing directly on the square, Siegel had picked the architect Sylvan Bien. Bien had designed the 1929 Carlyle Hotel, a handsome 40-story landmark tower on the Upper East Side at Madison Avenue and 76th Street. While managing to defeat Siegel's proposal, aided by a threatened zoning change (and a potential court fight) that would reduce height limits for buildings abutting squares, the Washington Square Association was diligently formulating a comprehensive and preemptive plan for postwar Washington Square—the Holden, McLaughlin Plan, completed on July 1, 1946.

The plan took as its purview the entire downtown region between Fourteenth and Broome Streets, and from Broadway to the Hudson River (fig. 6.26). It called for reclaiming the "obsolete" loft and tenement district that reached from south of the square to Houston Street for modern residential use; extending a giant mall from the square to Houston Street between Thompson Street and West Broadway, as an identifiable campus for NYU; zoning to prevent tall buildings around the square's perimeter; and aiming traffic, via expressways to the south and west, far away from the square. However, Robert Moses had other ideas. When La Guardia departed from office in 1946, leaving a dispirited Democratic Party, Moses had been powerful and popular enough to force a deal with the Democratic mayoral candidate, William O'Dwyer. Moses would endorse O'Dwyer if he would keep Moses in

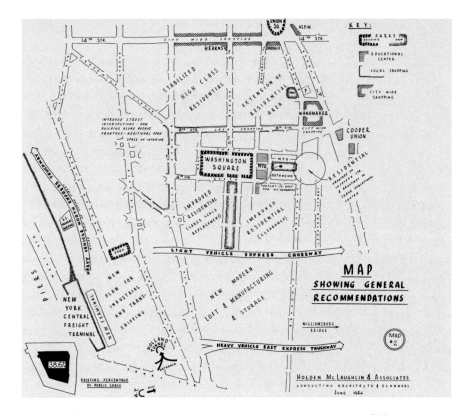

FIG. 6.26 The inauspicious Holden, McLaughlin Plan of 1946 led to community fights with Robert Moses in the 1950s and conflict later in SoHo over "improvements" to the south. Artist unknown. Author's Collection.

charge of the city's slum clearance and construction projects. O'Dwyer won, and Moses got his wish. And Moses still dreamed of a traffic artery through the square.

As real estate pressures escalated after the war, the Holden, McLaughlin Plan was subsumed into a larger vision that had gained force among city planners in dealing with blighted districts. Based on the World of Tomorrow and Pleasantvilles from the 1939 World's Fair, the idea was that any land rebuilt as residential districts should be connected by highways. "Obsolete," too, referred to housing that wasn't maximally "productive" in the modern sense of having high population density and low maintenance costs. Aiding the new vision, President Harry S. Truman signed the Housing Act of 1949, with its Title I provisions easing the cost of condemnation. (Under Title I, the federal government picked up two-thirds of the city's condemnation costs, permitting the city to turn the land over, at its discounted price, to private developers for reconstruction.) New York had Robert Moses, at the peak of his vast power, ready for the task.

By 1946, the postwar recovery was well along. All of the land south of Washington Square to Houston Street lay subject to demolition and redevelopment, and plans by two prominent institutions, NYU and the Metropolitan Opera, were cause for alarm.

In 1947, NYU purchased the Columbia University block (bounded by MacDougal Street, Washington Square South, and Sullivan and West Third Streets) for its Law Center. Neighborhood protests quickly erupted on two main grounds: the plight of nearly 300 tenants, many of them working artists, to be evicted, and NYU's continuing land grab for more control over the square. Signature-gathering and publicity by the Save Washington Square Committee, plus fierce opposition from a New York City councilman's campaign, was a temporary respite only, as NYU built the Law Center in 1951.

With NYU's main campus at University Heights in the Bronx, its expansion around the square had otherwise been uneventful. It had purchased and reused loft buildings to the east and southeast of the square, and had also acquired the Judson Church hotel. NYU's only new construction around the square had been in 1929, when it erected a Gothic-inspired 12-story edifice for its School of Education, on the north side of West Fourth Street just east of the square. However, with the GI Bill in full swing, all of its facilities were becoming strained by overcrowding. Between 1946 and 1949, the student body had grown from 47,155 to 70,376. NYU's town-gown squabbles with its Washington Square neighbors had only just begun.

Far more ominous for the square was the city's labeling of approximately 40 acres south of it—from the square to Houston Street, between Mercer Street and Sixth Avenue—as a slum. As such, the area would be eligible for slum clearance as a Title I project.

For the Italian community, which encompassed the western portion of the land from West Broadway to Sixth Avenue, their neighborhood was not a slum. Although their tenements were substandard compared to up-to-date housing, the residents still valued their family, ethnic, and religious ties to the location. Following World War I, the second generation had adapted to life in America, for example, by forming district political clubs instead of self-help societies. And the neighborhood was rejuvenated following World War II as returning GIs turned their energies toward local businesses and starting families. Nor did the businessmen in the light-manufacturing district to the east consider themselves as occupying an industrial slum. Most of the 173 loft and factory buildings, housing some 1,100 commercial or industrial firms, were in shabby condition. But they employed over 15,000 people and provided entry-level jobs, and they depended on cheap rents to survive. Some opposition to family and job displacement was voiced at the time, but none of this mattered in the forties to planners and politicians who were preoccupied with slum clearance.

An early developer for the central portion of the Title I project was the opera house's 1949 super-block plan, backed by Moses, for a major cultural mall (think Lincoln Center) covering the entire area south of Washington Square between MacDougal and Wooster Streets. The Metropolitan's feasibility study had chosen the Washington Square site over several others (all Title I projects), including sites at Columbus Circle and Lincoln Square. The proposed design would have encompassed a 4,500-seat opera house (the current Met seats 3,788); a 1,800-seat concert hall; a television building housing production facilities for the burgeoning new industry, revenue from which would help defray the opera's fixed expenses; and underground parking for

1,000 cars. Plans had been drawn up by the opera's architects, Wallace K. Harrison and Max Abramovitz, who would be the future designers of the actual Lincoln Center for the Performing Arts. Their renderings showed the building complex in the center of the approximately 21-acre site, flanked by two new north-south roads marked "Fifth Avenue East" and "Fifth Avenue West," primed for linkage through the square with the old Fifth Avenue.

By 1950, however, Moses and the Met had settled on the Columbus Circle (later Lincoln Square) area instead, and Moses had secured NYU as a developer for the Washington Square South project. NYU would get the northern strip between Third and Fourth Streets for its new buildings, and the rest of the Title I land would be developed with apartment houses. Moses's new proposal was presented to the city's Board of Estimate in January 1951. It perfectly captured his vision for Washington Square, as he had earlier explained in a letter to Burlingham: "I would eventually turn over to New York University all of the south frontage as part of their expansion plan, with the understanding that the buildings would be Colonial Georgian built around quadrangles and similar to those [NYU's Law Center] already under construction on the excellent plans prepared by Eggers and Higgins. I would rebuild all of the additional area south of the Square to [W]est Houston Street, and continue Fifth Avenue through the Arch or around it so that there would be a Fifth Avenue South."[26]

At first, other than a few polite inquiries from Baptist Church interests, there was little opposition to the Moses proposal, even though NYU's development would wipe out Stanford White's marvelous Judson Church and hotel. All that was to change over the next two decades, when intense strife over this and other urban renewal projects would kill most of the Washington Square South project, lead to the final defeat of Moses's plans to route traffic through the square, and lay the foundation for future preservationist victories.

Washington Square South and Manhattan's southern skyline, 1970. NYU's red-sandstone Bobst Library rises on Washington Square South (left) despite a gigantic fight with the community, but the rest of architect Philip Johnson's scheme for the square has been abandoned. To the right of Bobst, the Loeb Student Center can be seen; on its facade facing the square is sculptor Reuben Nakian's abstract *Birds in Flight*. In the center of the square, work is finally in progress on a traffic-free park redesign after decades of conflict between the neighborhood and the city over roads in the square. Just to the right of Stanford White's campanile on Washington Square South, one of the World Trade Center towers can be seen under construction, making its dramatic debut on lower Manhattan's skyline. Photograph by André Kertész. Courtesy of the Estate of André Kertész ©.

: : : : : 7

PROTEST AND TURNABOUT

1951–1978

HE 1950S IN NEW YORK CITY BROUGHT FINAL DISILLUSIONMENT to those who believed that real estate booms were not only a sign of progress but also salutary, that old structures would be supplanted by buildings as good or better than the ones they were replacing. A striking precedent that had lent credence to that assumption was the wildly acclaimed Empire State Building, erected in 1930 on the site of the majestic original 1890s Waldorf-Astoria Hotel, itself a visual improvement over the Astors' first Fifth Avenue houses, which had been built there in the 1850s. However, during the real estate boom of the 1950s, unlike those of earlier periods, the public generally came to detest what replaced those torn-down sites. By 1955, even the normally silent architectural community erupted with outrage when plans were unveiled to replace Grand Central Terminal with a 108-story skyscraper. At the same time, many were shocked to learn of Carnegie Hall's threatened destruction—the venerable concert hall was to be superseded by a flashy 500-foot-tall slab with a skin of bright vermilion panels and gold-tinted windows arrayed in a checkerboard pattern (fig. 7.1). With authority for Title I slum clearance projects concentrated in the hands of the ambitious and powerful Robert Moses—further empowered by the overall surge in real estate development during the early 1950s—shock waves reverberated throughout the city. One of the first areas hit was the Washington Square district.

FIG. 7.1 According to an August 7, 1957, press release by the architectural firm of Pomerance & Breines, the beloved Carnegie Hall would be razed in 1959 to make way for this 44-story, 500-foot-tall vermilion and gold skyscraper, surrounded by a sunken plaza lined with cultural exhibits. The late violinist Isaac Stern was in the forefront of the fight to preserve the 1891 hall. Courtesy of the Library of Congress.

FIG. 7.2 NYU's Vanderbilt Hall Law Center, looking east on Washington Square South from MacDougal Street, ca. 1964. Photograph by John Barrington Bayley. Courtesy of the NYC Landmarks Preservation Commission.

The newcomers to the Village after World War II were no different from those who had arrived in the 1920s; they loved the intimate scale and charm of the place and its many cultural landmarks such as the Brevoort and Lafayette Hotels. Yet the very attributes that drew new residents were threatened by the redevelopments undertaken to satisfy the need for new housing during a critical shortage. The clout of the Washington Square Association had been severely diminished by a political climate in which social connections played far less of a role, and new organizations—block associations, community boards, and the Landmarks Preservation Commission—would be needed to defend the Village turf. The sense of outrage over changes was felt by many in the city but nowhere more so than in the neighborhood of the square.

New York University had first upset the community in the postwar period with its Law Center on the southwest corner of the square (fig. 7.2). As the relatively benign full-block Georgian structure was rising in 1950 between MacDougal and Sullivan Streets, residents were somewhat calmed. Robert Moses had mandated that NYU construct low buildings facing the square, and the height of the new structures—a mere five stories—and their redbrick facades were a relief, even if the style would have looked far more at home in the reconstruction of Williamsburg, Virginia, than in downtown Manhattan. Then, in late December 1950, Robert Moses unveiled his 40-acre Title I project, Washington Square South, which included versions of NYU's Law Center building strung across the entire southern edge of the square, threatening massive population displacement. By October 1951 community opposition caused the project to be shelved. But across the square, on the old Rhinelander block at Fifth Avenue, one of the city's first white-brick apartment high-rises was being proposed, an alien intruder that would have far less relevance to its architectural setting than the Law Center. Hundreds of these white glazed-brick behemoths would be constructed, mainly in Greenwich Village and on the Upper East Side, in the 1950s and 1960s, and residents were horrified that one would be built on Washington Square.

A unique set of postwar conditions had led to the proliferation of these sterile-looking white-brick towers. Beginning in the 1930s, the city built blocks of redbrick public housing covering vast tracts opened up by slum-clearance projects, and white-brick buildings stood in sharp contrast to them. The color contrast to public housing was considered essential by developers, given that the plain, unadorned facades of the new white-brick apartment buildings might otherwise be confused with the equally unornamented exteriors of the public housing projects. (White-brick tower architecture was influenced by the recent arrival of the austere International Style, which was also cheaper to build.) Another salient design feature was the small balconies with which the buildings fairly bristled. Though they only cost the equivalent of a quarter of a room to build, in the 1950s lenders regarded them as equal to half a room when calculating property values, giving developers a bonus for balconies that was way out of proportion to their actual utility. Perhaps more to the point, they were not found on public housing. While Manhattan House, the first of these white-brick monsters, was being erected over a full city block bounded by Second and Third Avenues between 65th and 66th Streets in 1950, Samuel Rudin was pushing for a similar high-rise for Washington Square.

Rudin had picked up Joseph Siegel's 1945 property facing Fifth Avenue between the square and Eighth Street, but whereas Siegel had given up in the face of community protest, Rudin succeeded through compromise. Architect Harvey Wiley Corbett once again interceded, as he had done in 1939, to stop an insensitive remodeling of part of the Row. He induced Rudin to create a low, redbrick wing to maintain the facade plane and cornice line of Washington Square North, with the mass of the 22-story building concentrated in a white-brick tower behind it, set back from the square. While Rudin's compromise did not hew to the cornice line or to the nineteenth-century architecture as closely as its 1950s critics would have liked, the result—the apartment house known as Two Fifth Avenue, with a low, mock-Federal wing on the square—was considered a victory for early preservation (fig. 7.3).

Robert Moses turned out to be helpful, too, threatening Rudin with a zoning change for the square if the developer didn't comply with a setback. Although Moses still wanted to put a roadway through Washington Square, he believed that squares in general should be faced by low buildings and kept NYU from erecting overbearing buildings on the southern edge until he lost power under Governor Nelson A. Rockefeller in the mid-1960s.

Later critics have given Rudin's compromise decidedly mixed reviews. In 1964 Ada Louise Huxtable, architecture critic of the *New York Times,* called the low wing "a visual wound on the square that will never heal." Yet Paul Goldberger, Huxtable's successor at the paper, observed in 1979, "It may be heresy to say so, but the fraud comes off—it is good urbanism, respectful of

FIG. 7.3 Two Fifth Avenue from the square, shortly after the building's completion in 1952. Photograph by Fay S. Lincoln. Courtesy of The Pennsylvania State University, Special Collections Library.

the square and its neighbors."[1] Two Fifth Avenue was completed in 1952, and was the last modification to the north side of Washington Square. It has since become the home of many well-known New Yorkers, including Bella Abzug, Edward I. Koch, and master photographer, André Kertész, who shot many of his most acclaimed images of Washington Square from the balcony of his apartment.

The swift leasing success of Two Fifth Avenue appeared to open the floodgates for white-brick and other residential developments in the area. In 1958 Stewart House, a 369-family, 20-story white-brick high-rise, took over the full-block site of A. T. Stewart's original grand cast-iron building, part of the later Wanamaker's store. (Wanamaker's had given up its location there in 1954 because it was too far from the midtown concentration of high-end hotels and shops.) A pair of white-brick apartment houses covered the north side of East Fourteenth Street from Fifth Avenue to the Lincoln Building on Union Square. To the west, on Sixth Avenue, occupying the full west block-front between Twelfth and Thirteenth Streets, the 20-story white-brick John Adams, with 414 apartments, was erected in 1963. The smaller Lawrence House was built across Sixth Avenue on the northeast corner of Twelfth Street. White-brick or not—the second-class status of white-brick high-rises has been confirmed by their lower real estate valuations—these behemoths were residential rather than commercial developments, and they helped protect the environs of Washington Square as a residential neighborhood. Not all white-brick high rises were architectural mediocrities. On the northeast cor-

ner of Ninth Street, at 420 Sixth Avenue, a 13-story white-brick high-rise was
erected in 1958 without the obtrusive protruding balconies and with a recessed
central portion that makes the facade less monotonous. Number 420 is ac-
cented with horizontal bands of salmon-colored brick, acknowledging the
redbrick and stone bands of its famous neighbor, the Jefferson Market Courthouse, across Sixth Avenue.

A few other architectural misfits were built in the district during the heady
days of the 1950s when architects were experimenting with new forms under
the rubric of the International Style, and clients were happy to pay less for less
ornamentation. One of the first and largest was Lanes self-service women's
clothing store, a horizontal white slab floating over the southeast corner of
Fifth Avenue and Fourteenth Street (fig. 7.4). Designed by the architects
Cordes, Bartos & Mihnos in 1950, it covered 2–6 East Fourteenth Street,
through to Thirteenth. Numbers 2 and 4 had been the twin Italianate manors
of the shipping magnates Spofford and Tileston, with their ground floors long
converted to garish storefronts. The top two stories of the Lanes store's three-
story building were covered in glazed white brick, with the first floor set in to
form a sidewalk arcade. This gave the upper floors the weightless, suspended-
in-air appearance of the sort of pristine sculptural volume sought by International Style architects. Its three small ribbon windows were the only fenestration that the style permitted, but two signs spelling *Lanes,* at the first floor
corners made the building look more like an enormous gift box than an abstract modernist form. Today, the "floating slab" effect is entirely gone. A 1970
remodeling of the store into the New School's graduate center filled the arcade space with shops and changed the fenestration to rows of slit-like vertical windows with heavy moldings; the building awaits replacement by the
New School.

At the University Place end of the long Fourteenth Street block, the architect Morris Lapidus, who later in the decade became famous for his rococo
Fontainebleau and Eden Roc hotels in Miami Beach, designed a much smaller
store in the International Style mode in 1950. Lapidus created a two-story

structure with its University Place facade composed of glazed yellow brick and a long ribbon window at the top. On the Fourteenth Street side, a contrasting glass facade sported a distinctive short projecting tower with the flat roof demanded by the style. Originally, large letters identifying the business marred the Fourteenth Street side, but in 1998 the store was restored as a modernist gem in a row of much less distinctive neighbors.

Sailors' Snug Harbor began its postwar redevelopment in 1952 with the razing of the entire block bounded by University Place and Broadway, between Eighth and Ninth Streets. The demolition struck at the heart of the New York School artists' scene, which was centered around the Club at 39 East Eighth Street. Members of the group were forced to relocate nearby to the East Tenth Street block east of Third Avenue. The Club and all of the historic century-old structures, plus the Lafayette Hotel and a number of small-scale business buildings, fell to the wrecker's ball.

The new housing at least kept the scale and facade materials more in harmony with its surroundings and was a pleasant relief compared to the massive white-brick high-rises. Two low, six-story redbrick apartment houses without balconies, at 30 and 60 East Ninth Street, lined the ends of the block. Above the first floors, the massing of these structures has an inventive interplay of solids and voids, curved and angled facades, and integrated Art Deco–style fire escapes that still forms one of the more engaging of the modern neighborhood streetscapes. Stores occupied the ground floors facing Broadway and University Place, and a long one-story wing connecting the two buildings continued the line of stores on East Eighth Street. A 12-story apartment house was erected in the center of the block. Its covering was tan brick; otherwise it was similar to a white-brick high-rise, and it was well set back from the street. Across East Eighth Street, the smaller six-story redbrick apartment house that the trust had built in 1950 also had ground floor stores and a muted ziggurat facade broken up into solids and voids. Both sides form what is still a charming and architecturally interesting shopping street.

In 1954 the Sailors' Snug Harbor trust began work on the entire block to the west, bounded by Fifth Avenue and University Place between Eighth and Ninth Streets (fig. 7.5). Demolition commenced on the western end of the block, taking away the historic Brevoort Hotel and the Renwick house at No. 21, two of the most cherished sites on lower Fifth Avenue. In their place rose the tan-brick 20-story Brevoort apartment house, whose twist on modernist design was even more jarring than that of Two Fifth Avenue, diagonally across the street. For the Brevoort, the architectural firm of Boak & Raad created two 14-story balconied wings that encircled a central drive-in courtyard for automobiles. The tiers of deep corner balconies, the building's most prominent feature, were partially enclosed by the facade masonry, which created stark contrasts of solids and voids. Not as harmonious as the structures a block east, this new addition to the avenue, known as the Brevoort or No. 11, typified the failure of lesser International Style architects who honored abstract concepts

FIG. 7.5 The Brevoort apartment house from Two Fifth
Avenue, looking toward the
Brevoort's Fifth Avenue facade,
2001. Photograph by author.

of volumes and space over the need to fit in with the existing urban fabric. While the Brevoort maintained the avenue's facade plane and cornice line, and was sheathed in brick rather than glass, metal, or stucco, its style was thoroughly inappropriate for lower Fifth Avenue's mix of historical design motifs. The balconies in their original form (as the years have gone by, tenants have enclosed some of the openings) conjure images of gigantic waterwheel cups or chain-buckets used in mining, in contrast to the warm sense of habitability expressed by the Brevoort's neighboring 1920s apartment houses and early homes and churches.

On balance, the Sailors' Snug Harbor trust's full-block redevelopments in the 1950s could have been worse. However bland or discordant most of the architectural designs had been, at least the scale and density were not obtrusive, with the housing occupying much less space than the zoning permitted. However, with a new 1961 zoning law encouraging ground floor plazas by allowing additional height (six square feet of rentable floor space for each square foot of plaza), one of the trust's smaller blocks became a frightening early example of what harm the application of that law would bring. In *Shaping the City: New York and the Municipal Art Society,* Gregory Gilmartin sums up the result: "The notion of the street as an outdoor room was sacrificed as plazas turned the street wall into a jagged line; the ugly, scarred party walls of the old buildings were exposed to view; and the new towers, with all their volume concentrated in a single monolithic slab, dwarfed their neighbors."[2] The square block being described was bounded by Broadway and Mercer Street, between East Eighth Street and Washington Place.

In 1960, under the proposed new zoning guidelines, Rose Associates began developing the northern half of the entire square block with a 35-story tower and plaza called Georgetown Plaza—its name highlighting the new amenity. Completed in 1966, it dwarfed everything in the area, including Wanamaker's and One Fifth Avenue. The neighboring commercial building's party wall was exposed, and it left a gap in Broadway's nineteenth-century wall plane. Georgetown Plaza, at 60 East Eighth Street, was basically a white-brick high-rise, but it was double the usual height. David W. Dunlap, in *On Broadway*, describes the structure's obtrusiveness: "This monumentally bland buff-brick tower is disproportionately huge and set off in a plaza. The yellow balconies look like an afterthought."[3] Sailors' Snug Harbor completed the eastern end of its Brevoort block in 1965 (on University Place between East Eighth and Ninth Streets) with a 24-story version (minus a plaza) of its 1954 Brevoort on the western end. The Cedar Bar, which had served the New York School artists on the block for decades, was forced to close on March 30, 1963. (Its identically named successor, now situated a few blocks up University Place, has a different ambience entirely.)

During the 1960s, blocks of Sixth Avenue and miles of Third Avenue (where the el had come down in 1955) became host to residential and office towers with plazas. As the 1970s dawned and the city planners were beginning to grasp the extent of their mistake, a monolith similar to Georgetown Plaza named Hilary Gardens was crammed in next to it on the southern half of the block, at 300 Mercer Street. Completed in 1974, these two apartment houses were the only ones with plazas constructed in the district under the 1961 zoning.

West Eighth Street became threatened, when, by an apparent oversight, a 1961 change in city ordinances gave the stretch the same commercial zoning as that applied to Times Square. Large establishments such as department stores, bowling alleys, and auto showrooms, as well as conspicuous flashing electrical signs and displays, would be permitted. Yet zoning could only be changed with difficulty. Although a motion by just 20 percent of owners could force a vote, a unanimous approval by the Board of Estimate was necessary to make it effective. West Eighth Street landowners were able to influence at least one vote, which was to keep the less-restrictive 1961 zoning in place. They acted like most absentee owners anywhere, trying to get the best return on their investment. Explaining their stance, one prominent property owner felt West Eighth had already been diminished: "The narrowing of the sidewalks and the clutter of parking signs, traffic meters, and other street furniture have not helped to make the street a promenade."[4] In fact, though, the sidewalks had been narrowed in 1929 to accommodate increased motor-vehicle traffic when half of the roadway was still taken up by streetcar tracks. But the tracks had been removed in 1936 and the sidewalks could have been widened. (They now have been.) Neighborhood fears that West Eighth Street would become another Coney Island boardwalk seemed justified.

In the late 1950s, on Washington Square South, between Wooster and Thompson Streets, the architects Wallace K. Harrison and Max Abramovitz proved inept in their plans for NYU's Loeb Student Center, a much-needed recreational facility for the university's student population at the square. Forced, the school claimed, by a one-lot holdout on West Third Street to build a taller structure than originally planned, the architects designed a set-back ten-story glass curtain-wall tower on a raised concrete and glass platform; next to it was a low, angled, and curved redbrick structure containing an auditorium. To decorate the austere, windowless facade of the auditorium facing the square, the architects commissioned artist Reuben Nakian for an abstract sculpture later titled *Birds in Flight*.

Inspired by the pigeons and swirling leaves of Washington Square, Nakian randomly placed clusters of twisting aluminum plates along a diagonal line so they would appear to curl away from the wall in opposing directions. Installed in the spring of 1961, Nakian's large 28-by-45-foot work surpassed its host building in artistic merit and was the city's first major outdoor nonrepresentational sculpture. Until late 1999, when Loeb was razed and the sculpture dismantled, *Birds in Flight* served as a tangible reminder that the true "home" of the New York School was Washington Square. The Loeb Student Center was built on the site of Nakian's studio on the square; his had been a stone's throw away from that of fellow Armenian artist Arshile Gorky, whose first studio in New York was on the (pre–Law Center) southwest corner of Sullivan Street. Gorky and de Kooning influenced Nakian's turn toward abstract work in the 1930s; Nakian's subsequent free and gestural use of clay, terra cotta, plaster, and metal would establish his work as a sculptural correlative of the paintings of the Abstract Expressionists.

Critics castigated the Loeb center's design as "uninspiring," "awkward," and "pitifully weak." However, the center's relatively small size, compared to NYU's massive and controversial Bobst Library cube constructed directly across the street in the 1960s, probably spared it even more critical barbs than the center otherwise might have received. It was also difficult to get too angry over the Loeb center because it eliminated a ten-story factory loft within 56 feet of the square—the ugliest presence on it—at a time when the land southeast of Loeb was receiving, according to the *AIA Guide to New York City*, "[s]uperbuildings on superblocks. The antithesis of Village scale and charm."[5]

The Loeb Student Center sat at the northern end of what had been a large Title I project covering all of the land south of it to Houston Street. Loeb's modern architecture was a sharp break with the Georgian buildings originally proposed for the land between the square and Third Street. By December 1950, the firm of Eggers & Higgins had a redevelopment plan for Robert Moses, inspired by Le Corbusier's utopian towers-in-a-park housing scheme

W. JONES

FIG. 7.6 Robert Moses's 1956 version of his Washington Square roadway scheme, with a pedestrian overpass linking the halves of the bifurcated square. Artist unknown. Courtesy of the NYC Department of Parks and Recreation.

for the redevelopment of Paris in the 1920s. Their plan would have turned the entire area, except for the NYU strip, into a vast loop of mid-rise apartment houses like the earlier Peter Cooper Village and Stuyvesant Town (only the Eggers & Higgins buildings had balconies). The area to be affected ran from Mercer Street to Sixth Avenue and extended further south to Spring Street, west of a new South Fifth Avenue replacing West Broadway. Only the MacDougal-Sullivan Gardens block, St. Anthony's Catholic Church, and a small piece of the Minettas would have been spared. However, the section of the proposed project west of West Broadway would have demolished practically the whole parish of St. Anthony's. The Italian community was angered by this threatened desecration of home and church, and that part of the project was rejected by the Board of Estimate in October 1951. The plan's reduced area was bounded by the square and Houston Street but ran from Mercer Street to West Broadway instead of Sixth Avenue. Moses mounted a concentrated effort to give the project a Fifth Avenue address. (Possibly in fear of over-loaded streets, the Washington Square Association supported Moses's road-way, as they had his Bathmat proposal in the 1930s.)

Moses's new 1953 proposal for the smaller Title I project, which was to be undertaken in conjunction with NYU, featured three parallel 583-foot-long slabs of white-brick high-rises. The proposal was later changed to two slabs and three towers in a park, serviced by a multilane extension of Fifth Avenue through the square (fig. 7.6). By 1955, though, the local resistance had gained strength, including a valuable ally in the obstreperous new *Village Voice*, which quickly picked Moses and his roadway as its first major target. While the *Voice* was attracting big-league talent—Norman Mailer was an early writer for the paper—and gaining reputation and clout, the Title I program was coming under attack by other neighborhood groups, including some from Lenox Hill,

Yorkville, and Harlem. This opposition, coupled with profiteering within the Title I program (although not involving Moses himself) soon turned local politicians and key city officials against the roadway. Charles Abrams, a prominent lawyer, public official, and neighborhood resident, was a particularly important adversary of Moses on the issue.

Moses was weakened, and by 1958 Mayor Robert F. Wagner acted on the opposition's counterproposal for a trial closing of the square to automobiles. Moses's dire prediction that closing the square to traffic would only overload the surrounding streets was never fulfilled, and in 1962 the Board of Estimate finally voted down the roadway for good. Buses still used the square for a turn-around, but they, too, were excluded in 1965, and Washington Square was free of vehicles for the first time in nearly a century.

Community protest focused on Washington Square itself when NYU planned to create a modern campus there, replacing the nineteenth-century lofts it was using. Philip Johnson, then practicing a variant of the International Style, was hired by the university in 1964. With his partner, Richard Foster, Johnson was to design a group of buildings for Washington Square East and along Washington Square South between Wooster Street and West Broadway. This southern parcel, stretching to East Third Street and part of the Title I project, had already been demolished in the early 1950s. Certainly, NYU had no visibly identifiable presence on the square, and from its perspective, the perfect solution was a line of new buildings. The Washington Square community, though, took issue with the scale of the structures, which would cast a shadow on the square, and NYU's general dominance over the square. What Johnson and Foster had in mind was a 150-foot-high cube in the vacant lot between Wooster and West Broadway; its volume was big enough to stack three buildings the size of the Law Center in it with room to spare. It would be the district's third blockbuster following Wanamaker's south building and Georgetown Plaza.

Johnson and Foster's overall scheme offered a grandiose complex that would create a marriage between classical and modernist themes (fig. 7.7). For the square's east side, the architects planned the image of a single imperial edifice. The plan would replicate the scale of NYU's 1895 150-foot-high Main Building on the block south of Washington Place, with both structures sheathed in red sandstone and acting as wings of a 180-foot-high glass galleria covering Washington Place from the square all the way to Broadway. The red sandstone was meant to harmonize with the redbrick of the Row, the concave piers between pairs of windows hinted at classical columns, and a minimally defined cornice helped tie the wings together. Washington Square would thus become the forecourt of NYU's new presence, and the university's first addition facing the court would be Bobst Library. Bobst's design would be a variation on the proposed east buildings. The rhythm of the piers and the cornice line would be continued, but the library would have blank panels

FIG. 7.7 Philip Johnson's red-sandstone and glass additions proposed for NYU's campus on the square, with his glass galleria covering Washington Place (left), 1966. Courtesy of the New York University Archives.

where the east side had windows, and a central vertical section of windows would take the place of the galleria in the center of the east buildings.

As a first step, NYU attempted to get the blueprints for Bobst Library approved by the city because of the variances it required. The university proposed taking 40 feet from West Broadway (renamed La Guardia Place above Houston Street in 1967) for more width, and then adding 90 feet to the height limit for its new structures facing the southern edge of the square. By the time the university's request reached a vote on the Board of Estimate in 1966, scores of community groups were against its plan, and antidevelopment petitions containing tens of thousands of signatures had been received. The board vote was split—10 were opposed and 12 were in favor of the variances—but NYU got its library. Fortunately for the neighborhood, as a result of growing financial problems, NYU gave up on the rest of its overbearing design. There was irony and a Machiavellian twist to the Bobst episode, though, that would presage another controversy between the Village and NYU in the 1990s. Rather than building higher or more extensively underground, the university sought the 40-foot swath of La Guardia Place. That request put the community in a bind—a choice between the over-scaled library, or Robert Moses's despised bifurcating roadway scheme. If Bobst was not built, the roadway scheme might someday be resuscitated; building the library would not leave enough room for the road. When Bobst was narrowly approved in 1966, those who felt it was the lesser evil may well have made the difference.

Finally, Johnson's scheme for the square did not have the requisite design excellence nor even the necessary contextual considerations to succeed. Earlier, in the 1830s and 1840s, the architects Davis, Dakin, and Lafever created Gothic Revival buildings for the square's east side, and their romantic towers gave the square something of the look of a medieval hub. In the 1890s, Stanford White evoked the Roman forum with his arch and Judson Church buildings. Perhaps in Johnson's later postmodern phase he might have taken a cue from Milan's nineteenth-century galleria in the Piazza del Duomo and made inventive use of ornament based on Washington Square's existing commercial architecture. But the austere International Style he then espoused, even with subtle classical references, just could not meet the challenge at hand—to replace a large part of the square's masonry border with something compatible and magical.

Bobst Library's glowering mass shadows the square, ruins the effect of Alfred Zucker's Borgfeldt Building, and blocks southern perspectives from the square. Bobst nonetheless serves the university's needs with seating for 4,800 and space for 2.5 million books; its striking interior atrium relieves the structure's bulk for those inside and provides a sense of communality, acting as the university's town square. The library became even more important to the university in 1971 when it sold its University Heights campus (now Bronx Community College) to the city and consolidated its graduate and undergraduate departments of arts and sciences at Washington Square. NYU then built a much smaller modernist building on the southern edge of the square—the Hagop Kervorkian Center for Near-Eastern Studies—and, in the 1960s and 1970s, lined West Fourth Street east of the square with large buildings, including two red-sandstone compatriots of Bobst. The university did build a bland dormitory at 5–11 University Place between One University and the Merck Building, but otherwise it avoided conflict with the square's neighborhood activists during this period by reusing more old buildings and building new dormitories outside of the Washington Square district.

Ultimately, it was the cultural-political revolution exemplified by the Beats and the folk music revival of the 1960s, not the contractors' wrecking balls, that did the most damage to the character of the Washington Square district. Both the Beats and folkies brought a surge in tourism, including hordes of young people who were in search of entertainment and who were, increasingly, interested in purchasing—and selling—drugs. Associated crime and racial strife went up, leading to community protest groups and forcing a change in the neighborhood's tolerance for "different" behavior.

The original and iconic Beats—Allen Ginsberg, Jack Kerouac, and William S. Burroughs—first met on Manhattan's Upper West Side in 1944 at the start of their careers. Ginsberg was a 16-year-old freshman at Columbia University, unsure of his sexuality and talent for poetry; Kerouac was a 22-year-old star athlete and Columbia dropout working at odd jobs and writing; and Burroughs at 30 was studying the city's demimonde while cultivating a reputation as a connoisseur of the macabre. The three shared an affinity for New York City and a contempt for postwar America, "[a] society in . . . complete and utter denial of everything about itself that wasn't white, modern, middle-class, hardworking, God-fearing, flag-saluting, and American as Mom's apple pie," as writer Carlo McCormick recently put it. All of them developed groundbreaking new voices in their writings and performances while expanding their minds through drugs. "Our original use [of marijuana] was for aes-

FIG. 7.8 The Wilentzes' 8th Street Bookshop at 32 West Eighth Street, corner of Mac-Dougal Street, in 1954, with the Washington Square Book Shop across the street at No. 27. The view is northeast from the southeast corner of MacDougal. Photograph by Joseph Roberto. Courtesy of the New York University Archives.

thetic study, aesthetic perception, deepening it," wrote Ginsberg, who roamed the country proselytizing the use of drugs, free love, and Eastern mysticism as the bedrock of freedom and fraternity.[6] By the 1950s, they had become underground heroes, both for their iconoclasm in the arts and for their open defiance of convention. Important stops in the Beats' travels included San Francisco and Greenwich Village, where they discovered two friendly bookstores—City Lights in San Francisco's North Beach and the 8th Street Bookshop in the Village—that became gathering places both for the movement's icons and for its many followers.

At 32 West Eighth, on the southeast corner of MacDougal Street, the 8th Street Bookshop was a crucial part of many underground writers' literary life, functioning as a publisher, bookseller, promoter, way station, mail drop, friend, and sometimes employer. Ever since brothers Ted and Eli Wilentz opened their bookshop in 1947, their place had been a congenial common ground for readers and writers, including the Beats when they emerged in the 1950s (fig. 7.8). In 1960 the Wilentzes published *The Beat Scene,* a heavily illustrated poetry anthology that spread around the world not only the new poetry but also photographic images of the Beat lifestyle. As a center of avant-garde literature, the 8th Street Bookshop played a role very much like that of the Washington Square Bookshop in the teens and twenties. It closed in 1979.

Whatever cultural historians may decide about the positive contributions

FIG. 7.9 Allen Ginsberg (looking toward the camera) in Washington Square, with publisher Barney Rossett (with glasses and holding a document) and poet Gregory Corso between them, 1957. Rossett was a great help to the Beats in getting their work published through his Grove Press. Photograph by Burt Glinn. Courtesy of Magnum Photos.

of the artists who were part of the Beat Generation, one aspect of the counterculture they helped shape was undeniably pernicious: the glorification of drugs. In 1959, all of Eighth Street, but particularly West Eighth, was still an exciting neighborhood, of which philosopher and author William Barrett could enthusiastically write: "West Eighth Street is the main shopping and social center of the Village as a whole. One of the most vital and kaleidoscopically varied thoroughfares in New York, the street is lined with an art cinema, chic clothing stores, bookstores, nightclubs, arts and crafts shops, record shops and restaurants."[7]

A little more than a decade later, Eighth Street had been transformed from an asset to a magnet for drug users, drug pushers, and other criminals. Heroin and cocaine were the primary agents of this disastrous change, but some of its roots could be traced to the Beat scene around MacDougal and Bleecker Streets. In the late fifties, places like the San Remo, Café Rienzi, Café Figaro, the Kettle of Fish, and the Gaslight Café were already drawing crowds of young people from all over the region on Friday and Saturday nights, and countercultural energies were stirring in tamped-down cold war America. Experimental poetry and writing were an outlet for this energy (fig. 7.9). By 1959 the Beats' philosophy and lifestyle had become a national sensation. Allen Ginsberg's *Howl and Other Poems,* which had been confiscated by the San Francisco police in May 1957, was adjudged to have some redeeming "social importance" and was acquitted of being obscene on October 3.[8] Also in 1957 Viking published Jack Kerouac's *On the Road,* which became a bible for a generation of self-proclaimed dropouts. Two years later, Burroughs's *Naked Lunch,* with its graphic descriptions of drug use, sex, and violence, was published in Europe; it was banned in the United States until 1962. Comedian Lenny Bruce inspired the Beats in the 1950s with his incendiary brand of stand-up, attacking the political and religious icons of the day. He was arrested in the Café Au Go Go at 152 Bleecker Street in 1964 and would be at the center of the largest, costliest, and most fiercely contested and widely publicized obscenity trial in American history. His conviction was reversed on appeal, but by then it was too late for Bruce, who died of a drug overdose in 1966. He lived in the Marlton Hotel on West Eighth Street during his trial in order to be near his Beat supporters.

The Beats loved jazz, particularly the music of Charles Mingus, the innovative string-bass player and composer (fig. 7.10). Mingus's virtuoso solos and antiestablishment rants in the Village's jazz spots made him an area attraction even hotter than Jack Kerouac or Jackson Pollock, whose fame then seemed

FIG. 7.10 Pre-goateed Charles Mingus (left) playing at the Open Door, with Charlie Parker (saxophone), Thelonius Monk (piano), and Roy Haynes (drums), 1953. Jack Kerouac idolized Parker and claimed that his music inspired his writing style. (Parker died at age 34 from drink and drugs in 1955.) Photograph by Bob Parent. Courtesy of Dale Parent.

less certain. Many of the country's legendary jazz musicians, including Mingus, starred at the Open Door, the Five Spot, the Showplace, the Village Gate, and other Village venues after their 52nd Street shows. Mingus became more of a Village fixture after 1955 with his own band, the Jazz Workshop, and he was the quintessential Beat musician, often parodied on the Steve Allen show by TV comedian Louis Nye, with a turtleneck sweater and a beret added for effect.

Whereas the staid Italian community south of the square had tolerated the earlier bohemians, they became angered by the Beats and their too visible body of hangers-on, which was augmented, beginning in the 1960s, by the World War II baby-boomers who were then teenagers with some money to spend (fig. 7.11). Robert Moses's luxury Washington Square South housing was also seen as invasive. Not surprisingly, the Italians resented the huge influx of newcomers. The old espresso houses could not compete with the new ones, and local grocers and butchers began to be replaced by supermarkets. Outsiders opened pizzerias. The year 1959 saw young Italian toughs attacking homosexuals and blacks, particularly black men escorting white women; windows of establishments catering to the new crowds were smashed, and these places were shaken down by minor hoodlums and Mafia gangsters. Large numbers of policemen were added to the precinct's forces. The *New York Times* reported in September 1959 on "a sinister quality of hatred just under the carnival atmosphere created by blinking neon signs, jazz music, writers reading their poems, and crowds of young people" and the "sinister threat it poses to a peaceful way of life in one of the city's best-known neighborhoods" (fig. 7.12).[9] Later, in the 1960s, motorcycles added their sound to the nightly din, and during the day the bikes and their riders were concentrated around the arch in Washington Square.

Folk music was the biggest draw to Washington Square and the Bleecker-MacDougal Street haunts in the 1950s, and it brought in the largest number of outsiders to upset the Italian community. The square was the heart of folk

FIG. 7.11 (*top*) Tourist bus in Washington Square, mid-1950s. The view is northeast with One University (left) towering in the background. Photographer unknown. Courtesy of Hulton Archive / Getty Images.

FIG. 7.12 (*bottom*) The nighttime crowd on MacDougal Street in 1963. The view looks south toward the west side of MacDougal from a short distance below West Third Street. Courtesy of NYT Pictures.

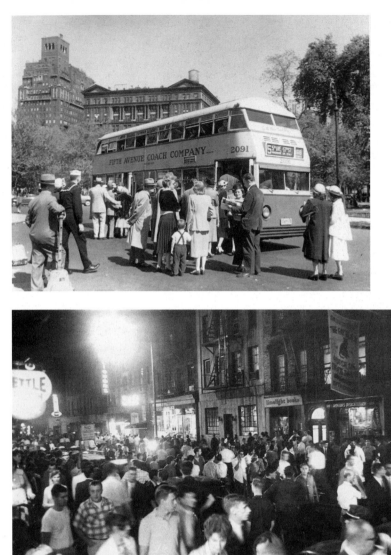

singing in the city and a springboard for talent (fig. 7.13). Sunday sessions in the square were run by Izzy Young of the Folklore Center at 110 MacDougal Street and Howard Moody, the burly, butch-cut ex-marine who was pastor of the Judson Church on Washington Square South. Moody had turned the church into a center for art, dance, and poetry, and a clearinghouse for civil rights and other protest movements of the time.

Big names appeared in the square during the 1950s. Robert Cantwell recounted the following in his book on the folk revival:

> As the numbers of folksingers increased [after 1945], the police attempted to control the crowd by dividing it into groups, many of whom formed around established figures [like Pete and Toshi Seeger] whose recordings were supplying the repertories for the amateurs: the Weavers, the Terriers, and the New Lost City Ramblers frequently joined the Sunday singing; Theo Bikel, Jack Elliot, and even

FIG. 7.13 Folk singing in the fountain area of Washington Square, 1959, David Sears is on banjo. Photograph by and courtesy of David Gahr.

FIG. 7.14 Young Edward Koch strumming his guitar in 1956, the year he moved to the Village. Photograph by Al Thaler. Courtesy of the LaGuardia and Wagner Archives, LaGuardia Community College / CUNY and the Hon. Edward I. Koch.

Woody Guthrie himself, in the early stages of his deterioration [from Huntington's disease], could be found there, imitated in his slouch, his old clothes, and his facial stubble by young would-be Okies who had to be told who he was.[10]

On March 27, 1961, after 16 years of unopposed Sunday-afternoon folk singing in the square, Parks Commissioner Newbold Morris banned singing there at the request of the Greenwich Village Chamber of Commerce. That came six days after Pete Seeger's conviction as a subversive influence by the House Un-American Activities Committee, which cast the ensuing protest as one against McCarthyism and brought national attention. At a subsequent demonstration against the ban on April 9, 10 protestors were arrested and 20 hurt. On Sunday, April 13, Howard Moody led a crowd of more than 500 people into the square. There was no opposition, and on the next Sunday, April 20, more than 2,000 singers, musicians, and fans again gathered in protest. Finally, on May 14, 1961, the ban was lifted by Mayor Wagner. City councilman and Washington Square resident Edward Koch had taken an early stance, although one opposed by his Italian constituents (part of his Greenwich Village district), by forming a Right to Sing Committee in 1960 (fig. 7.14).

Twenty-year-old Bob Dylan was drawn to the Village in early 1961 by Ginsberg and Guthrie, and he first lived at 161 West Fourth Street. He performed in the Café Wha? at 115 MacDougal Street, hung around the Kettle of Fish bar across the street at No. 114, and played in other coffee houses,

FIG. 7.15 Joan Baez (left), Bob Dylan (center), and Eric Anderson (right) in 1975 at Gerde's Folk City. Photograph by and courtesy of Mary Alfieri.

bars, and apartments. He opened for the late famed blues guitarist John Lee Hooker at Gerde's Folk City at 11 West Fourth Street before he became a feature there himself (fig. 7.15). After being discovered by music producer John Hammond, Dylan recorded the "anthems of a generation"—"Blowin' in the Wind," "Like a Rolling Stone," and "Visions of Johanna"—and went on to become a legitimate folk and rock artist for the ages. In 1966 Dylan bought two adjoining townhouses and combined them into one large residence at 92–94 MacDougal Street in the MacDougal-Sullivan Gardens block.

Bob Dylan met the young guitarist Jimi Hendrix in the Kettle of Fish in 1966. Dylan inspired Hendrix and was the catalyst who energized him to leave Harlem and a predominantly black audience to become part of the wide-open artistic community of Greenwich Village. Hendrix played in most of the Village hot spots—the Purple Onion on West Fourth Street; the Café Au Go Go and the Village Gate on Bleecker Street; the Night Owl Café on West Third Street; and the Gaslight Café, the Kettle of Fish, and the Café Wha? on MacDougal Street. In 1969, having achieved fame as an international rock-and-roll guitar star, Hendrix established his Electric Lady sound studio at 52 West Eighth Street. It was located in the large cellar space of the 8th Street Playhouse building, where, for decades, a Western-themed nightclub featuring square-dancing had once operated. There, Hendrix lavished a reported $1 million on construction and the latest recording equipment for use by his band and others. Hendrix had only begun to use his studio when, on tour in London, he died at age 24 from drug-induced heart failure in September 1970.

After 1968, Village tourism got an added boost when the prestigious Michelin Green Guides added New York City to its series. Washington Square, the Michelin authors proclaimed, was the "heart" of Greenwich Vil-

lage, which rated two stars. There, according to the guide, echoing Simone de Beauvoir's description 20 years earlier, one could find a decidedly unsinister section: "reminiscent of Montmartre, the Latin Quarter and St. Germain des Prés in Paris: a cosmopolitan crowd of tourists, 'intellectuals,' students and a dubious collection of beatniks, hippies and bohemians while, in the dimly lit nightclubs and coffee houses, blues and folk singers perform."[11]

At the same time that Howard Moody was creating an avant-garde culture center on Washington Square, he was also coping with the local teenage population, which was heavily into street gangs and heroin. He and Ed Fancher, one of the owners of the *Village Voice*, founded an aid center at West Fourth and Sullivan Streets. They were also involved with a coalition of antidrug agencies, and Fancher kept his paper abreast of the problem: the *Voice* reported the crimes the drugs caused, the activities of the coalition, and new ideas for antidrug measures. By 1964 the square had even acquired a "Junkie Row" as one of its prominent features (fig. 7.16). Quick to notice that the drug culture enjoyed a tolerant haven in the square and in the blocks around it, pushers staked out a length of pathway near the southwest corner of the green as their favorite local marketplace.

By 1965 the Bleecker-MacDougal Street mess had worsened, and for the first time West Eighth Street began to suffer the consequences. West Eighth had long been a main path from the subway, PATH stations, and bus stops to the Bleecker-MacDougal epicenter of the Beat scene, but in 1965 physical changes crept in that began to cheapen its retail mix. West Eighth Street had its own bars, restaurants, and nightclubs attuned to more mainstream 1950s and 1960s fare. However, two fast food joints, an orange-drink/hot-dog luncheonette, and a pizzeria replaced two neighborhood stores, a dress shop, and a pharmacy. More ominously, the Poster Mat, which originally sold just posters, glassware, candles, and pop art gifts at 16 West Eighth Street, began stocking drug paraphernalia in response to what its operator called "the 1960s marijuana explosion"; this dubious business development was soon to be initiated in other stores.[12]

In the 1960s the city administration exacerbated the woes of West Eighth Street and its surrounding neighborhood by an action and an inaction: dumping society's unfortunates in the area's single-room-occupancy (SRO) hotels and ignoring the continuing overcrowding and deplorable conditions in the Women's House of Detention. The SROs added to an alarming degree to the drug culture and rising crime rate already present. In 1970, then-congressman Edward Koch blamed Mayor John V. Lindsay for the SROs, which sorely tested the Village's liberalism. "There was a conscious decision by the administration in 1965 to make Greenwich Village wide open for every circus program imaginable," said Koch. Some "1,500 to 2,000 homeless single men on welfare, 90 percent of them black, many of them recently released convicts, . . . live in several run-down Village hotels and, . . . according to the police, are a major cause of the area's crime," reported the *New York Times* on September 28, 1970.[13] The trouble spots Koch and the *Times* referred to were some nineteenth-century hotels whose fortunes had been done in by more modern structures situated in midtown and by the automobile, which vastly widened the availability of lodging elsewhere. They included the Greenwich Hotel (the old Mills House No. 1, at 160 Bleecker Street), the Broadway Central, the Earle, the Albert, and the Marlton. There were 833 single men on welfare in the Greenwich Hotel, making up the majority of its residents, and they created a mini-crime wave of their own. Patrolmen in the Charles Street station made 700 arrests in Washington Square alone during July and August 1970, most of them on charges of public intoxication and drug possession. Seventy-five percent of those charged came from the Greenwich Hotel.

By 1970 a multitude of peddlers and panhandlers had made Sixth Avenue and West Eighth Street conspicuously unpleasant for passersby, and local businesses were being terrorized by a plague of holdups. Neighborhood residents avoided their Main Street. So severe were the social problems, added to skyrocketing commercial rents, that some local leaders believed that a continuation of the conditions could destroy the unique character of the historic neighborhood. The city had already begun closing Eighth Street to automobiles on Saturdays to help reduce the invading crowds of outsiders disturbing the quality of life for residents.

In combination with the SROs, the other festering neighborhood sore spot was the Women's House of Detention. Completed in 1932 with considerable municipal pride and built to hold 457, by 1938 it was already overcrowded with 688, meaning that two women were housed in many of the 10½ by 6½-foot cells. In the following year the Sixth Avenue Association was already campaigning for the prison's removal because of its noisy inmates. Loud interactions between the locked-up women and passers-by, friends, and relatives were frequent in the developing freak-show and carnival atmosphere at the Sixth Avenue and Eighth Street intersection, causing disgust at the scene as well as concern for the plight of the prisoners. Over the decades, conditions at the jail fluctuated between bad and terrible, with a record total of 750 inmates at one point. In 1963, the city finally began building a new prison on Rikers Island, and on June 13, 1971, the massive iron doors of the jail closed, and the last busload of the 422 inmates then incarcerated there moved to the new facility.

What to do with the building then became a contentious issue. One group wanted to sell it for use as a school, retirement home, or for another relatively socially redeeming purpose; others wanted it torn down and replaced with a new, lower structure (it overshadowed the landmark Jefferson Market Courthouse); and a third faction wanted the prison preserved because of its architectural merit. Yet the city administration was adamant about razing the building, and in 1973 Mayor Lindsay said at the ceremony for its demise, "I am delighted to fulfill a long-standing commitment to bring about the demolition of this prison. When it was built in 1932, it was the wrong kind of prison in the wrong place—a maximum security fortress in the middle of a residential community." By 1974, the Women's House of Detention was gone, and today the site is home to a lovely community garden. For the West Eighth Street merchants, though, the loss of the prison meant a loss of valuable business in a worsening economy. "Business is down 60 percent," said the operator of Wood Art, a frame and print shop at 11 West Eighth Street. "Those women had money. They were prostitutes, and their men used to come on this street to buy for them. They wanted clothes, and all kinds of things. That jail brought a lot of business here."[14]

The coup de grace for West Eighth Street merchants was not the loss of prison-based income but the 1974–75 recession that decimated small shops throughout the city. West Eighth Street's individually owned service stores—many of them distinguished by an idiosyncratic charm that had been a trademark of the street—went out of business or left the area. As New York City dug itself out of near-bankruptcy with critical help from the state, most of the vacant storefronts were replaced not by other service stores like dress shops, cleaners, hardware dealers, shoe repair shops, or food markets, but by impersonal chain stores, novelty shops, and establishments depending for a good part of their business on younger sensation-seeking tourists.

Throughout this long period of trauma for the city, crime rose, civil unrest grew and exploded in Harlem and Bedford-Stuyvesant in 1964, and students rioted at Columbia University in 1968. In comparison, Washington Square's problems looked small. Nevertheless, unruly behavior, often lasting until dawn and abetted by establishments (particularly on MacDougal Street) that kept illegal hours and used hawkers to rope in fun-seekers, was becoming intolerable to the neighborhood. The city's police responded to the disturbances on MacDougal Street and at other Village spots with saturation deployment, use of decoys, street closings, and other techniques that helped bring the neighborhood through the crisis. New York City's Tactical Police Force (TPF), which had been established in 1959, was key to the department's success and a model for the nation. Starting with an experimental squad of 75 men, it had grown to 944 by 1968. With independence from the precinct organization, the TPF could strike where necessary, and it was a prime factor in the city's critical strategy for defusing potentially explosive situations.

Police action was key, but increasing impatience on the part of neighborhood residents also assisted in quelling the MacDougal Street disturbances. In 1965, Koch formed the MacDougal Area Neighborhood Association (MANA), an organization that became 1,000 strong and was mainly drawn from the directly affected Italian Americans south of the square. By forcing the lawbreaking businesses into court and putting pressure on the administration to care more about the neighborhood than about the tourist business, MANA took important steps toward bringing relative peace to the area.

Student radicalism had little impact on the Washington Square district in the 1960s. NYU, still mainly a commuter school, had a few student protests, but they paled in comparison with those that ignited Columbia and other colleges and universities around the country. NYU chancellor John Brademas had it right when, in a television interview years later, he referred to the campus as "a hotbed of student rest."[15]

However, on March 6, 1970, one tragic reminder of the national trauma rocked the serene tree-lined block of West Eleventh Street between Fifth and Sixth Avenues when an explosion in the basement of No.18, one of five in a row originally built in 1844–45 by Henry Brevoort for his five daughters, almost totally destroyed the house. The place was owned by a wealthy businessman named James P. Wilkerson, who was then on vacation in the Caribbean. His daughter Cathlyn was identified as a member of the Weather Underground, an ultraradical faction of the militant antiwar campus group Students for a Democratic Society. The police investigation revealed that Cathlyn Wilkerson and 13 cohorts had turned the basement of her family's house into a temporary bomb factory. Of the five people in the house when the accidental explosion occurred, three were killed. Wilkerson and Katherine Boudin escaped the blazing house and went underground, disappearing for over ten years. Today, the sharply angled and pivoted front midsection of the reconstructed townhouse, designed by architect Hugh Hardy in 1978, is a reminder of the horrific event.

Criminal rowdyism in the Washington Square district reached a crisis in 1976, when a youth rampage in the square killed one person and injured 12 others. Twenty-seven young men were arrested in the incident, and 10 out of the 50-odd participants turned up by the ensuing investigation were later indicted. Even though drug-related crime did not abate until the 1990s, this 1976 tragedy seemed to be a watershed event. Afterward, the police paid more attention to the Village. Said Captain William P. Fortune, who was commander of the West Tenth Street station at the time, "Greenwich Village always has been the bastion of tolerance and liberality . . . As of late we've been going full speed in reverse. I've been asked 'Can't the police hassle these people?'"[16] Community attitudes were changing fast.

In addition to a loss of tolerance, the community felt a new pride in the square in the year of the national bicentennial; indeed, a reversal of fortune for the entire Washington Square district had begun on the social and historic preservation fronts. Neighborhood cleanup campaigns were organized, and residents increased their demands and kept up the drumbeat for stronger police protection. In response to the city's attempt to revamp the square in the early 1960s, the local citizenry showed early spunk, forcing a completely different design to be implemented. The spirit of protest so prevalent in the sixties led community boards and block associations to participate more in the city's decision-making process. For the Washington Square district, the turnabout began with neighborhood involvement in the development of the square itself.

During the 1960s the fate of Washington Square was controlled by Parks Commissioner Newbold Morris and whatever pressure the community could put on him. After 1962 the removal of the roadways in the square freed up 1.3 acres for new uses, and some kind of redesign of the square was in order. At the same time, its peacefulness and usefulness for the surrounding community were disturbed by the MacDougal Street crowd, welfare recipients in local SROs, and vagrants migrating west from the Bowery, then the nation's biggest skid row.

Jane Jacobs, the unorthodox urbanist and activist, had studied neighborhood squares in Philadelphia, Chicago, San Francisco, and New York City in the 1950s. By 1960 she had come to the conclusion that the best way to deal with undesirables was not to make or keep a space unappealing, or to limit access to it, but rather to make the area in question as attractive to as many others as possible. This idea became one of the main theses in her seminal 1961 book, *The Death and Life of Great American Cities.* In it, Manhattan's Washington Square was cited as one of the best examples of a successful square, particularly on account of its central fountain basin, which was used "inventively and exuberantly" by so many urbanites. Jacobs analyzed the appeal of

> the sunken concrete circular basin, dry most of the year, bordered with four steps ascending to a stone coping that forms an outer rim a few feet above ground level. In effect, this is a circular arena, a theater in the round, and that is how it is used, with complete confusion as to who are spectators and who are the show. Everybody is both, although some are more so: guitar players, singers, crowds of darting children, impromptu dancers, sunbathers, conversers, show-offs, photographers, tourists, and mixed in with them all a bewildering sprinkling of absorbed readers—not there for lack of choice, because quiet benches to the east are half-deserted.[17]

To encourage use, the city's standard design for a large space included discrete areas for diverse activities such as basketball courts, skating rinks, band shells, and playgrounds. Robert Moses had proposed the like for the square in conjunction with his roadway proposal in 1957, but the community had objected to most of these functions as inappropriate to the square's place in history. Newbold Morris, who was Moses's successor and ally, called in the landscape architect Gilmore D. Clarke for a new design. His firm, Clarke & Rapuano, had previously worked on Moses's roadway-in-the-square proposal. Possibly thinking that a more formal design for the square might satisfy the bluebloods to the north, Clarke came up with a plan featuring marble colonnades branching out from the sides of the arch, and expanses of lawns stretching east and west from the central fountain. Neighborhood residents objected again, wanting to retain spaces for the square's traditional activities without losing the basic layout of the square's pathways. In 1964 Mayor Wagner directed Morris to collaborate with a local committee of experts to produce an acceptable plan, and in 1967 the committee produced their recommendations for a design.

The main features of the new plan consisted of a large sunken plaza around the central fountain and an adjacent raised podium and smaller Garibaldi Plaza to the east for concerts. (Under the aegis of the Washington Square Music Festival, a summer concert series had been given in front of the Alexander Holley statue since 1953.) Small plazas occupied the square's corners, including the popular Chess Plaza installed during La Guardia's term, and another small plaza was laid out to the west of the statue of Holley. The focus on the fountain area, which expanded the performance space for folk singing, was the most contentious component of the new design. One group, termed the *old guard* by the *Village Voice,* wanted an ornamental fountain, but Jane Jacobs argued that "as soon as you have an ornamental fountain, you'll need a fence around it," and "you [the old guard] are ignoring the fact that we have here (in the fountain circle) one of the most remarkable things in America—an informal theater in the round."[18] One of the old guard suggested that Washington Square was not the place for a theater in the round. A vote on the issue at a community-wide meeting was split, with the chair casting its deciding vote in favor of the performance space. The subject of the square as a public city square or the neighborhood's private preserve still divides the community.

For lighting, the square's wonderful cast-iron "bishop's crook" lampposts were replaced by the 1950s "lollypop" lights, which were similar to those installed around the Washington Square Village housing complex southeast of the square. (At the time, cast-iron lighting was being replaced all over the city.) The renovation was completed on December 6, 1970, at a cost of $1,559,900; the square that is in place today remains basically the same. Some problems with the children's play areas needed fixing, but according to the press, the square's regulars liked the renovations.

Commentary by critics and writers over the years since has missed the real and growing value of Washington Square—its setting in the midst of skyscraper Manhattan. Former Parks Commissioner August Heckscher's book, *Open Spaces,* lays out the four key attributes of a "good square": its need to be part of a large city, its relatedness to the city streets, the diversity of its users, and its enclosure by a building wall that gives it form.[19] Washington Square meets the first three of these criteria superbly, but in the last, the square is spectacularly unique. Traditionally, the enclosure wall is created by the buildings facing a square, like the Georgian rows of London's squares, or the Federal, Greek Revival, and Italianate townhouses of early Washington Square. Stanford White's Judson Church complex and the arch remain the square's chief ornaments, but today, the square's form-giving wall is the magnificent Manhattan skyline, and the buildings immediately facing the square are reduced in importance.

Centrally located between the island's mountainous clusters of skyscrapers in the Wall Street financial district and midtown, Washington Square has not been hemmed in by overscaled developments on its periphery as have the other squares and spaces along Manhattan's spine, such as Battery Park, Bowling Green, City Hall Park, Union Square, Gramercy Park, Madison Square, Herald Square, Bryant Park, and Times Square. Indeed, the contours of Washington Square's periphery have been transformed from a wall into those of a bowl or amphitheater, an effect highlighted when the first version of Two Fifth Avenue was about to do it violence. On February 9, 1950, during the conflict between the neighborhood and developer Samuel Rudin, Henry H. Curran, a former Manhattan borough president and a prominent jurist, wrote in the *New York Herald Tribune:* "There is a tall building [One Fifth Avenue] on the Mews, a hundred feet behind the old row [the Row], which looks a little like an overgrown bottle of undoubtedly excellent hair tonic. It is not a happy interruption of the gentle upward slope of a bowl, but at least it stands back a little, just a little. The new building will be worse, a great deal worse. Dedicated to bulk, it will destroy forever a note of beauty that cannot be reproduced."[20] At the time the *Herald Tribune* published this, the Chase Manhattan Plaza, the late World Trade Center, the World Financial Center, and other downtown skyscrapers had not been constructed (fig. 7.17). Since the 1960s, when they first began to rise, their appearance has vastly enhanced the southern perspective from the square. The community had once fought NYU over height limits on Washington Square South because of loss of sunlight in the square. Now, the loss of the southern bowl contour is just as important.

In 1976 the architecture critic Paul Goldberger said that Washington Square's size fit "awkwardly" between the categories of a square and a park.[21] His criticism, however, misses an essential element of the distinction between the two—one that is only partly related to size. Urban parks, in contrast with squares, are landscaped spaces large enough to provide an escape from the city's streets and buildings: the visitor totally loses a sense that the trees and walkways are surrounded by a metropolis. In contrast, the visitor to a square can never forget that the space is an integral part of the urban fabric. This is certainly true of Washington Square. In the square, although it is larger than, say, Union Square, Gramercy Park, or Madison Square, the city is ever pres-

ent. Yet visitors to it do not feel oppressed or overshadowed by surrounding
skyscrapers.

Views into the north and south streets radiating from the square empha-
size the near and far bowl effect as buildings rise higher in the distance for
miles along the thoroughfares and are bejeweled at night by the lights of the
city. Today, these unrivaled perspectives are the square's chief amenities. The
stirring vista through the arch up Fifth Avenue became most dramatic when
the Empire State Building (at 34th Street) and 500 Fifth Avenue (at 42nd
Street) were completed in the early 1930s. Another magnificent view from the
square is south on West Broadway, past the restaurant row of SoHo, to the
awesome monoliths of the Wall Street financial district in the far distance—
a sparkling fantasy at night. East and west of the square, the bowl effect is
less pronounced, with Washington Place instead presenting glimpses into
the neighborhood's nineteenth-century architectural heritage. Eastward on
Washington Place is a passage to Broadway past the highly ornamented commercial 1880s and 1890s architecture created by Alfred Zucker and others. On
Washington Place West, through the 1920s apartment houses on the square,
the view takes in the lively assemblage of early-to-mid-nineteenth-century
houses stretching to West Street.

Indeed, no square in the United States, and perhaps in the world, surpasses
Washington Square in its combination of historic elements and high visual

drama, and in its centrality to one of the world's most vibrant cultural communities. So unusual has the setting of Washington Square become as Manhattan has grown around it but never overpowered it that it really has no peer. However, in the 1970s this famous square was in trouble.

By April 1973 crime was still on the rise in the city and the nation, and the parks department proposed enclosing Washington Square with a seven-foot-high wrought-iron fence "to combat muggings, vagrancy and vandalism" in and around it. As conceived, the fence would have eight gates connecting the paved walkways, making it easier for the police to exert control over the square's foot traffic. Residents, presumably from the old guard, had complained that their renowned square, "a magnet for the city's cultural underground on sunny Sunday mornings, has been swamped with derelicts, narcotics addicts and sexual perverts." However, the commanding officer of the Sixth Precinct, Capt. William Kelly, felt that "the main problem was not muggers, but vagrants and others who play musical instruments at night and disturb the residents."[22] Community Board 2, whose opinion was critical, unanimously opposed fencing the square, just as they had done in 1967, and the matter was dropped. The cry for fencing reflected the continuing division of community opinion about how much of a public versus private neighborhood preserve the square should be. It also revealed a lack of appreciation for Jacobs's theories and for real-life examples like Bryant Park, whose fortress-like design was the reason for its failure as a safe urban space. (Bryant Park, laid out in the 1930s, has recovered in the 1990s after a redesign based on Jacobs's and urbanist William Hyde Whyte's ideas. Whyte's later, more scientific observations paralleled and complemented Jacobs's work, and convinced him that the city should follow her suggestions for pushing out undesirables from public gathering places.)

An NYU sociology project studied the square in the summer of 1973. Among its conclusions, backed up by press reports, was that "[t]he dominant source of dissatisfaction is the lack of safety and the presence of undesirables [i.e., intoxicated and licentious bums, gamblers, panhandlers, pushers, and 'weirdos']."[23] But the study found that crime was much worse elsewhere in the city and that in the adjacent and comparably sized Ninth Precinct to the east, taking in the East Village, the crime rate was twice as bad. The NYU study was inconclusive on the value of a fence; however, it noted that one big problem in the square was dogs.

A dog run had not been included in the new design, and the law required that dogs be leashed and curbed in the square. The regulation was neither observed nor enforced, and the NYU study, while recognizing the value of dogs, cited the problems of excrement, competition for space, interference with adult games, destruction of grass and plantings, and danger to children. Part of the solution came after general disgust over dog waste in the city led to enactment of the clean-up, or "pooper-scooper," law in 1978. With that, and a dog run, the difficulty presented by dogs in the square has noticeably diminished.

The NYU study also stated that excessive numbers of tourists contributed to the bigger problems plaguing the square and the surrounding Village. "The Village suffers from an overload," the authors reported, "because there are so few comparable communities in the city—artistic and historic." By the 1980s, to the delight of tourists and the chagrin of many residents, the square's design had encouraged what was possibly the premier "found space" in America for street performers.[24]

Eighth Street, as convenient a route to Washington Square as to the Beat scene on MacDougal Street, also felt the ill effects of tourism. As Washington Square had a watershed year in 1976, 1978 seemed to be a turning point for the fortunes of West Eighth Street. Some stores had remained vacant since the 1974–75 recession, and fast food and other transient-oriented businesses dominated the street. However, on the prime southeast corner of West Eighth Street and Sixth Avenue, a major book dealer, B. Dalton, was planning to replace the worst of the fast food joints with one of its bookstores, and the company hired the local architect Edgar Tafel to design it. Besides designing the acclaimed community house for the First Presbyterian Church, Tafel had been on the Washington Square design team and had created its picturesque group of three small service buildings using redbrick facades and pitched slate roofs. For B. Dalton, Tafel again created a masterly new addition at an important site. Using redbrick facades, blind brick arches, plate glass windows, and a decorative brick cornice, he designed the two-story structure to fit comfortably among both its nineteenth-century and modernist neighbors. Construction, though, didn't begin until the spring of 1980, delayed "nine or ten months," according to Tafel, by Community Board 2's involvement in the design process.[25]

Toward Fifth Avenue on West Eighth Street, the original Whitney Museum, one of New York's art monuments, was again filled with artists, art students, and paint. Needing larger gallery and storage space, the museum had moved uptown in 1953, renting the building at 8 West Eighth to a succession of indifferent tenants who let it fall into disrepair. In 1967, however, the painter and teacher Mercedes Matter and a group of art students founded the New York Studio School of Drawing, Painting, and Sculpture and purchased the old museum building. Their endeavor had been championed by the legendary teacher, critic, and polymath Meyer Schapiro, who secured aid from several donors and a grant from the Ford Foundation. Both the New York Studio School and B. Dalton remained cultural anchors of West Eighth Street during the long wait for help from the Eighth Street Business Improvement District and Mayor Rudolph W. Giuliani's quality-of-life initiatives in the 1990s.

One important fallout of 1960s conscientiousness raising or "people power," was the impact on city planning. Whether issues concerned crime, dogs, tourism, new buildings, or anything over which the city could act, community boards continued to gain control over the years. *The Death and Life of Great American Cities* was also a potent call for neighborhood involvement

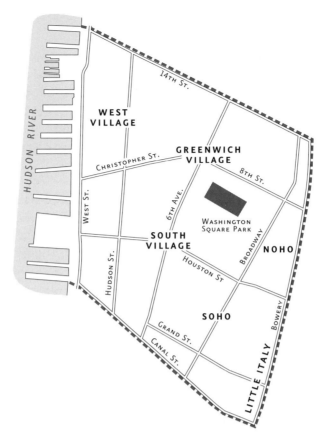

FIG. 7.18 Map of Community Board 2's neighborhoods and the principal streets, 2001. The old Fifteenth Ward occupies the upper-right quadrant. Map based on *Community District Needs—Manhattan, Fiscal Year 2001*, NYC Department of City Planning.

with administrative districts in cities. These districts would be a part of the municipal government to better coordinate the citywide service departments like the parks, police, and firemen. Under Mayor Wagner, a New York City charter revision in 1963 adopted the concept—59 planning areas with community boards were formed, including 12 in Manhattan.

Borders of the districts were drawn along historic or geographic boundaries. Community Board 2, which contained Washington Square, was made up of the old Fifteenth and Ninth Wards, then generally considered to encompass Greenwich Village. The board's southern edge extended to Canal Street because the city attempted to equalize the population count in the 59 districts, but even with the southern extension, Board 2 covered one of the city's least populated areas—some 80,000 people out of the city's then approximately 7.8 million (fig. 7.18). In addition to the Washington Square district (Fifteenth Ward), Board 2 picked up a chunk of the Lower East Side's Little Italy, more of the South Village's Italian neighborhood and blue-collar manufacturing zone, a thriving West Village gay community, and what historian Philip Campbell has described as the general Village populace of "artists and writers, sculptors and actors, editors and journalists, modern dancers and theatrical designers, poets and literary critics, political analysts and utopians, mystics and intellectuals, musicians and philosophers."[26] Board 2 also encompassed the site of Jane Jacobs's remarkable win over the city's Title I plan for high-rise housing in the West Village. This 1963 community revolt led by

Jacobs produced, instead, five- and six-story redbrick walk-ups spanning Washington Street between Morton and Bank Streets in what was a dreary commercial section. The 420 subsidized, middle-class apartments named the West Village Houses were meant to, and did, enhance the neighborhood diversity that Jacobs felt was essential to urban vitality.

Funding for boards was minuscule, with a maximum yearly allocation of $15,000, which was supposed to provide for projects like the hiring of architects and planners to conduct studies. A subsequent charter revision approved by voters in 1975 specified that the boards' advisory function be strengthened and expanded. Boards were given a formal involvement in approving neighborhood changes and a strong voice in making new recommendations, and, for the first time, they were given an annual budget of $60,000 with which to hire a district manager and a staff.

Block associations, which had grown in proportion to the number of structures replaced in the building boom of the 1950s and 1960s, also had a role to play in city planning. By 1975 Mayor Lindsay had almost 10,000 block associations and 62 community boards to be consulted when designing municipal projects. Inevitably, builders and developers complained loudly that realization of their projects was impeded by the new review process, but more effective community involvement in city planning had been achieved.

Block associations had been working to spruce up their neighborhoods since World War II, and they, like other activist groups, had mushroomed in the late 1960s. Using members' dues and monies raised from block parties and other fund-raising activities, they fought massage parlors and pornography bookstores, planted trees and flowers, installed security lighting, covered potholes, curbed (literally) dog litter, painted benches, and repaired sidewalks. Coalitions of block associations were formed, with clout directly proportional to the number of members in the coalition; the one covering Greenwich and West Villages had 34.

On the historic preservation front, still more of the neighborhood's older buildings were pulled down during the fifties, sixties, and seventies. Public indignation across the city was giving ever-growing support to preservationists, who were working to devise a landmarks law by 1965. In addition to the depredations of white- and tan-brick high-rises, two notable early buildings, the Tenth Street Studio Building and the Bible House, were lost to uninspired replacements in the 1950s. Fortunately, the Jefferson Market Courthouse and the Astor Library were saved through adaptive reuse and sensitive interior remodeling.

The Tenth Street Studio Building, Richard Morris Hunt's earliest extant architectural design, was razed in 1956. Its original function, to facilitate the marketing of its artist-residents' work, had long been taken over by dealers, and the number of people living in the old structure, which had never been fitted with modern plumbing, dwindled. No one came to the rescue of this remarkable building, and it was superseded by a nondescript apartment house.

Over on Astor Place, the Bible House had once stood with Cooper Union and other buildings of the 1850s as a showplace of New York, but in 1922 the Bible Society decided to send its printing out to commercial firms, and in 1936 the society itself moved uptown. "The building's old and outmoded, and the district's gone downhill," the Bible Society's real estate manager told a reporter in 1954. "So why not sell it?"[27] Cooper Union bought the Bible House and in 1961 replaced it with a bland building that houses its engineering school. Austere and out of context, the structure, clad in buff brick and stone, is mercifully only six stories high. Imaginative reuse of historic old structures was an alien concept in the 1950s.

In 1958, the Jefferson Market Courthouse became endangered when it lost its municipal function. By 1945, the city court had moved elsewhere, and the building was taken over in succession by the Public Works Administration, several civil defense groups, the Bureau of the Census, a health insurance program, and, last of all, a unit of the Police Academy. A developer was planning to erect an apartment house on the site, but this time effective opposition was able to save "Old Jeff." In 1959 this threatened loss inspired local political leader and architecture writer Margot Gayle and Judge Harold Birns, the city commissioner for housing and buildings, to fight for the courthouse's preservation by first repairing the works of the tower's huge four-faced clock and lighting it. They formed the Village Committee for the Clock on the Jefferson Market Courthouse, which was chaired by Gayle, in 1960.

By September 1961, the hands of Old Jeff's clock, which for years had remained stopped at twenty minutes after three, were moving once again. In celebration of the event, the tower's large fire bell tolled for the first time since Admiral Dewey's 1898 victory at Manila Bay. After 10,000 people and 500 businesses signed a "save the courthouse" petition and 62 organizations of all stripes backed the effort, Mayor Wagner became a strong supporter. Soon the New York Public Library, which had initially balked at the high cost of taking on the building, was persuaded to adapt Old Jeff as one of its branches. Architect Giorgio Cavaglieri was hired to supervise the exterior restoration and design the interior renovation, both of which were completed by 1967. Ada Louise Huxtable marveled at the success of the pioneering adaptive reuse, which she called "a study in organized public interest, dogged persistence, practical sentimentality and civic savvy—or how to make a determined group of citizens an effective force for the achievement of an objective generally considered hopeless." More recently, architect and writer Gregory F. Gilmartin summed up Old Jeff's value: "[W]hen Cavaglieri was finished, the library stood as an indictment of the modern library branches. They offered banal functionalism while Jefferson Market was graced by a generosity of scale and richness of craft that New Yorkers never expected to see duplicated in their lifetimes."[28]

While Cavaglieri was engaged with Old Jeff, he was also restoring the facade and renovating the interior of the Astor Library, which the impresario

FIG. 7.19 Joseph Papp, theater impresario and landmarking hero, at the Public Theater in 1985. Photograph by Richard Corkery. Courtesy of the *New York Daily News*.

Joseph Papp (fig. 7.19) had rescued from demolition by arranging for its purchase and transformation into the Public Theater. Its first production, the self-proclaimed "American tribal love-rock musical" *Hair,* made theater history in 1967 with its "six-piece rock band situated ten feet above the stage" and its "cheerful lack of [dramatic] structure."[29] Papp's theater on Lafayette Street became a popular downtown attraction with *Hair;* it mushroomed into an even more phenomenal draw after *A Chorus Line,* which began there and went on to run from 1975 to 1990 on Broadway with 6,137 performances (surpassed only by 7,485 by *Cats* in 2000). Papp used the profits from this fabulous moneymaker to subsidize more adventurous productions with less commercial appeal, and his theater became the nation's most important showcase for new playwrights. Papp's ingenious adaptive reuse of the Astor Library, together with the praise for the Jefferson Market Courthouse, severely challenged the prevailing real estate interests and proponents of architectural modernism. These victories reinforced the notion of enlightened preservation and renovation as a more than viable alternative to demolition and rebuilding.

New York City's 1965 landmarks law had been enacted in time to help Papp in his efforts to preserve the Astor Library. Yet the law had come into being only after a fight against entrenched ownership interests that had been responsible for the tragic razings of McKim, Mead & White's majestic Pennsylvania Railroad Station, one of the most significant building projects of the early twentieth century, and many other worthy structures. As a rising tide of public anger over mindless destruction made historic preservation legislation more palatable to politicians, a small band of preservationists searched for a way to shape a law that would withstand a strong challenge to its legal validity. Two impediments lay in the way of a landmarks law that would protect significant portions of a neighborhood as well as individual sites—the U.S. Supreme Court precedents on the matter, and the New York preservationists' sole concern for individual structures of historic merit, or "masterpieces," rather than whole districts. Charleston, Boston, and New Orleans had all established protected historic districts as early as the 1930s, and the courts upheld them. They did so, Gregory F. Gilmartin explains, "not because [these districts] preserved the beauty and historic character of neighborhoods, but because of more concrete and mercenary benefits: in return for surrendering a certain amount of freedom [in what changes they could make to their buildings], owners enjoyed increased property values, tourism flourished, and both the benefits and burdens fell on every property in the neighborhood."[30] These protected areas, such as the Vieux Carré in New Orleans, each contained a fair number of intact historical buildings. In contrast, early New York structures worth preserving were in scattered clumps. In addition, New York's preservationists had never even considered saving the architecture of entire districts until, in the late 1950s, a citizens' group in Brooklyn Heights took steps in that direction.

The U.S. Supreme Court and the lower courts had been in agreement that a community's policing power extended only to removing conditions "injurious to the public health, safety, morals and welfare." However, in 1954, in the case of *Berman v. Parker,* the Supreme Court ruled that it was definitely "within the power of the legislature to determine that the community should be beautiful" as well. *Beautiful* was the epoch-making word, and if beauty could be made, it could surely be protected, and the basis for a landmarks law was in hand. Enabling legislation was passed in New York State in 1956; however, the thorny issue of the role of city planners with respect to zoning, and the power the Landmarks Preservation Commission could wield when it came to protecting buildings, had to be resolved. With the success of Old Jeff being contrasted with the fate of Penn Station, which had been reduced to rubble, the City Council unanimously passed a landmarks bill in April 1965.[31]

Passage of the law made possible the last-minute rescue of the Astor Library, one of the new Landmarks Preservation Commission's first designations. A contract with a developer for an apartment house had already been signed, but the deal fell through, and the commission had one year to find a buyer or the designation would have to be rescinded. Joseph Papp bought the building just in time, and the Astor Library was saved.

Brooklyn Heights became the first historic district designated as a protected enclave by the Landmarks Preservation Commission. By the early 1960s a grass-roots preservation organization in the Heights, the first in the city to recognize the value of a whole area rather than individual sites, had done the work of documenting its case. It was persuaded to wait for an overall city law rather than separate legislation for a Heights district, and after the bill passed, the Heights was granted landmark status in November 1965.

It proved far more difficult to win a landmark designation for a Greenwich Village district. Its original 65-block proposed area, running from University Place on the east to Washington Street on the west, contained many buildings unworthy of protection. Furthermore, a number of the building owners were resistant to the idea of having permanent restrictions on the nature of the alterations that could be made to their property. A debate ensued that took more than four years and seven public hearings to decide: Should the protected area be comprised of 18 separate historic areas containing the most worthy structures within them (fig. 7.20) or should it be a single large district? The one-large-district model prevailed after general consensus was reached that unless the whole district, which was nearly 100 blocks, was covered, the smaller enclaves rich in genuine historic parts could well acquire wildly disreputable

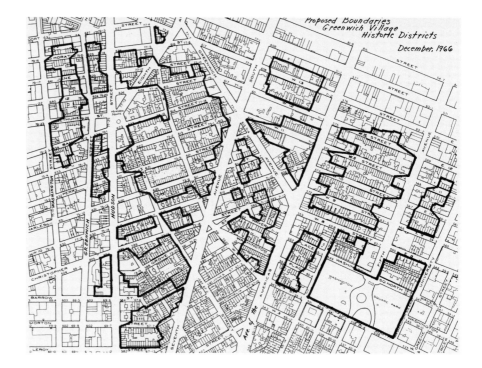

neighbors. The Landmarks Preservation Commission was concerned, however, that the larger district would be harder to defend in court. It took two years to document the full-sized area, and the Greenwich Village Historic District, covering the blocks north and west of Washington Square, was given landmark status in 1969. It remains the city's largest historic district, containing 2,035 buildings.

During the long period between the enabling Supreme Court decision in 1954 and historic district designation in 1969, two small groups of nineteenth-century townhouses within the environs of Washington Square were lost. In 1958, the First Presbyterian Church, seeing the inevitability of preservation, demolished two lovely houses designed by Alexander J. Davis at 12–14 West Twelfth Street for a future community center. Its architect, Edgar Tafel, did such a marvelous job creating a sympathetic addition to the church, even incorporating Gothic-inspired decoration into the building, that it won praise from the community and critics. The replacement of a block of four townhouses at 16–22 West Eighth Street in 1967 was markedly less successful. The Chisholm Real Estate Company erected a one-story commercial building containing five stores, constructed mainly to pay the real estate taxes until a more opportune time for redevelopment came along. Its overhanging roof with leaded dormers suggests an odd interpretation of English Tudor architecture, and while that feature distinguishes the structure from the other plain taxpayers on the south side of West Eighth Street, the other buildings constructed to meet similar financial exigencies together give that part of the street a somewhat snaggle-toothed appearance.

Without a strong test of the landmarks law, however, historic preservation was a shaky concept rather than a firm reality. A proposal by the Penn Central

Railroad to submerge Grand Central Terminal, a designated building, under a modernist 59-story slab created a test case that, despite the litigation risk (the court might rule against a law protecting beauty) could not be ignored. Architect Marcel Breuer's proposal for the new building was submitted for approval in 1969 and was unanimously rejected by the Landmarks Preservation Commission. The railroad, claiming economic hardship, sued, and after losing on appeal pursued its suit all the way to the U.S. Supreme Court. In 1978 the court upheld the landmarks law, and the Washington Square community, at least that part within the boundaries of the historic district, could feel secure.

As community boards, block associations, and the Landmarks Preservation Commission emerged and Robert Moses lost in his bid to put a road through the square, another Moses roadway scheme to the south had alarming consequences for a growing artists' community there. Redevelopment in the 1950s and 1960s wiped out most of the cheap studio spaces used by artists around Washington Square. Some relocated to the East Village, NoHo (the streets north of Houston Street between Broadway and the Bowery), and the old seaport district around Fulton Street and Coenties Slip, but many others moved to an industrial area south of Houston between West Broadway and Lafayette Street—today's SoHo. A final battle royal there in the late 1960s and early 1970s between neighborhood residents and planners did more than protect the Washington Square district's southern flank against the danger of continuing redevelopment. It also, on a much wider scale, changed the way cities are viewed and valued, which ultimately saved downtowns across the nation.

SoHo had spaces in its old manufacturing lofts that were cheap and big enough to accommodate the larger paintings, sculptures, and installations that were being created in the 1960s. To reconfigure loft buildings as studios and galleries solved the growing need for creating and showing the large-scale works promulgated by several generations of the New York School. SoHo offered the dealers more space for their money than was available in the established uptown gallery areas and facilitated interactions among artists, dealers, and clients who enjoyed the prospect of investing in new trends at their very source. The artists who lived in SoHo could also enjoy the inexpensive markets and restaurants of nearby Little Italy and Chinatown. Space was a bargain because the buildings had become outmoded for many types of commercial use, the land including SoHo had long been slated for urban renewal, and highways were making cheap suburban sites readily accessible. Landlords were happy to get anyone who would move in.

While the Wagner administration was holding off the threat of demolition under urban renewal, the inhabitants of SoHo faced two immediate problems. The lofts were neither zoned nor built for residential use, and a ten-lane roadway unveiled in 1959 was planned to replace Broome Street, cutting the heart out of SoHo. While the city worked to accommodate artists in areas zoned for manufacturing (accomplished in 1971), the roadway issue was far more intractable. Since the 1920s the roadway had been part of regional planning to link the East River bridges with the Holland Tunnel, and it had become a top priority with Robert Moses after the 1956 Federal Interstate Highway Act, which promised 90 percent federal funding for such projects. "In April 1960 the City Planning Commission approved the Moses route, called the Lower Manhattan Expressway, and determined that 416 buildings would have to be razed," meaning that the "2,000 housing units, 365 retail stores, and 480 non-retail establishments" contained within these structures would have to go, writes Charles R. Simpson in *SoHo,* his history of the neighborhood.[32] Community opposition was immediate and implacable.

Politicians representing SoHo marshaled large groups of elderly constituents who appeared at every expressway hearing to denounce the destruction of neighborhoods where they had spent their entire lives. In February 1961 liberal political reformers from the Villages jumped on the protest bandwagon. At one meeting, 300 people chose Jane Jacobs, who was about to publish *The Death and Life of Great American Cities,* as their leader. The Citywide Coalition Against the Expressway was born. The group's main strategy was to link its opposition to the cause of neighborhood preservation, which had the sympathies of the rest of the city. Mayor Wagner, given a hot political issue with costs and benefits that were difficult to fathom, stalled for time.

The city's top business and labor leaders were backing the expressway, including David Rockefeller, the head of the Chase Manhattan Bank. Rockefeller believed the bank's new 60-story aluminum and glass headquarters downtown between Pine and Liberty Streets would benefit from a highway nearby. Rockefeller and other chief executives of large corporations with interests in the area also planned to reinvigorate the financial district with the World Trade Center (built 1962–76), and they hoped that the expressway would facilitate their efforts by easing access to downtown. A powerful coalition of labor unions, desirous of the resulting downtown construction work and future service jobs, was also a strong expressway proponent.

John Lindsay, who succeeded Wagner as mayor in 1966, had opposed the expressway as a congressman, and Lindsay's antiexpressway stance helped get him elected mayor. Following a crippling transit strike in 1966, and with an impending sanitation workers strike, Lindsay reversed himself when the issue finally came up for a Board of Estimate vote in 1968 and 200,000 construction workers threatened to walk. The expressway was approved (fig. 7.21), but by then SoHo artists had joined the Jacobs coalition and vigorously organized the arts community.

The SoHo artist-activists named themselves the Artists Against the Expressway (AAE) and sought to publicize their plight. In December 1968, despite risk to themselves as illegal tenants in the old commercial buildings, the artists made the first count of their presence in the district, thereby giving a concrete identity to those who were facing grave injury from the expressway. "They found that twelve buildings were owned by individual artists, fourteen were artists' cooperatives, and one hundred and seven rental loft units were

FIG. 7.21 Paul Rudolph's dramatic design for the Lower Manhattan Expressway development, 1967. The view is east across Lower Manhattan from the Hudson River Tunnel. Courtesy of David Fishman, Robert A. M. Stern Architects.

used by artists—in all, a total of 270 units that had one and frequently more than one artist in residence."[33] The AAE pressured people known beyond the art world, as well as professionals from museums, colleges, and universities in the United States, Europe, and Japan. Representatives of these institutions flooded Mayor Lindsay and his administration with cables urging them to abandon the expressway plan.

An allied group, the Architects and Engineers Against the Expressway, revealed a fatal flaw in the expressway design. Much of the roadway would run below the water table, causing water pressure to force it up. Tunneling had reduced some of the expressway opposition, but the Lindsay administration was forced to solve the water-pressure problem by proposing the construction of housing and public buildings above ground in order to weight down the expressway. However, the 90 percent federal funding, which had made the expressway so attractive to many, would not cover this substantial additional cost. Another ally, the Scientists' Committee for Public Information, showed that expressway traffic would be a major polluter. Even the newly created Environmental Protection Agency joined the fray, producing its own report on dangerous traffic emissions.

Another potent force within the opposition was Margot Gayle, who in 1966 documented and publicized the historical value of many of the cast-iron buildings of the SoHo district. The ornate facades of these structures once stood as conspicuous examples of New York City's commercial and architectural supremacy. By the 1960s, they were nearly forgotten. James Marston Fitch, Columbia University's leading architectural historian and preservationist, threw himself into saving SoHo's cast-iron structures, and through him more cables from all over the world urging the area's preservation were received at City Hall. (The SoHo Cast-Iron Historic District, bounded by West Houston Street, West Broadway, and Canal Street, and ending to the east at Crosby Street, was designated by the Landmarks Preservation Commission in 1973.)

In a major public relations effort in June 1969, the AAE staged a protest rally involving 250 artists and their supporters at the Whitney Museum, with important coverage by the *New York Times*. But the outcome had already been decided. Mayor Lindsay, who had lost the support of his Republican party, badly needed the votes of Liberal and Democratic reformers, who were expressway opponents, in his 1969 reelection campaign. So Lindsay dumped the expressway, declaring it "dead for all time" on July 16, 1969.[34] The roadway was officially demapped by August, ending ten years of controversy. SoHo became an essential location on the sociological, cultural, and tourist maps of the city.

A year before the expressway was killed, in 1968, the fledgling Paula Cooper Gallery was the first to locate in SoHo, taking advantage of the convenient access to the growing number of artists there, the area's low overhead, and the large spaces that the new art demanded. Yet it was art dealer Leo Castelli's move to 420 West Broadway in 1971 that was crucial to the emergence of SoHo as the new center of groundbreaking art in New York. (Ileana and Michael Sonnabend, André Emmerich, John Weber, and Castelli all opened their galleries there on September 25, 1971.) Beginning in the 1960s, Castelli rose in the art world as the foremost champion and ultimate tastemaker of the Pop, Minimal, and Conceptual movements. Equally at home in the salons of Europe and the artists' lofts of lower Manhattan, he fostered the international acceptance of the young stars of these movements—painters like Jasper Johns, Robert Rauschenberg, Frank Stella, and Roy Lichtenstein—further cementing New York's role as the art capital of the world. Castelli's overwhelming success proved that SoHo's gallery space could accommodate the largest works being produced, and other dealers soon followed his path downtown.

Despite the migration of artists and galleries to SoHo, the neighborhood's stellar rise could never have been achieved without Mayor Wagner's foot-dragging on urban renewal south of Houston Street, which ensured the neighborhood's future. Wagner was neither indecisive nor a Moses lapdog, as some critics claimed; indeed, he outfoxed Moses on every critical issue facing SoHo and the Washington Square district. It was Wagner's approval of the square's trial closing to traffic, which proved that the neighborhood wouldn't be deluged with cars, that effectively killed Moses's beloved roadway scheme. Wagner also accepted community involvement in the square's redesign, was instrumental in stopping most of Moses's Title I projects in the area of St. Anthony's parish south of the square, and supported the drive for historic preservation. His adoption of community boards gave the city's mayoralty added muscle in countering Moses's (and others') disdain for "obstructive" old neighborhoods all over the city. Wagner is an unsung hero of Washington Square, second only to the square's creator, Mayor Philip Hone.

Although most residents of SoHo and the Village would have much preferred that the hordes of tourists stayed in other popular sites around the city, Michelin's promotion in 1983 of Washington Square to a two-star locale—the same rating as Times Square, the Upper East Side, and other attractions—was a sign of the community's success in protecting its precious neighborhood. SoHo got its first mention in the guide in 1974, following the historic district designation in 1973, and its success inspired scores of similar successes in and around New York and then around the country. Locally, the Ladies' Mile and the Flatiron districts, NoHo, TriBeCa, and the East Village were all infused with new life, placing Washington Square at the center of a thriving and exciting downtown Manhattan.

Aerial view looking northeast from above Sixth Avenue and Houston Street, 1999. Washington Square and its environs remain a respite from the gigantism prevailing elsewhere in the city. Fifth Avenue begins north of the arch between One (right) and Two (left) toward the upper left corner of the view, where nothing has been built on this stretch up to Fourteenth Street for 40 years. The neighborhood of the square is still a vibrant residential community with tree-lined streets. NYU's bulky Bobst Library occupies the block southeast of the square, throwing its substantial shadow onto it. The beautiful campanile of the Judson Church complex on Washington Square South still stands free of nearby tall structures, and the glass tower of NYU's Loeb Student Center, next to Bobst Library, has since been razed for a disputed replacement, higher and twice the Loeb's bulk. Photograph by and courtesy of Jeff Prant.

: : : : : **8**

REVIVAL

1979–2001

NOT SINCE ITS FOUNDING IN THE 1820S HAVE **WASHINGTON SQUARE'S** prospects looked brighter than they do today, even in the aftermath of September 11, 2001. In the late 1970s, while New York City struggled to overcome a national recession as well as its own real estate depression and near-default, another boom was gaining steam. This time, though, with much of Greenwich Village designated as an official landmark, the square was spared the large-scale redevelopment that occurred elsewhere. Megaliths erected during the 1980s and 1990s, notably those conceived by the developer Donald Trump for other neighborhoods, aroused the wrath of activist residents and drove consideration of a new citywide zoning law in 1999.

Crime rates in the city and country began to plummet in the 1990s, and Eighth Street, after a long decline, found new life after being designated a business improvement district. Washington Square and the areas surrounding it, which now include the East Village, bloomed as never before, in large part because protection of their authentic character and physical scale had been ensured. Strong preservationist goals were not shared by all, however, and the community remained vigilant. Groups trying to save their turf were dubbed *BANANAS* (Build Absolutely Nothing Anywhere Near Anything Standing) by urban planners bent on new development. Ironically, though, the very fruits of the preservationists' efforts—maintaining the integrity and increasing the popularity of the historic square and Village—encouraged tourism and new building wherever possible.[1]

One prominent site, the 90-foot-deep east blockfront at 360–374 Sixth Avenue between Washington and Waverly Places, had been vacant since subway construction in the 1930s and was being used as a parking lot. Part of the vast West Fourth Street subway station extended under a third of the lot, complicating any construction over it. Yet as the 1980s economy heated up, development became irresistible. In 1982, the Loew's theater chain kicked things off with a proposed multiplex cinema able to accommodate almost 2,000 people in four theaters and with stores at the street level. Whereas Loew's saw huge profits in locating a movie house directly over a major transportation hub, neighborhood residents feared that the proposal would draw packs of disruptive outsiders into what was still a quiet residential quarter. By 1984, facing the need for a zoning variance to operate a theater with more than 500 seats and in the face of community opposition plus the requirement for Landmarks Preservation Commission approval, Loew's gave up.

As the Loew's scheme floundered, other developers saw a grand opportunity for the construction of residential units. Here, in the middle of the Greenwich Village Historic District, where virtually nothing had been built for decades, demand was as hot as in other prime areas of Manhattan. Developer Philip Pilevsky took on the parking-lot challenge in 1984 with an apart-

ment house named Washington Court (fig. 8.1) and hired the architect James
Stewart Polshek, then dean of Columbia University's graduate school of
architecture, to design it. Polshek's design had to fit in with a mixture of
nineteenth-century Greek Revival and Italianate residences, some elaborately
remodeled; an 1830s Greek Revival church and a tall 1920s apartment house
across the avenue; and 1950s modern glazed brick and metal-and-glass commercial structures to the north and south. That was not all; no matter what he
created, the Landmarks Preservation Commission had to deem the design appropriate, even though there was no consensus on what architecture could
possibly meet that criteria.

Polshek's concept for Washington Court satisfied most of the community,
as well as the Landmarks Preservation Commission. He proposed a six-story,
28-unit apartment house surrounding an interior court, with ten street-level
retail stores facing the avenue. Its three-section main facade, predominately
clad in red brick, was Tudor in spirit, sporting chimney stacks, square bays
with relatively small-paned windows, and peaked triangular skylights. His
finely detailed and unusual design was, he said, "appropriate to the nature of
the Village, which is idiosyncratic."[2] Even before the construction scaffolding
was removed, 600 prospective buyers had signed up for the 28 condominiums.
Although critics who wanted a style close to that of the nineteenth-century
houses nearby were still unhappy, Washington Court won a prestigious Alfred S. Bard award in 1986 for excellence in architecture and urban design.

Over on Washington Square South, the neighborhood was not so lucky.
During John Brademas's term as New York University's president from 1981 to
1991, the university had been more or less respectful of the square, taking pains
to build underground rather than to add height to its buildings on the square.
New facilities were erected away from the square so as to avoid such con-
frontations with the neighborhood as the Bobst Library hullabaloo. However,

having laid low during the 1980s and 1990s, NYU brazenly sprang another
controversial proposal on the city and the Village in the spring of 1999. It proposed replacing Loeb Student Center with a more massive sun-and-view-
blocking building, the Kimmel Student Center, which would take up twice
the volume of space (fig. 8.2).

The university, despite its earlier commitments and conditions, claimed
Kimmel could be built "as of right." Was it hoping that its earlier commitments from the Moses era had been forgotten? On the basis of news reports,
it appeared that NYU president L. Jay Oliva desired to keep up with other important schools in constructing an extravagant and high-profile new campus
center, and was willing to thumb his nose at the local community to do it. In
an April 28, 1999, article titled "Schools Build Luxury Hangouts—Big-name
Architects Hired for Glitzy Student Centers," the *Wall Street Journal* reported,
"In lower Manhattan, New York University plans to start work this year on a
$70 million, 12-story building that architect Kevin Roche describes as 'a living
room for the students,' with a retractable glass roof on the top, and a 1,022-seat
theater. 'Students, I hope, will say, "Isn't this great" and they will want to
come here,' NYU President L. Jay Oliva says. Princeton University and Harvard's Business School are getting new centers, too."[3]

Determined to protect the real and growing value of Washington Square,
the community again rose in arms with a lawsuit against NYU (in which the
author of this book was a plaintiff). However, in March 2001, following more
than a year of legal wrangling, the university prevailed in court. Denying the
plain language of a 1967 board of estimate resolution requiring compliance

with the goals of the original project, the court once again proved that power and money trumped community activism and logic. Bobst Library and now the Kimmel Student Center will stand as overbearing intruders on this historic public space.

NYU's desire for ever-larger expansion reflected the greater wave of building outsized structures that had already swept over midtown and portions of the Upper East and Upper West Sides of Manhattan, and was threatening almost every area left unprotected by the city's landmarks law. Overshadowing NYU's attempt to bulk up on the square in 1999 was Donald Trump's effort to insert an 861-foot-high condominium in midtown, towering over the United Nations building and bothering some very well-heeled and celebrated residents of lower apartment houses nearby. This latest of Trump's behemoths was eminently symptomatic of what architecture critic Ada Louise Huxtable calls "creeping gigantism," a phenomenon that overtook real estate development in the 1980s and 1990s.[4] Work on a new citywide zoning law was initiated in 1999 to address the excesses of Trump and other developers, but the effort failed. Real estate interests and powerful institutions combined to defeat zoning changes, which they felt would unduly restrict their future expansion plans.

The charm of the older, low-scale downtown areas became all the more appealing when contrasted with the trend toward gigantism. Nowhere is the dichotomy sharper than in and around Washington Square. Physically, the neighborhood has changed little from the 1920s, but evidence of all of the quarter's storied eras is on display. Washington Square's elegant north side and the charming streets of townhouses west of the square and off Fifth Avenue to Twelfth Street are strongly reminiscent of the Fifteenth Ward's founding in the 1830s. Strolling through the quarter, the New York evoked by Henry James and Edith Wharton seems not so distant. Four early churches—St. Joseph's, Grace, Ascension, and First Presbyterian—continue to serve parishioners and add to the nineteenth-century ambience. On Sixth Avenue, the 1872 Jefferson Market Courthouse stands among modest buildings that existed when the food market was established there in the 1830s; today the market exists across the street in the current Jefferson Market and in Citarella, two of the finest food shops in the city.

Sailors' Snug Harbor, the once powerful trust that owned a huge 21-acre swath of the Village east of Fifth Avenue from Washington Square North to Tenth Street, sold the last piece of its property in July 1986. A favorable court ruling had permitted the trust to sell its land in 1976 (by the original terms of the 1801 endowment, the trust could not sell its property), and the trust's first sale in 1976 was the parcel on which the One Fifth Avenue apartment house stands. That time, however, was a bleak period in the city's history, and the $1,275,000, which the trust received for the sale in the depressed real estate market of the mid-1970s, could not even purchase one of the larger apartments in today's One Fifth Avenue cooperative.

On Astor Place, the Cooper Union and Astor Library buildings of the mid-nineteenth century remain part of the city's cultural life as well as reminders of the time when Astor Place was New York's cultural epicenter boasting premier theater, libraries, and philanthropic institutions. Also extant are two former Broadway hotels erected during the surge in hotel building around the time of the country's first World's Fair in 1853: the once ultra-fashionable St. Denis across from Grace Church at Nos. 797–799, and the Coleman House at Nos. 645–647, which held the first Pfaff's cellar restaurant, the gathering place for Henry Clapp, the King of Bohemia, and his band of unconventional revelers that included Walt Whitman.

Just east of Sixth Avenue, on the south side of West Eleventh Street, a small triangular plot with some original tombstones is all that is left of an 1805 cemetery. It had been established there by the Congregation of Shaearith Israel when its old burial ground at Chatham Square ran out of space, but it was left with this small lot when Eleventh Street was cut through in 1830. At the northwest corner of Washington Square, a magnificent English elm, which was planted in the late 1600s as part of a hedgerow lining an English colonial farm, still stands. Another interesting and highly unusual window into the past thrives at the northeast corner of La Guardia Place and West Houston Street, where the environmental sculptor Alan Sonfist created a 45-by-200-foot patch of greenery that replicates the rural makeup of Manhattan in pre-colonial days. Created in the years 1965–78, the flora abounding in the *Time Landscape* includes oaks, sassafras, maples, wild grasses, and flowers.

The arch in Washington Square, in addition to its ceremonial role, remains a proud symbol of the neighborhood's refusal to acquiesce to the commercial invasion at the turn of the century. Nearly all of the commercial structures east of University Place date from that era, including the one at 29 Washington Place where 146 garment workers died in the disastrous 1911 Triangle Shirtwaist Company fire. The gigantic, full-block 770 Broadway and a smaller building on the southeast corner of Sixth Avenue and Fourteenth Street were both built in 1904 as department stores and mark the sites of the retail empires begun by pioneering giants A. T. Stewart, John Wanamaker, and Roland Macy. Broadway between Houston Street and Union Square has many architectural souvenirs of the days when this stretch of the thoroughfare was the premier shopping district. Two of the best are James McCreery's former dry-goods store, built in 1868 on the northwest corner of East Eleventh Street and Broadway, and the ornate brick and granite former Brooks Brothers 1874 store at 670 Broadway.

Southwest of the square, the now-gentrified tenements attest to the influx around 1900 of Italian immigrants, whose labors fueled the city's spectacular industrial growth during the period. Judson Church, at the section's northern boundary, once bridged the worlds of the immigrants and the wealthy. It was built in conjunction with the arch—evoking, in concert with the square, the beauty of an Italian piazza, or when viewed from north of the arch the

FIG. 8.3 Kohn Pedersen Fox's rendering of the new Law Center annex, looking southeast from the pathways of Washington Square, 2001. The structure's barrel-vaulted upper portion is meant to soften the annex's visual impact on the Judson Church group and the square. Courtesy of Kohn Pedersen Fox.

grandeur of the Roman forum—and, with the adjoining hotel and campanile, still completes White's masterpiece of composition for the square. It, too, though, was endangered by NYU's depredations.

In the spring of 2000, on the heels of the Kimmel Student Center outrage, the university's law school proposed a 194-foot-high facility on the strip of land facing West Third Street, behind the Judson Church complex. This new structure, taller than even the Bobst Library and Kimmel Student Center, would wipe out the Edgar Allan Poe House at 85 West Third Street. Rising behind the church and campanile, it also would erase their silhouettes from the city skyline and obscure the view of them with the arch from across the square. Would anger over damage to an important literary landmark and to one of the most stirring vistas in the city make NYU's law school dean, John Sexton, reconsider? Poe scholars and buffs, including the Mystery Writers of America, historians of Stanford White and Beaux Arts architecture, and preservationists, together with most of the residents of Greenwich Village, were angered, but in early 2001 NYU sought compromise (fig. 8.3). Opposition to demolition had gained new strength from a growing protest within NYU's own faculty and the astonishing power of the World Wide Web. As word of the fight flashed through the national and international network of Poe fans, two websites sprang up to capture the outpouring of emotion by Poe devotees. Appeals to save the Poe House poured in to NYU from 20 countries, some as distant as Singapore and Sweden. Dean Sexton, with aspirations for NYU's presidency (which he obtained) and sensing a growing blot on the university's reputation from continuing fights with its neighborhood, changed course. Now, the proposed law school building will be reduced to 145 feet, preserving part of the historic view of the Judson campanile, and the facades of the Poe House and houses along Thompson Street will be recreated as part of the new design.

Southeast of the square, Robert Moses's Title I urban renewal project, with residential housing in two long slabs and three towers in a park, remains a complex of superbuildings on superblocks, the antithesis of Village scale and

charm. Plans to enliven the space around these stark edifices have met with limited success. In the early 1960s, Paul Lester Weiner, architect of the nearly 600-foot-long apartment slabs, and landscape architect Hideo Sasaki attempted to mitigate the austere effect of the structures by putting a complementary modernist courtyard between them. Sasaki combined shrubbery with a strong grid of trees and a spectacular fountain with five high jets to soften the 17-story units. Today, Sasaki's pioneering example of rooftop planting (the landscaping is over an underground garage) remains a gem of modernist design even though the fountain has been reduced to one jet. I. M. Pei, architect of the three 30-story towers, was more successful in his design than Weiner was with his slabs. Pei chose Picasso's monumental *Bust of Sylvette*, a 36-foot-high concrete sculpture, as the centerpiece of the group. Installed in 1968, *Sylvette* still holds its own amid the surrounding buildings (fig. 8.4).

Pre–World War I bohemian haunts can be found today in a few spots on MacDougal, West Third, West Fourth, and Eighth Streets, although nothing save its name on the remodeled Provincetown Playhouse marks its significance. That block of MacDougal, on the west side between the square and Third Street, contains some of the oldest houses extant in the Village. It remains little changed from the days of the Liberal Club and the Washington Square Bookshop, when Eugene O'Neill's early plays were staged in a tiny theater with wooden benches for seats. A short distance east on Third Street, only the facade of No. 85 (the Poe House) remains as a reminder of the Café Bertolotti, a top bohemian hot spot in the prewar period. Polly Holladay's first restaurant was located at 137 MacDougal before moving to 147 West Fourth

Street between MacDougal and Sixth Avenue, a block remaining virtually intact since that period. Number 147 and the West Fourth Street buildings across the street that once housed the Pepper Pot, the Samovar, and the Mad Hatter now contain the latest generation of eateries.

New York City is one of the chess capitals of the world, and since before World War I, the Village has been a magnet for grand masters, kids just learning the game, and aficionados. The first outdoor chess court in Washington Square was installed during La Guardia's administration, and the tradition continues to this day. Several scenes from the 1993 Hollywood film *Searching for Bobby Fischer* were shot in the square, and Fischer himself once played there in the 1950s. The Village earned its place on the city's chess map with the opening of Frank Marshall's chess club there. (Marshall was U.S. champion from 1909 to 1936.) First established in a room over the Pepper Pot at 146 (now numbered 148) West Fourth Street, the venerable club later moved to its current location, an 1839 townhouse at 23 West Tenth Street. Marcel Duchamp, who was obsessed with chess, played at the original Marshall's. Duchamp's enthusiasm for the game spread to his followers and spurred many Italian and French coffeehouses and cafés around the square to keep chess sets for their patrons' use, beginning what is another ongoing tradition in the area's eateries and bars.

Although East Eighth Street was transformed by redevelopment in the 1950s, evidence of the New York School scene survived on West Eighth. Hans Hofmann's school of painting occupied the front of the third floor of the 8th Street Playhouse building, today no longer a movie house. The New York Studio School currently trains budding artists in the old Whitney Museum space. Yet more than any other event or building, the biannual Washington Square Outdoor Art Exhibit associates the district with the artists' milieu that flourished on these blocks for generations. The outdoor show, which began as a work-relief effort for artists during the Great Depression, remains a Village attraction. As for the artists themselves, the neighborhood has become much too expensive for them; by 1999 a rapidly dwindling number of artists remained in rent-controlled quarters. (Nine artists in a former hat factory at 12–14 Washington Place made news in 1999 when NYU began to evict them in the university's latest expansion. The artists had been paying an average rent of $500 a month, whereas equivalent space in the area fetched $7,000.)

The Beat Generation left its mark on the square in its entertainment mecca at the intersection of Bleecker and MacDougal Streets and beyond. One of the most famous places on the Beat map in the 1940s and 1950s was the San Remo at 93 MacDougal. A seedy restaurant when the Beats discovered it, it is now the completely renovated Carpo's Café. Another well-known spot was the Rienzi, at 107 MacDougal, which is now a Thai restaurant. Today, an updated coffeehouse buzz emanates from Le Figaro Café on the southeast corner of Bleecker and MacDougal. The same feeling is to be found in the Minetta Tavern at 113 MacDougal as well as up the street at 119, where the

older Café Reggio hasn't changed much since 1927 (except that half of it is no longer a barbershop). Café Dante at 79 MacDougal also helps to maintain the old-world coffeehouse vibes dear to the Beats, in contrast to the proliferation of Starbucks and other Seattle-style coffee bars. A few of the Starbucks in the Village, despite their expensive coffee and mediocre pastries, do attract distinctly Village types, some of whom stay for hours on end in the easy chairs provided.

Music, poetry reading, and comedy joints were more prevalent 30 years ago. Nevertheless, the area south of the square continues to generate some of the old Saturday night sensation. On West Eighth Street, Jimi Hendrix's Electric Lady recording studio continues to rock with new engagements at 52 West Eighth, and the tradition is carried on by the Café Wha? at 115 MacDougal Street, the Bitter End at 147 Bleecker, the Bottom Line at 15 West Fourth, the Blue Note at 131 West Third Street, and the Village Underground at 130 West Third Street (fig. 8.5). Also hot are the newer Zinc Bar, at 90 West Houston, and CBGB-OMFUG (from "country, bluegrass, blues, and other music for uplifting gourmandizers"), which has been at 315 Bowery since 1973.

Only one of the bar-nightclubs on Eighth Street still jumped in the nineties, and its location at 40 West Eighth near the intersection of Mac-Dougal Street may account somewhat for its longevity. Long known as the Bon Soir during the 1950s and 1960s, it featured such gifted, then-fledgling performers as Barbra Streisand, Phyllis Diller, Joan Rivers, and Lenny Bruce. In late 1999, the club operated as 40 Flavors, and a recent guide to New York nightlife reported that "hip-hop is what you get at this small but cutting edge bar/club . . . The crowd is young and urban hip with dance moves that would make James Brown jealous."[5] In early 2000, 40 Flavors was not open for busi-

FIG. 8.6 Bowlmor, which occupies part of the large garage on the west side of University Place above East Twelfth Street, 2001. This stretch of University between Tenth Street and Union Square rivals MacDougal and Bleecker Streets in its concentration of restaurants. Photograph by author.

ness, and, given the quality-of-life issues that have attended this and other clubs in residential neighborhoods, community opposition may force the club's closure for good.

None of these businesses, alone or collectively, seemed a threat to bring back the circus atmosphere that permeated parts of the Village in the late 1960s. The Life Nightclub, which in 1999 took over the Atrium spot vacated by the Village Gate, plus an additional floor, was another matter entirely. For those seeking entertainment, Life's Miami-esque dance-club theme, with its wraparound neon bar, disc-jockey skybox, and sweeping dance floor, was a clubgoer's dream—and a civilian's nightmare. Quality-of-life complaints concerning the destructive effects of rowdy nightclubs were common in downtown Manhattan, but Life was the only such club in the central Village, and it soon aroused the wrath of locals. One of the protestors wrote, in a letter to the *New York Times,* that "[i]t is now a bridge-and-tunnel nightmare that spews hoards of drunk and high people onto residential streets that intersect Bleecker. The corner of Sullivan reeks of stale beer and urine, and when the club is in full swing, the sidewalk is impassable."[6] Instead of fighting, Life decided to move, and in April 2000 it resurfaced as the even splashier and higher-decibel Spa at 76 East 13th Street, still an "it" club, albeit in less community-sensitive digs.

At 110 University Place, one of the oddest nightspots can be found—of all things, a nightclub for bowling. Bowlmor Lanes, long a traditional bowling alley and a neighborhood fixture, had operated there since 1938. It took up two floors of the large and grungy parking garage on the west side of University between 12th and 13th Streets, with 40,000 square feet and 42 lanes (fig. 8.6). Bowlmor had survived the 1950s, even prospering by hosting televised bowling tournaments, when many other alleys had been squeezed out by more profitable real estate developments. In 1997, two entrepreneurs bought Bowl-mor and spent $2 million turning the place into a club for what they called "really cool bowling."[7] While the term *cool* may seem strange, if not sacrilegious, coupled with *bowling,* their concept emphasizes fun rather than the sport, and it works. Glow-in-the-dark bowling is a hit there, as a *New York Times* reporter discovered during a visit in March 2000: "Cradling an iridescent blue ball, I stare down toward a set of multicolored glow-in-the-dark pins. Red lights border my lane like airport runway beacons, and ceiling mounted 'black' lights render the world in dark shapes and electric whites. . . . I step up and roll . . . Upon impact, the pins detonate in an explosion of brilliant blues and greens, spinning and toppling over each other."[8] Computerized score-keeping, classy bathrooms, a disc jockey spinning rhythmic music from disco to show tunes, a full bar including pitchers of beer from six varieties on tap, a kitchen serving pizzas, salmon, lobster, and oysters, and scantily clad waitresses complete the new Bowlmor experience. The alley has attracted a crowd in their twenties and thirties, and, better insulated from the local residences, this club may last.

Restaurants line University Place north and south of Bowlmor in one of the largest concentrations of eateries in Greenwich Village. Other restaurant rows can be found on MacDougal and Bleecker Streets and Sixth Avenue. Restaurants have long been a source of sustenance and entertainment for residents and visitors alike, and socializing in restaurants is a distinctive trait of Village life. Most old and new restaurants in the Village fill the basements and first floors of former townhouses and tenements. Some occupy spaces in historic buildings that once housed hotels, stores, and business enterprises, or fill spaces in the ground-floor commercial strips of the newer apartment houses. They generally have the charm and intimacy associated with Village spots, in sharp contrast to the big tourist-oriented restaurants in Times Square and other areas that may as well be in Las Vegas as Manhattan. Today, residents of the Village still find themselves in a place that a lovely 1961 guidebook, *Where to Go in Greenwich Village,* said "has everything in food and drink for every taste, purse and nationality, from gourmet cuisine to Nedick's [today it's Gray's Papaya] frankfurters. It is probably the only place in the world, within so small a radius, which covers such a large variety of restaurants and entertainment possibilities."[9]

The Brevoort and the Lafayette, once beloved outposts of the downtown French community, are gone, but Provence and Chez Jacqueline at 38 and 72 MacDougal Street, respectively, Caffé Lure at 169 Sullivan Street, and Village at 62 West Ninth Street are now some of the bistros of note. Gonfarone's also perished, and only one of its two well-known circa 1900 spin-offs, Peter's Backyard at 64 West Tenth Street, existed recently as L-Ray, a Gulf Rim eatery serving Tex-Mex and Cajun dishes. The Italian tradition is stronger in 2001, with Il Mulino at 86 West Third Street, Ennio & Michael at 539 La Guardia Place, Da Silvano at 260 Sixth Avenue, Il Cantinori at 32 East Tenth

Street, and Lupa at 170 Thompson Street. Two other places have been around much longer as favorite neighborhood spots encrusted with old-fashioned charm—Gene's at 73 West Eleventh Street, going back to 1919, and the Minetta Tavern, which has been open at 113 MacDougal Street since 1937.

Two very old restaurant locations on Ninth Street still thrive as eateries. The Knickerbocker Restaurant, where the Lafayette Café used to be on the southeast corner of Ninth and University, is a jazz spot and popular neighborhood hangout. At 21 West Ninth between Fifth and Sixth Avenues, the Griffou Hotel restaurant—in operation from the 1870s and succeeded much later in the twentieth century by the well-known Nat Simon's Penguin Room, a steakhouse—is now Ocean's 21, a Rat Pack supper-club themed restaurant. Three other Village hotel dining rooms are left (several more serve as NYU dormitory dining halls), those at 24 Fifth Avenue and One Fifth Avenue (since the 1920s) and the North Square in the Washington Square Hotel (formerly the Earl Hotel).

One of the most notable restaurant sites in the city for over 50 years is the old Coach House location at 110 Waverly Place. It was a residence in the 1820s, the Wanamaker family's carriage house around the turn of the last century, and Helen Lane's tearoom before its famous run, beginning in 1949, as the Coach House under host Leon Lianides. In the 1950s, when fine dining meant French cuisine, his pioneering restaurant proved that a top eatery could be devoted to primarily American food. After Lianides's death in 1998, the place has begun a new life as the rave-reviewed Babbo, serving inventive Italian food under the celebrated chef Mario Batali and restaurateur Joseph Bastianich. (Lupa, on Thompson Street, is a less-expensive outpost of Babbo.)

Most recently, three developments by celebrity chefs have further brightened the restaurant scene around the square. In 2000, Dan Barber and Alex Ureña opened Blue Hill, with their refined American cooking, in the townhouse at 75 Washington Place. Jonathan Waxman's Washington Park, serving his signature American dishes, now occupies the dining spot at 24 Fifth Avenue, and the Babbo team has added One Fifth Avenue's space to their operation. Another notable culinary site bears watching. The century-old Peter's Backyard location (64 West Tenth Street) is currently vacant, and the leaseholder is searching for a top chef to open a new eatery there.

Off-Broadway theater (by Actors' Equity definition, productions in a venue with fewer than 500 seats) thrives in and around the Village, where there are now more companies, productions, and stages than there were in the 1950s and 1960s. Indeed, the vital Broadway theater district has moved back downtown, leaving, according to the late *New York Times* theater critic Vincent Canby, the precincts of 42nd Street "mostly as a glitzy, very dear sideshow."[10] Calling the complex of performance spaces in Joseph Papp's Public Theater, housed in the handsome old Astor Library, "still the most invigorating theatrical crossroads in New York," Canby contrasted today's Public with uptown venues: "Get there early on any night, have a coffee in the lobby and be turned

on by the enthusiasm and the variety of arriving ticket holders: white, black, Hispanic and Asian, young, middle-aged and old, backpacking students and tailored corporate types. It makes the preperformance crowd in the Vivian Beaumont at Lincoln Center look as genteel as the guests at a Buckingham Palace garden party. It also reminds you of what going to the theater was like 50 and 60 years ago: no big deal and possibly a lot of fun."[11]

Forty years ago, *Where to Go in Greenwich Village* summed up what had long been the shopping, restaurant, and entertainment scene: "If you've heard that many Villagers rarely go above 14th Street, this is the reason. They don't have to. It's all here."[12] Today, though, the northern limit is more than likely to be 23rd Street.

Amid its current surge in popularity, the square remains the vibrant hub of the Village: a people-watcher's paradise and performance space, as well as a place for quiet repose. Once on the route of major civic festivities, the square is now the spiritual center and gathering place for the colorful and increasingly popular gay pride and Halloween parades. In 1970, the first gay pride parade was a daring and hasty political protest by about 200 gays and lesbians marching up Sixth Avenue from the Village to Central Park. They were observing the first anniversary of an uprising against harassment by the police at the Stonewall Inn, a gay bar in the West Village. Today, the parade is a mainstream, celebratory Fifth Avenue event held on the last Sunday in June. It draws hundreds of thousands of spectators on its route south from midtown past Washington Square to Sheridan Square and the Stonewall Inn. The Halloween parade, created in 1974 by mask and puppet designer Ralph Lee, originally was a local affair too. It zigzagged through the West Village to West Tenth Street and then down Fifth Avenue to the square. As the parade's popularity caught fire, however, it became one of the city's major rites of fall, and now goes up Sixth Avenue from Spring Street to 23rd Street in Chelsea (fig. 8.7).

Long a center of protest, in 1997 the square, for the first time in 25 years, was not the site of the annual pot parade, which advocates the legalization of marijuana. In deference to the surrounding community, the first of May's annual smoke-in party has been preempted by Family Day, and the square is now virtually free of drugs.

While the deteriorating quality of West Eighth Street was a drag on the Village's present-day success, the fortunes of all of Eighth Street are about to change dramatically for the better. Business improvement districts (BIDs) arose in the early 1980s as neighborhoods sought better ways to effect positive changes. Block associations were limited in geographic scope and had to use their own resources for improvements, and community boards, which received some city aid, were big and served many constituencies. In the 1970s a new concept, special assessment districts (SADs), took root. SADs empowered groups to use money collected by the city for an improvement in a specific area, such as the designation of a shopping street as a pedestrian walkway. Each SAD required its own enabling legislation, a cumbersome process that the city and state soon sought to streamline.

After the fourth SAD had been approved, New York enacted in 1982 one general set of laws for city and state covering all future assessment districts, now called BIDs. Assessments are a surcharge on the real estate tax, typically of one to two percent. Fourteenth Street became the first BID, pushed by the heads of Guardian Life, Con Edison, and the New School, which were powerful local enterprises. Other areas quickly followed in seeking BID status, as good times mitigated the effect the new assessment taxes had on the affected property owners.

The 34th Street BID, which encompassed Pennsylvania Station, the Bryant Park BID, and the Grand Central BID, which included a stretch of 42nd Street, soon demonstrated how dramatically a judiciously deployed assessment could restore luster to streets and public places that had fallen from glory. Streets were swept, overflow from trash bins was bagged for disposal, graffiti was removed, uniformed but unarmed patrols reduced lawlessness, and revitalization projects like Bryant Park's renewal proved how effective the concept could be. Applications for new BIDs flowed into the city's Department of Business Services, and by November 1994 there were 33 BIDs in the city and 30 more in the works.

In 1993 a group of Eighth Street property owners, called the Village Alliance, formed a BID incorporating Eighth Street all the way to Second Avenue, with a short branch south from Sixth Avenue to Fourth Street. By 1995, the Village Alliance BID had launched a dramatic new proposal that incorporated many features of the Bryant Park model: Eighth Street sidewalks would be widened, trees planted, and historic lighting installed in an effort to transform the street into a user-friendly promenade.

Indeed, by 1995 the theories and experience of Jane Jacobs and William Hyde Whyte had amply shown the way in Washington Square, Bryant Park, and many other places, including the Champs-Élysées in Paris: the best way to handle the problem of undesirables is to make the area in question attractive to everyone else. Despite this evidence, some in the community feared that widening the narrow sidewalks would only worsen the problem of outsiders—particularly street people making a meager living as panhandlers, scavengers, and vendors, and an ethnically mixed pedestrian stream. The sociologist Mitchell Duneier described the human traffic at the corner of Sixth Avenue and Eighth Street in his excellent book, *Sidewalk:*

> Once the home of shops catering to white middle-class residents, as well as a tourist destination for white youths from other parts of the city, the street has undergone a major transformation over the past two decades. Today, it is the destination for blacks and Hispanics as well as whites. Like the white youths of the 1960s, say, these visitors come from neighborhoods with less exciting stores, movie theaters, restaurants, bars, and the like, than can be found in the Village. They move about the street among white youths from Long Island and New Jersey; older whites living locally in rent-controlled apartments; students, professors, and staff from New York University, the New School for Social Research, and Cooper Union; younger professionals of many races who have bought apartments in the Village; and gays of all classes and races.[13]

Supporters of the plan prevailed, and it was approved by Community Board 2 and the city in 1997. By December 2001 work was complete from Sixth Avenue to University Place.

On the housing front, settling in the central Village today is dear, and demand by refugees from the congestion and overdevelopment in upper Manhattan portend ever-higher prices for the limited stock of properties. One-bedroom, renovated cooperative apartments in prewar buildings on lower Fifth Avenue start at $500,000, and larger one-bedrooms on high floors with views sell in the millions. Scarce multibedroom apartments go for a million dollars and more, and townhouses list in the multimillion range. On University Place and Broadway near East Tenth Street, which is now an antiques center, 2,000-square-foot lofts sell for over a million. Rentals, where they can be found, start at $1,500 a month for a studio, with rents in the high thousands for buildings having doormen, elevators, and larger apartments. A triplex, two-bedroom former stable in MacDougal Alley recently rented for $10,000 a month.

As the fortunes of the square have risen, so, too, have those of the neighborhoods surrounding it. NoHo, once the eastern flank of the Fifteenth Ward, is today defined as the area between Mercer Street and the Bowery, north of Houston Street and south of Astor Place. Its grand ultrawide streets—Astor Place, Bond, Lafayette, and Great Jones—are what first lured the city's wealthy merchants north from their comfortable precincts below Canal Street in the 1820s and 1830s. At 29 East Fourth Street, the meticulously preserved Old Merchant's House, built in 1832, is one of NoHo's original residences, recalling the graceful living arrangements of a period when the surrounding blocks were filled with equally fine houses. That one of the very first of these merchant's residences remains standing, albeit with an altered first floor, is astounding. This miracle is the 1821 house originally built for James Roosevelt (Franklin Delano Roosevelt's great-grandfather) at 58 Bleecker Street, on the southeast corner of Crosby Street.

By the 1990s NoHo was becoming stylish, and its major streets acquired trendy acronyms—LoBro for lower Broadway, and BoHo for the Bowery below Houston. Like SoHo, NoHo had been a derelict industrial loft district settled by artists in the 1960s and 1970s, with fashionable shops and restaurants not far behind. One good reason for the area's high property values is that it still contains some of the city's best late-nineteenth-century commercial architecture.

Tower Records, in the Silk Building at 692–694 Broadway (at East Fourth Street), set off a retail resurgence and created lively street activity in 1983, but not everyone was pleased with the neighborhood's newfound popularity. One of NoHo's restaurants triggered an alarm in May 1994, when residents counted 21 limousines idling on the Bowery near a grungy former gas station at Nos. 358–364, on the corner of East Fourth Street. Remodeled as the Bowery Bar, the new place was hosting a Condé Nast office party prior to its actual opening. Community Board 2, the NoHo Neighborhood Association, and the NoHo Alliance opposed the restaurant for using a zoning loophole to operate. After all, converting the first floor of a multistory building to a bar required special city approval. Locals worried that with 47 other one-story structures in NoHo and SoHo, the area could turn into a 24-hour amusement park for the downtown demimonde. However, the local group didn't oppose the Bowery Bar's operation before the municipal Board of Standards and Appeals—the one entity that could revoke a building permit—fearing that a ruling against them might set an unwelcome precedent.

Though the Bowery Bar (since renamed the B Bar) sparkled for a few years as the city's top celebrity haunt, the neighborhood's worst fears didn't materialize, and most of NoHo became a historic district in June 1999. A part of NoHo that didn't get landmark status, the mixed loft and tenement section south of Bleecker between Lafayette and the Bowery, had nonetheless gone upscale. This trendy area is at the northern part of Little Italy recently nicknamed NoLiTa; centered on Elizabeth Street, where storefronts that went for $80 a month in the 1970s go for thousands today, the streets are thronged with shoppers looking for hip fashions and accessories.

High prices for apartments in NoHo in the late nineties highlighted in the Village a wider population trend—a new influx of moneyed celebrities. In 1983, the 12-story Silk Building had been converted from a silk garment factory to a residential and commercial condominium with Tower Records taking the ground floor. Rolling Stones guitarist Keith Richards bought a triplex of over 4,000 square feet for $700,000 in 1983 (sold in 1996 for $2.25 million),

and Cher also bought a 3,400-square-foot triplex, setting off a chain reaction of celebrities living downtown. By 1999, top loft space in NoHo was selling for millions of dollars, with the movie star Matt Damon paying $2.4 million for a 7,000-square-foot duplex on Lafayette Street near Astor Place.

A similar trend developed in the neighborhood's apartment houses, where numbers of single units were combined to form dwellings covering thousands of square feet. In One Fifth Avenue, the towering 1927 apartment house, as many as five apartments have been put together by wealthy owners to create extravagant spaces. Large space downtown, with room for luxurious amenities, is perhaps the biggest draw for moneyed buyers. "Uptown advantages moving south are transforming downtown from Chelsea to still-gritty Tribeca, into the new epicenter of the island's lush life," reported the *New York Times* on February 3, 2000, and the trend continues.[14]

Demand for upscale housing in the area spurred new residential construction in the early 1990s. In 1996, SoHo Court, a 12-story rental, was erected on the northwest corner of Elizabeth and Houston Streets, a site that once held a gas station. Although several blocks east of the formal boundary of SoHo, renters quickly signed up, paying $1,500 for a studio and $1,900 for a one-bedroom—surprisingly high prices for a nascent location competing with SoHo, NoHo, the Village, and other prime areas.

NoHo's northern end at Astor Place, one of Manhattan's major intersections, began receiving much attention in 1999 with plans for development by Cooper Union, the area's biggest landlord. Two works in metal are wonderful ornaments for the spacious Astor Place intersection of Fourth Avenue (the old Bowery), Third Avenue, and Eighth and Lafayette Streets, a site that may soon be dominated architecturally by a new building on one of Cooper Union's properties (fig. 8.8). On a small traffic island, sculptor Bernard Rosenthal's *Alamo* is a ten-foot-high, 3,000-pound black steel cube balanced on a point. Created in 1966–67, it was one of the first abstract sculptures to be permanently installed on city property. Previously a popular landmark and a magnet for graffiti and posters, it was stripped down and repainted in 1988, and is today under the care of Cooper Union engineering students. On a larger island covering the uptown Lexington Avenue subway stop sits a splendid 1986 recreation of an ornate 1904 cast-iron and glass kiosk that provides a sense of stepping into another era when entering and leaving the station. Some of these once ubiquitous structures that provided street level access to the early subway stations obstructed sight lines and became traffic hazards, so all were removed in the 1950s, early victims of misguided "modernization."

Among the most conspicuous features of Astor Place is a large parking lot (owned by Cooper Union), on which once stood the Beaux-Arts Brokaw Brothers men's store. For 35 years the college had been eyeing the space for development, and in 1999 the administration floated yet another proposal, the Astor Place Hotel. Ian Schrager, the celebrity hotelier and former manager of the Studio 54 dance club, was the proposed 99-year lessee, in partnership with a construction company, and he planned to construct his first newly built hotel there. The site is unique in Manhattan's gridiron, as the hotel could be seen for miles from uptown (a fact that once made the site home to the world's biggest billboard). The intersection of Fourth Avenue and Lafayette Street is also special in that it accommodates a sculptural ornament for Astor Place. Schrager, reported the *New York Times,* wanted something exceptional: a "shimmering design that would become a worldwide icon" for his growing boutique-hotel empire.[15]

After dumping a team of daring and highly acclaimed architects, who had taken nearly two years and cost a reported $2 million in fees, Schrager appealed to the famous architect Frank O. Gehry in June 2001. Computers had made possible the new sculptural forms of architecture—a development comparable in importance to the introduction of steel and glass a century earlier—and it was Gehry's Guggenheim Museum in Bilbao, Spain, that established computers as integral to designing cutting-edge, signature architecture for cities in the twenty-first century. For the Condé Nast Corporation's Times Square skyscraper (1999), Gehry had designed the company's restaurant—a Gaudi-like grotto of glass and blue titanium—and snazzy restaurants are a critical part of the boutique-hotel experience. Then, too, Gehry just might steal the thunder from French architect Jean Nouvel's innovative glass and steel Broadway Hotel being built in SoHo by André Balazs, a Schrager competitor. However, fate has again put a crimp in Cooper Union's plan. Schrager's hotel is now on hold in the wake of the World Trade Center tragedy, and the school is looking at other developers.

Nevertheless, in November 2001 Gehry released his proposed Astor Place Hotel design (fig. 8.9) for a *New York Times* article, "Welcoming a Return to Risk," which was a plea by the critic Herbert Muschamp for more venturesome architecture in the city. Gehry offered a stunning and witty Constructivist finial for the Astor Place intersection. Cascading stainless-steel-clad blocks partially conceal a 210-foot-high curvaceous glass sculpture. Critics had earlier discovered Ginger Rogers's swirling dress in Gehry's Nationale-

Nederlanden Building in Prague and Marilyn Monroe's billowing skirt within his proposed Wall Street Guggenheim Museum entrance. Does Gehry intend us to see the hat, scarf, and cloak of Isadora Duncan in the Astor Place hotel glass? Projected to contain 250 rooms, the design seems to fulfill Schrager's dream. Whether or not it will be built remains to be seen.

Cooper Union also envisions (shades of NYU) the entire Astor Place area as a campus, although a nontraditional one fully integrated with its neighborhood. By narrowing a part of Fourth Avenue and eliminating a piece of Astor Place, the college proposes a more consolidated green space for itself and the community. It also plans to replace its 1961 Engineering Building (the former site of the Bible House) and 1905 Hewitt Building (the former site of the Tompkins Market) with much larger structures. Part of the new structure on the Engineering Building block will rise 15 stories to be equal in height to the massive office building that was once the Wanamaker's department store. This land will be leased to a commercial enterprise, with Cooper Union occupying only three of the floors. The two-story Hewitt Building will be razed for a two-level nine- and ten-story replacement to be used by the college (except for a strip of stores on the ground floor facing Third Avenue). Cooper Union claims that it is strapped for funds and needs to upgrade its properties in order to better train its students within modern facilities. However, the adjacent East Village residents fear being driven out by haute gentrification, particularly as a result of an Astor Place hotel. Yet the trend toward a fashionable district is already well underway. The combination of the Eighth Street and Astor Place improvements has the potential to create an elegant new east-west axis for Greenwich Village, linking two of the Village's most fascinating sites—the beloved Jefferson Market Courthouse and Cooper Union at Astor Place.

To the east of NoHo and all around the old Fifteenth Ward—the East and West Villages, south of Houston Street, Union Square, and north of Fourteenth Street—old neighborhoods are chic. Lying east of the Bowery, the East Village occupies the area below Fourteenth Street east of Greenwich Village. Historically, the East Village covered the old Eleventh Ward, which was established in 1825 and ran from the Bowery to the East River between Fourteenth and Houston Streets, with Tompkins Square at its center. During the nineteenth century, these streets were known as Kleindeutschland. They housed a community of German immigrants then; in the twenty-first century, they are a raucous core of labor, left-wing, countercultural, and antigentrification protests. The East Village is, for the most part, a district of tenements, public housing, abandoned buildings, and vacant lots, but it remains low-scale compared to the colossuses so prevalent elsewhere. The spirit of bohemia so long a part of Village life is nowhere more evident than in the East Village, where artists and other creative types congregate in its eclectic mix of late-night bars and ethnic eateries.

By the 1990s, the East Village had also seen its rents soar. The news in 2000 was more about real estate deals, the newest boutiques and theaters, and what the hottest chefs were cooking up in Alphabet City (Avenues A through D), than about homelessness, drug busts, and death. No longer is the East Village the haven it once was for those priced out of Central and West Village housing, especially for artists and the young who flock to New York. One couple in their twenties, reported the *New York Times*, found a "fifth-floor walkup in the East Village that rented for $1,800 a month and featured two miniscule rooms off a hallway, a kitchen that was a converted closet and no living room. After seeing that, the pair decided to look in Brooklyn."[16] The long-dormant issue of opening a Second Avenue subway line is once again on the table, holding the promise of a far more extensive East Village Renaissance.

Northeast of the Bowery at Houston Street, a particularly desolate landscape presents itself, with only a few old buildings remaining on the Bowery. Here is large-scale urban renewal in progress, an issue that even now plagues the East Village, although it has subsided elsewhere in favor of adaptive reuse. In the 1950s, as part of a plan for another of Robert Moses's Title I projects named Cooper Square, the developers proposed razing a slice of the East Village—then part of the Lower East Side—from the Bowery / Third Avenue to Second Avenue, between East Ninth and Delancey Streets. This proposal unleashed the usual opposition from those who wouldn't be able to afford rents in the new development and who supported adaptive reuse instead.

FIG. 8.10 New Year's celebration at Sammy's Bowery
Follies at 267 Bowery, 1952.
Located slightly south of Houston Street, Sammy's was long a
place that gave the skid row
its *Beggar's Opera* appeal. Around
1910 a young banjo-playing
busker named "Izzy" Baline
(later Irving Berlin) could be
found performing in front
of Sammy's and other Bowery
dives. Photograph by Bill
Meurer. Courtesy of the *New
York Daily News.*

Over the ensuing decades the Cooper Square project first expanded and then shrank under continuous protest until, in the 1990s, only most of one full block on either side of Houston at the Bowery was still slated for demolition. In 1999 work was stymied when those fighting the project got an ally with some cachet in Kate Millett, the noted feminist author and artist. She had lived a little above Houston at 295 Bowery in a former Civil War–era hotel since 1973, when the Bowery was still synonymous with skid row, and in 1999 was renting two spacious lofts for the impossible total of $500 a month. Millett remained a vocal holdout until her building was demolished as part of a $230 million redevelopment consisting of a mixed-use group of five modestly scaled buildings. The project will have both low-income and market-rate apartments, stores, and green space. Construction began in 2001, ending the last major Manhattan urban-renewal fight with a legacy from the Robert Moses era.

Soon, nothing will be left of the Bowery that recalls its days as America's biggest skid row. Once, back in 1909, some 25,000 homeless derelicts lived along the Bowery and its el from Chatham Square to Cooper Square. Despite the notorious poverty and human misery displayed on its sidewalks and in cheap hotels, missions, late-night saloons, and brothels, some artists and writers found its *Beggar's Opera* aspect fascinating (fig. 8.10). A sense of that old Bowery can be found in Stephen Crane's sketches and novellas written in the 1890s, in Theodore Dreiser's novel *Sister Carrie* (1900), and in the dense, multifigured scenes that Reginald Marsh painted in the 1930s. Marsh's work captures the added impact of the cavernous el, which by 1917 had grown to cover the entire roadbed of the Bowery. Joseph Mitchell's 1940 profile of Bowery flophouses in the *New Yorker,* Simone de Beauvoir's 1947 observations in her journal *America Day by Day,* and E. B. White's classic 1948 essay "Here Is New York" also portray the strip at a time when godforsaken Depression-era homeless were being joined by legions of down-and-out World War II veterans. The el was removed in the mid-1950s, and the homeless are no longer concentrated in this one-mile, increasingly trendy stretch.

West of Sixth Avenue lies the old Greenwich Village, reflecting New York's Ninth Ward, although most writers since Anna Alice Chapin's somewhat fanciful 1918 book, *Greenwich Village,* the first mainstream book on the subject, have centered their Greenwich Village more on Washington Square. Even earlier, John Reed claimed the square as the heart of Greenwich Village in his poem, "A Day in Bohemia." Calling the Washington Square district the Greenwich Village of lore, as some of the papers and guides have begun doing recently, and keeping the area west of Sixth Avenue as the long-designated West Village makes better sense than lumping together the two quite different places. Confusion will likely reign for some time, as taxicab maps have the Greenwich and East Villages meeting at Fifth Avenue, with no West Village at all, while other maps label all territory from the Hudson River to Broadway as Greenwich Village.

Sixth Avenue defined that Ninth Ward and West Village demarcation, and today the avenue's landmark Jefferson Market Courthouse has a new ornamental iron fence surrounding its garden. Funds for the fence were donated by the city's foremost philanthropist, Brooke Russell Astor. (The widow of Vincent Astor, Mrs. Astor, age 101, retains the social aura and carries on the charitable traditions of the famous New York family who gave its name to Astor Place and the Astor Library.) Now the tower bell rings and the clock faces are lit, thanks again to the writer and preservationist Margot Gayle, whose valiant efforts helped save Old Jeff from the wrecker's ball in the 1960s. Extending west from Sixth Avenue almost to the Hudson River, real estate in the West Village is as costly today as in any prime neighborhood, and the area has remained remarkably unchanged. Most of the West Village is now protected as part of the Greenwich Village Historic District, while at its western edge battles are being fought over development.

An already high demand for housing in the West Village exploded in 1999, with site after site just beyond the historic district boundary slotted for new buildings. Nine apartment houses and two hotels are newly completed, under construction, or being planned from Hudson Street to the river in what the *New York Times* on August 29, 1999, called a "Developer's Gold Rush." The paper's David Dunlap paints the scene: "The question is whether this physical transformation will fundamentally alter the character of the West Village, a rough-edged amalgam of 19th-century industry and 20th-century artistry, of iconoclasm and neighborliness, of creative freedom and sexual license. New Yorkers who fled there to escape crush and buzz are distressed to see taxis full of fashionistas rumbling over the Belgian block paving with construction cranes on the horizon. What Jane Jacobs called 'an intricate sidewalk ballet' is turning into a duel for the future of the Village waterfront."[17]

Even though the new buildings were relatively modest in scale—the tallest two at 15 and 16 stories and the rest at 11 stories or less—they nonetheless overwhelmed the older building stock. And many potential sites remain. Village preservationists had originally hoped that the historic district limit might be extended to the river's edge; to that end they had conducted a building-by-building survey of the waterfront, but their efforts did not bear fruit. Those who prized the historic grittiness of the district and were not necessarily convinced that extending the district was the way to go were pleasantly surprised when some of the new projects employed design motifs from the old factories and warehouses.

A new park and the removal of two monstrously disfiguring structures helped produce the residential building rush. After decades of off-again, on-again plans for a park along the strip where the elevated West Side Highway once blighted the waterfront, the city and state finally approved and opened the first stretch of the park and the adjacent grade-level Route 9A between West Houston and Bank Streets in September 1999. This massive public improvement, scheduled to stretch from Battery Park City to 59th Street and estimated to cost in excess of $350 million, includes 13 recreational piers in its design and was extolled on its opening by Governor George E. Pataki as "the most magnificent waterfront park in America."[18] An abandoned freight railroad viaduct running parallel to the park a block inland was also dismantled below Gansevoort Street. It, like the West Side Highway, had long cast a perpetual shadow on the streets below and had depressed nearby property value. With these weights lifted from the West Village, its complete gentrification was perhaps inevitable. Yet, all in all, the basic character of the West Village has been maintained, largely through the dogged perseverance down the years of historic preservationists.

Seemingly a world apart is SoHo. In the 1970s one had a funereal feeling walking the streets of the struggling artist's community. Then, as now, its zoning limits and landmarks protection run from Crosby Street to West Broadway, below Houston and above Canal Streets. But present-day SoHo, the place found in guidebooks and advertisements, is a new phenomenon that stretches from Little Italy to Sixth Avenue and draws shoppers and strollers in droves to its shops, restaurants, and hotels.

As the average price of a 2,000-square-foot loft in SoHo shoots above $1 million, artists of small and modest means have migrated to old industrial neighborhoods in Brooklyn, Queens, and the South Bronx. (At the high end, prices in SoHo for the best penthouse lofts were nearing $10 million in 2001.) Despite this, and despite the exodus of many artists and galleries to Chelsea that began in the late nineties, there are still a relatively large number of art galleries in SoHo, and in the mid-1990s, 76 percent of SoHo's residents were working artists or were employed in arts-related fields. Community groups in SoHo have long fought to preserve low-rise, low-density zoning and to restrict any new residential construction to occupancy by artists. They also fought the first hotels as precursors to haute gentrification. However, as the trend of expensive retail stores replacing smaller businesses continues, preserving SoHo's original ambience will become an increasingly difficult task.

A bane to community residents has been the nearly century-old problem of billboard advertising, which continues to plague SoHo and adjacent NoHo. (This weed of art forms was banned in other prestigious neighborhoods.) SoHo and NoHo dwellers didn't fancy their neighborhoods becoming "Times Square south," but because these areas had been manufacturing districts, zoning did not prohibit billboards. When six giant ones were put up along Houston Street between Lafayette and Broadway in the spring of 1999 (five of them commanded entire building sides), one group took guerrilla action. More than a dozen signs were defaced. The mayor and city council members also took offense, and in December 2000 the city's zoning code was amended to restrict billboard advertising in combined commercial and residential districts like SoHo and NoHo.[19]

An example of what can be done as an antidote to the abhorrent billboards is *The Wall* (1972), a relief created by sculptor Forrest Myers that covers the windowless Houston Street facade of 599 Broadway and remains the unofficial gateway to SoHo. This lavender wall with 42 evenly-spaced turquoise beams jutting from it was commissioned by the Public Art Fund, a nonprofit group that sponsors public art around the city. A block and a half north on La Guardia Place between Bleecker and West Third Streets, a more traditional sculpture was unveiled in 1994: a vivid, larger-than-life bronze statue of feisty mayor Fiorello La Guardia stands on a granite pedestal on the eastern side of the block. Neil Estern, the sculptor, has depicted the intrepid politician striding forward, with hands clapping and mouth open as if he were leading a rally. The strip of land where the memorial stands, a leftover from Robert Moses's defeated Fifth Avenue South highway scheme, had become an unsightly dog run until the Friends of La Guardia Place landscaped it and commissioned the statue as its centerpiece.

Union Square, Washington Square's neighbor to the north and permanently linked to it by University Place, has had its own spectacular resurgence. Popular since 1976 when the city's largest green market was established there, Union Square is now a confluence of three recent developments in the city: Silicon Alley, the Flatiron District, and Ladies' Mile, all of which include the square in their geography. The Flatiron District teems with architecture, advertising, media, fashion, and photography firms. A number of Silicon Alley's Internet companies reside in spacious, state-of-the-art lofts near the square. Shoppers throng to the department stores (like ABC Carpets and Bed Bath and Beyond) housed in Gilded Age structures left over from the original Ladies' Mile. Fashion models, put up by their agencies in apartments near Union Square, add to the colorful mix of types and attire, making Union Square one of the best people-watching spots in the city. But Union Square's greatest claim to fame may still be its abundant year-round outdoor market, whose stalls overflowing with fresh produce and flowers draw people from all

FIG. 8.11 *Metronome* (2001), by Kirsten Jones and Andrew Ginzel, at One Union Square South. Photograph by author.

over the city. Award-winning restaurants abound in the nearby streets, five theaters have opened in the area, and the Guardian Life building has become a new luxury hotel.

The Zeckendorf Towers complex, complete with condominium apartments, offices, and retail stores, opened in 1987 on the site of the S. Klein's discount clothing store, an event that sparked the area's recent revival. Even before it opened, 90 percent of the 681 apartments had been purchased, with a typical 720-square-foot one-bedroom selling for $229,000. On the north side of Union Square, Barnes & Noble adapted the beautiful Queen Anne–style Century Building for a multilevel bookstore in 1995.

Facing the south side, at 1 Union Square South between Broadway and University Place, a 27-story full-block apartment tower was built in 1999 that also contains a music store, a consumer electronics store, and a 14-screen multiplex movie theater. Seen from across the square or down the long view-corridor from Grand Central Terminal, the tower features an arresting, if complicated, artwork on its main facade. Inspired by the immense sculptural clock surmounting the terminal, Union Square's abstract piece by the team of Kirsten Jones and Andrew Ginzel is called *Metronome* (fig. 8.11). Its most striking element is a huge wall of concentric circles of rippling brick symbolizing the expansion of energy as a metaphor for the earth's rotation. Steam spirals out of a hole in the center, and a long horn is positioned against the surface like a pendulum for visual and audio effects. Other time-related features of the design include a flashing digital clock and a rotating sphere of gold and black that mirrors phases of the moon. By a fortunate coincidence (the result was unintentional), *Metronome*'s large-scale, relatively flat, animated form evokes 42nd Street's dynamic billboards and thus commemorates the most important period in Union Square's colorful history. When America's show business was born there during the 1870s and 1880s, it was the Times Square of its day. *Metronome* occupies the very block where two of the era's most famous theaters—the Union Square Theater and Wallack's—once stood.

While the conversion of Union Square's commercial buildings to residential use had begun in the 1970s, it was the major overhauling of the square by the New York City Parks Department beginning in the 1980s that paved the way for the wave of new investment and development around its perimeter. Removing a screen of bushes and restoring lawns added sight lines, which dispersed the drug market and improved safety at night. Two new playgrounds brought back the sound of children's laughter. Historic district designation for Ladies' Mile now protects the area's lovely nineteenth-century commercial architecture, and in 1997 Union Square itself received national landmark status in honor of its role in labor history.

In addition to these protections, Union Square is part of the Fourteenth Street BID and the Flatiron District Business Association, which takes as its purview everything between Fourteenth and 23rd Streets, from Park Avenue South to Seventh Avenue. All of this has improved the quality of life north and south of Fourteenth Street and helped preserve the low-scale character of the neighborhoods up to 23rd Street, with the Flatiron Building as a sentinel standing guard against the tide of gigantism from midtown.

Residents of Washington Square and the ring of communities surrounding it would have been less satisfied had crime continued to rise throughout the 1990s as it had during the previous three decades. Fortunately, crime rates in the city peaked and steadied in the early 1990s, and while Greenwich Village was one of the less crime-ridden areas of Manhattan, drugs and disorderly conduct were claiming the streets. In 1990 sustained sweeps of Washington Square and other drug markets were made by the NYPD's Tactical Narcotics Teams, by 551 police-trained volunteer blockwatchers in Greenwich Village and the West Village, and by community patrols. For the patrols, increasingly desperate merchant groups and block associations brought in the Guardian Angels, a youthful anticrime group. A squad of four Angels and four community residents roamed the streets, harassing drug pushers, breaking up sales, and making citizens' arrests.

Sixth Avenue and West Fourth Street had become a particularly troubled spot. On August 5, 1990, at 2:00 A.M., a melee began on that corner when police tried to break up a group of about 200 with a boom box playing at full blast. Bottles were thrown at the officers in protest, and over the ensuing two hours, 84 policemen responded to the incident. Nine officers were injured, and nine people were arrested on charges of rioting, resisting arrest, and reckless endangerment. Several were also charged with weapons possession.

Over the next three years a plague of lawlessness infected Greenwich Village, as it did the rest of the city. However, Washington Square was famous

FIG. 8.12 *New York* Magazine, August 16, 1993. The arch is not normally floodlit with an eerie blue-green light. Cover photograph by Renato Rotolo. Courtesy of Renato Rotolo and *New York* Magazine.

and its residents vociferous, and the neighborhood's distress became a cover story—"The Village Under Siege" blared *New York* Magazine in its August 16, 1993 issue (fig. 8.12). Michael Gross lamented the "roving bands of graffiti-mongers," the "carousers on 8th Street—beer-swilling, obscenity-shouting hordes in boom-box cars," and the peddlers and vagrants on Sixth Avenue who "sell stolen goods and drugs, foul the neighborhood with garbage, urinate and defecate openly in the streets, and menace those foolish or brave enough to object to their behavior."[20] Ending on a positive note, Gross mentioned that the Village Alliance BID was being formed and that cops had begun Operation Silent Night, which involved Friday night ticketing of cars blasting their stereos and impoundment of the offending vehicles until the following Monday.

Although crime rates stood at near-record levels above ground, they were dropping rapidly in the city's subways under William Bratton, the transit system's police chief. He had established a new policing paradigm based on the "broken window" theory: one broken window in an abandoned building, left unfixed, would encourage stone-throwers to break the rest. Fix that pane, and any others that might become broken, and soon the building would no longer be a target. Subway fare-beaters became Bratton's "broken windows," and when strong and sustained enforcement led to apprehension of thousands of these miscreants, the whole subway environment began to improve. Fare-beaters, it turned out, were involved in much more serious subway crimes, and as arrest figures for this seemingly petty offense soared, crime in the subways began to plummet in all major felony categories—robbery, assault, and grand larceny—and the drop continues. This amazing quality-of-life and crime-busting achievement secured Bratton's position as New York City police commissioner in Mayor Rudolph W. Giuliani's new administration in 1994. Giuliani, a Republican, had won a squeaker race with his get-tough-on-crime message in an overwhelmingly Democratic city.

During the next 27 months, Bratton and Giuliani brought the same success to New York's streets, attacking all quality-of-life crime with the assistance of crime-statistics computer analysis, and the brilliance of Bratton's strategy and management made him the most famous cop in America. Gross's article had been picked up on by downtown politicians, and Bratton and Giuliani chose Greenwich Village to begin deployment of their new anticrime program, announcing the program's details at a news conference in Washington Square on March 12, 1994. The results of the pilot crackdown in Wash-

FIG. **8.13** A double-decker tourist bus heading east on
Bleecker Street after passing
MacDougal Street, August 2001.
Bleecker Street retains much
of its role as a downtown enter-
tainment and shopping spot.
Photograph by author.

ington Square and Greenwich Village, in which the police adopted a policy of
zero tolerance toward quality-of-life-offenses, were dramatic. Four months
later the program was extended to the entire city.

Overall city crime rates diminished to levels last reported in the 1960s, and
by August 14, 1995, *New York* was featuring Bratton and Giuliani on its cover
with the headline, "The End of Crime as We Know It."[21] (Crime rates also fell
nationally, as stricter overall law enforcement became the rule, but not as dramatically as in New York City.)

Video surveillance was introduced into Washington Square and other
areas to assist in breaking up drug markets and detecting illegal activity. Under
the watchful eye of the police and their surveillance cameras, the issue of free-
ranging dogs has subsided in Washington Square. It's also a quieter Village
and city, as police with decibel meters stop offending noisemakers, whether
they be boom boxes, booming cars, unmuffled motorcycles, or loud bars and
clubs. In the year 2001 serious crime rates continued to drop substantially, with
the city stressing quality-of-life arrests, while the nationwide decrease in crime
had stalled. Politicians take credit for the drop in crime and academics churn
out treatises on the causes. No one, however, can deny the overall benefits:
streets safer than they have been in a generation, increased growth, a residential real estate rise, and 38.4 million visitors in the year 2000.

South from the midtown canyon of Fifth Avenue, the spaciousness of the
square beckons American and foreign visitors alike. Double-decker tour buses
load up in midtown for a run down Fifth Avenue. As they descend from Murray Hill through sheer cliffs of commercial buildings, the Washington Square
arch emerges. Drawing closer, the scene changes as granite and limestone turn
to brick and brownstone amid gracious tree-lined streets and wide sidewalks,
with more open sky. Bicycles, skateboards, and roller-blades join the slowed-
down traffic.

While tourists—and the revenue they generate—are usually welcome at and around the square, double-decker buses (fig. 8.13) have posed a problem for some in the neighborhood. When they veered off of the avenues into the narrower side streets, and their top decks were eye- and ear-level with townhouse windows, residents said *enough*. These oversized vehicles were banned on West Ninth when complaints poured in that far too many buses, sometimes 40 to 50 an hour, had chosen their charming and leafy street as a scenic route. Many on West Ninth and other streets find these buses nothing but "intrusive, traffic-snarling polluters."[22] Yet today's jaunty colorful buses, introduced in 1991, continue a long tradition of tourism in the Village, with packed double-deckers going back to the World War I era.

With all of the change the square has undergone over the twentieth century, and despite the squads of tourists, Greenwich Village remains one of the city's most sought-after addresses. Its attractions appeal to the nation at large. Here, a bygone charm and elegance coexist with the vigor of youth, idiosyncrasy, and brash commercialism (fig. 8.14). Here, too, preservation goals can be achieved without foregoing all development and modernization. Such juxtapositions of seemingly disparate elements and objectives—the antithesis of the suburban mall—are increasingly found all over the country, and what's happening here is watched with keen interest. Many architects are recreating the old look of the romantic 1920s apartment houses and the proud, human-scaled, nineteenth-century commercial buildings, both of which have long been part of the neighborhood's essence. New real estate developments are eschewing mindless sprawl in favor of high-density, mixed-use projects with stores on the ground floor, apartments above, transit stops nearby, and delightful sidewalks for strolling—all signature characteristics of the Village.

In Greenwich Village, the buildings, spaces, and especially the Washington Square arch evoke the marvelous history of the place. Journalist and critic Harold E. Stearns was one of many who reminisced about their years in the Edenic pre–World War I Village and about the difficulty of recreating that lost past. "I think it is because it is our lost youth, when the world was young and amusing—that strange world before we entered the war and became one of the greatest nations on earth; the world when 'isolation' for us was a reality, at least as far as our feelings and hopes and memories could go. Sometimes I wish it could come back," wrote Stearns in 1935, several lost Edens ago.[23] The Village of the ages is still splendidly here. Into New York's urban fabric—a vast tapestry of sights, sounds, smells, identities, ideas, and ages—is woven the richness of that republic of Washington Square, today's Greenwich Village. Its citizens are a national model for preservation and protest, creativity and community, and the square's ever-vigilant protectors continue their watch, wanting to believe that its future finally seems secure.

The twin towers of the World Trade Center as seen through the arch from lower Fifth Avenue in the spring of 1998. It is early evening, and traffic peels off from Fifth Avenue onto Waverly Place. The Judson Church campanile stands to the right on Washington Square South. Photograph by and © Carolyn Schaefer.

⋮ ⋮ ⋮ ⋮ ⋮ ⋮

AFTERWORD

ON **S**EPTEMBER 11, 2001, TERRORISTS CRUELLY AMPUTATED A MAJOR piece of the Village's southern skyline. For a generation, no man-made structure in New York City, and perhaps in the world, captured the changing light of day as dramatically as did the twin towers of the World Trade Center. None glittered so brilliantly in the dusk and the night, nor served so unmistakably as a landmark for those approaching the city from afar. Cesar Pelli, architect of the adjacent World Financial Center buildings, said that he designed "a set of foothills beside the mountain, and now the mountain is gone."[1]

From the vantage point of Washington Square and the Village, the towers were a familiar and even reassuring presence. A glimpse from the square, or down the streets and avenues, made visitors instantly aware that they were looking south. The Eiffel Tower and Big Ben are landmarks for Parisians and Londoners, but we had a thrilling pair of giant exclamation marks befitting

Cooper Union's parking-lot site soon will receive its long-awaited development with 26 Astor Place, a 21-story apartment condominium designed by the prominent architectural firm of Gwathmey Siegel & Associates. According to Charles Gwathmey, the building is "an obelisklike object to mark one of the city's last triangular sites" and "a sculptural icon." It adds a striking eastern terminus to recent Eighth Street improvements and the promise of a bright future for historic Astor Place. Model courtesy of Gwathmey Siegel & Associates and the Related Companies.

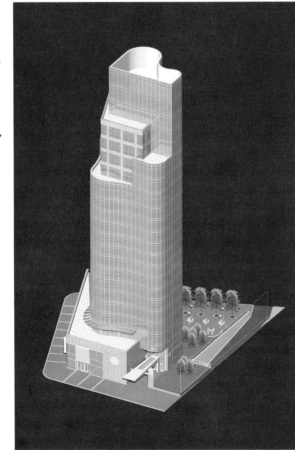

New York City. In the decades since they were built, the twin towers had become one of the main iconic views of the city, beloved by most residents, commuters, and tourists (although by some only grudgingly and in retrospect). They were unloved by our architectural critics and urbanists, who mistakenly claim that the towers' attraction and the affection for them derived solely from their bigness, and wish that the towers had never been built. Let us hope that the World Trade Center twins will be rebuilt using today's technology, and, if not, that something equally wondrous can replace them.

NOTES

These notes are for quoted sources only. Fuller citations are available at www.press.jhu.edu/press/books/titles/f03/f03haar.htm.

Chapter 1. Rise of the Square and Fifth Avenue

1. Henry James, *The American Scene* (New York: Harper & Brothers, 1907), p. 86; Henry James, *Washington Square* (New York: Harper & Brothers, 1881), p. 23.

2. "Commissioners' Remarks," in William Bridges, *Map of the City of New York and Island of Manhattan* (New York: 1811), p. 26, as quoted in John W. Reps, *The Making of Urban America: A History of City Planning in the United States* (Princeton: Princeton University Press, 1965), p. 299.

3. George E. DeMille, *Saint Thomas' Church in the City and County of New York—1823–1954* (Austin, TX: The Church Historical Society, 1958), p. 21.

4. John W. Francis, *Old New York; or, Reminiscences of the Past Sixty Years* (New York: Charles Roe, 1858), p. 25.

5. Barnett Shepherd, *Sailors' Snug Harbor, 1801–1876* (New York: Snug Harbor Cultural Center, in Association with the Staten Island Institute of Arts and Sciences, 1979), p. 15.

6. *Minutes of the Common Council of the City of New York, 1784–1831* (New York, 1917) of February 17, 1812 (p. 41) first questioned the size; minutes of July 25, 1815 (p. 262).

7. Ibid., minutes of February 26, 1827, pp. 229, 235.

8. "Celebration," *New York Evening Post,* July 5, 1826.

9. "Washington Military Parade Ground," *New York Evening Post,* May 10, 1828.

10. Philip Hone, diary, October 27, 1831. Hone's original diary is in the New-York Historical Society.

11. "Review of the Week," *New-York American,* May 27, 1837, quoted in LeRoy E. Kimball, "The Old University Building and the Society's Years on Washington Square," *The New-York Historical Society Quarterly* (1948), p. 17.

12. "Washington Square," *New York Herald,* July 13, 1837, p. 2.

13. James, *The American Scene,* p. 88.

14. "Growth and Prosperity," *New York Evening Post,* April 17, 1845; "The Second Avenue," *New York Evening Post,* January 14, 1846.

15. *New York in a Nutshell* (New York: T. W. Strong, 1853), pp. 107–108.

16. William Charles Macready, *The Diaries of William Charles Macready, 1833–1851* (London: Chapman & Hall, 1912), vol. 2, p. 419.

17. James, *Washington Square,* p. 23.

18. John F. Watson, *Annals and Occurrences of New York State, in the Olden Time* (Philadelphia: Henry F. Anners, 1846), pp. 362–363.

19. *Minutes of the Common Council* of June 27, 1832. The "park-as-lung" theory, an English import of the 1830s, held that verdant spaces such as parks and squares had therapeutic powers to purify the air and reduce disease-carrying miasma. Although absolute quackery and discredited by the end of the century, the notion didn't arrive soon enough to justify Washington Square. But it did help establish a reason for the existence of a central park, and in the 1870s it protected the square from having an armory encroach on its grounds. See Richard Sennett, *Flesh and Stone: The Body and the*

City in Western Civilization (New York: W. W. Norton & Company, 1994), p. 325; and Robert M. Fogelson, *America's Armories: Architecture, Society, and the Public Order* (Cambridge: Harvard University Press, 1989), p. 98.

20. James, *Washington Square,* p. 23.

Chapter 2. Empire Ward

1. "Editor's Easy Chair," *Harper's New Monthly Magazine,* June 1854, p. 122.

2. *New York as It Is* (New York: Disternell and Tanner, 1834), p. 12. This description compares New York's residences to "houses [in] the finest Cities of Europe," rather than to "European palaces," which was an overstatement in the previous 1833 edition of this guidebook.

3. Charles Dickens, *American Notes,* quoted in Bayrd Still, *A Mirror for Gotham: New York as Seen by Contemporaries from Dutch Days to the Present* (New York: New York University Press, 1956), pp. 122–123.

4. Austin Baxter Keep, *History of the New York Society Library: An Introductory Chapter on Libraries in Colonial New York, 1698–1776* (New York: DeVinne Press, 1908), p. 385, n. 2.

5. *The Diary of George Templeton Strong,* ed. Allan Nevins and Milton Halsey Thomas (New York: The Macmillan Company, 1952), pp. 269–270.

6. David W. Dunlap, *On Broadway: A Journey Uptown Over Time* (New York: Rizzoli, 1990), p. 92.

7. *The Diary of Philip Hone, 1828–1851,* ed. Alan Nevins (New York: Dodd, Mead & Company, 1927), p. 657.

8. "Tucseto" was reported by Doris Crofut in "A Brief History of the Town of Tuxedo" (1982) included in *Program for Centennial Celebration June 9, 1990* (Tuxedo Park, NY: 1990), courtesy of Tuxedo Park Associates.

9. *The Diary of Philip Hone,* p. 470.

10. "An Old Picture Gallery," *The World,* August 18, 1878.

11. Letter from Matthew Morgan to James Colles, December 11, 1843, quoted in Emily Johnston de Forest, *James Colles—Life and Letters (1788–1883)* (New York: privately printed, 1926), p. 189.

12. Nathaniel Willis, quoted in Paul Groth, *Living Downtown: A History of Residential Hotels in the United States* (Berkeley: University of California Press, 1994), p. 29.

13. "Places of Amusement," *Putnam's Monthly Magazine,* February 1854, p. 151.

14. Albert Parry, *Garrets and Pretenders: A History of Bohemianism in America* (New York: Covici-Friede, 1933), p. 23.

15. Ibid., p. 46.

16. Ibid., p. 57.

17. Susan Edmiston and Linda D. Cirino, *Literary New York: A History and Guide,* 1st rev. ed. (Layton, UT: Gibbs Smith, 1991), p. 45.

18. Justin Kaplan, *Walt Whitman: A Life* (New York: Simon & Schuster, 1980), p. 263.

19. Parry, *Garrets and Pretenders,* p. 43.

20. George G. Foster, *New York by Gas-Light,* ed. Stuart M. Blumin (1850; Berkeley: University of California Press, 1990), p. 159.

21. Richard Moody, *The Astor Place Riot* (Bloomington: Indiana University Press, 1958), p. 219.

22. "The Benevolent Institutions of New York," *Putnam's Monthly Magazine,* June 1853, p. 673.

23. Lois Beachy Underhill, *The Woman Who Ran for President: The Many Lives of Victoria Woodhull* (Bridgehampton, NY: Bridge Works Publishing Company, 1995), p. 309.

24. Theodor Griesiuger, quoted in Stanley Nadel, *Little Germany: Ethnicity, Religion, and Class in New York City, 1845–1850* (Chicago: University of Illinois Press, 1990), p. 104.

25. Thomas F. De Voe, *The Market Book* (1862; New York: Burt Franklin, 1969), p. 557.

26. James M. McPherson, *Battle Cry of Freedom: The Civil War Era* (New York: Oxford University Press, 1988), p. 609.

27. George J. Lankevich, *American Metropolis: A History of New York City* (New York: New York University Press, 1998), p. 117.

28. Alvin F. Harlow, *Old Bowery Days: The Chronicles of a Famous Street* (New York: D. Appleton & Company, 1931), pp. 533–534.

CHAPTER 3. SURROUNDING THE SQUARE

1. George E. DeMille, *Saint Thomas' Church in the City and County of New York—1823–1954* (Austin, TX: The Church Historical Society, 1958), p. 76.

2. Susan Edmiston and Linda D. Cirino, *Literary New York: A History and Guide,* 1st rev. ed. (Layton, UT: Gibbs Smith, 1991), p. 37.

3. Thomas Butler Gunn, *The Physiology of New York Boarding-Houses* (New York: Mason Brothers, 1857), p. 174.

4. Kenneth Silverman, *Edgar A. Poe: Mournful and Never-Ending Remembrance* (New York: HarperCollins, 1991), p. 243.

5. *The Diary of George Templeton Strong,* ed. Allan Nevins and Milton Halsey Thomas (New York: The Macmillan Company, 1952), vol. 4, p. 322; Timothy J. Gilfoyle, *City of Eros: New York City, Prostitution, and the Commercialization of Sex, 1790–1920* (New York: W. W. Norton & Company, 1992), p. 334, n. 6.

6. Francis R. Kowsky, *The Architecture of Frederick Clark Withers and the Progress of the Gothic Revival in America After 1850* (Middletown, CT: Wesleyan University Press, 1980), pp. 13, 109–118; "The Jefferson Market Monument," *New York Times,* May 9, 1877.

7. Moses Y. Beach, "Wealth and Biography of the Wealthy Citizens of New York City," *New York Sun,* 1845.

8. *The Diary of Philip Hone, 1828–1851,* ed. Alan Nevins (New York: Dodd, Mead & Company, 1927), pp. 110-111.

9. "Private Residences," *Putnam's Monthly Magazine,* March 1854, pp. 234–235, 237.

10. Beach, "Wealth and Biography of the Wealthy Citizens of New York City," p. 23.

11. "Progress of the City," *New York Herald,* February 26, 1845.

12. *The Diary of George Templeton Strong,* vol. 1, pp. 272–273.

13. "Miss Van Beuren Dies in Her Old City Home," *New York Times,* July 23, 1908; "Van Beuren Mansion Will Be Demolished," *New York Times,* August 7, 1927.

14. John W. Frick, *New York's First Theatrical Center—The Rialto at Union Square* (Ann Arbor: University of Michigan Research Press, 1983).

15. "Grand Fancy Dress Ball, At Brevoort Hall," *New York Herald,* March 2, 1840.

16. Ken Emerson, *Doo-da! Stephen Foster and the Rise of American Popular Culture* (New York: Simon & Schuster, 1997), p. 45.

17. E. W. Kramer, "Domestic Architecture of Detlef Lienau," Ph.D. diss., New York University, 1958, p. 213.

18. *The Diary of George Templeton Strong*, vol. 3, p. 101.

19. Herman Melville, letter to Evert Duyckinck, November 7, 1851, quoted in Edmiston and Cirino, *Literary New York*, p. 39.

20. Francis G. Fairfield, *The Clubs of New York* (New York: Henry L. Hinton, 1873), p. 43.

21. Will Irwin, Earl Chapin May, and Joseph Hotchkiss, *A History of the Union League Club of New York City* (New York: Dodd, Mead & Company, 1952), pp. 10–11.

22. Francis Brown, *Raymond of the Times* (New York: W. W. Norton & Company, 1951), p. 255.

23. Calvin Tomkins, *Merchants and Masterpieces: The Story of the Metropolitan Museum of Art* (New York: E. P. Dutton, 1970), p. 30.

24. See chapter 1, note 19.

CHAPTER 4. NARROW ESCAPE

1. John Moran, "Studio Life in New York," *Art Journal*, vol. 5 (November 1879), p. 343.

2. Henry C. Bunner, *The Midge* (New York: Charles Scribner's Sons, 1886), pp. 154–155. The Restaurant du Grand Vatel is thinly disguised as Charlemagne's.

3. Albert Parry, *Garrets and Pretenders: A History of Bohemianism in America* (New York: Covici-Friede, 1933), p. 93.

4. Rick Beard and Jan Seidler Ramirez, "A Spiritual Zone of Mind," in Rick Beard and Leslie Berlowitz, eds., *Greenwich Village: Culture and Counterculture* (New Brunswick, NJ: Rutgers University Press, 1993), p. 265.

5. "About the World," *Scribner's Magazine*, July 1896, pp. 129–130.

6. "The New Mercantile District," supplement to the *Real Estate Record and Builder's Guide* (New York: Clinton W. Sweet, October 25, 1890), pp. 3–4.

7. Paul Goldberger, *The City Observed: A Guide to the Architecture of Manhattan* (New York: Vintage Books, 1979), p. 64.

8. "The New Mercantile District," p. 3.

9. *Letters of Richard Watson Gilder (1844–1909)*, ed. Rosamond Gilder (Boston: Houghton Mifflin, 1916), pp. 181, 183, 213.

10. Paul R. Baker, *Stanny: The Gilded Life of Stanford White* (New York: The Macmillan Company, 1989), p. 169; "Making the Arch Permanent: Comments of the Press," *New York Commercial Advertiser*, May 10, 1889.

11. Arch Project Scrapbook, 1889–96, New-York Historical Society. Quoted in the *Real Estate Record and Builder's Guide*.

12. "Upon Historic Ground," *New York World*, May 30, 1890; "Famous Washington Square Home to Make Way for Apartment," *New York Times*, April 12, 1925.

13. Mariana Griswold van Rensselaer, "Fifth Avenue," *The Century*, November 1893, p. 10.

14. "Lower Fifth Avenue's Residential Stronghold," *New York Times*, July 30, 1905.

15. Gregory F. Gilmartin, *Shaping the City: New York and the Municipal Art Society* (New York: Clarkson Potter, 1995), pp. 1–2.

16. George B. McClellan Jr., *The Gentleman and the Tiger: The Autobiography of George B. McClellan, Jr.* (New York: J. B. Lippincott, 1956), p. 260.

17. "Two Sections of New York Seem Immune to Progress," *New York Times,* December 2, 1906.

18. "Steady Development of University Place," *New York Times,* June 11, 1905.

19. Leon Edel, *Henry James: A Biography* (London: Hart-Davis, 1972), vol. 2, pp. 188–189.

20. Dee Garrison, *Mary Heaton Vorse: The Life of an American Insurgent* (Philadelphia: Temple University Press, 1989), p. 36.

21. Hamilton Fish Armstrong, *Those Days* (New York: Harper & Row, 1963), p. 6.

22. Charles F. Peters, "When New York Dines à la Bohème," *Bohemian* (New York: Outing Press, 1907), p. 83.

CHAPTER 5. BOHEMIA U.S.A.

1. Cynthia Ozick, "1918–1927, Against Modernity—Annals of the Temple," in John Updike, ed., *A Century of Arts and Letters* (New York: Columbia University Press, 1998), pp. 53–54. The original name was "National Institute."

2. John Loughery, *John Sloan: Painter and Rebel* (New York: Henry Holt & Company, 1995), p. 120; John Sloan, quoted in B. H. Friedman, *Gertrude Vanderbilt Whitney* (New York: Doubleday & Company, 1978), p. 250; "The World of the Eight," *Arts Yearbook 1* (New York: Arts Digest, 1957), p. 76.

3. Mabel Dodge Luhan, *Movers and Shakers—Intimate Memories* (New York: Harcourt, Brace & Company, 1936), p. 83.

4. Lois Palken Rudnick, *Mabel Dodge Luhan: New Woman, New Worlds* (Albuquerque: University of New Mexico Press, 1984), p. 65.

5. Justin Kaplan, *Lincoln Steffens: A Biography* (New York: Simon & Schuster, 1974), p. 187.

6. "News of the Art World," *New York World,* February 8, 1914.

7. Rudnick, *Mabel Dodge Luhan,* pp. x, 86.

8. Hutchins Hapgood, *A Victorian in the Modern World* (New York: Harcourt, Brace & Company, 1939), p. 358.

9. Francis M. Naumann, *New York Dada 1915–1923* (New York: Harry N. Abrams, 1994), p. 106; Louise Varèse, *Varèse: A Looking-Glass Diary* (New York: W. W. Norton & Company, 1972), p. 127.

10. Rebecca Zurier, *Art for The Masses: A Radical Magazine and Its Graphics, 1911–1917* (Philadelphia: Temple University Press, 1988), p. 35.

11. Eunice Fuller Barnard, "Our Old Sport, the Parade, Is Waning," *New York Times Magazine,* May 19, 1929, p. 15.

12. Floyd Dell, *Homecoming* (New York: Farrar & Rinehart, 1933), p. 247

13. Floyd Dell, *Love in Greenwich Village* (New York: George H. Doran, 1926), p. 18.

14. Alfred Kreymborg, "The New Washington Square," *Morning Telegraph,* November 29 and December 6, 1914.

15. "How Greenwich Village Captivates City Wayfarers," *New York Tribune,* December 20, 1914.

16. Dell, *Homecoming,* p. 247; Hapgood, *A Victorian in the Modern World,* p. 198.

17. Kreymborg, "The New Washington Square"; Gorham Munson, *The Awaken-*

ing Twenties: A Memoir History of a Literary Period (Baton Rouge: Louisiana State University Press, 1985), pp. 41–42.

18. Jan Seidler Ramirez, "The Tourist Trade Takes Hold," in Rick Beard and Leslie Cohen Berlowitz, eds., *Greenwich Village: Culture and Counterculture* (New York: Museum of the City of New York, 1993), pp. 376–377.

19. Egmont Arens, *The Little Book of Greenwich Village* (New York: Egmont Arens, 1918), p. 31.

20. Louis Sheaffer, *O'Neill, Son and Playwright* (Boston: Little, Brown & Company, 1968), p. 332.

21. Susan Glaspell, *The Road to the Temple* (New York: Frederick A. Stokes Company, 1941), p. 254.

22. Kreymborg, "The New Washington Square."

23. Ibid.

24. "American Writers in Paris, 1920–1939," in *Dictionary of Literary Biography*, vol. 4, ed. Karen Lane Rood (Detroit: Gale Research Company, 1980), p. 4.

25. Ibid.

26. Ibid., p. 5.

27. "Manning for Saving Old Neighborhoods," *New York Times*, January 12, 1916; Elliot Willensky and Norval White, eds., *AIA Guide to New York City* (Orlando, FL: Harcourt Brace Jovanovich, 1988), p. 111.

28. "Demand for Washington Square Homes; Artistic Renovations of Old Houses," *New York Times*, August 26, 1917.

CHAPTER 6. HOME OF THE NEW YORK SCHOOL

1. Stephen Ruttenbaum, *Mansions in the Clouds: The Skyscraper Palazzi of Emery Roth* (New York: Balsam Press, 1986), pp. 86–87.

2. Ibid., p. 144.

3. H. I. Brock, "Number One Fifth Avenue," *The Arts*, vol. 13 (January 1928), p. 31.

4. Joel Schwartz, *The New York Approach: Robert Moses, Urban Liberals, and Redevelopment of the Inner City* (Columbus: Ohio State University Press, 1993), p. 17.

5. Howard Devree, "A Gallery-Goer's Week," *New York Times*, May 7, 1933.

6. George J. Lankevich, *American Metropolis: A History of New York City* (New York: New York University Press, 1998), p. 173.

7. Robert A. M. Stern, Gregory Gilmartin, and Thomas Mellins, eds., *New York 1930: Architecture and Urbanism Between the Two World Wars* (New York: Rizzoli, 1987), pp. 140–141.

8. Henry Adams, *Thomas Hart Benton: Drawing From Life* (New York: Abbeyville Press, 1990), p. 34.

9. Ibid.

10. Steven Naifeh and Gregory White Smith, *Jackson Pollock: An American Saga* (New York: Clarkson Potter, 1989), p. 635; Ronald Sukenick, *Down and In* (New York: Beech Tree, 1987), pp. 61–62.

11. *The Greenwich Village Guide* (New York: Bryan Publications, 1947), p. 63.

12. Simone de Beauvoir, *America Day by Day* (Berkeley: University of California, 1999), pp. 314–315.

13. Ibid., p. 33.

14. Grace Glueck, "Paying Tribute to the Daring of Peggy Guggenheim," *New York Times,* March 1, 1987.

15. Florence Rubenfeld, *Clement Greenberg: A Life* (New York: Simon & Schuster, 1997), p. 107.

16. Frances Stonor Saunders, *The Cultural Cold War: The CIA and the World of Arts and Letters* (New York: New Press, 1999), p. 277.

17. Lee Hall, *Elaine and Bill: Portrait of a Marriage* (New York: HarperCollins, 1993), p. 80.

18. Barry Miles, *Ginsberg: A Biography* (New York: Simon & Schuster, 1989), p. 127.

19. Terry A. Cooney, *The Rise of the New York Intellectuals* (Madison: University of Wisconsin Press, 1986), p. 117.

20. "Mabel's Comeback," *Time,* January 22, 1940, p. 80.

21. Thomas Bender, *New York Intellect: A History of Intellectual Life in New York City, from 1750 to the Beginnings of Our Own Time* (New York: Alfred A. Knopf, 1987), pp. 335–336.

22. Lankevich, *American Metropolis,* pp. 173–174.

23. Ibid., pp. 181–182.

24. Robert Moses, letter to Charles C. Burlingham, January 27, 1950, Box 99, The La Guardia and Wagner Archives, La Guardia Community College / CUNY.

25. "Washington Sq. Fights Park Plan," *New York Times,* March 30, 1935.

26. "Washington Square South—Slum Clearance Plan Under Title I of the Housing Act of 1949," January 1951, Box 91; Robert Moses, letter to Charles C. Burlingham, January 27, 1950, Box 99, The La Guardia and Wagner Archives, La Guardia Community College / CUNY.

Chapter 7. Protest and Turnabout

1. Ada Louise Huxtable, *Classic New York* (Garden City, NY: Doubleday & Company, 1964), p. 96; Paul Goldberger, *The City Observed: A Guide to the Architecture of Manhattan* (New York: Random House, 1979), p. 75.

2. Gregory F. Gilmartin, *Shaping the City: New York and the Municipal Art Society* (New York: Clarkson Potter, 1995), p. 429.

3. David W. Dunlap, *On Broadway: A Journey Uptown Over Time* (New York: Rizzoli, 1990), p. 102.

4. "Reply to Mr. Weinberg," *Villager,* November 11, 1965.

5. Gerard R. Wolfe and Carol Herselle Krinsky, "150 Years of N.Y.U. Buildings," *New York University Education Quarterly,* NYU sesquicentennial report (New York, 1981), p. 26; Goldberger, *The City Observed,* p. 77; Elliot Willensky and Norval White, *AIA Guide to New York City* (Orlando, FL: Harcourt Brace Jovanovich, 1988), pp. 114, 117.

6. Holly George-Warren, ed., *The Rolling Stone Book of the Beats* (New York: Rolling Stone Press, 1999), p. 367; Barry Miles, *Ginsberg: A Biography* (New York: Simon & Schuster, 1989), p. 97.

7. William Barrett, Hal Bowser, and Philip Campbell, *The New Guide to Greenwich Village* (New York: Corinth Books, 1959), p. 39.

8. Miles, *Ginsberg,* p. 232.

9. Robert Alden, " 'Village' Tension Upsets Residents," *New York Times,* September 29, 1959.

10. Robert Cantwell, *When We Were Good: The Folk Revival* (Cambridge: Harvard University Press, 1996), p. 287.

11. *Green Guide to New York City* (Lake Success, NY: Michelin Tire Corporation, 1968), p. 78.

12. Andrew Jacobs, "The Squeeze on Head Shops," *New York Times,* May 19, 1996.

13. Grace Lichtenstein, "Modern Perils Distress Old 'Village,'" *New York Times,* September 28, 1970.

14. Press Release, Office of the Mayor of the City of New York, October 9, 1973; Barbara Campbell, "Village Refrain: High Rents and the Passing of Charm," *New York Times,* October 9, 1977.

15. Videotape of the John Brademas interview, NBC Television News Archives, 1989.

16. Martin Gottlieb, "Village Leaders Want Precinct Head's Head," *New York Daily News,* September 18, 1976.

17. Jane Jacobs, *The Death and Life of Great American Cities* (New York: Random House, 1961), p. 137.

18. Mary Perot Nichols, "Old and New Guard Divide on Uses for the Square," *Village Voice,* June 7, 1967.

19. August Heckscher, *Open Spaces: The Life of American Cities* (New York: Harper & Row, 1977), p. 145.

20. Henry H. Curran, Letter to the Editor, *New York Herald Tribune,* February 9, 1950.

21. Paul Goldberger, "Metropolitan Baedeker: Washington Square," *New York Times,* November 19, 1976; Goldberger, *The City Observed,* p. 74.

22. "Fencing of Washington Sq. Park Studied," *New York Times,* April 6, 1973.

23. "Washington Square Park," a student report, Professors Patricia Sexton and Samuel Wallace, sponsors (New York University, 1973), p. 2.

24. Ibid., p. 41; Sally Harrison-Pepper, *Drawing a Circle in the Square* (Jackson: University Press of Mississippi, 1990), p. xii.

25. Gregory J. Perrin, "B. Dalton's to Open Store in West Village District," *New York Torch,* August 13–19, 1981.

26. Barrett, Bowser, and Campbell, *The New Guide to Greenwich Village,* p. 53.

27. Margaret Parton, "Memoryful Bible House Soon to Face Wreckers," *New York Herald Tribune,* September 24, 1954.

28. Robert A. M. Stern, Thomas Mellins, and David Fishman, *New York 1960: Architecture and Urbanism Between the Second World War and the Bicentennial* (New York: Monacelli Press, 1995), p. 1132; Gilmartin, *Shaping the City,* pp. 364–365.

29. Helen Epstein, *Joe Papp: An American Life* (Boston: Little, Brown & Company, 1994), pp. 213–214.

30. Gilmartin, *Shaping the City,* p. 357.

31. Ibid., p. 359.

32. Charles R. Simpson, *SoHo: The Artist in the City* (Chicago: University of Chicago Press, 1981), p. 139.

33. Ibid., pp. 144–145.

34. Ibid., p. 150.

CHAPTER 8. REVIVAL

1. Sasha Abramsky, "Manhattan: The Suburb," *New York,* February 1, 1999, p. 24.

2. Richard Severo, "Battle Over Cornices and Lintels Rages in 'Village,'" *New York Times,* August 28, 1984.

3. Linda Sandler, "Schools Build Luxury Hangouts," *Wall Street Journal,* April 28, 1999.

4. Ada Louise Huxtable, "Creeping Gigantism in Manhattan," *New York Times,* March 22, 1987.

5. *Shecky's BAR, CLUB and LOUNGE 2000 Guide* (New York: Hangover Productions, 1999), p. 105.

6. Letter to the Editor, "What Kind of Life Is This?" *New York Times,* October 25, 1999.

7. Chris Ballard, "On a Roll after Midnight, When Every Lane's a Fast Lane," *New York Times,* March 24, 2000.

8. Ibid.

9. Rosetta Reitz and Joan Geisler, *Where to Go in Greenwich Village: A Complete Guide to More Than 200 Places for Dining and Entertainment* (New York: Rosetta Reitz & Joan Geisler, 1961), p. 6.

10. Vincent Canby, "Where Even the Flops Have Zest," *New York Times,* November 7, 1999.

11. Ibid.

12. Reitz and Geisler, *Where to Go in Greenwich Village,* p. 87.

13. Mitchell Duneier, *Sidewalk* (New York: Farrar, Straus & Giroux, 1999), p. 116.

14. Elaine Louie, "Luxury's Expanding Frontiers: The New Dakotas Are Downtown," *New York Times,* February 3, 2000.

15. Charles V. Bagli, "A Hotel Alliance Splits Up, But Schrager Presses Ahead," *New York Times,* June 28, 2001.

16. Carole Zimmer, "Stars in Their Eyes: 'I Sort of Follow People Around. At Night I'm One of the Flock,'" *New York Times,* October 24, 1999.

17. David W. Dunlap, "In West Village, a Developers' Gold Rush," *New York Times,* August 29, 1999.

18. Douglas Martin, "City Opens 1st Section of New Park on Hudson," *New York Times,* September 27, 1999.

19. Denny Lee, "Billboard Haters Mar Many Signs," *New York Times,* August 29, 1999.

20. Michael Gross, "The Village Under Siege," *New York,* August 16, 1993, pp. 30–37.

21. Craig Horowitz, "The End of Crime as We Know It," *New York,* August 14, 1995.

22. Clyde Haberman, "Double-Decker Buzz: Fay Wray Lives There?" *New York Times,* December 6, 1998.

23. Harold E. Stearns, "When Greenwich Village Was Youth," in *The Street I Know* (New York: Lee Furman, 1935), p. 139.

AFTERWORD

1. Quoted by Paul Goldberger in "The Skyline: Building Plans," *New Yorker,* September 24, 2001.

INDEX

Morgan, Matthew, 49, 61–2, 97, *98*

Morgan, William F., 5

Morning Telegraph, 188

Morris, Newbold, 269, 275–6

Morse, Samuel F. B., xi, 20–1

Moses, Robert, xii; on bohemians, 228; on Greenwich Village, 244; housing of, upsets Italian community, 267; for low buildings facing square, 253–4; and Lower Manhattan Expressway, 287, 288; roadway and superblock schemes for square, *243,* 243–9, *244, 247;* roadway through square defeated, 263; and square designs, 275–6; superblock legacy of, 299–300; urban renewal legacy (Cooper Square) of, 313, 314; as Wagner opponent, 290; Washington Square South project, 260–2, *261*

Motherwell, Robert, 235, 238, 241

Mott, Valentine and Louisa Dunmore, 84

Mott Street, 65, 85, 87, 138, 164, *165*

Mt. Washington Collegiate Institute, *14,* 28

muckraking, *149,* 158, 161, 164, 169, 184

Mulberry Street, 75, 81, 85, 87

Multiple Dwelling Law of 1929, 212

Municipal Art Society (MAS), 154, 155, 246

Mural, 238

Murray, Hamilton, 13

Murray, James Boyles, *12,* 12–3, 17, *99,* 103, 104

Murray, John Boyles, 13

Murray family, *99*

Murray Street Presbyterian Church, 61

Museum of Modern Art (MoMA), 228, 231, 239, 241

Museum of Non-Objective Painting, 237–8

Museum of the City of New York, 215

Mutoscope Company, 140

Myers, Forrest, 317

Naked Lunch, 266

Nakian, Reuben, 222, *250,* 260

Nation, The, 199, 239

National Academy of Design, 21, 40, 63, 174, 175, 192

National Anti-Slavery Standard, 96

National Theater, 61

Ned Buntline's Own, 63

Neilson, Helena and William, 88

Neilson Place, 88

Neo-Georgian style, 215

New Deal mural program, 240

Newman, Barnett, 235

New Masses, 241

New Mercantile District, 128, 137

New School University (New School for Social Research), 224, *225,* 230, 241, 256, 307, 308

"New Washington Square, The," 188, 197–8

New York Academy of Medicine, 84, 124

New York Academy of Sciences, 40, 124

New York American, 19, 81

New York and Harlem railroad, 41, 73

New York as It Is, 36

New York Athenaeum, 40

New York City Armory Board, 124

New York Convention and Visitors Bureau, 210

"New York Daguerrotyped," 24

New Yorker, 7, 37, 133, 222, 314

New York Evening Post, 11, 15, 16, 23, 324

New York Evening Sun, 175–6

New York Gallery of Fine Arts, 40

New York Herald, 20, 62–3, 103, 112, 122, 140, 324

New York Herald Tribune, 277

New-York Historical Society, 40, 47, 324

New York Hotel, 49, 50, 97

New York Illustrated News, 53

New York in a Nutshell, 23, 24

New York Infirmary for Women and Children, 85

New York Is Like This, 221

New York Leader, 54

New York Magazine, 128, 320, *320,* 321

New York 1930, 230

New York Philharmonic, 63

New York Public Library, 6, 64, 109, 117, 119, 147, 175, 283

New York School: current evidence of, 301; and Eighth Street as Main Street, 230; and Arshile Gorky, 227; and Clement Greenberg, 238–9; and Peggy Guggenheim, 237; haunts destroyed by real estate development, 257, 259–60; and Hofmann School, 233; influenced by Surrealists, 241; inspired by Gallatin gallery, 222; and legacy of large works, 287; need for local bars and cafeterias, 224; as new style of painting, 206, *208;* occupies cheap flats, 210; of poets, 240–1; *Time, Life,* and MoMA support of, 239–40; and Waldorf Cafeteria, Cedar Bar, and the Club, *234,* 234–6, *235;* WPA support of, 229. *See also individual artists*

New York's First Theatrical Center—The Rialto at Union Square, 108

New York Society for the Prevention of Vice, 184

New York Society Library, 63, 101, *101*

New York State Board of Charities, 142

New York Stock Exchange, 95

New York Studio School of Drawing, Painting, and Sculpture, 280, 301

New York Sun, 95

New York Times: on Caroline Astor's guest list, *149;* on the Beats, 240; on bohemia, 54; on Burdell murder, 68; on cost of living in East Village, 313; on demand for apartments,

203; on developers in West Village, 315; on downtown theater district, 305–6; on Fifth Avenue parades, 185; on Lower Manhattan Expressway, 290; on MacDougal Street disturbance, 267; on Moses's scheme, 245; on nightclubs, 303–4; on outdoor art exhibit, 228; on risk in architecture, 310–1; on Springler farm, 105; on SROs, 272; on support of Lincoln, 122; on trees and the influx of trade, 152; on Two Fifth Avenue, 254; on Washington Square as a backwater and prospects for University Place, 156–7

New York Tribune, 96, 189

New York University, xi, *14, 19,* 28, 29, 63, *78,* 88, *99,* 120, 140, *141,* 150, 222, 245–6, 274, 301, 308; Bobst Library, *239, 250,* 260, 262–4, *263, 292, 295, 296,* 297, 299; controversy and compromise, 299; dormitory at 5–11 University Place, 264; dormitory dining halls, 305; founding, 18–22; Hagop Kervorkian Center for Near-Eastern Studies, 264; Johnson and Foster plans, 262–4, *263;* Kimmel Student Center, *296, 296,* 297, 299; Law Center, 187, 249, 253, *253,* 260, 262, 299, *299;* Loeb Student Center, *250,* 260, *292;* Main Building, *141, 219,* 241, 262, *263;* Medical College, 40; Moses's plans, 249, 253, 254, 261; Poe House and Thompson Street houses, 299; School of Education, 235, 248; student unrest, 274; town-gown battles, 248; University Heights campus, 248, 264

New York World, 47, 95, 148–50, 176, 179

Niblo's Garden, 108

Night Owl Café, 270

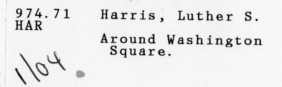